I0797301

HUBRIS

HUBRIS

PERICLES, THE PARTHENON, AND THE INVENTION OF ATHENS

DAVID STUTTARD

THE BELKNAP PRESS OF HARVARD UNIVERSITY PRESS

CAMBRIDGE, MASSACHUSETTS
LONDON, ENGLAND

2026

Printed in the United States of America
First printing

EU GPSR Authorised Representative
LOGOS EUROPE, 9 rue Nicolas Poussin, 17000, LA ROCHELLE, France
E-mail: Contact@logoseurope.eu

Library of Congress Cataloging-in-Publication Data

Names: Stuttard, David author
Title: Hubris : Pericles, the Parthenon, and the invention of Athens / David Stuttard.
Other titles: Pericles, the Parthenon, and the invention of Athens
Description: Cambridge, Massachusetts ; London, England : The Belknap Press of Harvard University Press, 2026. | Includes bibliographical references and index.
Identifiers: LCCN 2025032458 (print) | LCCN 2025032459 (ebook) | ISBN 9780674258471 cloth | ISBN 9780674303942 epub | ISBN 9780674303959 pdf
Subjects: LCSH: Pericles, approximately 495 B.C.–429 B.C. | Parthenon (Athens, Greece)—History | Parthenon sculptures—Political aspects | Athens (Greece)—Civilization—Political aspects | Athens (Greece)—Religious life and customs | Greece—History—Athenian supremacy, 479–431 B.C.
Classification: LCC DF277 .S78 2026 (print) | LCC DF277 (ebook)
LC record available at https://lccn.loc.gov/2025032458
LC ebook record available at https://lccn.loc.gov/2025032459

For Emily Jane

Let us go now to Athena's glistening land
to see the soil of Cecrops, so beloved, the home to such good men,
where they respect the sacred rites that must remain unspoken,
where the building that reveals the holy mysteries
welcomes initiates,
where offerings are consecrated to the gods of heaven,
where there are temples with high roofs and statues
and the most revered processions for the blessed gods,
and there are sacrifices crowned with garlands for the gods,
and feasts and banquets in their proper season.

—ARISTOPHANES, *CLOUDS*

CONTENTS

Maps x

Plans xiv

Introduction: The Girls and the Rock 1

1 Laying the Foundations 13

2 Powerhouses 43

3 Building Democracy 67

4 Burnt Offerings 91

5 City of Gods 120

6 Embracing Past, Present, and Future 146

7 Athens on the Cusp 168

8 Fractures and Fissures 198

9 The Road to War 225

10 Convulsions 248

11 Battle Lines 275

12 Catharsis? 297

Acknowledgments 323

Notes 325

Credits 373

Index 375

Map 1 The Eastern Mediterranean and Black Sea.

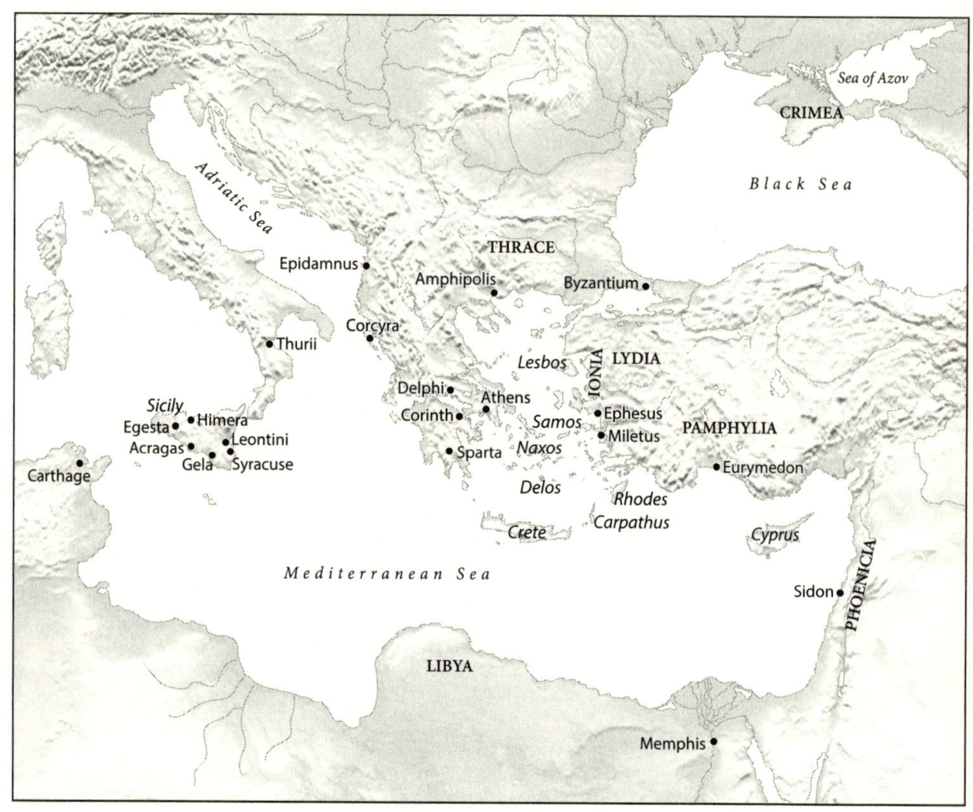

Map 2 Greece and Asia Minor.

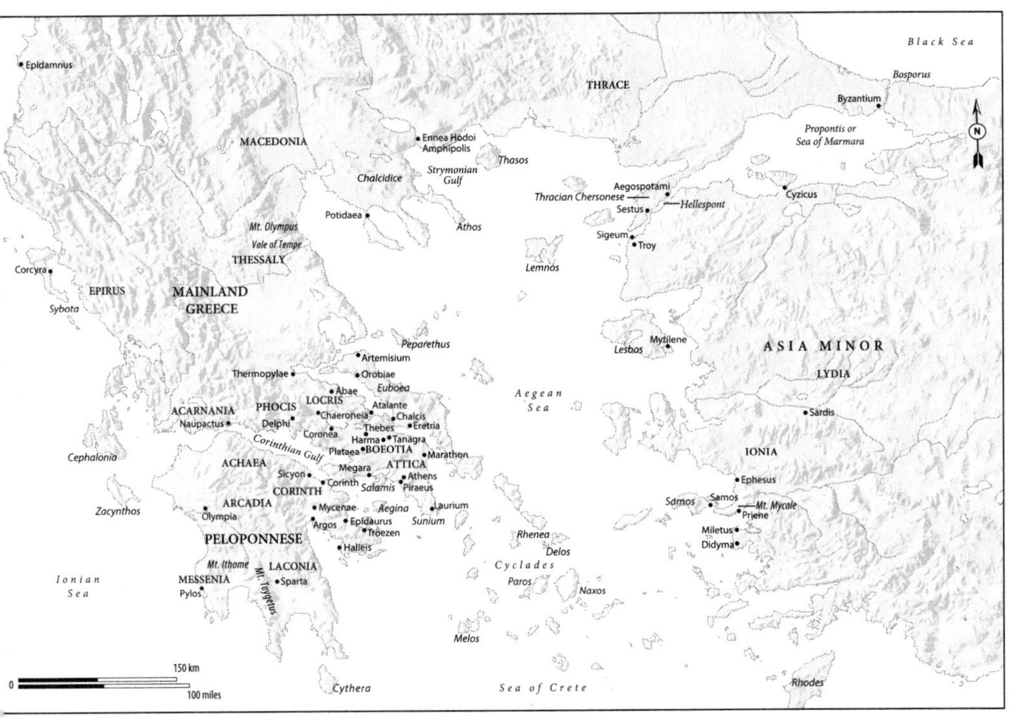

Map 3 Attica and environs.

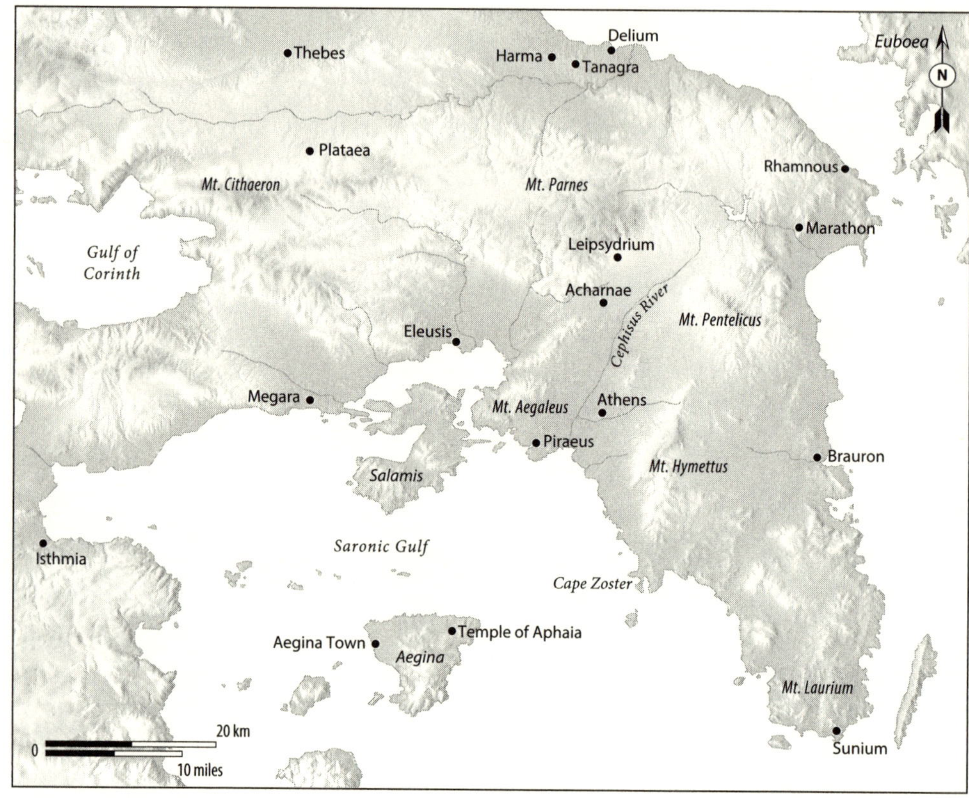

Map 4 Athens and Piraeus.

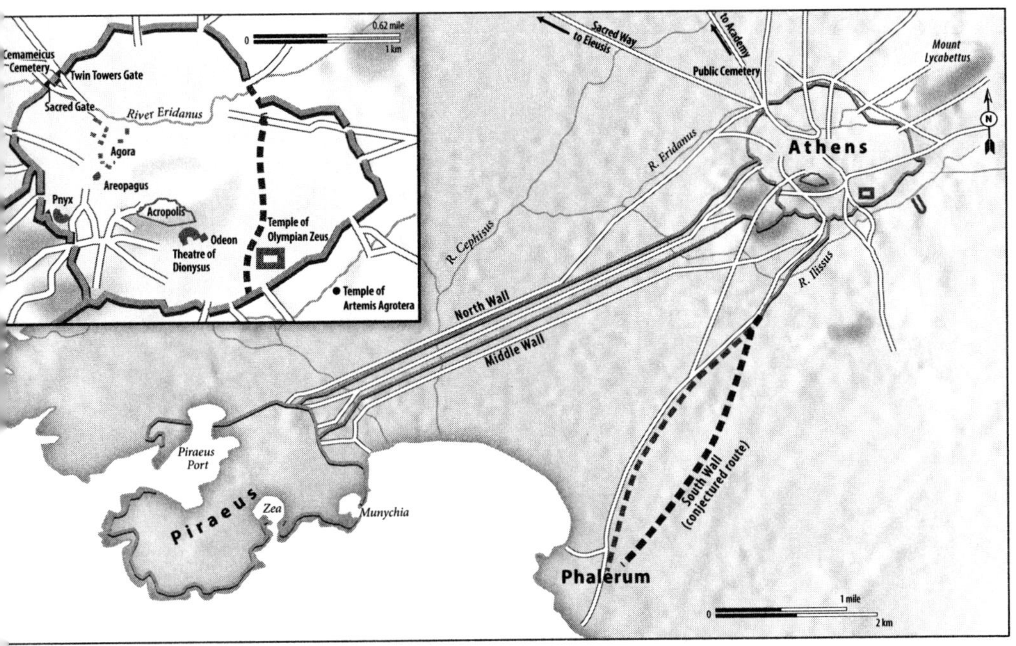

Plan 1 The Athenian Agora.

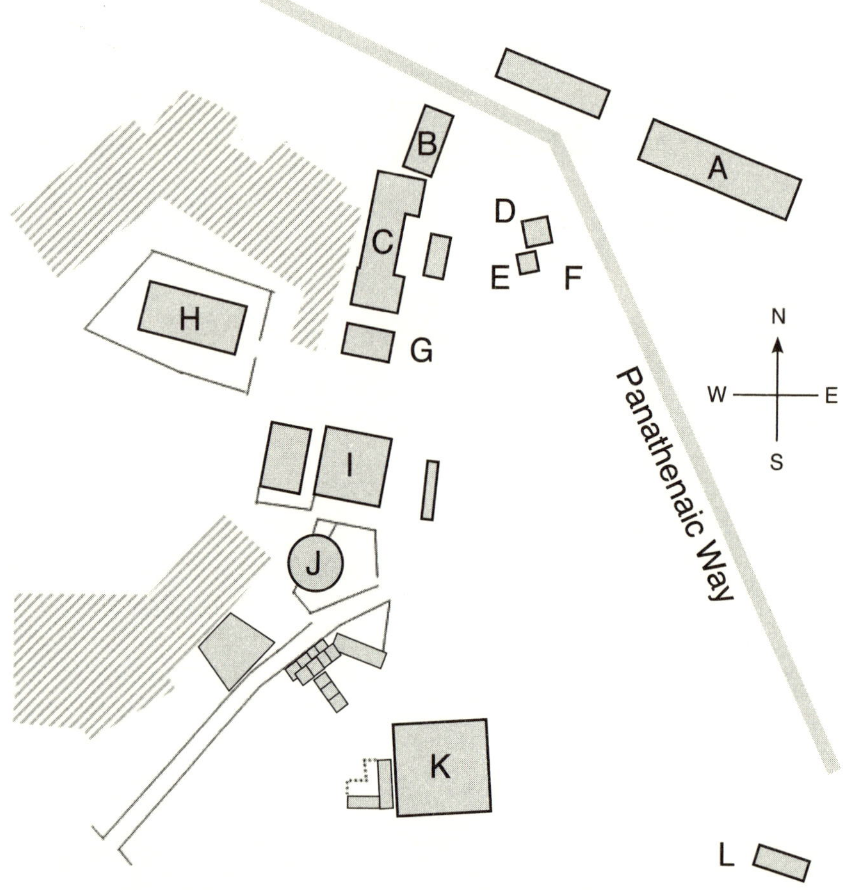

The Athenian Agora (with buildings mentioned in the text)

A	Painted Stoa (Poikile)	G	Temple of Apollo Patroos
B	Royal Stoa	H	Temple of Athena and Hephaestus
C	Stoa of Zeus	I	Bouleuterion
D	Leocorium	J	Tholos or Skia
E	Altar of Twelve Gods	K	Aeaceum?
F	Tyrannicides' statue?	L	Fountain House

Plan 2 The Athenian Acropolis.

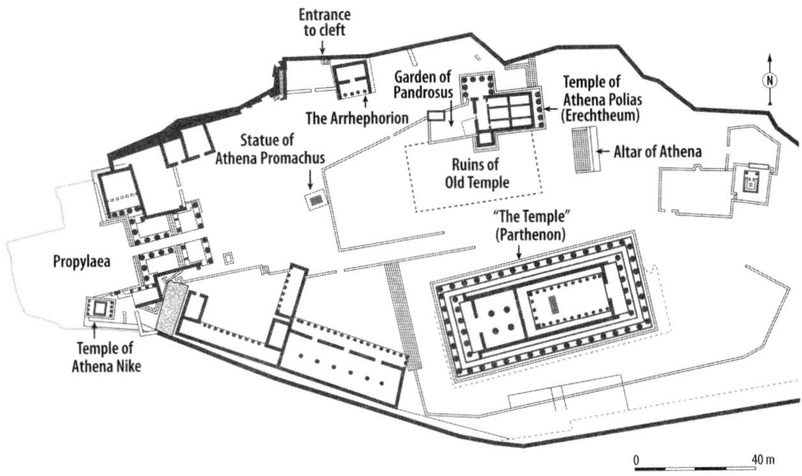

Plan 3 Plan of the Parthenon.

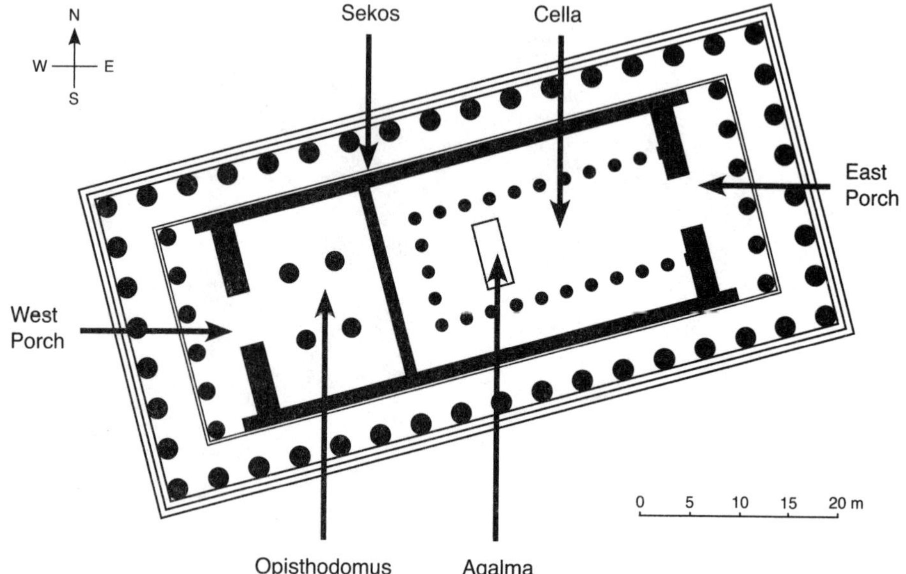

Plan 4 Architectural features of a temple.

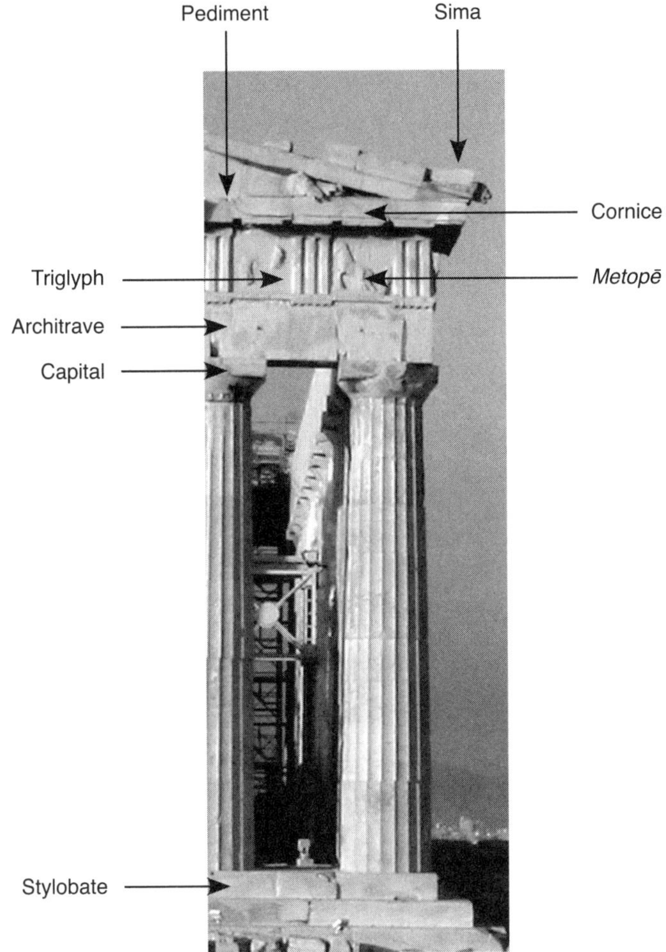

HUBRIS

On the Term *Hubris*

In classical Greek, *hubris* originally meant a deliberate and dishonouring transgression of status boundaries, often involving physical violence, with specific reference to the boundaries that were believed to separate humanity from the divine. In English, the definition has been broadened to include overconfidence or pride. In this book, readers should especially bear the former definition in mind.

INTRODUCTION

THE GIRLS AND THE ROCK

Athens, June/July 430 B.C.

If they were terrified, the two girls could not show it. For the past year, they had lived on the Acropolis as servants of the goddess, cloistered, with the hawk-eyed priestess of Athena Polias (Athena Who Protects the City-State) watching their every move, supervising their performance of each ritual, teaching them the skills they needed to fulfil their sacred duty. A great loom dominated the small building where they lived, and many of their waking hours were spent there, watching women work long skeins of blue and saffron-yellow wool that gradually transformed into a rectangle of cloth showing scenes of gods and giants locked close in combat for possession of the cosmos, with Athena in prime, central position, helmeted, her snake-fringed aegis slung about her shoulders, her right arm raised, about to spear her fallen enemy, Enceladus, who writhed, defiant, at her feet.[1]

Time had passed slowly, a blur of repetition in a circling of seasons as suns rose and set behind the high walls of their little compound, the one-roomed house and courtyard where the priestess granted them occasional permission to go out, play ball, and let off steam—they were, after all, just eleven years of age. But they were more than conscious of their status. Only the elite of the elite, the crème de la crème, could be considered for the most prestigious post a girl could hope to hold, as representative of all her people, a link with an ancient past, an expiation of a legendary guilt.

It was how they were to expiate that guilt that terrified them most. Time and again the priestess had gone over it, what they must do, and more importantly what they must not on any account dream of doing. Almost the first thing they had been shown when they moved in a year before had been the entrance to the chasm in the rock, the vulva-shaped cleft, from which a passage tunnelled down into the darkness. They could recall the earthy smell, the heat, the haunting quality of the stale air, as if left over from another age. And they could visualize the wooden treads that had been fixed into the crevice's grey walls, a staircase leading down into the very womb of the Acropolis.[2]

The priestess had done her best to reassure them. It would be dark, but they could take it slowly. They could not afford to fall. The main danger came halfway: a hairpin turn. But keep on going, and the air would change again. The light would become stronger, albeit the faint light of moon and stars, but still enough to help them see where they were going. Soon, they would hear familiar sounds, the nighttime city, stray dogs barking, distant revellers, perhaps even the low murmuring of women as they hurried to the fountain house to fill heavy amphoras of water, desperate to be back home before the dawn.

At least those women knew what they were carrying. Before they set out on their journey, the priestess would present the girls with *kistai,* circular lidded baskets, which they must carry on their heads down through the rock until they reached the cavern on the slopes of the Acropolis, at the lower end of the great gash. From there it was a brief brisk walk around the Peripatos, the road round the Acropolis, to the Gardens of Aphrodite, blossoming with a rich harvest of sculpted genitalia, where they would exchange their baskets for two others, in all respects identical, which they must bring back through the fissure in the rock, up the steep muscle-stretching steps, and, as the moonlight bathed the sky and glinted off the statue of Athena rising up beyond the compound wall, entrust it to the waiting priestess of Athena.[3]

And then their duties would be over. They would have lived up to the name by which they had been known for the past year: Arrhe-

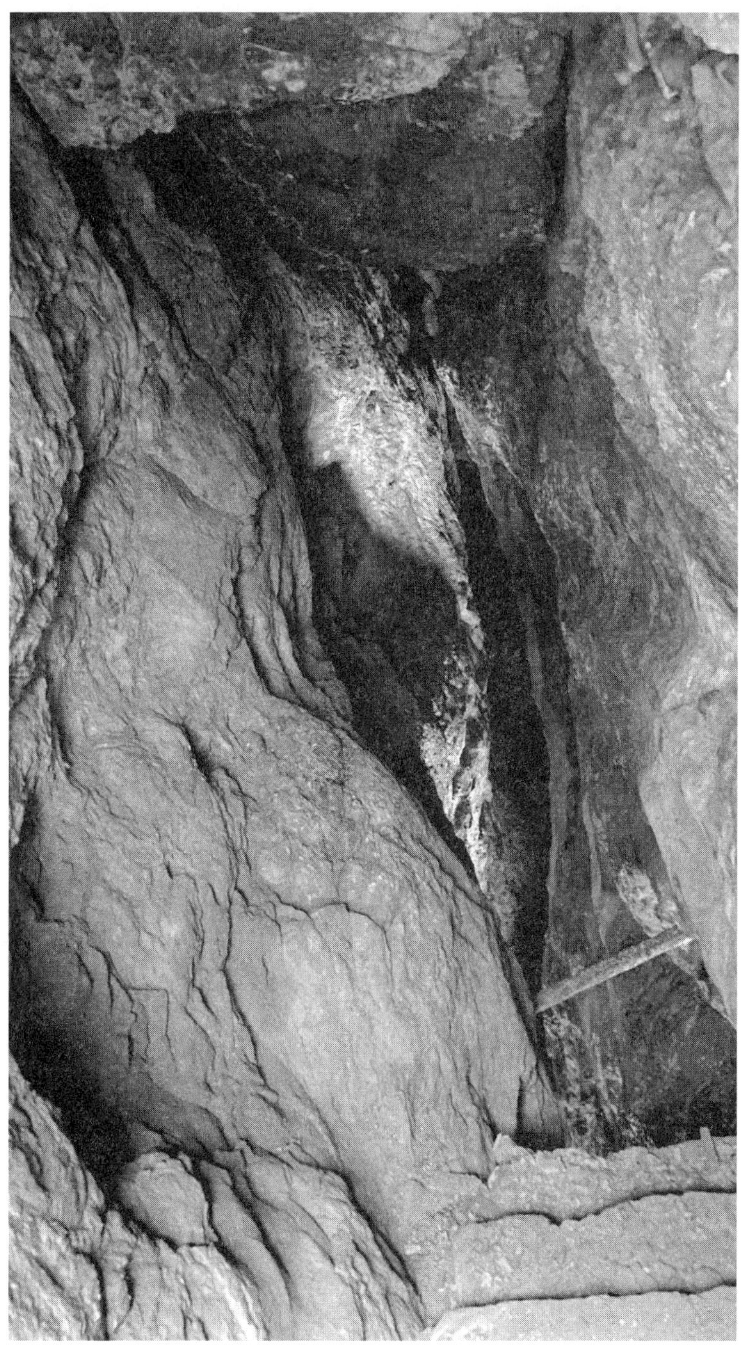

I.1 The entrance from the Acropolis to the fissure in the rock known as the Passage of the Arrhephoroi.

I.2 The Gardens of Aphrodite beneath the north face of the Acropolis.

phoroi, "those who carry something that must not be spoken of." Undoubtedly, they had both speculated about what that "thing" might be. They knew the story of the princesses, their predecessors, who, like them, were entrusted with a box, although it was Athena, not her priestess who had given it to them, with orders not to open it or look inside. But curiosity had overcome them. They disobeyed. And what they saw drove them insane: a newborn baby with, instead of legs, a scaly serpent's tail, conceived from semen wiped from Athena's thigh with wool and thrown down on the rock, a monstrous baby born from the Acropolis itself.[4]

Dropping the box, those princesses had panicked, running, stumbling in terror off the high cliffs to their death. Only their sister, the sublime Pandrosus, had obeyed the goddess, and it was to mark her sense of duty and do penance for her siblings' lack of it, that the Arrhephoroi performed their rituals every year, tending Athena's sacred olive tree nearby, watching the weaving of a robe from wool, the fabric soaked (in myth) with semen from which the monstrous child was born, living in a house above the entrance to the crevice, returning sacred objects through the rock to Aphrodite, goddess of generation, conveying sacred objects back through the vulvar tract of the Acropolis as if to a new birth—and overcoming their desire to raise the lid and look inside the basket.

As they dressed on that midsummer evening after sunset (for Greeks the start of a new day), shrugging on their special vestments, long robes that fell in pure white folds down to their ankles, the girls were justified in feeling fear. It was not just fear of what might be lurking in their caskets, though that was fearsome enough; or of the monsters they might encounter on their journey, creatures like the massive serpent which they knew lived near their compound or others which appeared to them in nightmares. It was the fear of what they would discover later that same day once they had discharged their obligation to the goddess, and their year as the Arrhephoroi was ended. For they had heard the news out of the lower city. Of war. Of plague. Of how the gods were abandoning Athens.[5]

Yet, the girls had done their best to keep those gods on side, not least by sacrificing a whole year of their young lives, marooned, imprisoned almost, on the rock—albeit in a gilded prison amid such awe-inspiring buildings and such vibrant statuary. They vividly remembered how at the start of their sequestered service they were taken to admire the frieze which had been carved high on the outer walls of the new temple, completed just a year before, and looking up excitedly saw set in pride of place above the stunning gold-and-ivory doors two sculpted figures—two young girls clothed in vestments that fell in pure white folds down to their ankles, sculpted Arrhephoroi presenting objects to a sculpted priestess, a mirror of themselves and of the duties that they must perform.[6]

If the role of the Arrhephoroi was so important—if they themselves were so important that men celebrated them in sculptures on Athena's temple—then they would overcome their terror and perform their duty without flinching. They would allow themselves to be absorbed into the rock, engulfed by darkness; and, after they had done what they must do, they would rise again onto the sacred rock of the Acropolis, transformed.

It was the sort of thing that made Athenians Athenian, as they had learned from myth and history and from the sculptures and the buildings that surrounded them. As Pericles, their "first man," had said just months before, Athens was the educator of all Greece. But cracks had been appearing in the city's confidence. Old certainties were being questioned. Already there were some who spoke of ancient curses being fulfilled or muttered about hubris being met by divine punishment. In the year the girls had spent on the Acropolis, war had come to Athens, and plague had broken out. People had been dying in streets and temples. The stench of burning corpses from incessant pyres was draped like a damp rag across the city, and there was no end in sight. And pious men were asking why the gods were angry. As the girls left the safe haven of their house on the Acropolis for the last time later that same day, they would discover that the educator of all Greece was facing a harsh lesson of its own.[7]

~ ~ ~

Today, images of the Acropolis are everywhere. The Parthenon is known across the world, a shorthand symbol, an icon for modern Greece, and in recent decades great care has been lavished on its curation. As columns have been cleaned and repaired, it has bristled with scaffolding as experts consider the extent of future restorations; an impressive museum has been opened to the south of the Acropolis exhibiting artworks from the temple with intelligence, ingenuity, and sensitivity; and all the while a great debate has gathered pace, as the Greek government demands the return of sculptures scattered far and wide across the globe (especially in London).

Such is the interest in the Parthenon and ancient Greece that in the twenty-first century A.D. not only do more people set foot on the Acropolis each year than visited in all of antiquity, but it is probable that more words are written about it in a day—perhaps even an hour—than have survived from the entirety of what we call the classical world. The paucity of our written sources is remarkable. Important documents have not survived—works such as a treatise written by the Parthenon's architect, Ictinus, or works by other practitioners referenced by later Roman specialists such as Vitruvius, which explored specific architectural refinements. And while we have fragments of the financial accounts—a marble slab recording construction costs for the temple and its towering gold-and-ivory statue—and while two generations later the orator Demosthenes praised "the beauty of the Parthenon," no contemporary literature explicitly explores the intention behind the building or its impact on Athenians and other Greeks. Only the late fifth-century-B.C. historian Thucydides comes close, observing that if Athens were to be abandoned but her temples left intact, "her appearance would suggest that she was twice as strong as she actually is."[8]

It is only in Plutarch's *Life of Pericles,* a work written half a millennium after the Parthenon was built, that we find an attempt to explain the motives for its construction, but we must handle this with care. Straddling two cultures, Plutarch was a Greek living in a Roman world, a product of his age, familiar with the Parthenon and its statue as it stood in his time but deeply influenced by the ethos of imperial Roman building programmes. So, although many inferences in his *Life of Pericles* may be correct, he tends to view the Parthenon project from a second-century-A.D. rather than a fifth-century-B.C. perspective, using anachronistic vocabulary and perhaps even imputing anachronistic motivations. As for his observations about its impact on those who first saw it, there is no evidence to suggest that they are anything but romantic speculation: "At the time all the buildings immediately seemed age-old in their beauty, while now, thanks to their energy they seem modern and newly made, so much does their constant freshness blossom, making them appear untouched by time, as if the ever-vibrant breath of an unageing spirit permeated every work."[9]

If Plutarch is gushing, our other major source, the roughly contemporary traveller, Pausanias, is frustratingly sparse and prosaic. In his *Travels Around Greece* he devotes a few brief sentences to the Parthenon and its statue, more interested in expounding his knowledge of griffins than in recording what he saw on the Acropolis; and, while his brief description of the temple's pedimental sculptures has proved invaluable to modern scholars, his reliance on an apparently ambiguous or ill-informed tour guide has led to misunderstandings of the statue's plinth which still persist today. At least Pausanias provides some detail, which is more than can be said for other writers of his era. Yes, Pliny the Elder tells us that the statue was made from gold and ivory, but other than that? Nothing. As for the third-century-A.D. biographer, Diogenes Laertius, all he contributes to the sum of our knowledge is that "the Parthenon at any rate is beautiful."[10]

Of course, we do have other valuable evidence: much of the Parthenon survives along with many of its sculptures, and although they are fragmented and disfigured their subject can be recognized. From Pausanias we learn that those on the east pediment showed Athena's birth, and the west her contest with Poseidon for the land of Attica. From autopsy we know that the four sets of *metopēs* (self-contained high-relief sculptural slabs set on the architrave above the columns on the outside of the temple) showed scenes of mythological battles, and that the continuous low-relief (Ionic) frieze that ran behind this outer architrave around the outside of the sekos (the temple's basic boxlike structure) roughly forty feet above ground level showed a procession—horsemen, charioteers, and worshippers—which culminated in a scene of five human participants surrounded by the twelve Olympian gods.

However, between recognizing subject matter and understanding its significance lies a world of difference. It is partly because of this that so much continues to be written about the Parthenon, its related buildings and their sculptures. For, while there are ongoing advances in our appreciation of the archaeology of ancient Athens and the architectural complexity of the Parthenon, and while it is generally recognized that the carefully curated subject matter of the temple's sculptures (many of them repeated, we are told, in details of the goddess's cult statue) was intended to project a message to both Athens and the rest of Greece, there is still no generally agreed consensus as to what that message was.

Yet, if we are to try fully to comprehend fifth-century-B.C. Athens, we cannot shirk from trying to comprehend the thinking behind the Parthenon's sculptures, since they encapsulate an image of the city which was being honed by its intellectual elite partly to project Athenian power, and justify imperialism, but partly, too, to find new ways to glorify its citizens. Carved in marble, they are both a record and a commentary as significant as Thucydides' history or Euripides' dramas.

The sculptures' structure, form and consequence can be appreciated at first glance, but, like their literary counterparts, a deeper understanding requires awareness of their own inner complexity and the external factors which helped shape their creation: the events, values, and beliefs of sixth- and fifth-century-B.C. Greece in general and Athens in particular.

For, the Parthenon was not created in a vacuum. Conceived in 449 B.C. and begun in 447, it was the centrepiece of an ambitious public programme whereby not just in Athens but throughout Attica temples and sanctuaries left ruined since being burnt some thirty-three years earlier by invading Persians were rebuilt to the highest specifications, many using the best, most costly materials. The timing of the project was significant. A year or so earlier, Athens had made peace with Persia, an event of huge significance, setting the city on a par with a great empire stretching all the way to India and positioning Athens as the leading power in Greece, something for which Athenians had striven over many years, a cause of celebration as they looked back on a remarkable six decades—most recently the acquisition of an empire, following their city's rebirth after Persian destruction, in turn following the overthrow of tyranny and the foundation of their boldly new experimental democratic constitution. The sense of can-do optimism, that anything was possible, which these events engendered, inspired and permeated the new building programme.

So, alongside ambitions for the future was a profound awareness of the past. The temples which the Persians burned had been constructed in the first two decades of the new democracy at a time when Athens had seen off not just an oppressive ruling family but concerted attacks from rival city-states. If the symbolism of the temples then had been profound, the symbolism of their postwar ruins had been profounder still, since during Persia's invasions, when many of those rival city-states had coalesced grudgingly into an uneasy alliance, Athenians had made the greatest sacrifice and borne the brunt of the destruction. At the same time, (they could argue, and they did) they had made the greatest contribution to Greek victory—on land at the Battle of Marathon; at sea at the Battle of Salamis. Thanks to their steadfastness,

Greece was free. Thanks to their resolution, their ruined city had been reborn from its ashes.

Many Athenians attributed their city's success to two main factors. One was its democratic constitution, in which every citizen of every class could participate at almost every level, attending every meeting of the Assembly, voting on every motion, and being eligible to hold most offices of state. The other was the favour of the gods. It was only thanks to their support and intervention and that of local demigods or heroes that they believed that Athens had prevailed against apparently insuperable odds; and the reasons for those gods', heroes', and demigods' support were their age-old love of Attica (evinced in myth and legend) and Athenians' unique character and piety. No other Greek city-state celebrated so many religious festivals, and the cityscape and landscape were alive with not just sanctuaries and shrines, but offerings paid for and consecrated by the state and private citizens, often in thanks for victory in battle. For most Athenians, the Parthenon was one such offering made to the city's patron goddess, Athena.

But not for all. The sixth and fifth centuries B.C. were a time of bold scientific discovery and intellectual growth. Through observation natural philosophers began to overturn old certainties, suggesting, for example, that heavenly bodies were not divine, but balls of fire or lumps of earth, and questioning the nature of the gods, their power and even their existence. Among those embracing such new ideas was Pericles, Athens' leading statesmen, the man (so we are told) behind the construction project of which the Parthenon was part. As a religious sceptic, his motivation for building temples to the gods must clearly have been different from that of pious believers. For him politics and the possibility for propaganda played a more important role than veneration, and surviving versions of his speeches lend credence to the idea that sculptors and artists working on the Parthenon channelled his carefully honed vision of a democratic Athens, where living citizens, through sacrifice and effort, attained a godlike status equal to that of the dead heroes of mythology. Designed to boost the city's self-esteem and standing in the eyes of others, this vision was not entirely new. While literature is silent on the matter, since the late sixth century B.C., the architecture of state buildings had consciously (and perhaps controversially) drawn on religious models in a manner that suggested that the demos (the civic body) and democracy were viewed as somehow godlike.

For so long as Athens prospered, the private sceptical beliefs of Pericles and his coterie, even if they were known publicly, did not really seem to matter. But just a year after the Parthenon was finished, Pericles' policies plunged Athens and her empire into war with Sparta and her allies; a plague killed a third of all Athenians, including Pericles himself; Athens' finances haemorrhaged; she suffered military defeats; and earthquakes rocked the city, cracking columns of the Parthenon, dislodging sculptures. To those opposed to Pericles, his politics, and policies, these misfortunes were proof of his misguided leadership and wrongheaded religious beliefs. Because of them, they argued, gods who once favoured Athens were angered: Apollo, god of plague, who killed thousands of Athenians; Poseidon, god of earthquakes, who razed large parts of the city; and Athena, who rejected her new Parthenon, suffering its damage as a sign of her discontent.

Following the plague and earthquakes, more new temples were quickly built—for Athena and Poseidon on the Athenian Acropolis; for Apollo on his sacred island, Delos. But for post-Periclean Athens it was too late. War with Sparta ended in defeat and the temporary suspension of democracy, and as Athenians took stock and questioned how such calamity had come to pass, many saw its seeds in the kind of thinking which Pericles had once famously embraced and Socrates still sought to promulgate. They could get rid of Socrates with little bother, but the sheer cost of Pericles' most famous monument meant that it must endure. So, the Parthenon remained on the Acropolis, a curious anomaly, a temple with no altar and no priestess of its own, more state treasury than religious building, which was why a century on from Athens' defeat a triumphant general could convert it into plush accommodation for himself and his pool of mistresses.[11]

For its original meaning and importance to be appreciated, then, the Parthenon must be seen within its wider context—the context of the Periclean building project and the building project in the early years of the Athenian democracy; the context of temple building throughout the Greek world, where religious structures and associated sculptures were used both to project power and to attract the approbation and protection of the gods; the context of shifting attitudes towards religion, of Athens' politics, her constitution, the two Persian invasions and her rise as an imperial power; and the context of the tensions which gave the city its identity but at the same time threatened to destroy it, tensions rising out of rivalries between diverse cultures, powerful families, classes, generations, and those whose vision of the world and mankind's place in it proved incompatible.

These themes weave through this book, as other themes weave through the subject matter of the sculptures we shall be discussing, themes such as mythology and cult, death and rebirth, civilization and hegemony, humanity, each one a constant background presence occasionally coming to the fore like a line of music in a fugue. But even the most complex fugue must be lucid to its listener, driving on with clear momentum until it reaches its conclusion, as accessible to the nonspecialist as to the expert. In a book with many strands of thought this can be difficult to achieve, but I hope that, by mixing historical narrative with architectural and artistic analysis, I might come close to doing so. For, despite the volume of words being written every day—perhaps each hour—about the Parthenon, I believe this book has something fresh to say, bringing a slightly different focus to and shedding a slightly different light upon not just the building and its sculptures but Athens in the course of the fifth century B.C. And because for the most part this is a book about not just a building programme or what happens when new certainties too quickly seek to topple old, but a city and the people who once lived there, we shall begin by visiting its democratic heart and meeting some of its key citizens as they gathered on a hill just west of the Acropolis some nineteen years before the two Arrhephoroi we have already met were dressing in their pure white robes to start their journey through the fissure in the rock. We shall begin one early morning in 449 B.C. as Athenians are pouring up onto the Pnyx for a much-anticipated meeting of their democratic Assembly.

1 LAYING THE FOUNDATIONS

Everything is full of gods.

—THALES OF MILETUS (QUOTED IN ARISTOTLE, *ON THE SOUL,* 411A7)

Athens, 449 B.C.

Already, like an evanescent dream, the darkness was evaporating, as sunrise gilded faces, arms, gesticulating hands, for a brief moment turning commonplace Athenians into glowing heroes. Alive with anticipation, through narrow moonlit lanes and alleys flickering with torchlight, they had gathered early on Pnyx Hill, conscious that today could represent a landmark in their history, a day when, even as they honoured their heroic past, they might quite literally begin to build a glorious future. On most of the roughly forty days each year, when the Assembly was held, the hollowed-out and banked-up auditorium was slow to fill as, half asleep, latecomers shuffled in with unenthusiastic yawns, resigned to hours of tedium, or, later still and breathless, stumbled up the slope, determined to avoid the crimson-paint-soaked ropes with which the Scythian archers, officers of law and order, rounded up whomever they caught loitering (imposing fines on anyone they later found with red-streaked tunics). This morning, though, with the sun already rising gold above Hymettus to bathe the city in its light and silhouette the plateau and sheer cliffs of the Acropolis, the Pnyx (quite literally "the congested place") was already packed to overflowing.[1]

1.1 The Acropolis (*right*) and Areopagus (*left*) seen from the Pnyx.

The city was a rumour mill, and word had leaked out from the Boulē, the deliberative Council which vetted every motion put before a vote of the Assembly, that Pericles himself was going to speak. He was a mesmerizing orator, whose appearances on Pnyx Hill were so rare that for some it was worth arriving early to get close enough to make sure they could hear him. As for his proposal—a massive building programme, which would bring employment to many hundreds, if not thousands of Athenians, and untold prestige to Athens—nothing like it had been mooted for nigh on half a century. No wonder that the atmosphere was so electric, a growing babble of excited voices as people jostled into place, all focussed on the Speaker's Platform, all trying to see if Pericles was there, all speculating about what precisely he might say.[2]

And then a sudden hush, the silence punctuated only by the bark of dogs from urban courtyards or cockerels crowing in cramped smallholdings or peacocks screeching eerily from far-off gardens of a rich ambassador, before the Pnyx was purified—a piglet carried squealing round the boundaries and sacrificed, its warm blood flicked across the seats of the executive officials, smoke billowing from burning incense, prayers offered to the gods and curses called down on the heads of enemies—a moment of shared contemplation before at last the public crier climbed the steps onto the Speaker's Platform and intoned the well-known formula, "Who wants to speak?" And then the hubbub of anticipation as a figure strode from the front row up onto the Platform and surveyed a sea of faces.[3]

Perhaps 6,000 people, between a fifth and tenth of all Athenian citizens, were gathered here, men mostly from the city or nearby Piraeus with its busy port, since those who lived in wider Attica, its towns and villages, its scattered farms and hamlets (if they had not camped out last night beneath the stars) would be hard pressed to make it into Athens for the dawn. Yet, many strata of society were represented here: potters and painters, metalworkers, some with workshops in the smoky Cerameicus district down in the valley below; stallholders and market gardeners; shoemakers who plied their trade beside the Agora, the public square that doubled as a marketplace beneath the Pnyx and the Acropolis; shipwrights, sea captains, and fishermen up from Piraeus' quays; an army (quite literally, as it was the duty of each citizen to fight when called to do so) of anonymous Athenians, but doubtless many, too, whose names are known to us—men such as the superstitious Nicias, rich from the silver mines at Laurium, or Sophocles, the pious, handsome dramatist, or the controversial musicologist, Damon, or Pheidias, the sculptor, or architects Ictinus and Callicrates, or Epizelus, the blind war hero, who swore that he had seen a demigod, or the young intellectual, Socrates.[4]

But this morning only one man truly mattered: Pericles, Xanthippus' son, the imposing figure with his dark curly hair and neat, well-barbered beard now standing, silhouetted on the Speaker's Platform. Instantly recognisable from his almost preternaturally large skull, his full lips, and his hooded eyes, not to mention the relaxed insouciance of his patrician demeanour, it was little wonder that those Athenians who did not call him by the nickname "Squill Head," referred to him as "The Olympian" or "Zeus." While, like the god, he tried to stay aloof, above the brouhaha of daily life, for more than twelve years he had dominated Athens both as a politician and as military commander, and the influence he wielded was enormous. At forty-five years old, already at the pinnacle of his career, soon to be considered the "first man of Athens," he dominated the most affluent and powerful city-state in the Greek world. So trusted was he to defend their interests that the working class of Attica—in Greek, the demos meaning both "the People" and "the poor"—now saw him as their leader, regardless of his wealth or the fact that, as a member of a landed family, the Alcmaeonids, he was born into privilege. Thanks to his intellect and charismatic oratory, proposals Pericles or (through him) any of his circle put to voters were likely to become state policy.[5]

This was not to say that Pericles did not have enemies, cautious landowners, old-school traditionalists, religious conservatives, deeply suspicious of his aggressive foreign policy and what they thought to be his overly progressive, populist ideas. But for the moment these men were leaderless. Just a year before, the elder statesman, Cimon, their respected champion, had died on campaign in Cyprus, and while his relative, Thucydides Melesiou (son of Melesias, so called to distinguish him from his cousin, the historian), showed clear potential, he still lacked the experience and nous to take on Pericles. It was one of many reasons why there could be no better time for Pericles to unveil a wide-reaching, radical proposal, which would (if passed) transform the face of Athens and her land of Attica forever.[6]

~ ~ ~

This much we can reconstruct with confidence from ancient sources, although even so some details are conjectured. That a building programme was proposed in 449 B.C. is certain, as is the process of the bill from its committee stage in the Boulē to the vote in the Assembly. But, while Pericles is widely credited with being its author and champion, we have no firm evidence that this is so. Plutarch, his biographer, who lived a full five centuries later, records that Pericles often had friends and allies bring his own proposals before the demos, Athens' voting citizens. But even the number of those citizens is un-

1.2 Bust of Pericles (Roman marble copy of a Greek original).

known, with modern estimates ranging from 30,000 up to 60,000. The capacity of the Pnyx is similarly open to question, though 6,000 seems likely. In this most participatory of democracies, only a fraction of those eligible were physically able to vote.[7]

While there was certainly a debate about the building programme, we have no record of the speech (or speeches) made by its proposer, or of those made in opposition. Nor do we know the arguments involved, or the proposed timescale or even the extent of the original project, although again we can make informed conjectures. We can be certain that every one of the Athenians packed on Pnyx Hill was familiar with three things which we can only grasp at—so familiar that they took them for granted: the democratic history of Athens spanning the past sixty years, and the part that Athens played in wider Greek affairs; the place religion held in their beliefs and daily life; and the role in Greek society of construction projects such as the one they were being invited to approve.

Without a clear-eyed understanding of them all, the proposal's impact, importance, and subsequent realization cannot be fully understood. So, before allowing Pericles to put his Parthenon and wider building project to the People, we must pause and delve deep into Athens' history and beliefs. Four chapters it will take, until we can return to this key moment and hit play, but unless we do the groundwork and are sure of the stability of our foundations, we shall never build a comprehensive understanding of the Parthenon and what it meant for Athens. For, like any work of art however timeless, the Parthenon was the product of its age and of the people who conceived it. And, since Pericles was chief among those people, it is through him and his experience that we shall start, sketching out his city's past, its religion and mythology, before we turn to the phenomenon of temple building in the light of Greece's history.

~ ~ ~

As the herald brought the vast assembly to order, it may well have seemed to Pericles as if his whole life had been leading to this moment and his motion to transform his city's fabric. He may have conjured early memories of Persian invasions, the first just over forty years before, the next just over thirty, for Pericles had lived through both. As a boy of five, he had experienced the terror as the Persian fleet approached, trailing in its wake destruction, fire, and death. He had seen his father strap on armour and march, grim-faced, with every other man of fighting age to Marathon to sacrifice his life, if need be, in what seemed a hopeless bid to hold back the invaders. He had shared his family's and city's jubilation when almost all these men returned, against all hope victorious, triumphant, standing tall, and a euphoric Athens sacrificed in celebration to her gods.[8]

Ten years later, now fifteen years old, he had experienced it all again: reports of a vast Persian navy nosing through the currents like a shoal of black sharks scenting blood; a monstrous army tramping west from Asia, so many men that they drank rivers dry; the order to abandon Attica and Athens—not through cowardice, but as a sacrifice, to let the land, the city, and its temples burn to form a firebreak, to give their allies time to regroup and rethink; weeping families at quaysides; bewildered women climbing into boats, clutching children tightly lest they lose them in the crowds; the short voyage to Salamis, the island where the fleet was based; and then, across the headland on that grim September day, the black smoke belching high into the pale blue sky and dissipating, drifting, no need to ask where it was coming from—the temple of Athena, the Acropolis, the sacred buildings on the sacred rock.

Days later, when it seemed that all was lost, boys like Pericles watched at daybreak from the beach on Salamis as Greek triremes rowed out into the bay; they heard the war cry echo from the cliff; they shouted their encouragement as warships of the allied Greek force splintered Persian hulls, and stared in thankful wonder as the enemy backed water, turned and fled; and they cheered the next year, too, when the rump of Persia's army left in Greece was cut down at Plataea on the same day (it was said) as on the other side of the Aegean Greeks, including an Athenian contingent led by Pericles' own father, won a crushing victory. Despite the passing of the years, Athenian memories were raw, not least of how, after the Persians were routed, citizens had filed subdued onto the Acropolis, its air still heavy with the charnel stench of death, to clear away charred wreckage and the faceless, brittle corpses of the stubborn men and women who had stayed behind, believing that by doing so they would save their city.

Even then, there was the constant consternation that the Persians would return. Which was why—to liberate those cities still controlled by Persia and remove the threat forever—Greek allies formed a league, whose leadership soon passed from overbearing Sparta to calculating, savvy Athens. It was perhaps the greatest turning point in Athens' history. Yes, it was chiefly thanks to Athens' fleet that Greece had smashed the Persian ships at Salamis. Yes, Athens' army almost singlehandedly had driven off the Persians at Marathon. And yes, Athens boasted her new democratic constitution, thanks to which (if recent history could be believed) she was invincible. But for Athens, one of the most dynamic merchant cities in the whole Aegean, possessed of Greece's strongest navy, to be the leader of a sea-based League meant untold opportunities for building wealth and power.

Athenians had responded with gusto. Thanks to effective leadership, irrepressible energy, unswerving self-belief, and conviction that the gods were on their side, they won resounding military victories, tightening their grip over the League until it mutated almost imperceptibly into a tribute-paying empire, and increasing the range and scope of their commercial interests until Piraeus' wharves and warehouses, and Athens' market stalls were packed with goods imported not just from the Aegean and the coastal strip of Asia Minor but from Carthage, Sicily and Italy, Egypt and Libya, and as far away as the Black Sea and Crimea. Meanwhile, although much of the city remained as unplanned and haphazard as it was before the Persian destruction (hasty rebuilding had preserved old networks of narrow streets and twisting lanes), the central Agora, a semi-sacred space where business could be done and spectacles performed, was lined with cool, impressive public buildings: colonnaded stoas; law courts; offices.[9]

But still three decades after the Persian invasions, despite Athens' newfound power and ever-growing wealth, her Acropolis (literally her "upper city"), her sacred heart, its temples torched by Persians, remained almost untouched. Preserved as a memorial, crumbling, pockmarked walls of broken buildings still protruded from long grass like fractured tombstones, some sufficiently secure to be adorned with offerings and trophies from past wars or lined with fragile statues still more-or-less intact and rescued from the rubble. Among them were the ruins of the holiest, most sacred building in all Athens—the Temple of Athena Polias, Athena of the City-State, once home to the xoanon, a venerable statue of the goddess, her arms stretched wide, a sacred vessel held in her right hand, an owl, her avatar, perched on her left. Hewn from olive wood (or constructed round a core of olive wood), it was so primitive in execution, that it was said to have once fallen from the skies, a gift from the goddess, imbued with her immortal energy to protect the people of her city, "light-infused and violet crowned, adored by poets, defender of all Greece."[10]

And so it had. Fleeing Athens, abandoning the sacred rock to Persian fire, the citizens had taken their xoanon with them, and, when the war was over, and the Persians gone, they brought it home again in triumph. Then, with the Acropolis repurified, they installed it in a temporary shrine, where, guarded by Athena's priestess, it gazed out every morning as the sun rose over the ruins, and the city woke. Knotty, gnarled the xoanon might be, but it possessed great majesty. Its head crowned with a golden diadem, gold earrings framed its face. A golden necklace hung about its throat, while clasped across its shoulders was a golden aegis (a magic snake-fringed goatskin), over which was slung a golden likeness of Medusa's severed head, the Gorgon, whose grim stare turned anyone it met to stone. A saffron yellow peplos clothed the xoanon, a woollen robe woven on the Acropolis by a chosen team of girls and dedicated to the goddess by the citizens of Athens, its fabric worked with figures in contrasting blue. They showed a legendary battle between gods and Giants, the Gigantomachy, in which Athena earned her spurs by cutting down the bloodthirsty Enceladus, as civilized Greek gods of Mount Olympus fought off the violent, nihilistic children of the Earth who were intent on their destruction.

The parallels between this battle and the Persian Wars were by now so well rehearsed that they seemed obvious.[11]

The same scene had appeared, too, on the destroyed Old Temple's eastern pediment, whose statuary had toppled in the fire. Contemporaries of Pericles had known it well. Created ten years or so before his birth, the first pedimental sculptures in the city to be carved from island marble, the first Greek public artworks to place the goddess centre stage, the first religious statement of the new democracy, they had highlighted Athena's role in keeping not just Athens but the very cosmos safe. All who had seen the composition could recall the power that emanated from the goddess—her hair painted auburn, her snake-fringed aegis red and blue, her metal spear tip and her jewellery glinting in the sunlight. Now more than ever, though these sculptures were destroyed, when they visited the vandalized Acropolis, driving flocks of sheep or herds of cattle to the altar to be slaughtered, devout Athenians knew that Athena had not abandoned them. For while their city had been ruined, they themselves had emerged stronger than ever. Which was why the war-torn landscape of the Acropolis possessed such potency. A testament to their goddess's protective love and to their own devotion and sacrifice, the sacred rock's three hectares anchored their sense of identity and linked past struggles with what they were convinced would be their glorious future.[12]

It was not just the Acropolis that Persians had burned. Throughout Attica fire had ripped through temples, leaving sanctuaries and altars blackened. But even by felling trees for fuel or setting up their bivouacs in the Agora, the invaders had potentially offended Attic gods, for many Greeks believed that gods were everywhere. As Thales, the philosopher from Greek Miletus on the western shores of Asia Minor, observed a century before, "everything is full of gods." And most Athenians agreed: gods strode the mountaintops and seas; nymphs lingered in the woods and rock pools; powerful spirits ruled the kingdom of the dead. At every turn most of mankind was constantly aware of them. As they left home or worked in fields, set sail, or marched to battle, most citizens felt a sense of certainty ingrained since childhood that they, their wives, and family must pay due honour to these gods, for they were dangerously mercurial.[13]

Like capricious human rulers, gods could be kind or cruel. All had their favourites, which was why it was so crucial to ensure their favour. While mankind might choose which stories to accept about the gods, invent new tales or even mock them (as they might mock a mortal leader such as Pericles), a shared belief in their existence and in their readiness to intervene in both the lives of individuals and the affairs of state helped underpin a sense of social cohesion. Gift-giving was essential to keep gods onside, and each god or spirit had their favourite gifts—a honey cake offered at a household shrine; a drizzle of sweet wine poured at a tomb; a sheep or goat or bull, its throat cut at an altar, its pale fat wrapped in skin and burnt, its fragrance drifting to the skies. To make proper sacrifice, to give proper gifts increased the chances that the deity would feel inclined to answer prayers or curses and lend support when it was needed most.[14]

But some locations were more sacred than others, and with its cliffs erupting some 500 feet above the olive-studded plain the Acropolis, a towering limestone outcrop, a rough ovoid in shape, was at once not just commanding but mysterious and numinous. Viewed from surrounding hills—the nearby Areopagus, Nymphs' Hill, the Pnyx and Muses' Hill, or conical Mount Lycabettus a mile to the northeast—or from the Attic plain, with its slow trickling rivers, Eridanus, Ilissus, and Cephisus, embraced by mountain chains (Aegaleus and Parnes, Pentelicus, Hymettus) that arced in a giant horseshoe west to east, it made for a commanding presence. Stand on the heights of the Acropolis, and gaze not only inland towards Attica but out across the sparkling Saronic Gulf, the purple silhouette of Aegina, the hazy folds and contours of the pale blue Peloponnesian massif rippling in the distance, the rugged hills of fateful Salamis stark in the morning sun, and that sense of power was multiplied.[15]

Primeval, impregnable, commanding, the Acropolis was sacred to Athena. But not to her alone. With its dark caves and jagged folds and upward-sloping plateau with access only from the west, for generations it had housed a host of sanctuaries, of which Athena's (while the most significant) was only one. At its highest point there was a walled-off open-air enclosure dedicated to the sky god, Zeus, the patriarch of the great family of deities who were believed to have their home on Mount Olympus, the highest mountain on the Greek mainland 250 miles northwest of Athens. Wielding power over the cosmos with his children, his wife, Hera, and brothers, Hades and Poseidon, Zeus, arbiter of justice, who, when riled, made heavens shake with thunder and blasted wrongdoers with his lightning bolt, was magisterial in his authority but lax in his morality. He enthusiastically pursued extramarital affairs with goddesses and mortal women, a tendency for which Athenians especially could hardly censure him. For among the children born from these liaisons was Athena.[16]

The story of her birth was well known to every Greek, a myth which, while it did not follow the same laws of nature that govern human conduct, they believed could easily have happened in the parallel, augmented universe of the divine. Having slept with the goddess Metis, whose name meant "wisdom" or "cunning," Zeus learned from a prophecy that any son he had by her would topple him from power. To forestall which, he swallowed pregnant Metis whole. As she approached full term, Zeus' head began to pound, and pressure on his skull grew more intense. Unable to find another cure, he ordered the blacksmith god, Hephaestus, to smite him on the forehead with an axe—and from his severed (but immediately healed) skull emerged Athena. One hymn praising her, the "grey-eyed goddess, cunning, and implacable, pure virgin, the brave saviour of cities," would later tell how:

> *Wise Zeus himself gave birth to her*
> *out of his venerable head, and she was clad in armour,*
> *golden, glinting. When they saw her, all the gods*
> *were struck with awe. At once, Athena leapt from*
> *aegis-wearing Zeus' deathless head, and stood before him*
> *brandishing a keen-edged spear. Mighty Olympus*
> *shuddered at the grey-eyed goddess' sheer strength, and the earth*
> *around it bellowed loudly. The sea boiled; dark waves rolled; and*

sudden foam erupted. For long, long hours the blazing sun god
reined in his swift-hooved horses until from her deathless shoulders
the maiden, Pallas Athena, removed her divine armour.[17]

Another hymn would play up her warlike attributes:

I begin to sing of Pallas Athena, who protects the city-state,
the dread goddess, who with Ares orchestrates the deeds of war,
the sack of cities, and the din of shouting, and the fighting.
She shields her people as they march to battle and come home again.
Greetings, goddess. Give us good fortune and blessedness.[18]

Time and again—before, during and after the Persian Wars—the citizens of democratic Athens believed they had been saved in battle by their terrifying, indomitable patron deity in recognition of their piety, which was why they valued especially three aspects of her nature expressed in different epithets: Athena Polias, "Athena, of the City-State"; Athena Promachus, "Athena, Fighter in the Front Line"; and Athena Nikē, "Athena of Victory." But the goddess had other concerns, too. The embodiment of wisdom, she was skilled in weaving, exulted in the arts, and especially (Athenians believed) loved Attica, the land which boasted Athens as its capital.

For Athenians—not just the mainly urban voters gathered on Pnyx Hill, but villagers and smallholders and farmers, whose livelihood came from the land—the soil of Attica had mystical associations. It was the fatherland, the giver of life, a place to be defended at the cost of their *own* lives, which in a solemn oath, as they passed to adulthood, its citizens swore to hand on to future generations "not worse, but stronger and better than I received it." It was, they believed, a land for ownership of which Athena had fought, too, when Poseidon, her uncle, despite his sphere of interest being the sea, earthquakes, and horses (all linked by their shifting, bucking motion), tried to claim it for his own. Legend told how both drove their chariots to the Acropolis and, ready to do battle, leapt onto the rock. But Zeus hurled a sulphurous thunderbolt, which exploded in a blinding wall of light, and ordered that the matter should be settled not by violence but by arbitration—albeit (wisely) not by him.[19]

Instead, he commanded the Athenian king, Cecrops, to leave his palace (also on the Acropolis) and sit in judgement, while the two gods argued their case. Each offered Cecrops and his people a gift. Poseidon thrust his trident deep into the rock, where a salt spring bubbled up, a miniature ocean, a promise that, if victory were his, Athens would be mistress of the sea. But Athena planted a sprig of olive in the rock's thin stony soil where, roots nuzzling down into the earth, its trunk grew thick, and breezes rustled in its glaucous leaves. The canny Cecrops was enchanted. With its prized oil, the olive tree could make his city rich. So, he awarded Athens to Athena, and she had been the city's patron goddess ever since.

For most Athenians, this was not mere myth but mystic history, as true and real as deeds performed a century before by their great-grandfathers, and kept alive, fine-honed through repetition across generations, perhaps slightly embellished, but containing an essential core of truth. There might be different versions, fresh details added by each teller, but, like the framework of more recent history, the basic story stayed the same, not least because Athenians possessed clear evidence that it was true, "tokens" left on the Acropolis by both gods for eternity. From deep within the rock a well of salt seawater could at times be heard to roar, while rising from its limestone surface, not far from where Poseidon's trident left its three deep scars, there grew a gnarled old olive tree, the very tree (Athenians maintained) which had been planted by Athena, the ancestor of every olive tree that shimmered throughout Attica, or was exported far and wide as part of what increasingly Athenians regarded as their civilizing mission to improve mankind's condition.[20]

But myth or mystic history showed that this mission could not be achieved without sacrifice. Cecrops' judgement did not end the two gods' rivalry. Angered by Athena's victory, Poseidon unleashed a tidal wave, engulfing Attica, annexing Athena's fiefdom, until only the Acropolis and a few surrounding hilltops stood island-like above the waves. Again, Zeus intervened. Poseidon backed down, and dry land reappeared, albeit now impoverished, but still he harboured deep resentment. Forbidden to strike directly at Athena, he ordered his mortal son, Eumolpus, king of grain-rich Eleusis on the Bay of Salamis, to attack neighbouring Athens, whose new king, Erechtheus, learned from an oracle that victory would be his—if one of his three daughters sacrificed her life.[21]

There are different versions of what happened next. All agree that one of the girls did sacrifice herself, and willingly. But even fifth-century-B.C. antiquarians could not agree about which one, or how she fitted into the complex nexus of dead maidens whose memory still haunted the Acropolis. Some said she was Aglaurus, but others called her Pandora, a name (meaning "All-Giving") which she shared with the first mortal woman—and which, as we shall see, was the alias of yet another Acropolis princess, and so the cause of much confusion in antiquity and now. Whatever her name, the noble maiden leapt to her death from the Acropolis, and in solidarity her sisters followed her. As prophesied, Erechtheus marched out to battle, and slew Eumolpus—at which Poseidon, enraged, rained down such blows on the Athenian king's head that he sank deep beneath the earth.[22]

Now even Poseidon was sated. He made peace with Athena, agreed to help her people, the Athenians, become rulers of the sea, and joining his name to that of his dead enemy consented to be worshipped on the Athenian Acropolis as Poseidon-Erechtheus. Meanwhile, Eleusis recognized Athenian sovereignty over everything except the conduct of her annual initiation ceremonies—in Greek, "Mysteries"—whose secrets were so arcane that only certain priestly families might reveal them, but whose promises gave mankind hope. Once more, location and religion met in powerful synthesis, since the myth behind these Mysteries—one of the most potent in the entire Greek world, and one which Pericles was to harness in the visual imagery of his new building programme—was insolubly fused into the very limestone of Eleusis.[23]

The myth told of a young goddess, Korē ("Girl"). While picking flowers in a meadow, she was abducted by her lustful uncle, the Underworld king, Hades, who dragged her beneath the earth, where he called her his queen, Persephone. Meanwhile, her mother, Demeter, searched vainly throughout Greece, a flaming torch held in each hand, until, disguised, she reached Eleusis. Here, cheered by bawdy humour and a heady drink, she agreed to work for the royal household, and would have made its prince immortal by plunging him into a fire, had not his mother intervened in terror and prevented her. Only now did Demeter reveal her true identity. A sixth-century-B.C. hymn recounts how she commanded Eleusinians to "build me a great temple and an altar beneath it. . . . And I shall myself instruct you in my sacred rites, so that for all future time you might perform them with pure hands and appease my spirit." But once in her new temple, Demeter sat dejected, allowing the crops, whose growth was in her care, to fail. With famine came death, and, since mortals could no longer sacrifice, even the gods suffered. So, Zeus ordered Hades to return Persephone, and from a cavern in the Eleusinian rockface, escorted by the traveller god Hermes she reemerged into the light. At once, fecundity returned to fields and pasturelands, and in her joy Demeter showed the local rulers (including Eumolpus)

> *how to take care of her sacred rites, and she taught her sacred*
> *Mysteries . . .*
> *which no one might transgress or question or*
> *speak of since great veneration of the gods keeps the tongue silent.*
> *Blessèd is that earth-dwelling man who has witnessed the Mysteries,*
> *but he who is uninitiated and has no part in them never shares*
> *in such a fate when he is dead beneath the earth in misty darkness.*[24]

However, in the Underworld Persephone had eaten a pomegranate seed, because of which (the logic of the myth dictated) she was forced to return beneath the earth for four months of each year, and so experience a never-ending cycle of life, death, and rebirth. As crops were sown and harvested, the earth experienced this cycle, too, and it was not too great a leap of reason to suggest that human life might also follow such a pattern.

Whether initiation at Eleusis promised rebirth after death, or simply a better afterlife, many people—not just Athenians, but men and women, slaves and free from other poleis, too—were keen to undergo its complex rituals, even if this meant journeying twice to Attica, once for the Lesser Mysteries, a preliminary purification ceremony held in spring, and again for the Great Mysteries eighteen months later. Here, following registration in Athens' Agora and payment of not inconsiderable fees, they first travelled in carts down to the sea for rites of ritual cleansing and to sacrifice a piglet each to Demeter, before isolating in advance of initiation itself. Then, amid mounting apprehension and excitement, at the end of each September, as the parched earth became suitable for farming once again, they gathered at dawn at the city's northwest Sacred Gate before setting off along the cobbled road on a thirteen-mile procession, chanting hymns to Iacchus, one of the cult names of Dionysus, god of transformation, and carrying bacchoi, branches consecrated to the god, along the Sacred Way from Athens to Eleusis, and the terrifying initiation ceremony. Because participants were forbidden to reveal what happened there, we can only guess its nature, but oblique hints and allusions scattered across centuries of literature suggest that in the Telesterion (Initiation Hall), with great theatricality, initiates, dazed, disorientated, and maybe drugged, endured a spine-chilling cacophony of shouts and clashing cymbals, all in total darkness before, in a sudden blinding blaze of torchlight, they saw a vision of Demeter and Persephone, enthroned among them, receiving reassurance that, no matter how they had behaved on earth, in death they would experience prosperity and happiness.[25]

But for Athenians no sanctuary in Athens, Attica, or wider Greece could rival their Acropolis, not least because they all believed that they had ultimately sprung out of its soil: the Acropolis had once (quite literally, they thought) given them birth. The legend, which explained this, again featured Erechtheus, whose own miraculous birth involved Athena and Hephaestus. In many ways, each god was the other's mirror image: the virgin Athena, born from Zeus' head, was motherless;

Hephaestus was conceived by Hera through parthenogenesis; and while the lithe Athena was determined to preserve her maidenhood, lame, brawny Hephaestus, god of manufacturing by means of fire and sweaty toil, lusted to deflower her. Rebuffed on the Acropolis, he ejaculated over her bare thigh, at which the ever-practical Athena cleaned herself with a woollen cloth, then threw the soggy mess onto the ground, where semen seeped into moist crevices and impregnated Gē, goddess of the earth—and from a vulva-like cleft in the Acropolis, close to the plateau's northwest cliffs, emerged a biform baby with a snaky tail but human torso, head and arms: Erechtheus.

The sight evoked unusually maternal feelings in Athena, but, unsuited to motherhood, she placed the baby in a box, which she entrusted to King Cecrops' three daughters with instructions not to open it. Two could not resist temptation. Disobeying Athena, they glimpsed the monstrous baby, fled in terror, and jumped to their death from the Acropolis. But the third, Pandrosus, an archetype of female excellence, obeyed the goddess, thanks to which Athenians accorded her a special place in their religious hierarchy, worshipping her as a heroine (in Greek religion a special term for a human who, through great deeds became immortal) on the Acropolis in an open-air sanctuary, the Garden of Pandrosus, which also housed Athena's sacred olive tree. So close was the bond between goddess and heroine that Athenian religious protocol dictated that "whoever sacrifices a cow to Athena must sacrifice a ewe to Pandrosus." However, despite her status within Athenian religion, Pandrosus was sometimes known by another name: like Aglaurus, she too bore the alias "Pandora," and, since she is a key part of our story, to avoid confusion, we shall henceforth call her by both these names: Pandrosus/Pandora.[26]

When Erechtheus grew up, he sloughed off his snaky form, ruled Athens wisely and fathered children of his own, and it was from them that all historical Athenians claimed descent—a powerful affirmation that helped cement civic identity. Not only did it mean that, being autochthonous (in other words, earthborn), Athenians enjoyed a strong bond with the land and soil of Attica but that, through Erechtheus, each claimed direct descent from both Gē/Earth and Hephaestus, as well as an unusual familiarity with Athena, Erechtheus' foster mother. Simply put, the blood of all Athenians contained a spark of the divine.[27]

However, even such a potent myth as this had variants. Some claimed that the earthborn baby was not Erechtheus but Erichthonius, another king (whose name combined the words for "wool" and "earth"). But while originally the two were distinct figures, they became so fused in popular imagination that they were thought of as essentially two aspects of one character, a powerful, all-protecting spirit, worshipped on the Acropolis in the form of a sacred snake (and whom, for sake of ease, we shall refer to henceforth as Erechtheus). Myth told how, when Poseidon forced him down beneath the earth from which he had been born, Erechtheus changed back into his snaky form, and fifth-century Athenians believed that he lived on as a serpent, immortal now, on the Acropolis amid the ruins of his Bronze Age palace, emerging from its dark vaults to sup offerings of honey cake left by his priests.[28]

The channel in the rock from which Erechtheus was said to have emerged, a baby, was the focus of another ritual, which served not only to commemorate the virtues of Pandrosus/Pandora and atone for her sisters' disobedience, but to celebrate the cycle of birth, death and rebirth. It was also tightly bound up with Athena, her peplos (sacred robe), and her xoanon (olivewood statue). Each year at midsummer the cult statue was cleansed. Only women from one honoured family, the Praxiergidae, were entrusted with the rite, stripping the statue of its robes and crown and jewellery, wrapping it in cloths and, escorted by an honour guard of young men, riding with it in a wagon to the sea, where, far from prying eyes, two girls uncovered it and bathed it in the drifting waves while a priestess washed the sacred peplos. The entire day was considered dangerous for Attica, a time in which all business was suspended and nothing new could be begun, since, with the goddess absent from the city, her protection could not be assured. The only work done was the cleansing of her shrine, its floor swept, and the jars of oil that lit its lamp filled for the coming year. Then, as evening fell, a procession wound its way back to the city—ranks of young men, armour gleaming in the torchlight; women in their wagon; the statue, dried and wrapped, the peplos neatly folded—back to the Acropolis, where, alone again, the Praxiergidae set the statue on its plinth, replaced the jewellery, and rehung the robes.[29]

Hours later, two young girls performed another ritual. Known as the Arrhephoroi, for twelve months they had lived on the Acropolis in a house shared with the Athena's priestess, where they had watched the setting up of the great loom on which each year was woven a new peplos for the goddess. Now, on the night of the old peplos' cleansing, dressed for the last time in their pure white woollen robes of office, the Arrhephoroi finally earned their title—"carriers of things that cannot be spoken of," sacred objects (whose identity they did not know, and nor do we) contained in caskets, which they set firmly on their heads as they prepared to make a claustrophobic journey. Adjacent to their house was the entrance to the chasm from which Erechtheus had once been born, where a flight of shallow steps, wooden treads affixed into the rock, squeezed down into the pungent darkness, the very heart of the Acropolis. Down these the girls now picked their way, one hand keeping the precious load from slipping from their heads, the other pressed against the stone to steady them, until they reemerged at last into the evening air. The passageway came out into a cave at the bottom of the rock, near the Peripatos Road that circled the Acropolis. Along this the girls strode until they reached a grove, the sanctuary of Aphrodite, known here as "The Lady in the Gardens," shared with her son, Eros. Here they put down their caskets, picked up two others, identical to the first, and with these on their heads, climbed back up the claustrophobic staircase, back onto the Acropolis, where the priestess was awaiting them. These were their final duties. The ritual had transformed them. They could serve no longer. The sacred objects safely delivered, they changed out of their white robes and, dedicating their gold jewellery to the goddess, returned to normal life (and soon to marriage), while two other girls arrived to take their place.[30]

Embedded like so many rituals in a forgotten past, the passage of the Arrhephoroi through the rock was fraught with symbolism. The

1.3 The entrance to the Passage of the Arrhephoroi as it appears today.

"unspeakable things" they carried paralleled the "unseeable" baby Erechtheus, though unlike Pandrosus/Pandora's disobedient sisters the two Arrhephoroi, young, chaste, and dutiful, did not look inside their caskets. Their journey, too, recalled Erechtheus, their white woollen dresses evoking the semen-soaked wool which Athena threw into the chasm, their emergence back onto the rock through the same vulva-shaped cleft mirroring his birth, while their visit to the Gardens of Aphrodite confirmed the importance of fertility. Furnished in the late fifth century with a statue of the goddess by the master sculptor, Alcamenes, this little sanctuary is known to have been decorated with phallic symbols, and it is possible that these were what the caskets, too contained.[31]

Athens enjoyed no fewer than 120 days of festivals each year. Many others, too, revolved around fertility, such as the autumn Thesmophoria, where the remains of piglets, cast into pits in summer, were retrieved and used to mulch the crops. The Mysteries of Eleusis celebrated a similar descent and subsequent ascension, a young girl disappearing into the earth before returning, transformed, to bring new life. So, the journey of the Arrhephoroi, surrogates for every young girl in Athens if not the entire citizenry of Attica, marked the annual regeneration of Athens and the Athenians. Part of a continuum that stretched back to prehistory, it embodied the city's ceaseless renewal as it forged its path into the future, and it was rooted in one uniquely sacred space, which combined the chasm in the rock close to Erechtheus' shrine and Cecrops' grave, Athena's olive tree, the marks of Poseidon's trident, and the Temple of Athena Polias, in 449 B.C. still lying in ruins, stark evidence of Persian destruction.[32]

Such rituals were vital to the lives of the Athenians, providing a sense of rootedness and certainty, shared values, and shared identities. But, constantly mutating in their telling, the myths surrounding them were as susceptible to shifting fashions and priorities as any other aspect of society. Doctrine was less important than the correct performance of ritual, so the detail of myths, exchanged orally or enshrined in art and literature, could be manipulated to reflect or underpin new social values and political realities—and, since myth invariably formed the subject matter for their sculptures, temples were a useful public space on which a city could use myth to promote politics.

In 566 B.C., as she grew more powerful, Athens had brilliantly manipulated myth to her advantage. Keen to host a Panhellenic (all-Greek) festival to rival the Olympic Games and so attract Greeks from across the Mediterranean and Black Sea basins to worship and compete, Athenians established a quadrennial festival, the Great Panathenaea. But all festivals required a good foundation myth, and lacking anything more suitable, Athens elevated what until then may have been a minor folktale into a powerful legend about a turning point in cosmic history: the Gigantomachy, the battle between gods and Giants, part of an ongoing struggle for control over the earth and sky.[33]

The myth had a long backstory. It began with Ouranus, the sky god, and his consort, Gē, the earth, who bore Titans, terrifying creatures, whom from fear or loathing Ouranus forced back inside Gē's womb. But Gē rebelled. When Cronus, her youngest son, was born, she gave him an adamantine sickle, with which he sliced off his father's genitals, and so seized power. But Cronus learned that his own son would in turn usurp him, so—cruel like his father—he devoured every child his wife (and sister), Rhea, bore, until she could stomach it no longer. When their next son, Zeus, was born, she hid him in a cave, and, wrapping a stone in swaddling clothes, presented it to Cronus as if it was their child. When the tyrant swallowed it, he vomited, regurgitating all his eaten children, still undigested, and alive and well. Led by Zeus, they overthrew Cronus and his fellow Titans (a conflict called the Titanomachy) and seized the reins of cosmic power.[34]

Meanwhile Gē, impregnated by semen from Cronus' severed genitals, gave birth to a new race, the Giants, who stormed Olympus to avenge the Titans. But Zeus learned from an oracle that he would win if he enlisted help—from a race as yet unborn: mankind. So, he reached out across time and space, and he discovered Heracles, the mightiest of men, with whose help he faced down the Giants. As battle raged across the heavens, Athena pursued one Giant, Enceladus, far to the west, skewered him with her spear, scooped up the island of Sicily, and slammed it down on top of him. And then (according to Athenians' new version of the myth) in Athens, she celebrated her part in civilization's victory over anarchy by inaugurating games, the forerunner of their new festival, whose centrepiece was a procession onto the Acropolis where, with hymns and sacrifice, her people dressed her ancient xoanon in a robe woven with scenes that showed the battle. The Gigantomachy soon became a favourite theme in art. Sixth-century-B.C. vase painters showed the goddess slaying Enceladus, sculptors carved the moment into stone, while like myths of their autochthony, and legends telling of Athena and Poseidon's contest for the land of Attica, the notion that it was in Athens that Athena chose to celebrate her victory added to the city's growing prestige.[35]

There was one problem, however. Central to the Gigantomachy was Heracles. But Heracles was not Athenian. He did not even share Athenians' Ionian ethnicity. Rather he was a Dorian, ancestor of the two royal families of Athens' greatest rival, Sparta, and, while Athenians were happy to associate themselves with him, they needed their own rival hero. So, in the last decades of the sixth century B.C., immediately before the dawn of their democracy, they elevated one of their own legendary kings to the role of powerful, civilizing hero, whose values—caring for fellow citizens, protecting the oppressed, upholding the rule of law—aligned with those they claimed to be their own. He was Theseus, son of Poseidon.[36]

Among his many exploits—cleansing Attica of wrongdoers, slaying the Cretan Minotaur—two quickly became staples of Athenian art. The first was the Centauromachy, a battle with the half-horse Centaurs, who, maddened by alcohol, tried to abduct Thessalian women from a wedding. Part of the ongoing struggle of civilization over barbarism, with which Athenians felt such personal engagement, this battle saw Theseus fight valiantly beside his friend, the bridegroom, Peirithous, and local men (in the same way as Heracles had fought beside the gods). The second, the Amazonomachy, another battle in which Theseus prevailed, resonated in the public psyche even more. Here, Theseus saw off invading Amazons, independent-minded, physically tough warrior women from the Black

Sea's shores, who rejected men and sex—the antithesis of everything that an Athenian expected in a well-bred woman (let alone a wife). In response to Theseus' abduction of their queen, they marched on Attica, where, tattooed and trousered (for Greeks sure evidence of uncouth barbarism), they occupied the Areopagus, before in battle on the plain below they were defeated. For fifth-century Athenians, the parallels between this battle and their recent history (a foreign threat, trousered barbarians, the city's salvation) were dazzlingly clear. For Amazons read Persians; for the Amazonomachy read the Persian Wars; and for Theseus . . . ?[37]

King Theseus was not simply a fighter. He was a champion of justice, too. During his reign when, after civil war in neighbouring Thebes, the victors refused to let the enemy dead be buried (to Greeks an act of sacrilege), Theseus intervened, compelled the Theban ruler to back down and ensured that the bodies were interred. His sense of fairness, piety, and bravery made him the perfect Athenian hero, a proto-democrat, a true man of the People, who behaved not like a king but as a "first man." Myth told how he established Athens as a city-state, uniting the twelve towns of Attica under Athens' central control and the protection of Athena, an act of "synoecism" crucial to Athenians' idea of self. For, while many hundreds of other poleis—towns or settlements and their surrounding countryside—dotted the Greek-speaking world from Sicily to the Caucasus, at around 1,300 square miles in area, after Sparta, Athens was the largest polis on the Greek mainland.[38]

The polis was also one of the most geographically diverse. Bounded to the north and west by mountain ranges, it unfolded eastwards from the rich wheatfields of the Eleusinian Plain to the red-soiled, silver-olive-studded hills and plain of Athens, and on across the hills to the east coast which stretched from Rhamnous south along the marshy shore, haunt of the goddess Artemis, to the metal-rich mountains of Laurium and Poseidon's sea-washed cliffs of Sunium, before it dog-legged back across the low Piraeus promontory and on to the wide bay of Salamis, a mass of jagged blue-grey hills, until, full circle, it returned back to Eleusis.

Its people were diverse, too: sponge divers and fishermen dipping nets at dawn into the swell off Marathon; sailors tacking home past Paros, holds packed with fabrics, precious jewels and spices from the shores of Asia Minor; farmers at Acharnae yoking oxen to the plough; husbandmen tending vines with blood-black grapes at Icaria in the foothills of Mount Pentelicus; tradesmen setting up their stalls on quaysides or in market squares; metalworkers stoking smoky furnaces and potters turning vases which painters would adorn with scenes from life or legend; women carding wool or working at the loom or in the fields; wealthy landowners and the gaunt, ever-hungry poor; foreign settlers and citizens and slaves.

Like all Greek poleis (and all contemporary cultures across the Mediterranean, Egypt, and the Near East), Attica relied heavily on slave labour. As many as a third of its population were enslaved—men, women, children bought at auction from slave merchants of Thrace or captured in raids and after battle, traded on, transported, sold, and bartered to whoever liked the look of them and could afford to pay. Most families owned at least one slave; only the very poor owned none; some wealthy men owned well over a thousand, their price and life expectancy dictated by their skills. An older, educated male, if lucky, might be set to work as tutor to the spoilt children of a plutocrat; a woman, newborn baby dead, might suddenly become a wet nurse; a strong young man, his life ahead of him (until his city fell), might find himself forever fixing terrace walls or operating bellows in a smithy; while a brooding Thracian knowing no word of Greek might be condemned to crawl the claustrophobic tunnels of the silver mines; and pretty youths and girls might spent their adolescence dreading nightfall and the call to satisfy their masters' lusts and entertain his friends. Almost no Greek questioned the concept of slavery. It was simply a given, and, if he reflected on it at all, even the most compassionate Greek man would find himself agreeing with Thales, who gave thanks that he was born a human, not a beast, a Greek, not a barbarian, a male not female, a freeman not a slave.[39]

The polarity expressed in this world view was not unique. Most Greek males had no doubt of their innate superiority to not just animals but other human beings, not least their poorly educated, dangerously emotional womenfolk, whom, thanks to menstruation and the fact that they gave birth, men considered to be more governed by raw nature and in consequence less civilized than they. To them, the world was split between those who spoke Greek, and those who did not, people whom—because Greeks thought they sounded like so many sheep, forever bleating "bar bar bar"—they called barbarians, a term which, while originally value-free, acquired a patina of scorn. For, despite their many differences and the sheer extent of their diaspora, despite their gentle mocking of each other's dialects and their suspicion of their neighbours' politics, Greeks had a strong sense of identity, sharing, as one Athenian was said to have expressed it, "a kinship in blood and speech, the shrines of gods, the sacrifices that we have in common, the likeness of our way of life."[40]

He could have added one more element: their love of competition. Already back in the eighth century, when Greek settlers in Asia Minor or the islands of the east Aegean first adopted and adapted the Phoenician alphabet and wrote down their earliest and greatest epic poem, the *Iliad,* imagining a "neverworld" where allied Greeks fought Asiatic Troy, one heroic maxim had trumped all the rest: "Always to be best and to surpass all others." Motivating the hero, Achilles, it permeated subsequent Greek culture, inspiring military commanders, athletes, poets, and countless others in stadia, on battlefields, or anywhere two men or cities met. And nowhere was it felt more keenly than in Athens. Which was why Pericles could be so certain that his proposals would meet almost universal acclamation. For, while over the past decades Athens had become more powerful by the year—defeating enemies, acquiring a great empire, claiming to be the rightful hegemon of Greece—save for a few memorials and statues, her Acropolis with its xoanon housed in a quickly thrown-together shack looked down-at-heel.[41]

This look had served the city well. While in other poleis temples, as well as being religious buildings, served both as a reflection of their people's pride and a projection of their power, in Attica they had been left deliberately derelict, a message carefully curated for citizens and foreigners to see, that in the Persian Wars it had been only the Athenians who sacrificed their land to save Greece from enslavement. These ruined temples were not simply a stark memorial of everything Athenians had given up, but a sign of their unique role as liberators, a badge of pride for all they had achieved, for thirty years a warning of the threats that still might lie in store. Now, though, those threats were over. Only this year, 449 B.C., when, following Athenian campaigns in Cyprus, the Persian Great King agreed to end hostilities, he had chosen Athens as the polis which should sign the treaty on behalf of Greece. His choice made it official. For him, Athens was Greece's hegemon. So now, with the city's star in the ascendant, it was time to close one chapter and begin another, and it was in part to mark this new start that the construction programme was conceived, designed both to reflect the spirit of the age and to project a vision for the future—of Athens as the greatest city in the world, the founder of democracy, the home to men and women who, thanks to sacrifice and toil, had gained a status close to that of heroes.[42]

Greeks' definition of a hero was more specific than our own: either the offspring of a god (or goddess) and a mortal, or someone who was seen to wield power even after death, or (most ideally) both. Vase paintings and sculptures showed male heroes, often in the prime of youth, riding or accompanied by a horse (symbolizing wealth and aristocracy, a visual metaphor for their prodigious life and enviable afterlife). Theseus and Heracles, sons of Poseidon and Zeus respectively by mortal mothers, were archetypal heroes. Not only had they purged the world of criminals or monsters while still alive, but they continued to do so long after they were dead—as many contemporary Athenians could attest, believing they had seen them fighting by their sides as they dodged a hail of arrows and hurled themselves against the Persians' wicker shields at Marathon and other battles in the recent wars. Not that all heroes were benign. Apparent interventions forced many Greek communities to grant heroic status to the angry spirits of the often-violent dead—which meant paying them the honour due to demigods, giving them a sanctuary or shrine, a statue, sacrifices, and libations. As with the gods, the urge to worship heroes was driven by fear as much as by a sense of love, respect, or honour.[43]

Gods, demigods, and heroes: there were so many, and all demanded worship, whether at a local shrine or in a public festival. No other polis held as many festivals as Athens. In each of her twelve months, there was at least one large-scale public ceremony, each with its sacrifice, many with processions, most for the city as a whole, some for specific gender or age groupings. Largely following the seasons, they included harvest festivals in honour of Demeter and Persephone; winter festivals to mark the turning of the year, where performances were staged in recognition of the god of transformation, Dionysus; festivals of sowing and planting; festivals to please Athena; and festivals to soothe the dead. Days of each month were also sacred to specific gods or heroes: the first to Selene, the moon; the third to Athena; the fourth not just to Heracles and Hermes but to Eros and Aphrodite; the sixth to Artemis; the seventh to Apollo; the eighth to Poseidon and Theseus. Familiar to all Athenians since birth, these festivals and dates, ingrained into their psyche, linked their lives firmly to the rhythm of religion.[44]

Some Athenians might argue that this link went deeper. While there were differences between the hero and the common citizenry of Athens (not least that heroes were, by definition, dead), there were intriguing similarities. Like heroes, Athenians claimed ancestry from gods; collectively they, too, could boast miraculous achievements; they, too, could rightly claim that, overcoming what once appeared insuperable odds, they had quite literally saved their world by beating off the Persian threat, and (in their own version of the Gigantomachy) upheld those central values of civilized society: justice; order; harmony. While other Greeks had fought beside them, only Athenians had made the supreme sacrifice, abandoning their land, so that their cause could win. Only they had watched their city die, before being resurrected like a phoenix soaring from the flames, shaking out the ashes of destruction from its spreading wings.

The citizen as (future) hero in a reborn city: it was a powerful vision, and there was no better moment to embrace it. Following the

Persian invasions times had been tough. Fiscal priorities had been dictated by the need to reconstruct the city, protect borders, finance overseas campaigns. Despite annual incomes from the silver mines and taxation of subject states, it was thanks only to war booty that, in the 460s, the city's finances had begun to turn a corner. Even if the ruined temples had not been piquantly symbolic, Athens would have been hard pressed to rebuild them. But now that the Persian threat was lifted, budgets could be reallocated. Of course, there would still be wars—for Greeks life without war was unimaginable—but for the first time in decades the moment seemed ripe to transform Athens, to make her the glittering imperial hub that she deserved to be, acclaimed by her inhabitants, approached with awe by subject states and enemies. And at the heart of this vision were the temples.[45]

Greek temples were not just about religion. Although they were intended to delight the gods and to attract their power, they were equally important as a medium through which a city might project its own authority, influence and wealth, signs of divine favour, since it was only through the gods' approval and support that it enjoyed sufficient capital to fund such costly structures. Indeed, by 449 B.C., temple building was the architectural equivalent of an arms race, as cities tried to trump their rivals and gain favour with the gods by raising ever larger, more expensive, more impressive buildings. And not just cities: powerful families, too, and powerful individuals. In Athens no one knew this better than Pericles himself, whose family and their associates had been involved for well over a century in some of the most impressive temple-building projects seen in mainland Greece, curating the sculptures which adorned them to project their vision of the world, using their kudos to enhance their standing and their city's. So, since temples had such historical and political significance, it is to them that we must turn next, for, unless we appreciate them fully, we cannot hope to understand the Parthenon, its associated buildings, and the impact for both good and ill it was to have on Athens.[46]

2 POWERHOUSES

Always to be best and to surpass all others.
—HOMER, *ILIAD*, 6.208, 11.784

Like gods, religious sanctuaries were everywhere. Sometimes they were natural phenomena—just outside Athens a spring bubbling beneath a tree was consecrated to a river god and water nymphs, furnished with statues of young girls, and piled with votive offerings. Elsewhere a sanctuary might simply be a demarcated area of hallowed land just large enough for worshippers to gather in the open air and offer sacrifices at an altar. Even in 449 B.C. the Sanctuary of Zeus on the Acropolis was such a place, and Athenians knew countless others dotted around villages and towns and rural settings across the Attic countryside. Then there were the more elaborate cult buildings. In the Bronze Age, while self-contained shrines did exist, most were connected to royal palaces, chapels where the great and good might commune with gods on behalf of subject peoples. The Bronze Age palace, whose foundations could be seen on the Acropolis, almost certainly contained such a chapel, but in the seventh century B.C., as many monarchies gave way to powerful aristocracies, and kingdoms became poleis, monumental wooden temples independent of a dwelling place became part of the religious landscape, their designs inspired and influenced by buildings seen by Greek traders, diplomats or mercenaries serving in Egyptian and Near Eastern armies, their alfresco altars the focus of increasingly public sacrifices.[1]

Although, at roughly 100 by 25 feet, some were imposing, each was fundamentally a box, or sekos, invariably with just one room, the inner sanctuary or cella, housing the cult statue and belongings of whichever god or gods were worshipped there. All strove to be distinct. Set on a level stylobate (pavement) sometimes atop a stepped platform, some had columned porches, but the most elaborate (and expensive) were peripteral—which is to say, their colonnade (or peristyle) enveloped all four sides, enlarging the building's footprint, allowing for a wider, taller, more impressive roof, and adding grace and airiness to their appearance. Almost all were richly decorated. Their shallow triangular pediments (or gables) were brightly painted, their apexes embellished with acroteria, their corners with antefixes, while above their columns the entablature was studded with brightly coloured *metopēs,* self-contained plaques, whose subject matter might show scenes familiar from mythology, each positioned between the exposed ends of roof beams, which in turn were carved with the three deep vertical ridges, which gave them their name, triglyphs.[2]

Around 580 B.C., however, there was an architectural revolution. The islanders of Corcyra became the first Greeks to build a peripteral temple from stone. Their motivation was complex. Dedicated to Artemis, both the temple and its massive altar were a statement of not just piety and wealth but defiance towards the Corcyreans' hated mainland cousins, the Corinthians. A century and a half previously, when mainlanders and islanders began establishing new poleis across the wider Mediterranean and Black Sea, Corcyra had been founded

2.1 One of the pediments from the Temple of Artemis in Corcyra.

from rich Corinth. Like all such settlements, Corcyra was expected to acknowledge the authority and customs of her metropolis (or mother city), but almost from the start there was bad feeling. Escalating animosity led to the first recorded sea battle in Greek history, and it was as relations soured still further that the Corcyreans, determined to flaunt their independence and superiority, built their temple.[3]

Nestling on a lush plateau with a fine bay to the west, and the sea and distant mountains of the mainland to the east, it was imposing, and it set a precedent for all ambitious Greeks to follow. Resting on a two-stepped platform, its east-facing cella housing the cult statue was furnished with a back room and front porch. And, while at 113 by 31 feet the sekos—its wooden ceiling, almost 50 feet in height, supported by two rows of ten internal columns—was slim, the surrounding colonnade (seventeen columns by eight, with two more flanking the porch) enlarged its footprint and so made the building more proportionate and pleasing.[4]

High-relief sculptures set into both pediments showed the same subject: a running Medusa, the Gorgon whose glance turned anyone to stone, clad in a short tunic, snakes coiling round her waist and darting from her shoulders, a ghastly grin erupting from her staring face. Her death was clearly imminent, since beside her were her children, the human Chrysaor and the winged-horse Pegasus, born from her blood, when Perseus, the hero, slew her. Crouching leopards flanked her, along with scenes of fighting: Zeus launching a thunderbolt against a cowering enemy (perhaps a Giant or Titan); an old man (perhaps Troy's King Priam), skewered in the neck by a spear, enthroned beside a dying younger man.[5]

With scenes from the Trojan War shown on some *metopēs,* one concept united all these sculptures—victory: the victory of Greeks over Trojans, of Zeus over Giants or Titans, of Perseus over Medusa, all metaphors for Corcyra's victory (or longed-for victory) over Corinth. At the same time, Medusa's stare, repeated on fired-clay plaques hung high around the outside of the building to glare across both sea and island heartland, was a powerful apotropaic. Combined with the building's confident extravagance, it carried a blunt warning: meddle with Corcyra at your peril.[6]

Forty years later, the Corinthians responded in kind. In 540 B.C. they built a slightly larger stone temple of their own for Artemis' twin brother, Apollo, which overlooked their city's agora. With tapering monolithic limestone columns, it was also more sophisticated, since its stylobate swelled almost imperceptibly from each corner to the centre, a phenomenon inspired by earlier Egyptian architecture and known as "upward curvature." Its purpose was both practical—to let rainwater drain more easily—and aesthetic: seen from a distance, a perfectly flat stylobate appears to sag in the middle; upward curvature counters this illusion, giving the impression of a straight line.[7]

Internally, too, the temple's sekos differed from its Corcyrean counterpart, containing not one outward-facing room but two, each entered through massive heavy doors: the east-facing cella with its cult statue of Apollo, and a smaller west-facing opisthodomus (literally, back chamber), whose purpose is uncertain. Facing the setting sun, associated by Greeks with death, it may have contained a shrine to the local hero, Sisyphus, founder of Corinth, who according to legend tried to triumph over his mortality, briefly imprisoning the death god, Thanatos, before being killed by Ares, god of war; but he had already arranged that his corpse be left in Corinth's agora unburied, so, arriving in the Underworld, his soul persuaded Hades to send it back to earth to organise the funeral. Once returned, however, Sisyphus stayed put, and only when Zeus intervened, sending Hermes Psychopompus (Hermes, Escorter of Souls), did he relinquish life, to spend eternity

2.2 The Temple of Apollo at Corinth.

pushing a boulder uphill towards the light, forever thwarted when it rolled back down before it reached the top. Heroes such as Sisyphus, who visited the Underworld (Theseus and Heracles both did so, too), played a special role in Greek religion. Rooted in the cycles of the agricultural year, legends recounting their return to life—like Persephone's, so central to the Eleusinian Mysteries—offered hope to Greeks contemplating their mortality.[8]

The opisthodomos of Corinth's Temple of Apollo may also have been a treasury, a strong room housing an eclectic mix of bullion, booty, and sacred artefacts, as well as private dedications—perhaps even rare coinage from Lydia, whose King Croesus had recently established the world's first mint. Housed in temples or templelike constructions, whose hefty doors and wood or metal grilles between the columns of their porches promised security, such treasuries were fast becoming part of the religious landscape, not least at Panhellenic sanctuaries. Crammed with priceless artworks or weapons dedicated as thank offerings for victory, they occupied prime positions at Delphi and Olympia, a provocation to the rest of Greece, a proclamation of the kudos of the cities which erected them.[9]

Among those cities was Corinth's neighbour, Sicyon, which, too, boasted a rich mythology. It was here that Prometheus outwitted the gods, persuading them to accept as sacrificial offerings not an animal's meat but its bones wrapped tight in fat and burned. But, for Pericles, Sicyon had more immediate significance: Cleisthenes, its early sixth-century ruler, was his great-great-grandfather, and his energy and vision passed through the generations. An astute politician and propagandist, Cleisthenes reshaped his city's laws, reorganised its social structures, and transformed it into a cultural and artistic hub. He also made his mark in wider Greece, allying with Alcmaeon of Athens (from whom Pericles' family, the Alcmaeonidae, was named) to wage a sacred war, protecting pilgrims journeying to Delphi—and financed from booty taken from defeated enemies they built a massive terrace for Delphi's first stone temple.[10]

At home in Sicyon, Cleisthenes built his own peripteral stone temple, while at Delphi he erected a stone treasury with *metopēs* showing legendary scenes of overseas adventuring and contests. Its prize exhibit was the chariot with which in 582 B.C. he won the race at Delphi's newly founded Pythian Games, before setting up his own equivalent games at Sicyon. He was victorious at Olympia, too, and around 575 B.C., after a chariot victory there, he invited the most eligible men in Greece to Sicyon for a year of competitions. Their prize was the hand of his daughter, Agariste. Two Athenians surpassed the rest, but when Hippocleides, a member of the Philaid dynasty, disgraced himself with a display of drunken dancing, Cleisthenes declared the winner to be Megacles, the son of his old friend, Alcmaeon. Hippocleides' flippant response—"Does Hippocleides look like he's bothered?"—became a common proverb, and true or not, it was a story which Pericles must have known since childhood. Not only were the happy couple, Megacles and Agariste, Pericles' great-grandparents, but their marriage helped to rehabilitate the Alcmaeonidae, since, thanks to an earlier Megacles (known today as Megacles the Elder) and an incident involving a temple, the family was thought to be accursed. The episode cast a long shadow and informed Greek views of not just Pericles himself but by extension his brainchild, the Parthenon.[11]

Late seventh-century-B.C. Athenian politics were the preserve of a sometimes-uneasy coalition of powerful rival families, whose leaders decided policy in council, whose social equals rubber-stamped those policies in an elite assembly, and whose members shared high offices of state. But in 632 B.C., one of them, Cylon, tried to seize total power. He had laid the ground carefully, allying with the ruler of neighbouring Megara, and consulting the Delphic oracle, which advised him to stage his coup during the "great festival of Zeus." As an Olympic victor, Cylon assumed that this meant the Olympic Games. So, that August, with most of Athens' great and good out of the city, he seized the Athenian Acropolis, the traditional seat of power.[12]

The Athenians refused to obey him. Instead, they besieged the Acropolis, forcing their would-be master, now their prisoner, to sweat it out in searing heat on the unforgiving rock, until (realising that the oracle must have meant another festival of Zeus) Cylon and his henchmen, supplies of food and water gone, began negotiations with the magistrate in charge of civic business, who that year was Megacles, family head of the Alcmaeonidae. Despite promises of safe passage, the rebels took no chances. Believing that (like electricity along a wire) it would transmit her power, they tied one end of a long rope around Athena's xoanon (then housed in a wood-and-mudbrick Temple of Athena Polias with two limestone pillars at its porch). Then, careful to keep contact with the rope, they shuffled off the Acropolis. But when they reached the Areopagus, whose caves were said to house the Furies or Erinyes, baleful goddesses of retribution, the rope broke. For Megacles the Elder it was a sign. Athena had abandoned the conspirators. He ordered the Athenians to bind the revolutionaries in chains and led them to the marshes by the sea, where, executed, they were buried, still shackled, in a squalid grave.[13]

Yet Athens remained edgy. Amid rumours of ghosts wandering the streets, rival families took advantage of the growing hysteria and levelled accusations against Megacles the Elder and his family. Killing Cylon's men despite the promise of safe conduct was, they said, a crime against the gods. The Alcmaeonidae were cursed; they had polluted Athens; and they must be punished. In a court of law, 300 men from rival families passed a grim sentence: on a Cretan exorcist's advice, they exiled not just Megacles the Elder but all his family, too, alive and dead—even graves were emptied of remains, their contents carried out across the border.[14]

Neither for the first time nor the last, Athenians had weaponized religion for political advantage, but the fallout was far reaching. The Alcmaeonidae's absence created a power vacuum. The situation grew unstable. Neither Dracon's tough new penal code, nor Solon's constitutional reforms succeeded in restoring harmony. So, in 596 B.C. Solon persuaded his peers to recall the Alcmaeonidae, and when just two years later Alcmaeon, the new head of their family, won the Olympic chariot race and brought kudos to his city, it seemed to all but his most trenchant critics that the curse must have been lifted, since otherwise Zeus, the Games' patron, would never have countenanced his victory. For now, the notion of the curse was set aside. As Pericles discovered to his cost, however, it was not forgotten.[15]

Alcmaeon was charismatic. Tradition told how, visiting Asia Minor and the Lydian capital, Sardis, some years later, he so charmed his host, the rich King Croesus, that the monarch promised him as much gold as he could carry. When Alcmaeon stuffed his robes with gold dust, filled his mouth with it, and poured it into his long hair and beard, Croesus, delighted, sent him home with double the amount. However he acquired it, it was partly through his wealth and family ties that Alcmaeon formed his close relationship with Cleisthenes of Sicyon, and that Cleisthenes chose Alcmaeon's son, Megacles, to be his son-in-law. But the "unbothered" Hippocleides, Megacles' defeated rival, was rich and powerful, too, and, despite his louche display of dancing, he was appointed Athens' archon (or chief magistrate). Perhaps his reputation as a showman worked to his advantage, since one of his duties in his year of office (566/5 B.C.) was to oversee the consecration of a new stone Temple of Athena Polias. Another was to preside over the first-ever celebration of the quadrennial Great Panathenaea (a name deliberately chosen to impress).[16]

For centuries each August, Athenians had celebrated a Panathenaic ("all-Athenian") Festival—a mix of contests, games and feasts, all centred on the sacrifice of a hecatomb (of around 100 cattle) to Athena on the Acropolis—but, as its name suggested, it was a purely local affair. Now, keen to project Athens' power, her leading families announced that every four years the annual Attic festival would be replaced by a new larger celebration, open to all Greeks, with the existing programme augmented to create a heady mix of sacrifices and processions, dance contests, music competitions, athletic games, and hippic races.[17]

Athens was not the only city to introduce ambitious games. In 582 B.C. two Panhellenic festivals intended to rival the Olympics were founded (Delphi's quadrennial Pythian Games, and two-yearly Isthmian Games near Corinth) with a third following soon afterwards in 573 B.C. (the biennial Nemean Games). Like temple building, hosting Panhellenic games was evidence of status. Hence Athens' inauguration of the Great Panathenaea in 566 B.C. But from the start there were significant differences: while participation in other Panhellenic festivals was open to any Greek male citizen (provided he was not religiously polluted by being, for example, a murderer), some parts of the Great Panathenaea were restricted to Athenians alone. Moreover, while in the other games victors were awarded crowns of olive, laurel, or celery, at the Great Panathenaea (in keeping with athletic games in Homer's epics, on which they were also modelled) victors won more generous prizes: cash and amphoras of olive oil from Athena's sacred trees, each painted with an image of the goddess. In other words, while other festivals stressed common bonds, the Great Panathenaea spoke to Athens' individuality and exclusivity. And underpinning everything was Athena's starring role in the newly reworked, painstakingly curated story of the Gigantomachy.[18]

References to the myth punctuated the festival, acts of commemoration in which only Athenians could take part. The *apobatēs* contest, where helmeted warriors, each carrying a heavy shield, leapt off fast-moving chariots before racing on foot across the finishing line, emulated Athena's advance into battle. The *pyrrhichē,* a war dance by teams of armoured young men, mimicked Athena's victory dance over the fallen Enceladus. And the procession onto the Acropolis of handpicked Attic residents—armed citizens, their womenfolk and children, as well as metics (settled incomers)—culminated in the presentation to Athena of her new peplos, the woollen robe woven with scenes of battle.[19]

But another legend permeated the Great Panathenaea, too: the legend of Erechtheus (a.k.a. Erichthonius), progenitor of all Athenians. According to the festival's foundation myth, it was he who founded the first Panathenaea, devised the *pyrrhichē* to celebrate Athena's victory, and invented the four-horse chariot so central to the *apobatēs* race; while Athena's peplos was a tangible reminder of the wool used by the goddess to wipe off Hephaestus' semen, which, thrown into the chasm in the rock, resulted in Erechtheus' birth. Harnessing myth as propaganda was common throughout Greece and not thought to disturb the gods, especially when they were honoured as lavishly as at the Great Panathenaea. But in the 560s B.C. this was not the only way that the Athenians were celebrating their patron goddess. On the Acropolis they were erecting an elegant new building. Proud, provocative, peripteral, it was a limestone Temple of Athena Polias. The first stone temple not just on the Acropolis but in Attica, it was almost 50 feet tall, with an overall footprint of 143 by 70 feet, a sekos of 112 feet by 44 feet and twelve by six external columns—and, while not the largest temple yet to be constructed, with two colonnaded porches and not two but four distinct inner chambers, its layout was one of the most complex.[20]

Roughly square with six internal columns, its east-facing cella, home to the ancient xoanon, was conventional enough. But on the western side, instead of the one-roomed opisthodomos, familiar from Corinth's Temple of Apollo, a shallow rectangular lobby gave access to two inner rooms. Each had dual functions, part treasuries, part chapels, and, while Sisyphus was honoured in the Corinthian opisthodomos, here a multiplicity of gods and heroes was revered. Chief among them was Poseidon-Erechtheus, that fusion of old enemies now sharing a temple with Poseidon's one-time rival, Athena. In both cases, hostilities were over; from strife had emerged harmony and strength. Athenians must have hoped it was a metaphor. The

2.3 The snake-tailed Tripartite Being from a pediment of the first Temple of Athena Polias on the Acropolis.

focus of worship was on the great altar facing the east door, and, since access to the interior was restricted, many may have been unaware of the temple's unusual floorplan. Yet, all could see the vivid, vital sculptures on its pediments, each topped by an acroterion, an eye-stopping, self-standing statue of a long-fanged, lolling-tongued Medusa, her features painted blue, black, red, and green. The pediments themselves drew inspiration from Near Eastern art. On one, huge sculptures of two lions mauled a stricken bull; on the other two lion-cum-lionesses sank teeth into the rumps of fallen calves. Both were visions of raw power: the power of the aristocratic lion; the power of Athens.[21]

Flanking the central scene of the west pediment were writhing snakes, but their counterparts on the east pediment were very different: to the left a sea creature, its scales picked out in red and blue, being wrestled by a naked human, the configuration of whose muscly legs and buttocks echoed the monster's fishy undulations; to the right a strange, serene, tripartite being—three bearded human heads, each with a fleshy smile, atop three well-formed torsos ending in a snaky tail, each coiling round the other to create one triad, indivisible. Perhaps a trinity of early earthborn kings or an allegory for the three constituencies of Attica (the coast, the country, and the city), one held a rippling wave, the next a flame, the third a bird, symbols of water, fire, and air. Master these gifts, and Athens would be strong indeed. The temple's marble *metopēs,* too, replete with four-horse chariots and exotic creatures such as panthers, spoke of power, while their style, so reminiscent of Near Eastern artworks, positioned Athens as a powerhouse equal to such glittering realms as Lydia, where Alcmaeon had more than held his own at Croesus' court.[22]

It was a two-way relationship. At Sardis, capital of his Lydian empire, Croesus was strengthening his own cultural links with Greece, sending rich gifts to Apollo at Delphi and hiring a Greek architect to build a Greek-style temple to the Asiatic goddess Cybele (identified by Greeks with Artemis). A surviving model hints at its hybrid appearance. Housing a cult statue—Cybele flanked by two snakes, her body bejewelled, her right hand clasping her long dress, her left outstretched, a lion nuzzling her breast—its Greek silhouette was enhanced by a new style of slim, graceful columns. Each topped by a capital, whose twin volutes softened its profile and lent a sense of flow and rhythm, they are the first Ionic columns on record. The model suggests, too, that the sekos's outer face was decorated with three rows of painted sculptures. On one long wall, a lower band showed crouching lions, while on each of the two upper rows women walked in procession towards the temple doors; on the other wall, girls, running men, and dancing women likewise approached the entrance. But the back wall displayed scenes and characters from Greek mythology: Heracles fighting the Nemean lion; Pelops driving a chariot; a centaur; Agamemnon murdered by his wife and her lover. Some of these images may have been universal, but all were chosen carefully. Croesus was as keen to forge links with Greece as Greece was to forge links with him.[23]

Annexing Greek Ionia in the 560s B.C., Croesus helped fund an Artemision, a huge peripteral Temple of Artemis, at Ephesus. Two details were extraordinary: its length of 377 feet and width of 150 feet meant that it could not be fully spanned, so its cella was roofless; and its statue showed the goddess in full Asiatic guise, more Cybele than

Artemis, her dress adorned with signs of the Babylonian zodiac, her chest festooned with severed testicles. But otherwise the temple was pure Greek—if on an epic scale. Paid for by Croesus' gold, a double colonnade of 98 columns, each almost 40 feet tall, enveloped the sekos, with eight more supporting the deep porch. On many of the lower drums were carved and painted life-sized figures: men and women dressed in sumptuous clothing, their hair meticulously styled, some with panther skins slung over shoulders, many bearing offerings and ritual vessels, all walking in procession accompanied by horses and sacrificial cattle. As time passed more details were added, a frieze showing a procession of male and female worshippers, chariots and horses, sculpted lions and oxen, a seated assembly, Amazons, a Centauromachy. But Croesus was not alone in using his own wealth to advertise his piety. While work at Ephesus was underway, on nearby Samos the potentate Polycrates built an even more colossal temple of his own to Hera, 30 feet wider than Croesus' Artemision. Polycrates was what Greeks called a *tyrannos,* a term coined from the Lydian *tûran,* meaning "absolute ruler," who was neither appointed nor elected but seized power by force. In the sixth century B.C. the word was value neutral, and many *tyrannoi* were thought to govern well.[24]

Among them was Peisistratus of Athens, a brilliant general who, in 565 B.C. (the year after the consecration of the Temple of Athena Polias and inauguration of the Great Panathenaea) following victory over neighbouring Megara, annexed the island of Salamis. In some ways Peisistratus was a forerunner of Pericles (who was said to look like him), and his impact on Athens' psyche was profound. Three times he tried to become *tyrannos,* the first time by guile. In 561 B.C., faking an attempt on his life, he gained permission to employ private security, a bodyguard of young men armed with clubs, and (like Cylon) seized the Acropolis before being driven out. The second time he used diplomacy, a deal that had him marry Megacles' daughter in return for Megacles' support. His entry into Athens was pure theatre—riding in a four-horse chariot, a tall woman beside him, spear in hand, high-crested helmet glinting on her head, and wearing dazzling armour, apparently the incarnation of Athena in her role as *apobatēs* (but, in fact, a girl called Phya). While undeniably kitsch, the pageant was perfectly thought through, its imagery borrowed from vase paintings showing Heracles arriving on Olympus apotheosised and escorted by Athena. The honeymoon did not last long. When he learned that Peisistratus, who, already had sons and heirs, was avoiding making his bride pregnant, Megacles turned against him. Again, Peisistratus went into exile.[25]

The third time he left nothing to chance. Through interests in gold mines in northern Greece, he funded a mercenary army, and, backed by rich friends in Thebes, Argos, Naxos, and Thessaly, in 546 B.C. his fleet beached on the Attic coast at Marathon, where his family owned estates. It was nothing short of a military invasion. Megacles and a hastily assembled army of Athenian patricians were defeated, and for the next three and a half decades Peisistratus and his sons, Hippias and Hipparchus, dominated Athens. But despite his strong-arm tactics, his rule was not tyrannical. Later generations considered it a golden age, and Pericles learned much from how Peisistratus had governed.

From the start, Peisistratus cultivated a populist image. Instead of a palace on the Acropolis, he constructed a large townhouse with a central courtyard and fine reception rooms on flatlands north of the Areopagus, from which with boundless energy he set out to build a fair and equitable society. He offered farmers generous, low-interest loans; he established a proto-police force (the brigade of Scythian archers); he appointed peripatetic judges to ensure equal access to the law for inhabitants of both the city and wider Attica; he constructed an aqueduct that carried water from the Attic hills to an elegant new city-centre fountain house; and he installed political strongmen around the Hellespont to guard the sea-lanes, through which grain ships from the Black Sea sailed each autumn, ensuring that Athenians would not go hungry.[26]

He also built temples—though not on the Acropolis, that age-old focus of both temporal and religious power. Instead, he marked the dawn of a new age, by bringing Athens' gods down from the rock into the city. Facing his palace was a flat expanse of land, studded with wells and dotted with buildings, the Public Fields, the site of games and gatherings, where spectators sat on temporary bleachers to watch events associated with the Panathenaic Festival, including the procession from the Twin Towers Gate amid the tombstones of the Cerameicus along the packed-earth road to the Acropolis. Here Peisistratus raised two temples, one for Zeus, the other for Apollo Patroos, "Ancestral Apollo," an aspect of the god becoming ever more important thanks to international power games.[27]

Legend told of an Athenian prince, Ion, sired by Apollo in a cave beneath the Acropolis and fostered at Delphi, who not only helped cement ties between Athens and Eleusis (where he died), but fathered a dynasty of children, an ethnic group called after him, Ionians. Promulgated zealously by the Athenians, the myth had profound implications. The Greek world contained different ethnic groupings with distinct dialects and rituals, and one of the largest were the Ionians. With cities on the coasts of Asia Minor and Aegean islands and in Sicily and southern Italy, all recognised Apollo as their patron god. So, for Athenians the myth of Ion seemed heaven-sent. Already at the start of the sixth century, Solon used it to claim Athens as de facto metropolis and rightful hegemon of every Ionian city. Now Peisistratus furthered that claim by seizing Delos, the legendary birthplace of Apollo, and site of a quadrennial festival famous for its games and dances, where "the heady scent of fatty sacrifice" burnt on its celebrated "Altar of Horns." As a hymn to Apollo declared,[28]

Your greatest joy is Delos. Here, to honour you,
Ionians in long flowing robes assemble
with their children and modest wives;
in boxing and in dancing and in song
they call you to their minds, delighting you in contests.
To see Ionians thronged there, you'd think them
ageless and immortal,
gazing on their beauty,
delighting in the men and the deep-bosomed women,

in their sleek ships,
in all their treasures.[29]

Delos bristled with treasuries and shrines, many dedicated by islanders from nearby Naxos: an impressive avenue of marble lions which overlooked a sacred lake and venerable palm tree, believed to have been gripped by Leto as she gave birth to Apollo; a propylaeon (gateway); a stoa (colonnade); and a temple, revolutionary in its design since not just its slim columns but even its roof were made of marble, while outside, beside its north wall, a statue of Apollo, four times life-size, clasped a metal bow and arrow.[30]

But Naxos' glory days were over. Defeating it, Peisistratus installed a puppet *tyrannos*, and seized control of Delos, where, to mark the shift of power, he oversaw a purification ceremony, including the removal of all graves from the sanctuary, with their contents reburied on the far side of the island. Next, backed by convenient oracles, his builders began work on a new temple from poros stone (soft, marly limestone) shipped from Attica. Geographical constraints meant not only that it needed to be modest in size (a mere 52 by 53 feet in area) but that unusually its cella—part sanctuary, part strong room—faced west towards Apollo's altar and the sacred harbour. Its visual impact was striking. As worshippers sailed in, this building, set defiantly between the Naxian temple and the sacred lake, was testament to Athens' power, a sign that times were changing.

For much of her previous history, Athens had been a minor player. Now, thanks to its growing military might, its architecture, and its festivals, the city was becoming a vibrant international religious and cultural hub. But for the ambitious Peisistratus there was always more that could be done. So, he turned to a god who shared many of his attributes: the flamboyant, subversive Dionysus, god of wine and transformation. His worship took many forms, but during the Attic winter he was associated especially with drama—specifically at this period with tragedy, an artform which Athenians believed evolved from narrative hymns or dithyrambs, sung and danced by choruses in Dionysus' honour. They claimed that it was Thespis of

Icaria (an Attic village where Dionysus reputedly planted the first vine) who first assumed the role of protagonist, peeling away from the chorus and interacting in character with fellow performers. Soon Thespis and his troupe were touring local festivals, performing from the back of a wagon, but it was Peisistratus who harnessed tragedy's potential.[31]

In 534 B.C. he inaugurated the annual Greater or City Dionysia, a dramatic festival straddling the vernal equinox, when the weather became calm enough for sailing. Soon its performances attracted not just Athenians but overseas visitors and delegates. Like the Great Panathenaea, it involved processions and sacrifices, prayers, and feasts, but its unique focus were tragedies staged in the Public Fields, where audiences sat on wooden bleachers in clear sight of Peisistratus' palace. Part sacred ritual, part musical entertainment, part spectacle, part artform, part vehicle for exploring difficult ideas, like Homer's epics they offered an enticing vehicle for exploring the human condition, and, while other cities developed their own forms of drama, there was something about Thespis' brand of tragedy that was intensely powerful.[32]

Another festival, which Peisistratus promoted and where Dionysus played a central role, was the Eleusinian Mysteries. One of the god's cult titles was Dimētōr, "Twice Mothered," and twice he escaped death: still an embryo, he was rescued from being immolated with his mother, and sewn into his father Zeus' thigh until the time came for his birth; while later, as a child, he was ripped apart by Titans before being reconstructed and revitalized. His experience of death and resurrection saw Dionysus Dimētōr, god of the grape, worshipped alongside the two grain goddesses, Demeter and Persephone (or Korē), at Eleusis, home to the Mysteries, where thanks in part to Peisistratus' clever marketing, Greeks from other poleis increasingly desired to be initiated, a constant flow of visitors to Attica, a boost for traders, and a welcome revenue for Eleusinian priests, who charged initiates a hefty fee.[33]

Peisistratus may have planned to enlarge the Telesterion, the Hall of Mysteries, but he did not live to see work started. He died in

528 B.C., passing his authority to his sons, Hippias, a pious devotee of oracles, and the creative, cultivated Hipparchus. It was they who erected the new hall with its portico, its 88-foot-square poros-stone cella, its fine, tiled roof supported by 22 interior columns, and its acroteria carved from Parian marble. It was not their only project. Soon another aqueduct and fountain house provided water for the city; a fine wall embraced the hero-shrine of Academus a little to the north; a stone temple enhanced the precinct of Dionysus south of the Acropolis; and after years of planning, around 515 B.C., by the banks of the Ilissus a huge new Temple of Olympian Zeus, Athena's father, was beginning to take shape. At more than twice the footprint of the Temple of Athena Polias on the Acropolis, it was set to be the largest temple on the Greek mainland, a rival to the monumental temples of Hera on Samos and Artemis at Ephesus. Its cost was stratospheric.[34]

Hippias and Hipparchus had learned well from their father, and they knew how to keep rival families happy. They allowed appointments to key public posts of men such as Miltiades, from the powerful Philaid family, and Cleisthenes (named from his grandfather), who had succeeded his late father, Megacles, as head of the Alcmaeonidae. They knew, too, how to attract creative talent into Athens, poets such as Simonides, whose choral songs were legend, Lasus, a virtuoso on the lyre, who wrote the first recorded music treatise, and Anacreon, whose was so famous that, when Polycrates, his patron died, Hipparchus immediately sent a ship to fetch him to Athens, where his flamboyant fashion sense caused a sensation. Hipparchus, too, wrote poetry, morally improving messages which he had carved on country herms, square pillars topped with sculpted heads of Hermes, and equipped with erect phalluses, which served as markers between outlying towns and villages and a new Altar of the Twelve Gods within sight of the tyrants' palace: "A reminder from Hipparchus: as you walk, think proper thoughts"; "A reminder from Hipparchus: don't cheat a friend."[35]

These were not Hipparchus' only forays into literature. During the 520s B.C. he commissioned a definitive "Athenian" text of

Homer's *Iliad* and *Odyssey,* whose worldview formed the bedrock of Greek identity. His family knew these epics well. A local festival on their estates at Brauron included contests for the rhapsodes ("ode-stitchers"), who performed the entire poems in relay. Now Hipparchus added this competition to the Great Panathenaea—with one proviso. All rhapsodes, no matter where they came from (and many were international superstars), must use his new authorized version. To incentivize them to learn no other, he offered a significant cash prize, a brilliantly calculated move. With the odd line inserted to enhance his city's role at Troy, Hipparchus' edition of the poems was soon being sung from Sicily to the Black Sea. Athens was on her way to claiming for herself a reputation as (to use a phrase that Pericles would later coin) the educator of all Greece.[36]

As their standard of living improved, many Athenians must have viewed the future with some optimism. With Hippias taking care of politics, widely circulating, newly minted coins, stamped with Athena's owl, the city's "corporate logo," were evidence of a buoyant economy. Meanwhile the flamboyant Hipparchus could be relied on to enliven cultural life, not least the pomp and ceremony of the Great Panathenaea. But it was at that festival in 514 B.C. that everything suddenly changed.[37]

Before sunrise as spectators filed onto the bleachers, Hipparchus was weaving through the hubbub of the Public Fields to the Twin Towers Gate, where the procession was assembling, when—near the Leocorium, a hero-shrine for three more girls, whom myth said sacrificed their lives for Athens—two men attacked him. A sudden flash of knives, a blade thrust upwards through a belly, a downward slice across an unprotected neck, and it was over. Too late, stunned bodyguards snapped into action. Some tried to staunch Hipparchus' wounds; others tackled one of the assassins and bludgeoned him to death; still others pushed through throngs of onlookers, hot on the heels of the surviving murderer, as he elbowed his way to safety. Free from the crush, he fled through empty streets, but there was no escape. Cornered, he was taken in for questioning.[38]

When news of the assassination reached Hippias at the Twin Towers Gate, he reacted speedily. No one knew if the killing was part of a wider plot. Hippias, too, might be a target. Security was paramount. Yet, the procession must go on. A murder at a festival was sacrilege, but to cancel the parade would be unthinkable. Athena must be served. So, following a thorough search for hidden weapons, Athens' men and women, suspicious and subdued, trudged dazed and nervous along a Sacred Way fraught with potential danger, blindly observing ritual until a fatty reek of sacrifice wreathed the Acropolis.[39]

That evening, as choirs of young girls danced and sang hymns for the goddess on the rock and in the city families gathered to eat sacrificial meat, Hipparchus' surviving killer was interrogated. His name was Aristogeiton and, like Harmodius, his youthful coconspirator and lover, he belonged to an obscure family from the eastern hinterlands of Attica. His story was all too human. Hipparchus had desired handsome Harmodius, and when the younger man rebuffed him, he invited Harmodius' sister to be a basket bearer in the Great Panathenaic procession, a prestigious role reserved for elite girls, who, faces caked with white flour to protect them from the sun, carried the bowls and instruments of sacrifice up onto the Acropolis. But, when she turned up for rehearsal, Hipparchus ridiculed her, mocking her low birth, sneering that a girl like her would never be invited. Burning with shame, her spirit broken, she told Harmodius. Hipparchus' fate was sealed.[40]

So first rumour, then tradition, and then history maintained, but, since Aristogeiton did not survive interrogation, the truth cannot be known. Gossips suggested that the assassination was part of a wider conspiracy, that Hippias was the intended target, that, with him dead, accomplices would neutralize his bodyguards, and rally the Athenians to rise up and overthrow the tyrants' family—but that when the lovers saw a fellow plotter talking with him at the gate, they panicked and, too early, killed Hipparchus. Whatever the reality, the killing changed Hippias. His rule became more autocratic, and as Harmodius and Aristogeiton morphed into folk heroes, he saw conspiracy in every shadow.[41]

Perhaps he was right to do so. Perhaps Hipparchus' murder was more than just an act of simple thuggery. Perhaps it really had been part of a failed coup. Certainly, Cleisthenes wasted no time in trying to seize the moment. Despite being wooed by the Peisistratids, he had never been their lackey, and now he showed his colours. Rallying supporters, he fortified Leipsydrium, a hilltop in the furrows of Mount Parnes, and fomented revolution. But the rebels were no match for Hippias' mercenaries. Weakened by siege, they were routed. As Cleisthenes and his fellow Alcmaeonidae melted into the maquis, his foot soldiers slunk back home to sing sad songs in secret:

Alas, Leipsydrium, you traitor!
Such good men you destroyed.
Brave fighters and true patriots,
They showed their noble pedigree.[42]

While Hippias' regime dissolved into a reign of terror and his lieutenants hunted down and executed his opponents, Attica sank into a bleak, totalitarian dystopia. But his enemies were indefatigable. Leipsydrium had taught a vital lesson: since Hippias had clung to power with the support of foreign mercenaries, they would use foreign aid to oust him. With stony resolution, Cleisthenes set to work cementing a formidable alliance. He began by courting Apollo. His family had a long association with the god at Delphi. It was his grandfathers, Alcmaeon of Athens and Cleisthenes of Sicyon, who had built Apollo's temple. But in 548 B.C., that building had burnt down. To fund its larger, grander successor, Delphi's priests embarked on an ambitious sponsorship campaign, persuading a consortium of Greek states to foot much of the bill. Even Egypt's pharaoh Ahmose II sent crates of alum to be monetized, with profits added to the fund. But after thirty-five long years, work had stalled. Partly because the building's enlarged footprint needed massive terracing, the project had come in over budget. The coffers were empty.[43]

For Cleisthenes it was a golden opportunity. He made the Delphic priests an offer they could not refuse: the Alcmaeonidae would pay for the completion, building the entire east façade from not limestone (like the rest of the temple) but expensive Parian marble. And if in return, when any Spartan consulted the oracle, the priests decided to add lines to its reply suggesting that the god wished Sparta to free Athens from the tyranny of Hippias, that was entirely up to them. The project was ambitious, the logistics complex: blocks of marble hewn from quarries in the heart of Paros, transported to the sea and loaded onto merchant ships; the voyage of 300 miles around the long peninsulas of southern Greece before being hoisted into ox carts for the lumbering climb—2,000 feet up—to the sanctuary at Delphi, where cliffs resounded to the ricochet of hammer upon chisel, and where, as columns rose, and form emerged from shapeless rock, the full extent of Cleisthenes' designs became apparent. He had used both sets of pedimental sculptures to broadcast to all Greece the strength of Delphi's links with Athens and (by implication) its backing for her liberation.[44]

Facing the forecourt with its generations-old inscriptions ("Know Yourself" and "Nothing in Excess"—more profound than any of Hipparchus' maxims), the east pediment showed Apollo in a four-horse chariot surrounded by a crowd of mortal favourites, entering Delphi for the first time to take possession of the sanctuary. Legend told how he had sailed from Delos to the Greek mainland, disembarked in Athens, and travelled with Athenian hosts along the very mountain road that Cleisthenes had taken from Leipsydrium. It was a clever choice of myth, rich in implication: it was Athenians who first welcomed Apollo; it was Athenians who brought the god to Delphi; it was Athenians, specifically the Alcmaeonidae, who helped finance the old temple and its replacement; so, it was Athenians, specifically the Alcmaeonidae, who were shown with Apollo on the sculptures. Far from being cursed, the Alcmaeonidae were Apollo's favourites. The western (limestone) pediment was equally provocative. It showed the Gigantomachy, the legend associated with Athens' Panathenaea, which—since Hipparchus was slain at this festival—was beginning to assume a new, political significance. A century later, Euripides imagined a group of Athenian sightseers admiring these very pedimental sculptures:

Look at the battle of the Giants on the stone façade!
—Friends, I'm looking at it.
Do you see her [Athena] brandishing her Gorgon-shield
against Enceladus?
—I see Pallas, my goddess.
What now? The blazing thunderbolt
so devastating in Zeus' hands
who shoots from afar?
—I see it. He is turning warlike Mimas
to ashes in his fire.
And Bacchus, loud-roaring, with his
rod of ivy—no weapon, that—
is slaying another of the sons of Earth.[45]

Again, the parallels were clear: now Athens' tyrants were the giants; like the gods' cause, Athens' people's cause was just; and all right-minded Greeks should help them.

If this story of how Cleisthenes suborned the Delphic priests (the first recorded case in history) is true, he was playing a dangerous game. Perhaps, however, it was a slur invented by disgruntled rivals, keen to perpetuate the idea of the Alcmaeonidae as godless cynics, appropriating religion and religious art for their own political ends. But what cannot be denied is that the plan worked. Goaded by the god (or by his priests), pious Spartans attacked Attica by sea. But Hippias was ready. With a thousand Thessalian cavalrymen—mercenaries all—he scythed down the Spartans and their general, driving the survivors to their ships. But still the Delphic priests persisted, and in 510 B.C., on the eve of the next Great Panathenaea, Sparta's king, Cleomenes, marched north. On the plain near Eleusis, he found Hippias' army, and in the tumult of battle, the Thessalian horsemen lost their nerve, wheeled their snorting horses, and galloped for the safety of the hills.[46]

Hippias fled to Athens and shut himself behind the Bronze Age walls of the Acropolis, trusting in his allies to fend off a siege. He was overconfident. His family was arrested as they tried to escape Attica, and he was served an ultimatum: leave Athens within five days or they die. He chose to save their lives. As Hippias sailed, an exile, east for Sigeum in Anatolia, where his half brother had been ruling for two decades, Pericles' great-uncle, Cleisthenes, rode home to Attica in triumph. He had helped to liberate his people, deploying every weapon in his arsenal—force, persuasion, guile, the wealth to build a temple and the cleverness to turn it to his own advantage—to rid his city of oppression. Yet, he knew that this was not enough. Attica was plagued by instability. To reach its full potential, for its citizens to live in harmony, for the Alcmaeonidae to prosper, its entire means of governance needed to be overhauled. It was time to reinvent not only Athens but her very way of life.[47]

3 BUILDING DEMOCRACY

Some call it democracy, others whatever else they please, but it is actually an aristocracy backed by popular support.

—PLATO, *MENEXENUS*, 238C–D

Revolutions are by their nature destabilizing. The coup that ousted Hippias was no exception. As rival groups fought for power, politics became increasingly unstable. There were two main factions. One was championed by Isagoras, an Athenian aristocrat who was wedded to returning to the oligarchic status quo which had prevailed before Peisistratus and cultivated close relations with Sparta (though rumour said his wife enjoyed still closer ones with Sparta's King Cleomenes). The other was led by Cleisthenes.[1]

In exile, Cleisthenes had honed radical ideas, perhaps inspired by memories of partisans, who fought beside him at Leipsydrium. Uniting all of them had been the dream of seizing their own destiny and claiming their autonomy, and while they had included landed rich, many had been artisans or peasants; men who loved their families and villages, the very soil of Attica; men tired of taking orders from the privileged elites; men of the demos, that anonymous, vast mass of poorer citizens, who individually had little influence, but united could be formidable—and Cleisthenes had a plan to harness its power. Little evidence survives for these crucial years, and none is entirely reliable, but, elected to high office, Cleisthenes apparently convinced sufficient colleagues that the only way to build a future free from civil strife was to give more power to the People and implement a new, progressive constitution. Called *isonomia,* "equality under the law," it would soon have a catchier name, *demokratia,* "the power of the people," "the power of the poor," "democracy"—and it changed how every citizen viewed both himself and his relationship with the state.[2]

Previously, a citizen's identity had been defined entirely by his patrimony—"x, son of y"—a system promoting loyalty to family. But to achieve real social cohesion, that loyalty needed to be focussed on wider Attica. So, Cleisthenes created a network of 139 "demes," small districts, each with its own administration, whose names were added to the name of each of its citizen inhabitants ("x, son of y, of deme z"). Groups of demes were then combined to form a body called a *trittys* ("third"), so named because each *trittys* was in turn teamed with two others from different areas of Attica to form one of ten new tribes (*phylai*), each containing one "third" from the coast, one from the city, and one from the countryside. From now on, his tribe would form the basis of every Athenian citizen's life, informing everything from where he sat in the theatre to his place in the battleline, and compelling diverse communities, which had once been bitter rivals, to work together for the common good.[3]

To add gravitas to this new dispensation, Cleisthenes sent delegates to Delphi to ask Apollo to assign each tribe a name. From a hundred possibilities, scratched on shards of pottery and placed into an amphora, acting for the god the priests drew out his choices, each name connected to Athens' legendary history. Some were so obscure that few even in Attica had heard of them. But that was not the point. What mattered was that Apollo had helped shape Athens' constitution. It was a major propaganda coup. Thanks to Delphi's standing as a diplomatic hub and font of gossip, news of the god's approval quickly spiderwebbed across the Greek-speaking world.[4]

The tribes would also form the backbone of Athenian politics. Each provided fifty members annually (500 men in all) to serve on the central Council (Boulē), and for a tenth of their allotted time each tribe served as Council "presidents," with roughly sixteen men on twenty-four-hour duty in case of an emergency. Part of the Council's role was to prepare motions for discussion at the Assembly (Ekklesia), now open to all citizens, who would ratify or reject them by a show of hands. Moreover, while senior magistrates (archons) were still elected from the highest echelons of the elite, and roles such as generalships, which required experience and skill, were subject to appointment, many more citizens could now hold offices of state. But with new power came new accountability: at each year's end, every official was subject to a rigorous enquiry, the *euthyna* (making good), a strict examination of his conduct, especially his financial probity. Although women and metics still had no say in politics, and although slave-ownership remained unquestioned, the new constitution represented a seismic change. Unsurprisingly it met strong opposition. Not least from the now sidelined Isagoras, who scuttled south to Sparta, complaining that this dangerously anti-oligarchic charter was not what they envisaged when they helped rid Attica of Hippias. Landed aristocrats all, the Spartan warrior-elite heard his catalogue of woes with growing dread.[5]

Ironically the Spartan constitution was not so far removed from Cleisthenes' democracy. Said to have been implemented by a legendary lawgiver, Lycurgus, it, too, gave every citizen a voice in government—quite literally, since issues were decided not by a show of hands but by shouting (the loudest loudmouths won). However, since only men of wealth, land and long pedigree could be enrolled as citizens, it was in reality an oligarchy. There was no Spartan lower or even middle class. Those involved in commerce and manufacturing were technically not Spartans at all. Called *perioikoi* ("dwellers in surrounding areas"), they lived in scattered towns and villages across Spartan-controlled Laconia and Messenia, and while locally self-governing, they were required to obey the Spartans' rules, to pay their taxes and to do their bidding with no say in state policy. More powerless still were helot serfs, the indigenous population enslaved centuries before when conquering Spartans migrated from ancestral Dorian heartlands. Dangerously resentful, yet a vital part of economic life, helots outnumbered their overlords by perhaps ten to one, a menacing enemy within the very bounds of Sparta.[6]

The Spartans voted noisily to smother the Athenian experiment at birth. But there remained one problem: even Sparta's patron god, Apollo, had backed *isonomia*. Isagoras' solution was a neat one: if Cleisthenes could utilize religion, so could the Spartans. On his advice, apparently concerned for Athens' welfare, they reminded the Athenians that, thanks to the massacre of Cylon's followers a century before, the Alcmaeonids were accursed. For Athenians to prosper, the leading Alcmaeonid Cleisthenes must again be exiled. A blatant threat, it exploited Athenians' innate fear of Sparta. Memories of the Spartan intervention that toppled Hippias were raw. Athenians had met the dead stare of Sparta's warriors and been grateful that their spear tips were not aimed at them. As for the curse, gods and spirits were a real and constant presence, and spiritual pollution was considered so contagious that, unless its source was driven out, it could infect a whole community. Indeed, each summer, Athenians held a ritual to purify the land of such pollution. Believing that appearance reflected moral worth, they chose two scapegoats, the ugliest man and woman they could find, paraded them around the streets and beat them with green branches before chasing them out of the city, perhaps even to their death. So, in the unstable atmosphere of post-coup Athens, once its seeds were planted, fear of the Alcmaeonid curse blossomed.[7]

Prudently, Cleisthenes left Attica. But Isagoras smelt blood. With his eye on tyranny, he knew that other rivals too must be removed. So, together with Cleomenes and a band of Spartan bodyguards, he rode into the city to proclaim the banishment of 700 families—and the dissolution of the democratic Council. For Athenians, so recently emancipated, this was a step too far. The scales fell from their eyes. They had let themselves be duped, but now despite the danger, they refused to obey. Outnumbered, Cleomenes, Isagoras and their supporters retreated . . . to the Acropolis, where they found themselves besieged. Living with them on the sacred rock was the priestess of Athena Polias, and, as the days dragged on, Cleomenes, increasingly frustrated, found her dozing in the temple's portico. He demanded that she let him in. But he had met his match. Her reply became legendary: "Stand back, Spartan foreigner! Do not set foot in this holy place. It is sacrilege for Dorians to cross this threshold." With condescending arrogance Cleomenes pushed past her, through into the temple, where he rifled through its archives and looted sacred books of oracles, an outrage, and a desecration. In doing so, he lost the moral argument. By appealing to the laws of sacrilege, he had orchestrated Cleisthenes' exile. By breaking them so readily himself, he exposed his own hypocrisy. Just two days later, he conceded defeat. Granted safe passage, he and his humiliated Spartans slunk out of Attica; Isagoras' supporters were arrested, tried, and executed; and Cleisthenes, and the 700 exiled families, including the Alcmaeonids, returned to a hero's welcome.[8]

But celebrations were short lived. Bent on revenge, and determined to bring Athens to heel, by 506 B.C. the Spartans were again advancing on Attica. They had amassed a terrifying alliance—Corinthians with whom they would invade from the southwest; Boeotians and Chalcidians, whom they had primed to sweep down from the north in a classic pincer movement. With its future hanging on a thread, Athens put its new constitution to the test. The Council proposed a general mobilization; the Assembly approved the motion; Council members circulated call-up lists prepared from newly drawn-up registers of tribal- and deme-members; generals met in conclave; armed men mustered in the Public Fields; and, with trumpets blaring, the Athenians marched out to battle. The generals had taken a high-risk gamble. Calculating that to fight on two fronts simultaneously was suicidal, they had opted to concentrate their power against the Spartans and Corinthians and then, if they defeated them, to turn and face the others. It was a big "if." The Spartans were the greatest fighting force in Greece. And, when the first javelins were thrown and swords were drawn, who knew how many land-owning Athenians would willingly lay down their lives for a constitution that safeguarded the poor? Across the saddle of Aegaleus they marched, and down into the wheatfields of Eleusis, home to the great Mysteries, where Hippias had been defeated, where Erechtheus had fought and died, and there, arranged for the first time in new tribal battalions, untrained, untested, a ragbag army in a mishmash of unmatching armour, they gazed out at their Spartan counterparts, grim warriors, their long hair oiled and lustrous, their beards full, top-lips shaved, bronze helmets, armour, spear tips and round shields all glinting in the sunlight, their cloaks and tunics all identical, the dull red of fresh blood, and in command their two kings, Cleomenes and Demaratus, sure proof of the sheer magnitude of their resolve.[9]

And so, with the adrenaline of apprehension pounding in their brains, Athens' democratic army waited in the warm sun for the order to advance. Instead, what happened was extraordinary. Instead of lowering their helmets and hefting spears, the Corinthians broke rank, turned, and set off back along the sea road out of Attica. Confusion in the Spartan ranks. Then King Demaratus, too, gave the order to stand down. All that Cleomenes could do was follow where his retreating colleague led. In the absence of a military explanation why such hardened soldiers had backed down, pious Athenians believed that they had witnessed a miracle: the first time that the new democracy had mobilized for war, the gods had intervened—on Athens' side at one of the most sacred sites in Attica.[10]

Not that they could celebrate. Boeotians and Chalcidians were preparing to join forces to invade from the northwest, and they must be stopped. Through mountain passes, and by dusty roads, across vast plains, the jubilant, awestruck Athenians marched at the double. They encountered the Boeotians first—in fields near Harma, a town whose name meant chariot—with such impetus, such passion, such belief in their invincibility that they smashed straight through the enemy lines and, once the choreography of slaughter was completed and the theatre was secured, discovered they had seized some 700 prisoners. But still the victors pressed on to the Euripus Strait, whose treacherous waters separate the mainland from Euboea, and by nightfall they had slaked their bloodlust on the Chalcidians. It was an extraordinary achievement: one enemy army routed without a blow being struck; two victories in battle in a single day; the rich farmlands of Chalcis annexed; huge ransoms raised from prisoners-of-war.[11]

The gods deserved great praise, especially Athena. To mark her role in their great triumph, the Athenians dedicated to her their prisoners' shackles, and, paid for from booty and ransom, commissioned a thank offering—a bronze statue group, a chariot and four horses, standing proud on the Acropolis "on the left as you go through the gate," set on a plinth of dark blue-grey limestone from Eleusis, and bearing the inscription:

> *Sons of Athenians brought swarms of Boeotians*
> *and Chalcidians to heel in the workshop of war*
> *and quenched their hubris in dark chains of iron.*
> *They erected these horses to Athena as a tithe.*[12]

No detail had been left to chance—especially not the statue's subject. On a simple level, the chariot was a visual reference to the site of one of the two victories: Harma. But there was more to it than that. By the late sixth century B.C., chariots were used not in war but in the upper-class pursuit of racing, and statues of chariots and horses were often dedicated to the gods in thanks by wealthy victors. So, this appropriation of an aristocratic image was a provocative political statement, setting the People, the poor, the demos on a par with kings and oligarchs, while celebrating Athens' military and moral superiority in verses trumpeting the punishment of hubris with iron shackles.

But the epigram could mark only the Boeotians' and Chalcidians' defeat since it was from spoils from these encounters that the statue had been raised. Because Athens' other, equally significant encounter—at Eleusis with the Spartans and Corinthians—had involved no fighting, it had resulted in no spoils. There was technically no victory to celebrate. But there was the enemy's miraculous retreat, most likely prompted by intervention of Eleusis' gods, and by using Eleusinian limestone for the statue's plinth, the Athenians could allude to this event, too, in their monument. This, furthermore, was the limestone through which Persephone emerged reborn to bring new life, which even the uninitiated might see as paralleling Athens' own rebirth, a victorious democracy, after decades of tyranny. It was the first time Eleusinian limestone was used on the Acropolis, but it would not be the last. Thanks to its connections with both the ancient, otherworldly message of the Mysteries and the first victories of the new democracy, for generations it would play a central role in statuary and architecture.[13]

The chariot dedication also marked a major shift in policy towards the Acropolis. While the Peisistratids had largely left the rock alone, the democrats reclaimed it for themselves, dedicating offerings and constructing buildings, symbols of defiance and self-confidence. The greatest symbol of them all was the Temple of Athena Polias. The two-day occupation of the Acropolis by Isagoras and Sparta's King Cleomenes—men threatening bloodshed, voiding bodily wastes, defying the priestess—had defiled the sanctuary, causing such gross spiritual pollution that religious experts could find no rituals strong enough to decontaminate the temple. Instead, they insisted that it be demolished, and a new building erected on its site.[14]

As the first temple built under the new democracy, paid for by the People not the rich elite, it was a celebration of Athenians' relationship with their presiding goddess, protectress of the city, at whose Great Panathenaic Festival the two tyrannicides had killed Hipparchus, and struck the first blow for democracy. The project must have had a sponsor to propose it to the Council and steer it through the Assembly, an architect, a budget, an administrative infrastructure, and a huge workforce. But no records survive. All that we know is that the temple occupied the same foundations as its predecessor with the same layout, that its height was marginally increased, and that its entablature, its sima (guttering) adorned with ram's head finials, and its pedimental sculptures were all carved from not poros stone (as in the previous temple) but Parian marble, the same material that, thanks to Cleisthenes and the Alcmaeonids, now graced the east face of the Delphic Temple of Apollo.[15]

Combining tradition and modernity, the subjects of the pedimental sculptures were well chosen. With more than a nod to its predecessor, the west pediment showed two lions tearing at a bull. But for the first time on the Acropolis the east pediment drew on mythology. It showed the Gigantomachy, spotlighting Athena's slaying of Enceladus, the foundation myth of the Great Panathenaea. Recently the subject had

3.1 Athena fights in the Gigantomachy on the pediment of the early democratic Temple of Athena Polias on the Acropolis.

appeared on other sacred buildings throughout the Greek-speaking world (including, of course, Delphi's Temple of Apollo), but nowhere was its relevance more potent than at Athens, where Athena killing a hubristic giant and thus ensuring the Olympians' supremacy, could be taken as a metaphor for democratic Athens' overthrow of Hippias, and the two lions savaging the bull could be interpreted as standing for Harmodius and Aristogeiton assassinating Hipparchus.[16]

It was not the only way that the tyrannicides were celebrated. In the Public Fields near the Leocorium, where their attack had taken place, the People erected a bronze statue group, two life-sized figures, commissioned from the leading sculptor, Antenor. One was a bearded older man, the other a smooth-cheeked youth; both clutched a weapon; and as befitted their heroic status, both were nude. It is unlikely that they were truly recognizable portraits, but there could be no doubt as to the men's identity. Lines written by Simonides (once the tyrants' favourite poet) drew on imagery from the Eleusinian Mysteries with their sudden blaze of torchlight speaking of new life, proclaiming:

> *Great was the light that flared for the Athenians*
> *when Aristogeiton and Harmodius killed Hipparchus.*[17]

Like its subjects, awarded now by public decree "honours equal to those of gods," the monument was revolutionary. Unique in concept and daring in its context, for over a century it was the only statue of mortal men permitted by law to stand in the Agora. For the Agora is what the Public Fields had now become—Athens' commercial, legal, and administrative heart, a quasi-sacred space with its own rules and regulations, its boundaries delineated by inscribed marker stones, its tightly controlled gates flanked by lustral basins, so that all entering might purify themselves, part sanctuary, part civic centre. We do not know what prompted the Assembly to relocate the Agora, or who proposed the move, though the latter is not simply an accident of history. In the early democracy, individual ego was deliberately suppressed. What mattered were the collective wishes of the People, and those wishes were ambitious. Over the next quarter century (505–480 B.C.), the scale and vision of the democratic building programme surpassed all that had preceded it.[18]

Even as the Temple of Athena Polias was being dismantled and rebuilt on the Acropolis, in the new Agora below, drains were dug, and homes and workshops demolished. Among them was the tyrants' palace, reduced like their regime to dust and rubble, its site repurposed and reclaimed—as the democratic Bouleuterion, the Council Chamber, as conspicuous for its iconoclastic architecture as for its revolutionary purpose. Essentially square (76 by 78 feet), the building was divided into two unequal parts: a shallow south-facing portico and the large rectangular chamber with ranks of wooden benches arranged against yellow limestone walls pierced at regular intervals by high windows. Because of its size, the building's revolutionary hip roof was supported by strategically placed columns—five (linked by high metal security grilles) at the entrance to the portico, three at the entrance to the chamber, and five in the chamber itself. It was the first secular hypostyle (or columned) hall in mainland Greece, but what made it even more unorthodox were its Doric frieze of *metopēs* and triglyphs, and its Doric columns and capitals, all details previously reserved for religious buildings. While their use in a civic Council Chamber was potentially shocking, their message was clear: there was something special, something spiritual, something approaching the divine about the democratic constitution, and if its architecture blurred the boundaries between the sacred and the secular, so be it.[19]

The Council Chamber was not the only innovative new construction in the newly relocated Agora. A few hundred yards to the north, near the Sacred Way that led to Twin Towers Gate, was built a stoa, a colonnaded arcade, to house the office of the Archon Basileus ("King Archon"), the magistrate whose remit embraced justice, civic sacrifices, a festival of Dionysus, and the Eleusinian Mysteries. Previously stoas were associated exclusively with sanctuaries. This stoa was the first designed for nonreligious purposes, and like the Council Chamber the "Royal Stoa" (named for the King Archon) drew heavily on religious architecture. With its Doric columns, trigyphs, *metopēs,* and tiled terracotta roof, it looked more like a temple than a government office. Which was precisely the point. It was thanks to Athena and the gods that Athens was liberated, democratic, and victorious. Athena permeated every organ of the state. It was only fitting that civic architecture should nod to the sacred.[20]

A torrent of building work marked these heady years: a temple to Hephaestus, ancestor of all Athenians, on the hill above the Royal Stoa; a temple to Dionysus south of the Acropolis, with a nearby theatre space where (mirroring the rectilinear arrangement in the Council Chamber) benches could be set out on the hillside—far safer than the temporary grandstand in the Agora, which collapsed with injury and loss of life in 496 B.C. New fountain houses were constructed, too, and law courts, an altar of Aphrodite, and a temple to Triptolemus, the harvest hero of Eleusis, who toured the earth, his chariot drawn by dragons, teaching mankind the art of agriculture, an Athenian helping civilize the world. But one existing project lay abandoned. By the banks of the Ilissus, the Temple of Olympian Zeus, dreamchild of Hippias and Hipparchus, sprawled unfinished, its huge foundations and its stunted ranks of still-unfluted columns just a few drums tall. For centuries the site would languish, overgrown and empty, a place of haunted memories, a crumbling memorial, a deterrent to despotic hubris.[21]

While temples and stoas celebrated democratic Athens' relationship with her gods, the sheer scale of one project transformed the cityscape still further: the huge open-air auditorium built into the hillside as a meeting place for the Assembly, which thanks to its popularity earned the nickname "Pnyx," "congested." Much effort went into its construction. Homes were dismantled; on the higher slopes unprecedented volumes of soil were excavated, while lower reaches were infilled with many thousand tons of earth and rubble packed behind a high retaining wall; the ground was tamped and smoothed; and gradually the hill was reshaped, a shallow semicircular bowl that curved up from its central focal point, the Speaker's Platform. Accommodating some 6,000 men, the auditorium was vast, but even so (as we have seen) it could hold only a fraction of Attica's citizenry. Thanks to the constraints of space, Athenian democracy could be fully participatory in name only. Not everyone who was eligible could vote. Distance, work pressures, serving on campaign might all prevent a man from attending the Assembly, but that was not the point. The possibility was there for everyone to help shape policy and determine their own lives.[22]

They found a perfect venue, too, for honouring their dead. By the broad avenue that led out to the Grove of Academus, one of the most enchanting and delightful Athenian suburbs, they consecrated land to house a public cemetery, where any man who sacrificed his life in battle, be he wealthy statesman or humble peasant farmer, would be buried with solemnity, the war dead for each year interred together in their tribal plots, their names recorded for posterity, all venerated at the grateful state's expense.[23]

Throughout all Attica, thanks to a democratic building programme outstripping in ambition anything yet seen in the Greek-speaking world, the landscape was transformed. No tyrant ever thought so big. From coastal plains high into mountain folds, demes (linked by networks of new roads begun under the tyrants and continued by the People) built their own alfresco auditoria with seating arranged in rectilinear rows. Used both for secular political assemblies and for religious dance or drama, these multifunction venues spoke to the symbiosis between religion and state, and the conviction that the gods would favour and protect democracy. Thus, while military mountain fortlets secured passes into neighbouring Boeotia and Megara, in sanctuaries along the coastal fringe of Attica, a chain of temples was created as a sacred palisade, a spiritual threshold guarded by the gods. Their positioning was far from accidental. At Rhamnous, opposite Euboea, near the Boeotian border, Athenians built a pair of temples—one for Themis, goddess of tradition, law, and justice; the other for Nemesis, "winged goddess, blue-eyed unbalancer of life," the scourge of hubris, punisher of mortals who transgress the boundaries that separate mankind from gods. Twenty-eight miles south at marshy Brauron, once part of the Peisistratid estates, they built a temple to the goddess Artemis to house an ancient talismanic statue, while a further twenty-eight miles south of that on the beetling promontory of Sunium, they began another pair of temples, one for Athena atop a grassy knoll, the other (the first peripteral temple outside Athens itself) for Poseidon rising proud and gleaming on the clifftop. A similarly spaced sequence of sanctuaries protected Attica's south coast: along with Leto and her twins, Artemis and Apollo, Athena safeguarded Cape Zoster, twenty-five miles west of Sunium, while a further twenty-five miles on from there was numinous Eleusis, the mysterious portal to the underworld, whose gods Demeter, Persephone, and Dionysus had intervened to turn the Spartans and Corinthians to flight. Like the Temple of Athena Polias on the Athenian Acropolis, Eleusis, too, had been

3.2 Cape Sunium topped by the ruined fifth-century B.C. Temple of Poseidon.

defiled by Spartan occupation, which was why it, too, must be demolished and rebuilt—larger.[24]

Under the democracy the importance of Eleusis rapidly increased as the Assembly voted to improve access to the Mysteries for anyone who had the time (and money) to take part in the preliminary rites, procession, and initiations, by constructing a new Telesterion. Its design was impressive: a shallow porch (resembling a stoa with twelve Doric columns) led into a vast chamber, at 82 by 88 feet almost square, its foundations hewn out of the limestone bedrock, its roof supported by twenty-two interior Ionic columns, its inner walls flanked by nine tiers of shallow steps, from which initiates observed the sacred drama of Demeter and Persephone enacted each September by the priests. Urban Athenians would have recognized three architectural details: the Telesterion's porch resembled the Royal Stoa, its interior resembled that of their Council Chamber, while, outside, the sima's rams' head finials were exact replicas of those on the Temple of Athena Polias. Deliberately, the architect had linked these four significant buildings, highlighting their hierarchy in the network of sites, sacred and secular, that interlaced through Attica like a protective web. But these were not the only architectural echoes. Consciously or not, the lower bands of limestone, on which not just the Telesterion but the towered gates and mudbrick walls that ringed the sanctuary were built, evoked the plinth on the Athenian Acropolis, part of the Harma statue group evoking Athens' bloodless victory at Eleusis over the Corinthians and Spartans.[25]

But while the democratic building programme brimmed with confidence, one inconvenient truth threatened to disturb its vision of utopia. Back in the spring of 507 B.C., with Attica threatened by invasion, the Assembly had sent a high-level delegation to Sardis. Once the seat of Alcmaeon's friend, Croesus, forty years earlier the city had been subsumed into the fast-expanding Persian empire and transformed into a regional capital, whose satrap (governor) was answerable only to the Great King, Darius, himself. The reason for the meeting was to seek a military alliance. Perhaps led by Cleisthenes, the ambassadors enjoyed a favourable reception. The Great King, his satrap assured them, would happily enter an alliance—if, in turn, the Athenians sent him one amphora containing Attic earth, and another containing Attic water. The diplomats agreed, but back home the Assembly erupted in righteous anger. Somehow it had passed the envoys by that for Persians gifts of earth and water were symbolic not of an alliance but of voluntary surrender to their empire. The diplomats had just agreed to hand over their polis to the most powerful tyrant in the known world. But Athens had just driven out one overlord. She had no wish to submit to another. So, the Assembly overrode the envoys' promises; no amphoras were sent; Cleisthenes played no further part in history; and the Athenians did their best to forget the entire episode.[26]

They had enough to occupy them nearer home. Just twenty-five miles south of Athens, the hostile island of Aegina (later called by Pericles "the eyesore of Piraeus") dominated the Saronic Gulf, and in the aftermath of Harma it allied with Boeotia, launching sleek warships to torch defenceless villages and homesteads on Attica's south coast, and even burning installations at Athens' port of Phalerum. The conflict had been sparked in part by statues, and, as it escalated, the arms race of architecture accelerated.[27]

In around 625 B.C. (chronology for this period is insecure), the Delphic oracle had advised Epidaurus, Aegina's metropolis, to stave off famine by dedicating statues carved from cultivated olive trees to two local fertility goddesses. The Epidaurians requested wood from one of Athens' sacred groves, in return for which they promised to make annual offerings on the Athenian Acropolis. But the Aeginetans (like the Corcyreans at odds with their metropolis) stole the statues and took them to their mountain sanctuary at Oea. That year the Epidaurians sent no gifts to Athens—they said that, since the Aeginetans now possessed the statues, the obligation lay with them—and, when the islanders refused to honour the commitment, Athens dispatched her ships. The result was a disaster. Only one Athenian survived, and (according to much later sources) his story was remarkable. Reaching Oea unopposed, he and his comrades found they could not remove the statues from their bases. Superstitious and impatient—why were the goddesses resisting?—short tempers frayed. Then, mayhem, thunder, earthquake. The statues sank to their knees. Swords scraped from scabbards, blades slashed through flesh, blood sprayed, and the sole survivor ran in panic to the sea. Somehow, he crossed to Phalerum. When he told his comrades' widows how their husbands, maddened by the gods, had slaughtered one another, the grieving women tore the long-pinned brooches from their dresses and stabbed him to death. The Aeginetans told a different tale: in the chaos of the earthquake, they had massacred the terrified Athenians.[28]

While this episode was largely cleansed from Athens' communal memory (which recalled only success), it was clearly a major defeat. But it is also an important insight into not just a forgotten history but Greek popular beliefs about statues. While the urbane historian, Herodotus, our only source, dismissed the tale of kneeling statues as implausible, he admits that others might think differently, since many thought that statues did quite literally embody the divinities they represented, and could even show emotion. In times of stress they sweated, trembled, groaned, for statues were not simply sculptures: they were earthly avatars of the divine.[29]

Years later, still nursing hatred towards Athens, Aegina escalated hostilities—but not through war; through temple building. In the 510s B.C., they constructed a new limestone temple for Apollo just outside their city, importing Parian marble for its pediments (the material used by the Alcmaeonids at Delphi)—while high in the mountains in the northeast of the island with clear views over the Saronic Gulf to Attica and Athens they erected a provocative new temple to Aphaea. A local variant of Artemis, Apollo's twin, she had long been worshipped here, but in 510 her wooden temple was destroyed by fire. Its limestone replacement, columns stuccoed dazzling white with details highlighted in vibrant paintwork, was a masterpiece of delicate proportions and elegant roof ornaments (sphinxes and curling lotus flowers ablaze with colour, their tall stems flanked by smiling maidens). Inside, light filtered through thin marble roof tiles into a spacious, airy cella, its ceiling supported by a two-storeyed colonnade, where Aphaea's new statue stood behind a wooden railing, her original wood-and-ivory cult statue (saved from the fire) set on a stone plinth to its left. But it was the pedimental sculptures that were most calculated to provoke Athens since they boasted Aegina's superiority in not one but two Trojan wars.[30]

Athenians featured rarely in the myths of Troy—unlike the Aeginetans, whose mythical King Aeacus helped Apollo and Poseidon build Troy's walls. But, when the Trojans failed to pay them, the gods demanded that they sacrifice their princess to a sea monster. Only Heracles' arrival saved her, but he, too, was cheated of his reward, so he led an army into Asia. With him was Telamon, Aeacus' son, now king of Aegina. He breached the walls and, once inside, the Greeks (in Homer's words) "made desolate the streets." In recognition, Heracles gave the princess to Telamon, who took her home to Aegina, where she bore him a son, Teucer. This was the war shown on the new temple's east pediments with Heracles and Telamon placed almost centre stage. But not quite. At this place of honour stood an even more important figure—not Aphaea or her alter ego, Artemis, but Athena,

3.3 Figures from the west pediment of the Temple of Aphaea on Aegina.

giving her support to both Telamon and his homeland, Aegina. Athena dominated the west pediment, too, where Telamon's heir, Ajax, and his half brother, Teucer, confronted their Trojan enemy in the conflict familiar from Homer's *Iliad.*[31]

It was perfectly pitched propaganda. Challenging the Athenians' aggressive narrative that they were the gods' chosen people, and that Attica was the gods' chosen land, the Aeginetans were channelling the power of Aeacus' family, the Aeacidae, whose relics (housed in a hero-shrine, whose walled enclosure shimmered with olive trees beside their harbour) they believed brought victory in battle. Indeed, when the Boeotians asked Aegina for military aid in their own ongoing war with Athens, instead of sending troops, the islanders loaned them their prized relics. Even Boeotia's defeat could not dull the reputation of the relics or the Aeacidae—Athenians, declaring that (like all right-thinking divinities) the Aeacidae were clearly pro-Athens, appropriated the heroes for themselves, and built their own Aeaceum in the new democratic Agora, a thank offering for victory and an invitation to Aeacus and his family to quit Aegina and take up residence in Athens. Athens' Aeaceum and Aegina's Temple of Aphaea showed how art, sculpture, and architecture could be weaponized. By honouring Athena on their temple's pediments, the Aeginetans aimed to trump Athens' Temple of Athena Polias and secure the goddess's support; by building an alluring sanctuary for Aegina's dynamic hero, Athenians hoped to weaken their enemies.[32]

Athens, meanwhile, had been honing and promoting her own superhero, Theseus. Hipparchus may have commissioned an epic poem, the *Theseis,* but ironically his death and Hippias' expulsion made Theseus seem more relevant. While Theseus had been a king, with just a little ingenuity he was recast as a proto-democrat, ruling wisely, justly, with his people's willing consent, an exemplary "first man," who united Attica and pioneered a model of political cooperation not seen again until the days of Cleisthenes. Moreover, his mission chimed with that of democratic Athens. Upholding morality, helping the distressed and championing the underdog, he freed his fellow citizens from paying tribute to the Cretan king, defended Athens from the Amazons, fought lawless Centaurs, exterminated brigands, and strove unceasingly to civilize the world. By the end of the sixth century, Theseus, once a minor demigod, was becoming equal to the Panhellenic Heracles, his doppelgänger, and his inspiration, in some of whose adventures he now played a leading role. So, let the Aeginetans boast of their Aeacidae. Athens' Theseus could more than match them.[33]

But could he match the Persians? While Athenians were trying to forget their promise to send earth and water to the Great King, Persia's empire had been thriving. It had emerged from nowhere back in 550 B.C. when Cyrus, king of the tiny province of Anshan, annexed a string of mighty kingdoms: Media and Babylon and Croesus' Lydia, whose vassal Greek poleis fringed Asia Minor's Aegean coast. By 530 Cyrus' son, Cambyses, had conquered Egypt; by 513 Darius, his successor, had seized the Indus valley, campaigned beyond the Danube and extended his command of the Aegean coast as far as northern Greece. Such sprawling territories required tight administration, and with unerring skill Darius strengthened his network of satraps, provincial governors who oversaw taxation and enlisted men for Persia's army, ever conscious of the need for sensitivity when dealing with their subjects' traditions and beliefs.[34]

The Persian Empire managed to accommodate a vast range of religions—Hinduism; Judaism; the worship of the Babylonian god, Marduk; Egypt's host of animal-faced deities; the Greeks' unruly pantheon of gods. For Darius the greatest was Ahura Mazda, Lord of Wisdom, paradigm of truth and justice, god made manifest to man as fire. Opposing him was Angra Mainyu, the Evil One, the lord of demons, purveyor of the Lie. With both gods locked in an eternal cosmic struggle, Darius saw it as his earthly duty to do Ahura Mazda's work by imposing order—whether that meant making equitable laws or cultivating orchards, fields, and well-irrigated gardens or exterminating Angra Mainyu's fiendish agents, be they savage beasts or traitorous men. Already, Darius' predecessor, Cyrus, had held all Greeks in deep suspicion, describing them as men who met in agoras and "lied to one another under oath." But so long as they did not threaten Persian stability, Darius readily accepted the rich gamut of his subject nations' people and their gods—not least Apollo, like Ahura Mazda lord of light and fire. When he learned that in Ionia Apollo's sacred gardeners were required to work unconsecrated land, the Great King was quick to reprimand the local satrap.[35]

But in 500 B.C. Darius' problems with Ionia became more serious when Aristagoras, his puppet tyrant of Miletus, proposed what seemed a failsafe plan. Wealthy Naxos had just staged a revolution, expelling its oligarchic government (installed by Sparta in a blow to Athens twenty-four years earlier), and declaring itself a democracy. It seemed the perfect time for Persia to intervene with a special military operation to return the oligarchs to power, bring Naxos under Persian control, and secure a valuable bridgehead to the Greek mainland (which Darius was already planning to invade not least to punish the oath-breaking Athenians). Things turned out very differently. Aristagoras squabbled with Darius' general; the Naxians took refuge behind strong city walls; and when a lengthy siege resulted in the Persian navy's ignominious withdrawal, Aristagoras knew that he would shoulder the blame. To save his skin, he hatched another plan. Stepping down as tyrant, he declared Miletus a democracy, stirred up a populist revolt throughout Ionia, and sailed to mainland Greece to canvas help in throwing off what he now described as the oppressive Persian yoke.[36]

As protocol dictated, he went first to the most powerful city, Sparta, but here he was rebuffed—not unsurprisingly, given his betrayal of the Spartan-leaning oligarchs, and Sparta's suspicion of all things democratic. In Athens, however, eight years into her own democracy, Aristagoras was welcomed warmly. Addressing the Assembly on the building site that was Pnyx Hill, he evoked legendary Ion (father of all Ionians), claimed (wrongly) that Miletus had been founded by Athenians, elaborated on shared blood ties, and made increasingly quixotic promises, "guaranteeing whatever came into his head" and mesmerizing all who heard him. They were receptive anyway—these were precisely the circumstances in which Theseus, champion of the underdog, would himself have intervened—but Aristagoras' appeal to their emotions and sense of kudos was so well pitched that, joined by five triremes from Euboean Eretria, twenty Athenian warships were soon racing east.[37]

In Miletus they joined forces with the Ionian democratic army, before cruising north to Ephesus and the eager road across the scrubby hills to Persian Sardis. For Athenians, familiar with tales of Croesus and Alcmaeon and the gold-dust that had made the Alcmaeonidae so wealthy, Sardis inspired avarice and awe: a steep well-walled acropolis that towered above a jumble of wooden thatched-roofed houses; the workshops and refineries for gold panned in the River Pactolus, which frothed and tumbled through the city; the narrow streets and alleyways; and rising tall and elegant above the hubbub, Croesus' Temple of Cybele with its Greek design and walls adorned with scenes from Greek mythology.[38]

As Persia's satrap cowered on his acropolis awaiting reinforcements, the Greek liberators set to work, swarming through the city, smashing doors and windows, overturning oil lamps, heedless of the flames now catching the dry thatch or black smoke rolling through the lanes, conscious only of the moment, the shouts and screaming, the townspeople of Sardis appearing through the murk, attacking them as they themselves fell back, advantage lost and impetus exhausted—as through a firestorm raining red-hot cinders the Greek liberators turned and fled. Only when they had outrun the enemy did they stop and turn and see through billowing smoke the Temple of Cybele, roof buckling, rafters shattering, fire pouring up the walls and flooding through the sanctuary, devouring priceless treasures, sacred relics, and exquisite artworks. To burn a temple even accidentally was a crime against the gods, forbidden by Greek rules of military engagement, and it boded ill. Soot-blackened, shocked, subdued, they tramped back to the coast, but on the plain near Ephesus the Persians found them. As their infantry advanced in adamantine ranks, their cavalry smashed in foaming waves of blood against the fleeing Greeks.[39]

In the Assembly, Athenians spoke no more of ties with the Ionians or of their zeal to spread democracy. They voted to play no further part in the revolt, and for five years they watched as cities fell. In 494, Miletus, the last stronghold, was taken, its menfolk slaughtered, its women and children led captive to the marshes of the River Tigris, before at nearby Didyma the pious Persians torched the Temple of Apollo. Perhaps they thought it was polluted by the demons of the Lie, so needed to be purified in flames. Or perhaps it was their vengeance for the fire at Sardis. Whatever the explanation, it was clear that Persians now considered Greek temples to be legitimate targets. It was clear, too, that, with Ionia subdued, Darius would not let Eretria and Athens escape unpunished. When a playwright dramatized *The Capture of Miletus* at that winter's Festival of Dionysus, the Athenian audience erupted, stopped the play, and fined him for reminding them of their own troubles.[40]

In truth, Athenians had long realised that war with Persia was inevitable, and for so many reasons: Darius' ambition to extend his empire west; their own broken promises of earth and water; their role in the Ionian Revolt. For Darius, Athenians were sacrilegious rebels, who must face the punishment he had imposed on such men in the past: "I sliced off his nose, his ears, his tongue. I blinded him. I kept him tied up at the gates and all could see him. . . . I impaled him on a pole. And in the camp, I flayed his close confederates."[41]

So, when, in 492 B.C., just two years after the capture of Miletus, Persian warships were seen sailing west along the north Aegean coast, purportedly for Attica, Athenians certain of the consequences of defeat—the end of democracy; the enslavement of their daughters, wives and mothers; their own death or torture—made anxious sacrifice and prepared for war. Then, unexpectedly, their prayers were answered. As Persia's fleet rounded the promontory of Athos, storm winds blew in from nowhere; huge waves swamped decks; ships foundered; hulls splintered on black rocks; men and horses, flailing in the roiling tide, were hunted down by terrifying sea monsters. The gods had intervened on democratic Athens' side.[42]

The threat was over. But not for long. Next year Persian emissaries came to Attica with an ultimatum and two empty amphoras. Athens could still repent. Send Darius Attic earth and water, and he would overlook her misdemeanours. Refuse, and he would destroy her. The Athenians did not hesitate. They dragged the Persians from the Speakers' Platform, dragooned them down the hill and flung them into the barathrum, a deep pit where criminals were left to die. To murder an ambassador broke every law, but Athenians had passed the point of legal niceties. They had burnt their bridges. They would fight and maybe die. But they would never surrender. Meanwhile other Persian delegates were touring Greece. Not to be upstaged by Athens, the Spartans threw Darius' envoys down a well, but other poleis were less spirited. The Aeginitans—prompted by hostility to Athens as much as by self-interest—readily filled twin amphoras and promised everlasting loyalty. Darius had long realised that the Greek world was fissured. Now he was testing fault lines, exposing fractures, and exploiting them more artfully than anyone before.[43]

By August 490 B.C., everything was in place. Confident of victory, the Persians set sail directly west for mainland Greece. At Naxos they met no resistance. As islanders scattered for safety, Persian troops poured through their streets, corralling stragglers, looting, vandalizing, before next morning, booty stowed in transport ships, they torched the city, and from the water watched as sacred fire swept through the public offices and homes—and temples, too—of this, the richest and most vibrant island in the whole Aegean. Then they set course for Delos, the sacred heart of the Ionian Greeks. The priests had fled, but they were easily tracked down—and coaxed home with reassurances of safety. The birthplace of Apollo, god of light, had not been contaminated by contact with Angra Mainyu. So, the only fires the Persians lit on Delos were on its massive altar, an offering of staggering extravagance, seventeen tons of frankincense, whose perfume drifted out across sea. And, like the stench of burning Naxos, this scent of incense carried a compelling message: those who opposed would be destroyed; those who cooperated need not fear.[44]

The message was repeated on Euboea at Eretria, whose citizens had joined in the attack on Sardis. After seven days of siege, two venal Eretrian aristocrats unbarred the gates, and the well-established process was repeated: men, women, children rounded up to be sent east to slavery; homes and warehouses ransacked; temples, stripped of statuary and treasures, engulfed in flames. And then the Persians set sail for Attica—not south, round Sunium for Phalerum, but across the straits to the Peisistratids' ancestral estate of Marathon, its marshlands sacred to Artemis, where an old man hobbled, sneezing, down the gangplank and stepped onto his native soil: after twenty years, Hippias was home. His presence revealed Darius' intentions: Athens, Attica, and mainland Greece were to become a Persian province with Hippias its satrap. While other defeated peoples were allowed to keep their constitutions, Athenians most certainly would not. Unless there was a miracle, unless the gods came to their aid, the days of their democracy were numbered.[45]

4 BURNT OFFERINGS

Hear me, you, War Cry, daughter of war, overture to spears,
to whom the city offers up her men in the sacred sacrifice of death.
—PINDAR, FRAGMENT 78

For Pericles and Athenians, what happened in those days at Marathon and in the years that followed was the stuff of legend. Outnumbered at least two to one, they were essentially alone. Only Plataea, a tiny city in the badlands between Attica and Thebes, had promised her support, and after the defeat of Naxos and Eretria, the chance of victory seemed slim. Yet, these were the same Athenians, who had faced down Spartans and Corinthians and beaten the Boeotians and Chalcidians thanks to their bravery and their gods' support. They would not waver now. As time accelerated, much must have seemed a blur. Runners were sent with messages to other poleis inciting them to action, but none returned with good news. Only the runner, Pheidippides, rebuffed by Sparta (adamant she could not march until Apollo's festival was over), offered a dull glimmer of hope. In the mountains of Arcadia (he said) he had encountered the god, Pan, who bade him "ask the Athenians why they neglected him, although he showed goodwill to them, had helped them in the past and would help again in future." So, Pan's name was added to the growing list of gods to whom Athenians made sacrifice—Athena Promachus, Apollo, god of the Ionians—while to Artemis, goddess of Marathon, they vowed to sacrifice a goat for every Persian they killed.[1]

And then the strapping on of armour; the march to Marathon; the camp beside a shrine of Heracles; prayers to the hero to support them; long days of waiting, staring at the enemy across the plain; the sunrise of that morning; Miltiades, one of their generals, who claimed to be descended from Aeacus, barking out the order to attack; time telescoping so it seemed they must have run the mile and more, so soon did they emerge out of the cloud of arrows to crash, a wall of bronze, against the Persians' wicker shields, to slash with swords and lunge with spears, frenzied by the war god, Ares. Many swore that they saw other gods and heroes, too, fighting there beside them: Heracles and Theseus; a local demigod, Echetlus, scything at the Persians with his plough; a phantom warrior, the very sight of whom struck one Athenian, Epizelus, permanently blind.[2]

And so, the mêlée bulged and buckled, until the moment came that comes in such encounters, when the victors know that they have won and the vanquished can think only of survival. Somehow the Athenians had managed to surround their Persian enemy, kettling them in Artemis' marshes, a mass of helpless, frightened men, and chasing those who tried to flee down to the beach, splashing through surf towards the Persian ships that even now were putting out to sea to set course south, their destination: unprotected Athens. The field of Marathon was won, but danger was not over. A desperate forced march across the saddle of Pentelicus saw Athenians take up position at another sanctuary of Heracles close by the city, where already Persia's warships were nosing near to shore. But then the enemy fleet stopped. It came no further. All night it sat at anchor, and next morning it was gone, sails hoisted, scudding home for Asia.

Against all odds the threat was over. Alone of all Greek poleis, Athens (and Plataea) had seen off the Great King's might. The city had survived—and many saw the Persians' flight as evidence that Athenian democracy, as victorious against barbarians as against Greek enemies, was special, singled out, protected by the gods. Within hours, Sparta's hoplites, fresh from their religious festival, reached Attica. Too late to share the kudos of victory, they were instead conducted on a battlefield tour, impotent sightseers forced to

4.1 The Sōros, the grave mound of the Athenians at Marathon.

gawp as their triumphant guides rehearsed their tactics and showed off their booty and the piled-up corpses of 6,400 Persian dead. But it was to Athens' fallen that the site belonged. The Assembly passed a vote to honour them like epic heroes, their remains collected and cremated on the battlefield and laid to rest not in the public cemetery but at Marathon itself beneath a towering earthen mound, the "Sōros," 40 feet tall, 165 feet in diameter, with ten marble slabs around its base, one for each tribe, each bearing the names of that tribe's fallen, 192 names in total—while nearby the eleven slain Plataeans, like the countless slaves who fell fighting for Attica, were buried beneath their own communal grave mound. All these grave mounds were deliberately modelled on descriptions in the *Iliad,* as was the committal service for the war dead with its speeches and sacrifices, its libations poured to gods, its solemn dedications to the fallen. Their message was simple: despite what the pediments of Aeginetan temples might maintain, Athenians were the true heirs of the Greeks who fought at Troy.[3]

The grave mounds formed just part of a long process of memorializing the Athenians' extraordinary victory and transforming the landscape of Marathon into a sacred park. Where Persia's lines first broke, they set up a marble column, a lasting version of the usual trophy (a suit of captured armour mounted on a frame) with which Greek victors marked a battle's turning point, while on the Sōros, carved in marble, they displayed an epitaph commissioned from Simonides, the People's laureate:

At Marathon Athenians fought in the front line for Greece,
and scattered the gold-garnished Persians' power.

Just two lines long, its implications could not have been clearer: Athenians—not Spartans, Aeginetans, or men from any of a multitude of rival poleis—had sacrificed their lives for all of Greece. Who, then, but Athenians should be recognized as leaders of the Greeks?[4]

And everywhere—publicly and privately—Athenians gave thanks to their gods for victory. At the Panhellenic sanctuary of Olympia, they dedicated a Persian helmet incised with the inscription, "The Athenians consecrated this to Zeus, when they took it from the Persians." It was not the only helmet offered there. Miltiades, who gave the fateful order to advance at Marathon, sent his own helmet to Olympia, its cheek guard bearing the laconic dedication, "Miltiades to Zeus." Listing neither patronymic, tribe nor polis, as if Miltiades believed he stood unique, apart from family or city ties, his name familiar to all (including Zeus), the helmet's dedication risked seeming hubristic, but it was not unique. At Marathon itself, he made a further offering, a statue bearing the inscription:

Miltiades set up this statue to me, Pan, the goat-hooved Arcadian,
who fought against the Persians and stood as Athens' ally.[5]

Athenians had good reason to thank the god who whispered to Pheidippides his words of hope. Countryfolk had long believed that Pan caused sudden terror to descend on sheep and cattle, sending them skittering across hills, but at Marathon it was not animals he panicked, but the entire Persian army. So now, in thanks, on the Acropolis'

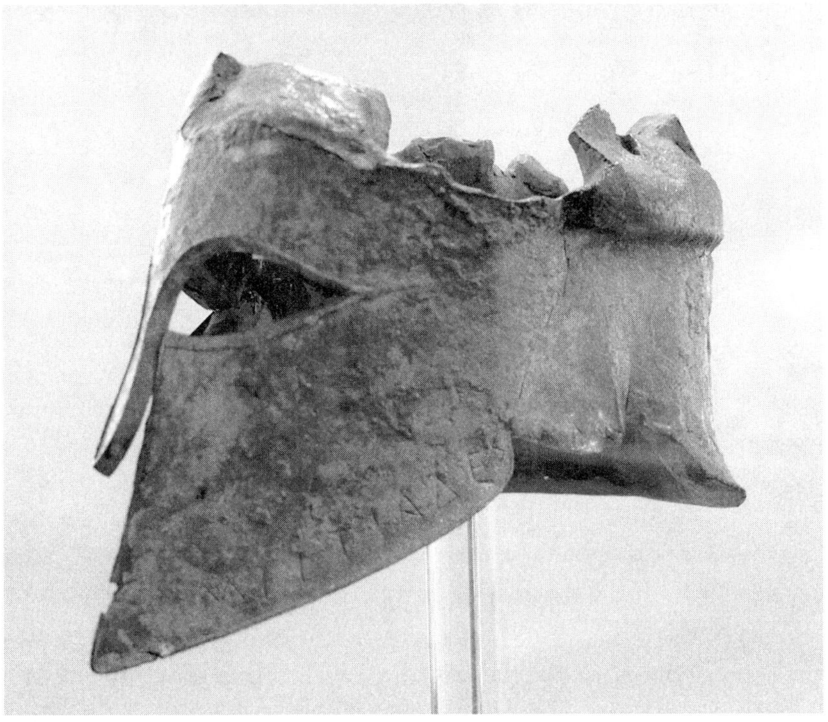

4.2 Miltiades' helmet dedicated after Marathon to Zeus at Olympia.

northwest slope, in an appropriately rustic cave, near which (myth said) Apollo fathered Ion, the People consecrated a new sanctuary to Pan, the wilderness god coaxed deep into the city's heart. Nor did they forget their vow to Artemis: a goat for every Persian killed. But with so many Persians dead, Athenians had insufficient goats to spare. Instead, they reached a compromise: they would pay off their debt in installments, 500 goats a year, and dedicate a temple to the goddess in her guise as huntress, Artemis Agrotera, who turned her arrows on the Persian bowmen and trapped them in her marshes.[6]

As for her twin, Apollo, at Delphi below his temple's towering platform on a bend in the Sacred Way, the People used a tithe from their war booty to complete a treasury already started, built from Parian marble, whose inscription stated simply, "Athenians to Apollo from the first fruits of the Persians at Marathon." Clean, simple, with two pillars flanking its doorway, its pedimental sculptures mirrored

4.3 The Treasury of the Athenians at Delphi.

those on Apollo's temple: the west displayed a Gigantomachy, the east a god's epiphany—though this time not Apollo's but Athena's—while *metopēs* showed Heracles, beside whose sanctuaries Athenians encamped before and following the battle. But Heracles was not the only hero honoured. A further set of *metopēs* showed Theseus on his mission to civilize the world. Athenians believed that both had fought beside them at Marathon, as for the first time now the two stood side by side in sculpture, the hero of Attica beside the hero of all Greece, equals in status and prestige.[7]

But the greatest dedications of them all were reserved for the Athenian Acropolis. In nominal command at Marathon had been Callimachus, appointed by lot, not merit to the ceremonial office of War Archon. Trying to live up to his auspicious name (it meant "Good Fighting"), he lost his life in battle. But before marching to Marathon, he pledged an offering to Athena, should she grant victory, a pledge which the People proudly honoured. They erected an Ionic column almost twelve feet high on which they set a marble sculpture of Iris, the winged messenger goddess, fifteen feet tall, adorned with metal jewellery, a metal caduceus (or herald's staff) glinting in her outstretched hand, and an inscription running vertically within two flutings of the column's shaft:

Callimachus of Aphidnae dedicated me to Athena—
I am the messenger of the immortal gods of Mount Olympus—
Callimachus, Athenians' War Archon, who fought
at Marathon for all the Greeks:
this monument is given by the sons of Athens.

Once more, the message sounded clearly. This was not merely an Athenian victory (or even a joint Athenian-Plataean victory, although no mention of Plataeans here). It was a Greek victory—won solely by Athenians.[8]

Yet the greatest gratitude was owed to Athena herself. So, her people voted through a dazzling new temple on the Acropolis to celebrate their close relationship with her and help project their power. Sited just south of the remodelled Temple of Athena Polias, with a footprint of roughly 77 by 220 feet and a colonnade of six by sixteen Doric columns, it would both dwarf the older building and dominate the skyline, and in the years following the battle it started to take shape: its platform of local marble from a quarry opened just a few years earlier on Mount Pentelicus, with a bottom step of Kara limestone encasing its tight-packed poros core; its cella with two rows of ten internal columns supporting wooden rafters; its four-columned opisthodomos; its pedimental sculptures and its *metopēs*. All needed time, money, and skill, and for now it seemed that Athens had them all.[9]

But what she lacked was unity. Neither democracy, equality before the law, nor free speech had ended rivalry and quarrelling. Nor did victory at Marathon. Instead, it brought new allegations and infighting. One target were the Alcmaeonidae, whose enemies accused them of being Persian agents, flashing signals from their shields to Persia's fleet as it threatened unprotected Athens following the battle, a ridiculous suggestion but one calculated further to undermine the "cursed" family's credibility. Yet the family, which suffered most, were the Philaids: when Miltiades, their head, whose hubristic dedications had not gone unnoticed, failed to punish Paros for supporting Persia, he was tried, fined heavily, and thrown into prison, where he soon died of his wounds, a squalid end for such a stellar general. Undoubtedly the charges brought against him (including profanation of a sanctuary of Demeter) were trumped up by political opponents: his prosecutor was, like him, a scion of the landed aristocracy, a ruthless young Alcmaeonid, Xanthippus, father of the young Pericles.[10]

But already a new breed of democratic politician was emerging, epitomized by the populist Themistocles, who urged Athenians to focus on the sea. In the late 490s, following the destruction of Miletus, their main commercial rival, he had persuaded them to relocate their port from Phalerum west to Piraeus, whose bay and promontory offered not just one but three safe harbours, where warehouses and port facilities were already taking shape. Construction was beginning, too, on military works—with good reason, since hostilities with Aegina showed no sign of abating. Shortly before the Persian invasion, an Aeginetan boarding party intercepted Athens' sacred warship, kidnapping its crew and passengers on their way to Sunium and a festival of Poseidon. For Attic waters and the Attic shore to be so vulnerable was unacceptable, and Themistocles kept urging the Athenians to build a larger, more efficient navy. But to construct one ship was costly. To build a fleet would mean a vast outlay, and the People had other priorities.[11]

Then, in 483 B.C. in one of the labyrinth of claustrophobic tunnels that burrowed deep into Mount Laurium near Sunium, a slave made what for the Athenians (though not for him) would be a life-changing discovery: the richest seam of silver Attica had ever seen, its yield for the first year alone projected to be little short of two and a half tons. The find sparked great excitement. The mines were state-owned; their revenue belonged to all Athenians; and if shared equally, each citizen's dividend would equal more than a month's wages, repeated every year for years to come. The Council drafted a motion. The Assembly met. But before a vote was taken, Themistocles stalked, burly, shaven-headed, bull-necked, onto the Speakers' Platform.[12]

In the aftermath of victory at Marathon, Themistocles had weaponized the power of ostracism, a mechanism intended to reduce the risk of tyranny, whereby the People had the option every spring to exile one leading citizen for ten years (after which he could return, his property and reputation still intact). The first ostracism vote was held in 487 B.C., its (soft) target one of Hippias' few relatives still left in Athens, but, as his confidence increased, Themistocles had orchestrated a fresh ostracism almost every year to bring down rivals. In 486 B.C. Pericles' uncle (yet another Megacles) was ostracized; in 484 B.C. it was the turn of his own father, Xanthippus, whose exile young Pericles almost certainly shared. With such men neutralized and the economy more buoyant than ever, there was no better time for Themistocles to set out his vision: a huge fleet of warships to protect the coastline from Aegina's attacks, ensure the safety of merchant shipping, and set Athens' navy on a par with her victorious army.[13]

It was a costly and ambitious plan, but thanks to revenue from Laurium, Athens could afford it. Moreover, it would benefit so many citizens. Each of 200 warships, manned by 200 Athenians (170 oarsmen plus deck crew and marines), would employ 40,000 citizens and metics, as well as countless slaves, not to mention teams of shipbuilders and other craftsmen with immediate effect. Most of the crews would be the city's poor, a detail which passed no one by—not only would the fleet provide a steady income, it would ensure that men unable to afford armour could play an equal role with the elite in both defence and conquest, a truly democratic proposition. Athenians liked nothing better than a grand project, and few could be grander than this. First introduced to Greece in the late seventh century B.C., a new design of warship, the trireme, was the must-have acquisition for cities with maritime ambition. Around 130 feet long and 20 feet wide, with a draught of just three feet, capable of impressive bursts of speed and endowed with almost gymnastic manoeuvrability, it was a deadly killing machine, a torpedo powered by the muscle of three banks of oarsmen, guided by its helmsman standing in the stern, and tipped with a three-pronged bronze-sheathed ram designed to punch a hole into an enemy hull and leave it wallowing and helpless, its crew an easy target for marines and archers stationed on deck. In countless battles it had proved its worth, as tactics became increasingly well honed: fleets of triremes, fighting as a pack, encircling their prey or tearing through the enemy, then swinging round and pouncing from the rear.[14]

A show of hands, and the proposal passed—with such enthusiasm that it was little wonder that its chief critic, Aristeides, was ostracised within a year. All Attica was abuzz. Supervisors were appointed, answerable to boards of overseers chosen annually by lot. Materials were sourced, purchased, transported: oak, pine, fir, ash, mulberry, and elm, each chosen for its own specific qualities to make the massive keels or tiny dowels or all-important oars; pitch from trunks and roots of conifers for rendering hulls watertight; linen and flax for ropes and cables, sails and canvas awnings to protect the oarsmen's backs from the harsh sun; leather for waterproofing portholes and protecting upper rowing frames; iron for grappling hooks and anchors; tin and copper for the bronze sheath moulded to the wooden beak, the deadly ram; and marble from Pentelicus, carved into defiant eyes to glare from every prow beneath a golden figurehead, on each trireme the same—Athena helmeted, a Gorgon glaring from her snake-fringed aegis. Each task meant teams of specialists: shipwrights and carpenters; stonemasons; metalworkers; women weaving sails or twisting ropes; the minds of many thousands focussed on one overarching project. And as each ship was finished, its crew was trained: long days at sea, hands blistering, backs aching as frustration turned to pride, and oarsmen learned to operate as one, and watchers from the shore saw their new fleet of triremes skim the water like a flock of circling birds.[15]

Not a moment too soon the landlubbers of Attica had learned to ride the waves. For already news of enemy ships mustering and armies gathering suggested that the fleet would soon be tested—but not against Aegina. Against Persia. For ten years Persia had been preparing for a new invasion. A series of events had held it up—Darius' death; rebellions against his successor and son, Xerxes—but in 480 B.C., with the new Great King at its head, a massive army, so large that Greek spies could not count it, marched north from Sardis, while 1,200 warships shadowed it by sea. On mainland Greece, many poleis were already offering their amphoras of earth and water. Boeotia backed Persia; Argos, after Sparta the most powerful city in the Peloponnese, declared neutrality; and, when those few states still willing to resist sought help from friends in Crete and Sicily, they were rebuffed. Their determination, nonetheless, was adamantine. For now, they shelved their differences. Athens, Sparta, Corinth—old rivals swore to fight as one. Ostracized statesmen—Megacles, Xanthippus, and Aristeides—were recalled to Athens. The allies might be few, but they were ready to protect their freedom to the death.[16]

The danger grew increasingly apparent by the day—the Persians had bridged the Hellespont (it took their fighting men and baggage train full seven days and nights to cross); they had sliced a canal across the isthmus at Mount Athos to avoid the treacherous circumnavigation of the cape; and in northern Greece they were drinking rivers dry. An ill-planned allied mission north to Tempe to try to halt the Persians' advance was hurriedly aborted, and suddenly, with Boeotia, Thessaly, and Macedonia embracing the Great King, the Athenians with stomach-lurching horror realized that there was nothing standing between them and the vast Persian army—except their bravery, their ingenuity, their gods. With mounting apprehension, the Assembly sent delegates to Delphi to ask Apollo what to do.

The oracle operated on only the seventh day of every month (and even then, not in winter). So, opportunities to question it were few. Moreover, no petitioner could access the inner sanctum where the oracle herself, a local woman, sat in a cauldron raised on a tripod high above a fissure in the rock, from which strong gasses leached to mingle with the fumes from burning bay leaves, until intoxicated and hallucinating, she began to moan unworldly sounds—to be translated by Apollo's priests into polished hexameter verse, written down and read to the petitioner. Her message now was chilling:

Timewasters! Why sit here? Flee to the furthest corners of the earth!
Leave your homes and the Acropolis, that your city circles like a wheel!

The head will not remain in place, no, nor the body—
neither feet nor hands nor torso.
All is ruined. Fire and Ares, rushing god of war,
who bears down on you in his Syrian chariot, will lay you low.
He will shatter many other high-towered citadels—not yours alone—
and consign many sanctuaries of deathless gods to all-consuming fire.
Gods stand sweating, trembling in fear as over rooftops
black blood surges: they know that suffering is inescapable.
So, leave my sanctuary, and veil your heads as you prepare to suffer.[17]

The vision was apocalyptic: Athens destroyed; her people slaughtered; the Acropolis consumed in flames. But bold, brash, never balking at a fight, Athenians would not accept defeat, not even from a god. They demanded a better answer, threatening never to leave the temple until they got one, but to die there if necessary, and so pollute its sanctity, disturb the god, and spark a serious religious crisis. Small wonder, then, that when the priests emerged a second time from behind the ornate curtain, their words were (marginally) more optimistic:

Athena cannot completely win over the heart of Olympian Zeus
though she begs him incessantly with many prayers and all her guile.
Yet I shall give you this second response, adamantine and
unchangeable:
although the rest of Attica and all the
sacred gullies of Cithaeron shall be overrun,
wide-seeing Zeus shall give Athena one inviolable stronghold,
for you and for your children: the wooden wall.
So, do not wait for the great hordes of cavalry and infantry from Asia.
Do not stay still but turn. Withdraw.
The day will come when you will face him.
God-like Salamis, you will bring death to women's sons,
when grain is scattered, or the harvest gathered in.[18]

In Athens, these words provoked passionate debate. Athena's intervention the Athenians could understand. She was their patron goddess; they were her favourites. It was natural that she should intercede with Zeus, her father, and that, given Athens' piety, Zeus should provide a path to safety. But what was the "wooden wall," the "one inviolable stronghold"? Traditionalists maintained it was the ancient stockade surrounding the Acropolis, but progressives took a different view. For them the wooden wall meant their new ships' hulls. Apollo's graphic images of the Acropolis ablaze as torrents of black blood broke over rooftops showed they must not stay and fight in Athens but evacuate before the Persian army reached them. To do so—to abandon Attica, their homes, and their most sacred sanctuaries—would be not cowardice but piety, born out of trust in the divine, a willingness to give up everything to follow where gods commanded, and so take to the sea.[19]

With the wealthy reluctant to abandon their estates and homes, and the poor, with less to lose and more to gain, convinced that their salvation lay in their new fleet, it took an act of ritual drama to break the stalemate. Its setting was the Temple of Athena Polias on the Acropolis, its protagonist Miltiades' son, Cimon, who, permission granted by the priestess, entered the cella's hushed half-light and, with a prayer for victory, laid his horse's bridle, symbol of his landed aristocracy, at the feet of Athena's xoanon, before, with not a backward glance, he left the temple and, his comrades following behind him, marched down to Piraeus and the ships. The new head of the Philaids, he had declared his backing for Themistocles and his strategy to empty Attica and fight at sea. Where Cimon led, most of the city followed—including, the Athenians believed, their gods and heroes. According to Athena's priestess, the sacred serpent, Erechtheus' earthly incarnation, too, abandoned the Acropolis, leaving its offerings of honey cakes untouched; and with it went the goddess.[20]

A decade earlier Themistocles had argued that it would make sound economic sense to relocate the city from Athens to Piraeus, but such was their attachment to the Acropolis, that Athenians rejected his suggestions. Now, thanks to Apollo's oracle, close to the entire population of Attica—women, children, the elderly, citizens, foreign residents, and slaves—left their homes to board the boats that took them overseas to Salamis and Troezen and Aegina, where islanders, with a newfound determination to show a bold, united front, welcomed refugees, who had so lately been their enemies. So, as Attica and Athens emptied, homes and fields and olive groves and vineyards and public buildings so symbolic of democracy—the Pnyx, the Council Chamber, stoas in the Agora, the lawcourts, new warehouses, shipyards at Piraeus, temples finished or still incomplete—silent and abandoned, waited for the Persians.[21]

There was no stopping them. After only a few days, a taskforce led by Sparta's King Leonidas to slow Persia's advance at the key pass of Thermopylae was massacred—an outcome as shocking as it was predictable. At once, the allied fleet, commanded by a Spartan (despite Athens' contribution being by far the largest), left its forward base at Artemisium on the north tip of Euboea. It had already acquitted itself well, engaging the enemy in battle, and capturing or sinking a clutch of Persian vessels, many of them damaged in a recent storm, when winds from Thrace sent rollers smashing into unprotected rowing benches, swamping decks, and snapping moorings, driving hulls against dark, jagged coastal rocks. Athenians knew who to thank for this destruction: as at Athos twelve years earlier, Boreas, the wind god, son-in-law of King Erechtheus, had intervened by wreaking havoc on a Persian fleet.[22]

As the Greek navy backed water, heading for the Bay of Salamis, the Persians entered Phocis, and reports of their atrocities kept multiplying: towns, villages and farmsteads torched; temples looted; sanctuaries burned; young women gang-raped to death. And now they were being feted in Boeotia. Stationed at Salamis, the Greek commanders argued violently. The Spartans and Corinthians were worried that the Persian army would breach the wall thrown hastily across the Isthmus of Corinth and so enter the Peloponnese. They itched to leave, but somehow Themistocles dissuaded them, arguing that Apollo would never have called Salamis "godlike" unless the island was destined to see the turning point in Greece's struggle. Tempers frayed. The Persians crossed into Attica. The spoliation began. In empty hillside hamlets, abandoned coastal villages, and silent ghost towns, Xerxes' men methodically, mechanically began their orgy of destruction, and, as centuries-old homes were set alight and buildings redolent of the democracy were torched, black smoke boiled across beloved landscapes. And then they entered Athens, where, setting up command headquarters on the Areopagus, Xerxes laid siege to the Acropolis.[23]

A few Athenians had stayed behind, convinced that the "wooden wall" meant the Acropolis' palisade, certain that Athena would not allow her citadel to fall—furnished as it was with all its statues of young girls with enigmatic smiles, memorials to Harma and to Marathon, scaffolding around the half-completed temple, its sanctuary to Zeus, its iconic Temple of Athena Polias. Even it was empty now, its xoanon removed for safe keeping, along with any other treasures that could be carried. Everything now left had proved immovable: objects because they were too large or heavy, people because they were too stubborn. For days these few endured as blazing Persian arrows thumped into the palisade. But they could not hold out for ever. A crack team of Persian mountaineers scaled the sheer east face of the Acropolis, unbarred the heavy wooden gates and let the Great King's troops pour through. Slaughtered at Athena's altar and in her temple's cella, not one Athenian was left alive. And then the looting, and the vandalism and destruction as—roof buckling and rafters shattering, fire pouring up the walls and flooding through the sanctuary, and roof tiles crashing to the ground—they purged Athena's temple in Ahura Mazda's flames. From Salamis and Aegina, the refugees could see the black smoke bellying from their Acropolis and drifting high into the September sky, and their trauma can scarcely be imagined. They had abandoned everything that gave them their identity—homes, graves of their forefathers, hero-shrines and temples, their Acropolis, the very soil from which they were convinced they had been born—and all that they could do was watch it burn.[24]

It was their darkest hour.

But then, a miracle.

Among the polyglot barbarians who occupied the city—Persians and Medes, Egyptians, Ethiopians, Phoenicians, Babylonians, Thracians and Sacae, Arabians and Libyans, and tribesmen from the far-off Indus Valley—were quisling members of Peisistratus' family. One of them was Hippias' cousin ostracized just seven years before, who now hoped to govern Greece. At sunrise next day, Xerxes ordered them to sacrifice on the Acropolis. But as they picked their way across the smouldering ruins heavy with the acrid stench of smoke and blistered flesh, they saw that from Athena's sacred olive tree, scorched, blackened in the flames, there grew a new shoot, green and healthy and already 18 inches long. For them and for the crews of Athens' triremes, when they heard of it, there was no doubt: it was a sign from Athena. Her citadel might be destroyed, her temple lie in ruins, but her power was indestructible. Her people would prevail. Athens would rise again.[25]

But how? The allied generals were squabbling; morale was ebbing by the hour; and, with all talk of sailing for the Isthmus, the Athenians desperately needed to stiffen Greek resolve. They began by seeking divine help. At dead of night, they ran the Persian blockade and sailed to Aegina, smuggling the sacred relics of Aeacus and his family back across the sea to Salamis, a powerful talisman to set beside Athena's xoanon, an inspiration to the allies to remain. But then more news: the Persians were on the march; they were heading for the Isthmus; the battlefront was moving west. Panicked Spartans and Corinthians vowed to sail next morning. Themistocles objected. Tempers flared. Harsh words. Themistocles, snapped one Corinthian, had no right to dictate policy—he was a man without a city. Mirroring the words of Apollo's oracle, Themistocles' response was magisterial. And revolutionary. Athenians, he said, did not hold bricks and mortar in such high regard that they would let themselves become enslaved. "We have the greatest city in all Greece—200 triremes that even now stand ready to help save you if you would be saved. But if you leave us exposed again, the Greeks will soon discover that Athenians have got themselves a city that is free and a land that's better than the one they left behind." Rather than withdrawing to the Isthmus with the craven Peloponnesians, the Athenians would sail to Italy and found a city there, since Athens' essence lay not in buildings or material possessions but in her people, and ideals, and her connection with her gods. And when, as soon as he stopped speaking, the straits of Salamis began to boil, and tremors shook the island, it seemed that this connection was confirmed. Poseidon, god of earthquakes and the sea, had given his approval.[26]

It was not the only omen. By chance, this was the day on which in peacetime the procession made its way from Athens to Eleusis for the Mysteries, a key date in the religious calendar. So, when the Greeks on Salamis saw a dust cloud drift across the bay towards them from the mainland as if kicked up by 30,000 people walking on the Sacred Way and heard a noise like a loud voice boom across the straits, they convinced themselves that, rather than being evidence of Persia's army marching west, the voice was a divine voice chanting the initiates' hymn, while the dust cloud was a portent that in the coming battle the Eleusinian gods—Demeter, Persephone, and Dionysus—would stand with Ares to fight beside the Greeks against the Persians.[27]

But victory called for human intervention, too. That evening Themistocles sent a faithful Persian slave to the Great King with false intelligence: that Themistocles himself had switched sides; that the allies were about to cast off in the darkness and sail with all speed for the Isthmus; that, should the Persians intercept them, the Greeks would easily be overcome. All night the Persian fleet patrolled the entrance to the straits, increasingly frustrated, increasingly exhausted, but only in the morning as the sun rose did the allies put to sea, their war cry ricocheting off the cliffs: "Forward, Greeks! Set free your fatherland! Set free your wives and children. Set free your fathers' gods, and spirits of your ancestors. The contest is at hand, and it is all to fight for!"[28]

Triremes swung into the bay, oars feathering the swell, and then, first blood: a Greek vessel ramming a Persian; warships darting like a shoal of fish across the water—at first a glassy calm, then ruffling until, as the breeze stiffened, the sea turned choppy and the Persian ships began to lurch and buck and wallow, prows colliding, oar snagging oar, until all that their crews could think of was escape. But their now-sluggish vessels made for easy targets. Some did break through and rowed like fury for the open sea and the race back home to Asia, but many others were corralled, mere floating wrecks, their crews, a mass of helpless, frightened men, speared "like tuna fish" as they tried to swim to safety or butchered as they crawled onto the shore. The wooden wall had done its work. Thanks to the Athenian fleet, the Greeks had won the day.

Thanks, too, to the gods. Just as at Marathon, so at Salamis men swore that they had seen them: Athena, swooping as her avatar, the owl, through the Greek camp to settle on the rigging of Themistocles' flagship; a Salaminian demigod, transformed into a serpent, swimming beside Athens' fleet. Together with Poseidon's earthquake, the voice and cloud of dust that drifted from Eleusis, Apollo's oracle about the wooden wall, his revelation of Athena's intercession with Zeus to save her city, her omen of the sprouting olive tree, Boreas' winds that wrecked so many Persian ships at Athos and at Artemisium, the god-sent breeze that stirred the seas at Salamis—clear evidence was everywhere of the gods' intervention, enhanced by news of Boreas' latest feat: his gales destroying Persia's pontoons across the Hellespont. In the days following victory at Salamis, the Greeks had felt a nagging fear that ships used for these bridges could be used to launch a new offensive. But not now.[29]

To crown this sense of triumph came news of another victory. Sicily, too, had been invaded—by Carthaginians, whose Phoenician ethnicity meant they were related to many sailors in the Persian fleet. But outside the besieged town of Himera on Sicily's north coast, a relief force from Greek Syracuse had massacred most of the Carthaginian army, while, as it fled, the enemy fleet had been destroyed by storm at sea. It was a nail-biting victory, made even more significant when calculations were performed suggesting it had taken place on the same day as the Battle of Salamis. Fanciful though this may seem, it is entirely possible. But the precise date did not matter. What mattered was that both invasions, timed to coincide, had failed.[30]

With autumn nearing and supply lines shattered, Xerxes began the long march home, albeit leaving an impressive army in the north of Greece to regroup and campaign next spring, which was why, when refugees returned to Athens, they found many homes still ominously intact. For the Persians, defeat at Salamis had merely been a setback. They would return. And when they conquered Attica, they did not wish for it to be a wasteland. Nonetheless, signs of their brief occupation were everywhere—the ruins and corpses on the Acropolis; the empty plinth in the denuded Agora, from where the statues of Aristogeiton and Harmodius had been carted off to Persian Susa. But there was still much to give thanks for, sacrifices to be made and dedications offered to the gods in thanks for victory.[31]

Three captured Persian ships, hauled from the sea, were each dragged to a sanctuary and consecrated—one to Zeus at Salamis, where a chorus of Athenian youths led by a handsome young wrestler called Sophocles performed the victory hymn; another to Poseidon atop the cliff at Sunium near his now ruined temple; and the third, also to Poseidon, at the Isthmus, where the allies met to allocate the aristeia (prizes for bravery in battle). The individual award went to Themistocles, while that for the best polis went to Aegina—which for Athenians was not just controversial (a decade earlier Aegina had sided with Persia) but a calculated snub. No city had fought more valiantly than Athens; no land had sacrificed as much as Attica.[32]

By winter, Athens' discontent with her ungrateful allies was so intense that the Persians sensed an opportunity. They sent an emissary, Macedonia's obsequious King Alexander, with a seductive offer: Xerxes would forget the past, let the Athenians keep their democracy, give them whatever lands in mainland Greece they might desire, rebuild their temples at his own expense—on one condition: that they became not vassals but allies, enjoying a special and unique relationship with Persia. If not, Xerxes would obliterate them. Perhaps anticipating terms (though surely none so generous as these), Athenians had invited Spartan envoys to the Assembly meeting, and their response, a panicked bluster, part accusation (the war was Athens' fault), part cynical appeal to a political ideal in which they did not share (tyrant-hating Athens should have no truck with Xerxes), fell far short of the commitment the Athenians were looking for (that in the coming year Sparta and her allies would help to defend Attica from Persian invasion). Only their brief peroration—"in barbarians there is neither trust nor truth"—struck a chord in men grateful for being born Greeks not barbarians, freemen not slaves. However fractured the Greek world might be, when contrasted with Persia, its values seemed more compelling than ever.[33]

The Athenians' replies to both Sparta and Persia were imbued with deep religious faith. To Alexander: "So long as the sun keeps to his course, we will make no pact with Xerxes. We shall fight him without ceasing, trusting in our gods and heroes, whom he scorned when he burned their temples and their statues." To the Spartans: "There are so many strong, compelling reasons to prevent us [from supporting Xerxes]: first, the burning and destruction of our gods' temples and statues, atrocities that we must punish to the last degree. . . . And those things that unite all Greeks: one blood, one language, our shared sanctuaries, our sacrifices, and our shared way of life." Central to both replies was religion, a strong sense of outrage at the burning of the temples, a conviction that the gods were on their side.[34]

Next spring, the Persian army, said to be 100,000 men, again marched south; flotillas of small boats again evacuated all noncombatants from Attica; and Greek allies were again mired in argument. And then, a breakthrough: too late to save Attica, but perhaps in time to safeguard Greece, their generals agreed to march north of the Isthmus to face the enemy on land in one last existential battle. As the Persians withdrew from Attica, the allies exchanged oaths of loyalty at the great altar at Eleusis before, sacrificing to the gods of death and rebirth, they passed through Cithaeron's canyons to Plataea, where the Persians and their Theban allies were encamped. A first Persian attack, a Persian commander killed, and then long days of waiting. Attrition. A Greek supply train intercepted, massacred; provisions dwindling. More Persian attacks. A hail of arrows. Death raining out of August skies. The Spartan general, Pausanias, mishandling a redeployment: confusion and resentment. And the Persian army poured out in a haze of dust across the dried-up riverbed, the slanting morning sunlight glinting on their spears, as they slammed hard into the unready Greeks, still trying to reach their new positions, following Pausanias' commands. As the Spartans waited agonizingly for priests to pronounce prebattle sacrifices auspicious, it was every polis, every fighter for himself; and then the clash of armies; screams of wounded men and horses; stench of blood and shit, until the word gushed through the lines: the Persian general was dead. The Persians were fleeing; and the allies, crazed with bloodlust, were racing after them.[35]

It was all over. As Persian survivors evaporated into the soft August night to slog back home through Thessaly, incredulous Greeks vented months of pent-up anger on Boeotian captives and celebrated as only a triumphant army can. Soon they had fresh news of victory. In Ionia near Mount Mycale in a battle fought, as at Plataea, near a sanctuary of Eleusinian Demeter, the Greeks had crushed those Persian troops, who had accompanied King Xerxes home to Asia the previous autumn. In twelve months, two Persian armies and the Persian fleet had been destroyed. The threat to mainland Greece was lifted—if not forever, then for many years to come.[36]

But the two Persian invasions had changed Athens and the Greek world profoundly. The physical signs were obvious: in Attica the Persians had vandalized most of what they had left standing after their first occupation, destroying homes, smashing water pipes and cisterns, fulfilling Xerxes' threat to wipe out Athens, should she reject his terms. Psychologically, too, the ground had shifted. For Athenians returning to their city, their broken buildings and scorched earth were battle scars that they could wear with pride, hard proof of sacrifices made to safeguard Greece. And paradoxically what filled them with the greatest pride were their burnt temples. Especially potent was the ruined Temple of Athena Polias, its ruins a reminder of how the goddess of the city-state had helped to save her people, how, like them, she had withdrawn from Athens, how she, too, had sanctioned the destruction of her home, her temple, for the common good. Athena, the maiden warrior, had truly stood beside them, fighting with them in the front line, and with them she had been victorious.

In verses on a stele at Plataea, Simonides remembered those Athenians who made the ultimate sacrifice:

If the greatest part of bravery is to die a splendid death,
Fortune allotted this to us above all other men.
For we strained every sinew to ensure that Greece was free
and now we lie here, vouchsafed a good name that will not grow old.[37]

As after Marathon, so now Athens was claiming credit for Greek freedom. But she was not alone. Corinth's epitaph for her dead at Salamis told how they sacrificed their lives "to save all Greece, when she stood balanced on the razor's edge"; Megara's cenotaph erected in her agora, commemorating all the battles of the war, told how her sons died "striving to sustain the day of freedom for both Megara and Greece"; but Sparta's verses for her fallen at Plataea struck a very different note. They read:

These men adorned their fatherland with a glory that can never be extinguished,
before enveloping themselves in the blue-black cloud of death.
Though they have died, they are not dead: their bravery brings them glory,
and leads them back to earth from Hades.[38]

No mention here of liberating Greece. Instead, a striking, metaphysical reflection. By laying down their lives in battle, the ninety-one Spartans who fell at Plataea had undergone a transformation, becoming, if not divine, immortal, not confined to the underworld, as was usual for the dead, but capable of returning to earth. Although the poet did not use the word, they had become, in Greek terms, heroes, men who, through bravery in life, transcended death. It was a bold, provocative assertion, whose influence would be profound, not least in Athens, suggesting that through self-sacrifice contemporary Greeks could achieve—and, indeed, had achieved—a status equal to such legendary

4.4 Modern reconstruction of the Serpent Column with (*behind*) the Temple of Apollo at Delphi.

warriors as Achilles, Theseus and Heracles. While initiation at Eleusis promised a blessed afterlife in Hades, death in battle could somehow offer more: a return to earth.

The epitaph formed part of Sparta's sustained drive to emphasise her leadership at the expense of Athens. Two others at Thermopylae continued this campaign. While one extolled her soldiers' sense of duty ("Stranger, report this to the Spartans: we lie here obeying orders"), a second was more political. It read:

Here, against three million,
four thousand Peloponnesians once fought.[39]

Exaggerating the size of Persia's army, and ignoring the part played at Thermopylae by Thespians, and Malians, and Phocians, and Locrians (none of them Peloponnesians), the epitaph spoke volumes. Athens might promote her own role in the war, but more than one could play at that game. The race was on not only to shape history but to be recognized as Greece's saviour and, in consequence, her leader.[40]

For now, that leader remained Sparta—as evidenced in the most prestigious monument of all. While Greek allies used booty from

Plataea to dedicate a fifteen-foot-tall bronze statue to Zeus at Olympia, and a bronze nine-foot Poseidon at the Isthmus, at Delphi by the courtyard of Apollo's temple they erected a tall bronze column in the form of three coiling bearded serpents, whose heads (mouths gaping, fangs bared, forked tongues lolling) supported a huge gold cauldron. Inscribed into the pillar were the names of every polis that had fought the Persians, thirty-one in all. Sparta inevitably topped the list. It was her admiral and general who had commanded the Greek forces. But more significant was who came second: the Athenians, relegating the Corinthians to third place (and the Aeginetans to a lowly sixth). It must have prompted some rejoicing in Athena's city, since, far from being a simple catalogue of allies, the list was in effect a league table, a snapshot of who held the greatest power. That Mycenae, once citadel of Agamemnon, mighty in Homeric epic, now nothing but a goat-swarmed village, was nowhere near the top was poignant but instructive. Times changed. Cities rose and fell. A century before, Corinth or Sicyon would easily have taken second place to Sparta. But not now. Now Athens eclipsed both.[41]

But Athens was still dangerously exposed. The Persian invasion had left her defenceless and suspicious of her one-time allies. So, no sooner had the Persians fled than Themistocles enthused the People to begin another major building project—not ships this time, but city walls. The Spartans had attacked before. They could attack again. Speed was essential. Every resident of Attica must be involved. Perhaps there really was a Spartan threat, but, even if not, his thinking was clever, uniting every stratum of society—every able-bodied man, woman, and child; every citizen, metic, and slave, 300,000 people—in one project, shoring up a new security from the rubble of defeat. And rubble was everywhere, ready to be used. Broken columns; stone slabs; marble blocks and statue bases; grave markers: all were collected to be built into the lower courses of the wall that snaked five-and-a-quarter miles around the city, to rise in places 32 feet high and 10 feet wide.[42]

Even as the wall's foundations were being dug, a Spartan delegation confirmed Athenian suspicions. Addressing the Assembly, its arguments—that, should they return and occupy the city, the Persians could use the walls for their defence—were disingenuous. So was its reiteration that only the Isthmus could be properly defended, and reassurance that, come the next invasion, the Peloponnese would welcome Attic refugees. In fact, Sparta's fear was palpable, and rightly so: Athens' new fleet threatened to upset the status quo; her courage in the recent war confirmed her fighting spirit. But until the walls were finished, the Spartans must be kept onside. Sailing to Laconia, Themistocles played for time, while in Athens Sparta's delegates were held as hostages. At last, with the wall at a safe height, Themistocles returned home to watch its facings being rubbed smooth, doors hung on each of thirteen gates, roofs tiled, and windows shuttered, crenelations set in place. The first great democratic building project following the Persian War, its significance could not be exaggerated.[43]

Only now could the city be rebuilt, as unplanned and haphazard as before—a warren of lanes and alleyways, windowless walls facing tamped-earth streets where the sun scorched roofs of single-storeyed houses, and puddles pooled in fetid shade. While administrative buildings were swiftly raised again, the sanctuaries were deliberately left in ruins, testament to Athens' sacrifice. Most powerfully curated of them all was the Acropolis. Especial care was lavished on the area around the ruined Temple of Athena Polias. Amid a shambles of shattered roof tiles and blackened rafters, some architectural elements survived from both this and the half-built Marathon temple—unfinished column drums, triglpyhs, uncarved *metopēs*. None could be reused in a building, but they could be repurposed, built into the new marble wall raised round the outer edge of the Acropolis. Organized by category—the temple drums arranged like columns side by side, triglyphs and *metopēs* alternating laterally as on a building—they were sited in the section of the north wall closest to the Temple of Athena Polias, with elements abutting the Arrhephorion, the home of the Arrhephoroi.[44]

The Arrhephorion itself was hastily rebuilt. Despite the devastation, worship needed to continue unabated, not least the weaving of the peplos for the goddess which took place in this house, and the

4.5 *Metopēs* and triglyphs built into the north wall of the Acropolis above the cave at the lower end of the Passage of the Arrhephoroi.

girls required accommodation. So, above the cleft that penetrated deep into the rock, with its staircase leading down into the darkness, a one-roomed building was erected with a high-walled courtyard, where Athena's elite servants could resume their cyclical routines in respectable seclusion, and life could begin again. Meanwhile, close by, many of the statues smashed by the Persians, snapped at the ankle as they toppled from their bases, were devoutly laid to rest in deep pits, a cemetery of smiling marble maidens, their paint still fresh and vibrant, offerings to Athena embedded in her rock.[45]

The Arrhephorion was not the only new construction. Across the levelled earth, near the graveyard of broken statues, stood Athena's olive tree, whose regeneration had inspired embattled citizens and increased their sense of reverence and awe. Once the site was cleared of rubble, they enclosed it and the neighbouring Garden of Pandrosus with a wall, which abutted to the east the sanctuary of Pandrosus/Pandora's legendary father, Cecrops, to the south the platform of the ruined Temple of Athena Polias, and to the west a new compact stoa, through which was the sole means of access. Also connecting the garden with the outside world was a narrow pipe, drilled into the marble wall, to drain off any overflow of water from around the sacred olive tree. This water was then collected, stored, and used in ritual, since by coming into contact with the roots, it had acquired its own distinctive sanctitude.[46]

A few other building works were deemed so essential that they could not be postponed: in the ruined Temple of Athena Polias' opisthodomos, a temporary shrine was raised to house the sacred xoanon; the altar was repaired; the Propylaeon gateway was shored up to guarantee security for the Acropolis. Yet, apart from new memorials and statues to the goddess, the rock would be, for thirty years, a curiously empty, haunted place, where insects thrummed amid wildflowers and lizards scuttled across baking stone, but not a single temple would be built.[47]

However, there was one ruined statue with such potency that it could not be simply swept aside—the bronze chariot and horses raised after victory at Harma. Now in the shadow of the Propylaeon, its plinth of blue-grey Eleusinian limestone newly polished, a replacement was installed, while in the Agora new statues of Harmodius and Aristogeiton were set up, commissioned from two craftsmen, Critius (pupil of one of the original sculptors) and Nesiotes, whose name, "Islander," appealed to sea-going Athenians. Both statue groups had such profound significance, not simply memorials of past glories, but markers of the city's unique character and the qualities that made her great: her people's drive and energy, their determination never to be cowed, their willingness to fight against the odds, their readiness to sacrifice their lives to overcome aggressors and oppressors.[48]

Yet, notwithstanding the defiance of these statues, the truth was that the Persian invasions had devastated the Athenian economy. The destruction of homes, the smashing of equipment, too heavy to be saved, and the loss of countless animals meant that it would be years before the polis could recover. Not even booty seized from Persian tents and corpses at Plataea or the ongoing revenue from Laurium could compensate. It would later be suggested that one reason why it took so many years before the temples were rebuilt was that among

4.6 Roman copy of the replacement statue of the tyrannicides erected after the Persian Wars.

the oaths the allies swore before Plataea was one promising to leave in ruins sanctuaries burned by the Persians. This oath may be fictitious but even were it genuine, Athenians could simply not afford another major building programme. Their infrastructure needed to be reconstructed. Funds needed to be gathered, and the public purse refilled, and the quickest way to do this was through war. The choice of enemy was clear. The Persian threat needed to be neutralized—though not in Attica or mainland Greece but wealthy Asia, where the potential spoils of war were unimaginable.[49]

5 CITY OF GODS

Shining city, crowned with violets, song-worthy famous Athens, the defence of Greece, the city of gods.

—PINDAR, FRAGMENT 76

Spearheading the new campaign was Xanthippus, Pericles' father. Officially he was representing the Greek alliance, but it was already clear that the wartime coalition was so strained that it was unlikely to survive the peace. The first rifts appeared soon after victory at Mycale when, in a war council on Samos, the Spartans, chronically reluctant to campaign far from home, disingenuously suggested that, since Ionia was certain to remain a flashpoint, the best way to prevent renewed hostilities with Persia was a population exchange—between Persians, including their sympathisers, in the north of Greece and the Ionians. Such was Xanthippus' rage that the Spartans not only backed down but agreed with him that the Ionians should be admitted into the alliance immediately, despite their having fought for Persia only weeks before. It was the Spartans' first mistake.[1]

Their second was to sail home to overwinter, leaving Xanthippus in theatre in command. He lost no time in sailing with his new Ionian allies north to the Hellespont to cleanse the straits of all Persian presence. As Greek ships approached, the Great King's governor took refuge behind the walls of Sestus on the northern shore. A lengthy siege. The city fell. The Hellespont was in Greek hands. And with it all the Thracian Chersonnese—where they found the cables used to lash together Persian pontoons across the Hellespont. Xanthippus sent these home to the Assembly, which was already finalizing plans for a new stoa to display war booty. But not in Athens, at Delphi, beneath the terrace of the Temple of Apollo.[2]

At 87 feet long and 10 feet wide, its wooden roof supported by an Ionic colonnade of pillars made from Attic marble hewn from Mount Pentelicus set on bases of Parian marble, the stoa, part secular, part religious, was designed to resonate with Athens' nearby treasury. Their dedicatory inscriptions resonated, too. While the treasury bore the legend, "Athenians to Apollo from the first fruits of the Persians at Marathon," the new stoa—crammed with spoils from Salamis, Plataea and Mycale, not to mention those newly liberated cables—was inscribed: "Athenians dedicated this stoa, armaments and ships' figure heads taken from the enemy." Athenians, not Greeks; the enemy, not Persians. But who was that enemy? Officially Xanthippus had been acting in the Hellespont on behalf of an alliance led by Sparta. So, arguably, it was not just Persians, whom Athens had deprived of booty, but Spartans, too.[3]

If the appropriation of the cables was controversial, more serious was Xanthippus' treatment of the captured Persian governor of Sestus. Rather than ransoming him as was the norm, he crucified him on a promontory near the European head of one of Xerxes' bridges, forcing him to watch as locals stoned his son to death. By any standards it was a barbarous act, but Athenians attempted to excuse it by arguing that the Persian had ransacked a local hero-shrine of Protesilaus, claiming him to be an enemy of Asia, which in a sense he was—according to mythology, Protesilaus was the first Greek casualty of the Trojan War. But, if the governor could situate the current conflict in the context of age-old hostilities, telescoping time for his own purposes, so could Xanthippus. By punishing the Persian for impiety and avenging Protesilaus' killing in the Trojan War, he was acting doubly as Greece's champion.[4]

Nonetheless the episode was chilling. Herodotus places it a few brief paragraphs before the end of his chronicles, leaving readers with disturbing questions. Was this a just close to long centuries of East-West aggression? Was it to let Athenians behave like this that allied Greeks had fought? Such conduct was not just shocking, it was un-Greek. It smacked of hubris, too. And hubris in the end was always punished by the gods. It is the last recorded exploit of Xanthippus, member by marriage of the cursed Alcmaeonids, the father of Pericles. But it set the tone for what would come.

Meanwhile, the Spartans made their third mistake. Next spring, they sent a new commander east, Pausanias, whose bungling tactics at Plataea had almost cost the Greeks their victory. Not that he acknowledged this. When the serpent monument was first set in place at Delphi, he saw to it that it carried the vainglorious inscription: "After defeating the Persians, I, Pausanias, the Greek general-in-chief, dedicated this memorial to Apollo." Outraged, his fellow Spartans and their allies had the words erased, to be replaced by "Greece's liberators dedicated this when they freed their cities from grim slavery," and it was this inscription which accompanied the list of cities. Now at newly liberated Byzantium, Pausanias, drunk on power and, freed from the constrains of Spartan life, embracing all temptation, grew more louche and autocratic by the day. Athenians and Ionians swapped stories—how he accidentally killed a girl forced to his room to pleasure him, freed Persians to ingratiate himself with Xerxes, was plotting to betray Greece in return for marrying the Great King's daughter. Meanwhile, his treatment of his allies grew more arrogant, his punishments more savage, his rage should any colleagues question him more vexing. The Ionians could take it no longer. They asked Cimon and Aristeides, Xanthippus' replacements in office, to write to Sparta's ephors requesting that they recall him. Remarkably the ephors agreed, but instead of sending a replacement they meekly passed command of the alliance to Athens.[5]

This was the Spartans' fourth mistake, and it resulted in the greatest shift in the relationship between Greek poleis in generations. With Sparta gone, her Peloponnesian allies, reluctant to be led by Athens, lost enthusiasm. Which passed responsibility for continuing the war with Persia to the Athenians, a situation they moved quickly to exploit. Within months, Aristeides was presiding over an extraordinary ceremony. At Delos, he led delegates from Ionia and Caria, the Hellespont, Thrace and the Aegean islands, representatives of over 250 poleis, all dressed in richest finery—robes embroidered, tunics dyed, hair curled, adorned with gold armbands and headbands, pins and brooches—intoning oaths which, one by one, each solemnly repeated: that they would in perpetuity share common enemies and friends with Athens. An attack on any member would be considered an attack on the whole League. Should the League decide to go to war, the entire alliance would be mobilized. The implications were enormous, not least for Athens. Invaded by neighbours or by Sparta, she would no longer be alone, while, in wars of her own making, she could field a staggeringly large army.[6]

Alive to the theatricality and power of ritual, Aristeides contrived that as they ratified their oath, each envoy dropped a red-hot iron bar into the sea, swearing that, until the metal floated to the surface, his polis would keep its word. As one by one the spitting iron bars sank, and hymns were sung and prayers were chanted, and the stench of sacrifice engulfed the island, all recognized the deep significance of what they had just witnessed: the creation of a new power bloc, the "League of Athens and Her Allies," today more often called the "Delian League." It was the culmination of a tortuous journey, which had seen Athens briefly intervene on the Ionians' behalf at Sardis, then watch from the sidelines as their cities fell, fight against them in the Persian Wars, welcome them back into the Greek alliance, and finally exploit their renewed loyalty in the founding of the League.[7]

Among its first acts was to build a new Temple of Apollo at Delos, the island's third, whose strong walls, massive doors, and metal grilles embedded between both porches' columns betrayed one of its chief purposes: to serve as the League's treasury. Built not in Athens but on Delos, dedicated not to Athena but to Apollo, and paid for not by the Athenians but chiefly by their allies, it was nonetheless the first sacred construction project spearheaded by Athens in the postwar years, a marker for a reimagined future, where thanks to her constantly expanding influence, Athens might claim leadership of not just the alliance but all Greece. Among the treasure it would house was the annual fee paid by League members (assessed by Aristeides, but essentially the same as what most had paid as tribute to the Persians). This budget required close supervision. So, each year the League appointed ten commissioners, whose title, Hellenotamiae, "Treasurers of the Greeks," laid claim to a wider remit than they possessed. Their composition, too, raised questions and revealed intents. All were Athenians, one from each tribe, accountable not to the League but to the Council and Assembly of Athens.[8]

If Athens' allies could not see how Athens might exploit the League, her enemies most surely could. Furious at being wrong-footed, Sparta's hot-blooded warriors demanded action, and only with great difficulty did their elders manage to avert a war, arguing that, while Athens had stolen a march on them, nothing had really changed. Sparta needed her army close to home. The helot threat remained. The homelands required constant vigilance. Moreover, with the League protecting mainland Greece from Persian attack, there was no necessity for Spartans to risk fighting far off in the east for the kind of power and booty which had debauched Pausanias. Better to keep what they had, preserve their honourable way of life, and let Athens shoulder all the work and risk corruption from her plunder.[9]

As for the plunder they themselves had taken at Plataea, the Spartans earmarked some for a new building project of their own, a stoa to commemorate their victory. Sited in their agora close to the council chamber and the ephors' offices, its design was remarkable, its long roof resting not on columns but on larger-than-life marble statues. Each portrayed one of Xerxes' lieutenants (including Queen Artemisia, who fought at Salamis, and the general, Mardonius) identified by accompanying inscriptions—once threatening commanders condemned to play a servile role, their honour degraded, their memory debased, metamorphosed to support a stoa's architrave. Inspiration may have come from Persia itself. Far to the east at Naqš-e Rostam in the ancient heartlands of Fars, on the cliff face housing Darius' tomb a carving, 75 feet high, showed the Great King standing on a dais facing a fire altar while the winged Ahura Mazda hovered in the air above him. But holding up the dais were not legs or pillars. Instead, representatives of each of Persia's subject states strained to raise the heavy structure high above their heads. An inscription spelled out their identity, a litany of names including "Yauna" (Ionians, or Greeks) and "wide-sunhat-wearing Yauna." "If you should ask 'How many peoples did Darius rule?,'" it read, "look at the sculptures of these men who hold his throne. . . . The Persian spear has been thrown far. . . . A Per-

5.1 Detail of Darius' tomb showing subjects supporting a platform on which the Great King is making offerings to Ahura Mazda.

sian has waged war far from Persia." But now the tables had been turned. In Sparta it was no mere representatives but leaders of the Persian Empire who supported the roof of the stoa of victory.[10]

The Spartans were not the only Greeks to use the human form in such a way. At Delphi, two caryatids, sculpted female figures with plaited hair, dressed in long, flowing robes and clutching offerings in outstretched hands, already supported the porch roof of the Siphnian Treasury built around 525 B.C., but during the 480s B.C. the idea of substituting bodies for pillars was embraced with gusto, not least by Sicilians of Acragas. Following victory over Carthaginians at Himera, financed from spoils and reparations, they raised a massive temple to Olympian Zeus, the largest in the entire Greek world, into niches between whose columns they inserted thirty-eight huge limestone statues, 25 feet tall, and all identical. They represented Atlas, the Titan condemned to stand forever in the mountains of North Africa supporting the heavens on his shoulders, a punishment for fighting with the gods, a perfect allegory for the vanquished Carthaginians. Meanwhile, the Syracusan tyrant built two trophy temples of his own to mark his city's role at Himera. Almost identical, both were dedicated to Athena. One was set beneath the town of Himera itself beside the river, where Syracusan cavalry cut down Carthage's general as he sacrificed to his sea god. The other, at Syracuse, towered magisterially above chic, sophisticated buildings near the entrance to the city's harbour, light filtering golden through its thin marble roof, a well-polished shield capping its pediment to catch the sun and flare, a beacon for ships out at sea, a promise of safe haven.[11]

So, the temple race continued, as poleis vied to outdo one another, mark victory in war and seek divine favour. On mainland Greece, to celebrate another military triumph, citizens of Elis built a Temple of Zeus at Olympia. With an area of 230 by 68 feet, it was by any standard massive, and its sculptural decorations were magnificent. Soaring more than 68 feet high and crowned with gilded tripods and gold statues of the goddess Nikē (Victory), its *metopēs* traced the twelve labours of the Panhellenic hero, Heracles, while its marble pedimental sculptures carved in the most modern style combining three-dimensional plasticity with heightened realism, were breathtaking in design and execution. The east pediment showed one of the foundation myths of the Olympic Games, its setting underlined by the inclusion of a local river god at each of the two narrow vertices, while on the west Apollo, poised and perfect, stretched out his right arm to impose order on the chaos of the Centauromachy.[12]

These sculptures marked the start of a new trend in temple art—away from the orientalising stiffness of aloof archaic statuary towards a new, dynamic, thoroughly Greek suppleness, where drapery revealed the human form, and the human form revealed emotion. Following a lightning strike that damaged their Temple of Aphaea's east pediment, the islanders of Aegina embraced it, too, removing the old sculptures (but preserving them in an adjacent exhibition hall) and instead installing figures full of energy and motion, whose costumes drew strong visual parallels between the Trojan and the recent Persian Wars, foregrounding Aegina's commanding role in both.[13]

For Athenians, despite their pride in Attica's burnt ruins, such moves by rival poleis to propagandize temple art were deeply irritating.

To their mind, the Delian League, not Aegina, was the true heir to the allied Greeks at Troy—as they were clearly demonstrating. Under Cimon's energetic leadership, deadly shoals of triremes crisscrossed the Aegean, expelling Persian garrisons, amassing slaves and booty, and bringing coastlines and vital sea lanes under their control. Military and economic though Athens' motives were, she used these victories to amplify her narrative that she was fighting in the vanguard of an existential war between the west and east whose origins stretched back to Troy. After one campaign, the Assembly voted to erect three monumental herms beside the Sacred Way inscribed not with morally instructive maxims (like Hipparchus' herms) but with words applauding military triumph. One praised Athens' generals, another her fighting men, while the third and longest drew parallels between Cimon's recent victories and the Trojan War:

Once from this city with the sons of Atreus
Menestheus led Athenians to the sacred plain of Troy.
Homer records how—of all Greeks in their close-fitting armour—
he was the best at stationing his men for battle.
So, it is no small thing to call Athenians
experts in deploying both the arts of war and strengths of men.[14]

Athenians play a small role in the *Iliad;* Menestheus was no Achilles; but Athens was determined to link past and present as she claimed a central role in Greece's future.

So, she turned once more to Theseus, her homespun hero, whose character and exploits chimed with her emerging postbellum identity. He, too, a proto-democrat, exterminated wrongdoers, freeing his city from a foreign empire before uniting Attica, as Athens had united Greeks within the Delian League. His values were those claimed by contemporary Athenians—compassion, justice, piety—and both he and his son Demophon ("Voice of the People") fought to uphold them. So, when an oracle commanded Cimon to find and repatriate Theseus' bones, past and present once more met in perfect synchronicity. Guided, he claimed, by Zeus' bird, the eagle, Cimon discovered a gigantic skeleton, which with loud fanfare he entombed in a newly renovated shrine, a mausoleum built of ashlar poros blocks, approached by shallow limestone steps, sited not on the Athenian Acropolis but "in the heart of the lower city" on the south side of the Agora, and decorated with majestic paintings. Commissioned from the master, Micon, they showed episodes from Theseus' life: the Amazonomachy; the Centauromachy; his confirmation as the true son of Poseidon. Challenged to prove his divine parentage, he dived beneath the waves to find a ring. The painting showed the moment he resurfaced, the ring held high in triumph, a gold crown on his head, a gift from Poseidon's queen, Amphitrite, proof that the god, his father, would make him and his descendants masters of the sea.[15]

Theseus' hero-shrine spoke to Athens' sense of destiny, and in the decades following the Persian Wars, the city truly seemed unstoppable. In victory after victory, pious Cimon and the Delian League thwarted the renewed invasion plans of Xerxes and his successor, Artaxerxes. In 468 B.C. on one day in Pamphylia at the mouth of the River Eurymedon, they destroyed the Persian fleet and Persian army, amassing booty beyond their wildest dreams. Just twelve years earlier, Athenians had been compelled to leave their land and city as the Persians advanced; now, agreeing in a treaty to keep his navy out of the Aegean, even the Great King acknowledged their invincibility. Which called for further offerings and artworks. At Delphi, funded from booty, they dedicated a bronze palm tree, life-sized, with gold fruit hanging from its branches. A replica of the sacred palm tree growing beside the lake at Delos, it married piety with politics: colonizing its branches were gold owls, symbols of Athena (and her coins), while from the tree's crown, gilded, rose the goddess herself, modelled on her xoanon in Athens, her dominant position matching Athens' domination of the League. Part thanks offering to Apollo, the League's patron, for victory at Eurymedon, part testament to power, it encapsulated a growing sense of Athenian ambition.[16]

It was a message broadcast in the heart of Athens, too. On the north side of the Agora, Cimon's brother-in-law funded a new stoa, over 100 feet long and 40 wide, its colonnade providing a fine view of the north face of the Acropolis with its upper courses peppered with those unfluted column drums and *metopēs* and triglyphs, a ghost temple signifying Athens' sacrifice. Housing three enormous panel paintings, the stoa quickly gained the nickname Poikile (Painted). Each the work of a leading artist (Micon, Polygnotus, and Panaenus), they all depicted battle scenes linked by one great overarching theme: Athens' fight for victory and justice in the conflict between east and west.[17]

Taken from left to right, the triptych formed a journey linking mythological and real history. The subject of the first panel, the Amazonomachy, was the furthest removed in time. The original is lost, and, while no descriptions survive, it was likely later copied by sculptors and vase painters, who showed Athenians engaging with horse-riding, trouser-wearing female warriors, their costumes a visual link with Persia's cavalry encountered by Athenians at Plataea and Eurymedon. The fighting was depicted in full flow, but all knew its eventual outcome: Athens, led by Theseus, would win. Theseus' influence was felt, too, in the second painting set a generation later. On one level triumphalist, its subject matter, the Sack of Troy, was potentially problematic, since many victorious Greeks behaved with such barbaric hubris that they provoked gods' anger. In the absence of any visual or written record, the description of another "Sack of Troy," also by Polygnotus, provides one tantalizing detail, since this showed Theseus' son, Demophon, rescuing his grandmother, Aethra, taken as a slave by Helen when she sailed to Troy. Were the scene included in the Painted Stoa (as it surely was), the parallels between Aethra (enslaved by Spartan Helen; held in Asiatic Troy; freed by an Athenian) and the Athenians and their League allies (subject to Spartan hegemony, occupied by Asiatic Persians, freed by Athens) could not have been clearer—a new layer added to the layer of east-west conflict. Theseus himself reappeared in the third painting, a romanticized recreation of the Battle of Marathon. A description survives:

> [On the left] the battle is evenly matched, but at the centre of the fighting the barbarians are in flight, shoving each other into the marshes, while at the right of the painting are Phoenician ships and Greeks slaughtering barbarians as they try to get aboard. Here, too, is the figure of Marathon, the hero from whom the plain is named, and Theseus rising from the earth, and Athena, too, and Heracles.[18]

The spirit of Theseus, Athens' once-and-future king, pervaded the entire triptych, and his appearance in the painting of Marathon, alongside not just Heracles but Athena, confirmed his status as Panhellenic hero. The triptych confirmed Polygnotus' status, too. Originally from Thasos, in lieu of payment he requested—and gained—full Athenian citizenship.[19]

It was a sign of the regard in which great artists were held, and among the greatest was an up-and-coming sculptor, Pheidias, brother of Panaenus, one of the triptych painters. The post-invasion years were an exciting time for a young sculptor as the orientalising school beloved by the Peisistratids gave way to more heroic realism. Experimenting with contrapposto, masters such as Critius (who worked on the tyrannicides' replacement statue) helped liberate the human form, imbuing bronze and marble bodies with a sense of natural fluidity and energy. Pheidias may have spent some of his apprenticeship in Critius' studio. Tradition has him study in the workshop of Ageladas of Argos, too, a magnet for a brilliant new generation of creative minds, including Myron, creator of the discobolus (discus-thrower), and Polycleitus, whose dynamic sculptures betrayed years of observation and research in mathematics, symmetry and balance to determine the ideal human proportions, distilled in his now-lost *Canon.* Fragments shed light on his painstaking technique: "Gradually perfection comes about through many numbers." "If one casual element is omitted or included wrongly unsightliness results."[20]

While Polycleitus strove for perfection in the human body, Pheidias gave it a sense of the divine. Even as a young man, his genius was recognized. Following the Battle of Eurymedon, when he was perhaps still only in his twenties, Pheidias had won the prestigious contract for a bronze statue group. It was the Assembly which signed off the commission, but the victor Cimon's influence was plain to see. Installed at Delphi at the entrance to the sanctuary it took the form of thirteen figures, an honour guard beside the Sacred Way: seven Attic tribal heroes; Athens' last king, Codrus; Philaeus, founder of Cimon's family, the Philaids; Theseus, whose bones Cimon repatriated; Athena, goddess of Athens, and Apollo, god of Delphi and the League; and flanked by them one mortal man—Miltiades, victor of Marathon, Cimon's father. An inscription on the podium named each character and proclaimed that they had been funded out of booty. But not booty from Eurymedon. From Marathon.[21]

It was clever propaganda, rehabilitating Cimon's father's memory, linking Cimon's victory with Marathon, spotlighting Athens' and his family's role in shaping history. But the Marathon Monument showed Pheidias' flair, too, in working to a bold, sophisticated brief. After Plataea, the Spartans claimed of their fallen that "though they have died, they are not dead: their bravery brings them glory and leads them back to earth from Hades." Now Pheidias' statue group went further, implying that Miltiades' virtue and bravery had led him, a mortal Athenian, not simply back to earth but to commune with gods, on a par with Athens' semi-divine heroes. It was an idea that Pericles would embrace with gusto.

As Pheidias' reputation spread, commissions flooded in: a statue of Athena Areia (Warlike), just over 25 feet tall, for her temple at Plataea, its body carved from wood encased in sheets of wafer-thin gold leaf secured by tiny golden nails, its face, and hands and feet sculpted from Attic marble, its lips reddened, its grey eyes glaring from beneath a shining helmet; and at Pellene in Arcadia another gilded statue of the goddess, her flesh formed this time not from marble but from ivory. Chryselephantine (gold-and-ivory) statues were not new. At least three were badly damaged in the Delphic temple's fire of 548 B.C. But cost made them a rarity. Sourcing and importing ivory was expensive; unscrolling tusks, then flattening and treating them to make them malleable was time consuming and demanded expertise; ensuring that the ivory did not dry out and crack was problematic—but luckily for Pheidias, this statue was set up above a subterranean chamber, damp air from which provided the humidity the ivory required.[22]

On the Athenian Acropolis three more of his statues stood amid the ruins: a bronze Apollo in his guise as "Locust God" (either a response to a real but unrecorded plague, a reference to a legend telling how Apollo drove clouds of locusts out of Attica, or an offering in thanks for how he helped expel the Persians); a bronze Athena, paid for by Athens' colonists on Lemnos, showing her bareheaded, a broad circlet set on her short, curly hair, her aegis slung across one shoulder, a young warrior at rest, one hand gripping a spear shaft, as, cheeks suffused with a soft rosy blush, she gazed in rapt, defiant concentration at the helmet that she cradled in the other—an enigmatic composition (was she returning from the fight or arming before battle?) but thought by many to be Pheidias' finest work; and the Athena Promachus.[23]

A companion to the Lemnian Athena, the Promachus was erected like the Marathon Monument at Delphi after the Battle of Eurymedon. It showed Athena mid-combat, her aegis slung across her shoulders, on her head a gleaming horsehair-crested helmet, her shield strapped to her left arm, her right hand wielding a long spear, her lunging pose an echo of the sculpture which once stood on the pediment of the Old Temple. Facing the entrance to the Acropolis, its base angled towards Salamis, it was to date the tallest statue in the city, rising thirty feet into the air, the sunlight glancing from it visible to sailors as they hoved across the gulf into Piraeus. Close inspection revealed further details: the Centauromachy embossed onto the shield (by now visual shorthand for the Persian Wars, linking Theseus' exploits with those of his descendants); and the inscription on its plinth commemorating Athens' triumph at Eurymedon over Persia's fleet and army:

Ever since the sea split Asia from Europe
and maddened Ares poured into the cities of mankind,
nothing like this was ever won by men who live on earth:
victory on a single day on land and sea.[24]

Bronze masterpieces such as these required not just great artistry, but, given the size of the creative team, painstaking logistics. As sculptor, Pheidias oversaw each project through every stage: making drawings and maquettes; creating a wax original to be encased in plaster, melted and drained off through sprues before, heated to 2,552° Fahrenheit (1,400° Celsius), liquid bronze was poured into the cavities of the resulting mould and, once cooled, the plaster casing was removed; smoothing the statue; polishing it; and rubbing colouring into its gleaming surface. It was Pheidias, who was responsible, too, for sourcing raw materials, for organizing their delivery, for employing an army of contractors, metal workers, marble cutters, engineers to hoist the statue up onto its plinth. And it was he who must ensure that every project came in on time and budget.[25]

Pheidias had a genius for capturing the zeitgeist, and through unrivalled statuary projecting an image to the world of Athens and her League united and triumphant. The hard truth was very different. Almost no sooner was the Delian League formed than old fault lines fissured in Athenian domestic politics. On one side was the populist Themistocles, hero of Salamis, propounding his vision of radical democracy and trying to export it to wider Greece. In 476 B.C., at the first Olympic Games after the battle, encouraged by his reception (spectators rose as one to cheer him as he entered the stadium), he incited the crowd (in vain) to remove the Syracusan leader, debar him from the chariot race and tear down his tent because he was a tyrant. He did everything he could to frustrate oligarchic Sparta, too, weakening her dominance of the old Panhellenic Council, by finessing the readmittance of Thebes, Thessaly, and Argos, their prior alliance with Persia or their neutrality eclipsed now by their readiness to stand up to the Spartans.[26]

But the world was changing. As Cimon and Aristeides, aristocrats both, won a string of victories, Themistocles, tiresome, self-satisfied, and always harping on about the war years, metamorphosed into yesterday's man. When he constructed a new Temple of Artemis Aristoboule (Giver of Good Counsel) in an Athens suburb, the People's patience snapped—they believed he was alluding to his own good counsel, by which he boasted he had won the Persian Wars, and they

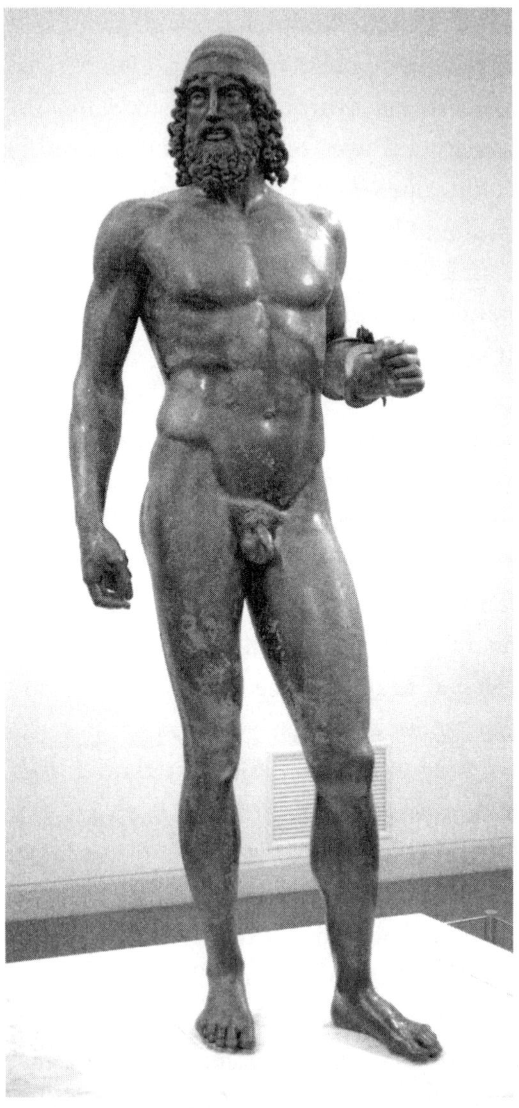

5.2 A fifth-century-B.C. bronze statue of a warrior, one of the two "Riace bronzes."

accused him, too, of setting up a statue of himself inside the cella. In Spring 471 B.C. they trooped into the Agora to use the mechanism that Themistocles himself had weaponized to such effect and ostracized him. Even then his enemies were not satisfied. In Athens and Sparta, they found—or fabricated—evidence that he was plotting with the disgraced Pausanias to betray Greece to Persia, install themselves as tyrants, and take vengeance on their enemies. Sentenced in absentia to death, Themistocles fled—to Persia, a prized defector, like Hippias growing old in luxury. As for Pausanias, taking refuge in the Spartan Temple of Athena, its walls shimmering with bronze plaques, he found himself besieged without food or water. At last, weak, parched, and starving, he was dragged out to die, lest his passing should pollute the holy shrine.[27]

Of greater concern, however, was the future of the League. In 468 B.C., just ten years after its inception, the Naxians, resentful of paying tribute and in breach of their oaths, announced that they were leaving. This was something the Athenians could not allow. If Naxos seceded, the whole League might collapse, leaving Athens as vulnerable and isolated as before the Persian Wars. A siege and a capitulation saw Naxos' city walls destroyed, and loyalty restored with threats and promises. Once more the gods had favoured Athens. But only three years later gold-rich Thasos, too, rebelled. For two long winters, Cimon laid siege to the city, and when at last the Thasians surrendered, it was on the harshest terms: their walls torn down; ships confiscated; mining interests passed to Athens; payment to the League increased; a huge indemnity imposed to pay for the Athenian campaign.[28]

By now all Greece could see that, once a voluntary coalition, the Delian League had mutated into an Athenian Empire. The transition had been insidious. Tasked with supplying ships, men, and money, many allies (as they still euphemistically were known) had preferred instead to translate all their contributions into cash, leaving the Athenians to build, maintain and crew the costly triremes. But as Athens' fleet increased in power, and her ambitions grew, her allies' needs and wishes seemed increasingly irrelevant. As their treatment of Naxos and Thasos showed, while Athenians might pride themselves in being staunch democrats at home, they were increasingly imperialist when dealing with the League. Increasingly they felt the gods' approval. Even victory on Thasos was won thanks to Poseidon. Early in the siege the islanders requested help from Sparta, which was poised to intervene by launching raids on Attica, when without warning a huge earthquake struck. As rocks rained down from the high mountains, buildings across

Laconia collapsed with massive loss of life. It was the moment that the helot serfs had prayed for. They were potentially a daunting force: 35,000 of them had fought beside their masters at Plataea. Now, armed with whatever weapons they could find, they marched on Sparta. But even as aftershocks convulsed the high crags of Taygetus and the lush Eurotas valley, the Spartans rallied, and the helots, cowed, abused, dehumanized for generations, fled to the mountains of Messenia, their ancient heartlands, where they fortified the high plateau of Mount Ithome and dug in for war. For Athens the Spartan threat was over.[29]

The earthquake had saved Cimon's operations against Thasos, but it would ruin Cimon. An avid devotee of all things Spartan (one of his rhetorical techniques was to demand, "what would Sparta do?"), he championed power sharing, encouraging the two main mainland poleis to respect each other's spheres of influence and work together for the common good like "two well-matched horses pulling one chariot to victory." Back from Thasos, he led a taskforce on a goodwill mission to help Sparta, but when the Spartans rejected his intervention, he found himself exposed to his political enemies, a cadre of newly resurgent radicals coalescing round their charismatic leader, Ephialtes. And among these young progressives was Pericles.[30]

Now thirty-two years old, Pericles had worked hard to achieve political success. His father, Xanthippus, had died soon after his return from Sestus passing his wealth and social standing to his two sons. But it was only Pericles who showed ambition. Already in 472, in his early twenties, he had funded a dramatic tetralogy by Aeschylus, which included a tragedy, *Persians,* reimagining Xerxes' defeat at Salamis through the eyes of the king's mother and court. Pericles' role in the production was fortuitous. Athenians paid no income tax, but each year elite citizens were tasked with financing one specific area of public life, such as maintaining a trireme and its crew, funding tribal dinners, leading delegations to the Panhellenic games, financing a gymnasium, supporting the Arrhephoroi, or acting as choregus—funding choruses and plays for the dramatic festival. Lavishing money on their staging was a sure crowd-pleaser, and, since *Persians* called for sumptuous eastern costumes, carriages, and wagons, not to mention a necromantic scene involving Darius' ghost, Pericles had plenty opportunity to use his money to spectacular effect.[31]

Even more striking than the staging was the sophisticated script. Rather than let his audience simply gloat over its defeated enemy, Aeschylus explored the two sides' shared humanity, suggesting that, supporting pious Greeks, the gods had punished Xerxes' arrogance. "When hubris flowers," Darius' ghost observes, "it bears rich fruit—blind recklessness, a bumper harvest thick with tears." Nonetheless, a rich vein of patriotism ran through the play. Messenger speeches gave a stirring account of the Battle of Salamis and the Persians' retreat. The Chorus of Persian elders reflected on how democratic Athenians "are not slaves of any man—nor vassals either," and how "the gods protect the city of Athena." Darius' ghost advised his Persians, "Do not campaign against the Greeks, not even if your numbers are superior—the very land is on the side of Greece," warning that their fallen at Plataea will be "a silent witness—even to the third generation—that they must not think too big." But most arresting of all was the dead king's reasoning for why the Persians' expedition ended in disaster: "When they got to Greece, they felt no scruples about looting ancient wooden statues of the gods or torching temples. They smashed altars, tore down statues of divinities from plinths, and shattered them. So, since they acted so outrageously, they are suffering no less outrageously in turn."[32]

So, only just an adult, Pericles found his fate entwined with that of Athens' temples. But for the next decade, he followed what for young aristocrats was an unremarkable, well-trodden path, perfecting his forensic skills, honing his oratory, perhaps serving as archon, and gaining military experience when, alongside Ephialtes, he led the fleet out to patrol the east Aegean. It is impossible to gauge Ephialtes' influence on Pericles, but it is small wonder that, as the great-nephew of Cleisthenes, founder of Athenian democracy, Pericles embraced Ephialtes' populism, while, as Xanthippus' son and heir, he did all he could to sustain his family's feud with the conservative Philaids, and their current head, Cimon.[33]

For years Cimon's star had burned brightly thanks to his military success, the projects for which his victories had paid, and his own innate generosity. Throwing open his estates, he had encouraged the poor to pick fruit from his orchards. He had hosted regular dinners for every member of his deme. He had championed public works to ease the lives of every citizen, planting plane trees in the Agora to give shade to those doing business there; enhancing the Academy gymnasium with olive groves and artificial streams; draining the marshes between Athens and Piraeus; and reinforcing the south wall of the Acropolis in preparation for the fast-approaching day when public sentiment and strong finances meant that Athens could again consider building a new temple to Athena.[34]

Yet, even before Cimon's disastrous Spartan intervention, Pericles had worked to undermine him. He accused the elder statesman of gross dereliction of duty while on campaign on Thasos—in that he failed to punish Macedonia's King Alexander for supporting Persia—and of accepting bribes. Both accusations were absurd, but, with the trial the talk of Athens, and in the light of Sparta's recent plans to attack Attica, it was a useful barometer to discover to what extent the People were losing faith in the pro-Spartan Cimon. In the event the trial was a damp squib. Pericles simply stood, read out the charges and sat down again, content to let Cimon vent his outrage, and make a blustering defence of his own record. But his acquittal was irrelevant. What mattered was that fault lines between Cimon's camp and that of Pericles and Ephialtes were exposed, not least regarding Sparta. Increasingly Cimon seemed on the wrong side of history. So, when he marched home, rebuffed by earthquake-stricken Spartans, and an ostracism vote was mooted, its outcome was a foregone conclusion. Cimon was exiled, and Pericles and Ephialtes were ascendant.[35]

Already they had been flexing their muscles, not least by clipping the wings of the elite Council of the Areopagus. As Cimon's conservatives became more vulnerable, Ephialtes drove through a motion stripping it of many of its ancient powers, including some judiciary responsibilities, instead establishing public lawcourts where up to 501 Athenians, chosen by lot, would sit as judge and jury in trials, none of which would last for longer than a day. This ruthless emasculation of one of the last bastions of the elite was also powerfully symbolic:

after a decade in the doldrums, following Themistocles' disgrace, progressive democracy was back on track, spearheaded by a new generation of champions, determined to remove all vestiges of privilege, and turn Athens into a true city of equals.[36]

To celebrate both this and Cimon's ostracism, Ephialtes or his followers put forward plans for a new residential building in the Agora for use by members of the democratic Council, where delegates could meet, and eat, and sometimes sleep. Architecturally it was ambitious. Adjacent to the Council Chamber, this Tholos (built of limestone and mudbrick, its walls plastered, smooth and gleaming) was a round building, whose conical pitched roof with elegantly intersecting tiles lent it the nickname "Skias" ("Sunshade"), and whose appearance was deliberately reminiscent of the tents put up at Panhellenic games for ritual feasting. Yet, even more striking than its appearance was its location: where farmers from Acharnae and fishermen from Rhamnous now banqueted the night away, once stood the palace of the tyrants.[37]

The construction of the Tholos was overshadowed by an act of violence—a bloody corpse discovered in the early morning, knifed in an alleyway, the victim: Ephialtes. His killer or killers were never found, but one man benefitted more than any other from his death, the brilliant, inscrutable, aloof patrician, the Alcmaeonid Man of the People, who had been hiding in his mentor's shadows for so long, perhaps the intellect behind his every move, but keen now to occupy the limelight: Pericles. He had worked hard to win the People's trust and favour, honing his image as the cool Olympian, guarding his privacy, shunning social events, appearing in public only when necessary, maintaining tight self-discipline, and taking care at all times to betray not even the remotest flicker of emotion. And now the stage was his.[38]

Charismatic, persuasive, and with no real opposition to speak of, Pericles recalibrated Athens' foreign policy, maintaining her aggressive stance vis-à-vis Persia, but now no longer caring if her blatant expansionism provoked Sparta. Thessaly and Argos had recently allied with Athens. Now Megara, too, for many years a Spartan ally, joined the Athenian confederacy, allowing Athens' fleet the use of a

5.3 The foundations of the round tholos in the Athenian Agora, with the Temple of Athena and Hephaestus on the low hill behind.

strategically vital port on the Gulf of Corinth, cutting out the need to circumnavigate the Peloponnese when sailing west, and providing a useful base from which to threaten cities on the north Peloponnesian coast. But still Athenian ambitions grew. In 460 B.C., when an envoy asked the Assembly for help in ending sixty years of Persian rule in Egypt in return for a share in the country's rich resources, Pericles backed by the People responded eagerly. A fleet of 200 triremes sped down to the Nile—and victory. The next that the Assembly heard, the Persians were under siege at Memphis.[39]

Nearer home, an Athenian offensive in the Argolid had spiralled into all-out war with Aegina and Corinth, victory for Athens' fleet, Corinthian attacks on Megara . . . and now Athenians were laying siege to Aegina. Their casualties were high. One tribe mourned 107 men "fallen in the same year fighting wars in Cyprus, Egypt, Phoenicia, Halieis, Aegina and Megara," figures which, if replicated throughout Attica, would mean more than a thousand dead. However, far from denting their ambition, such sacrifices seemed instead to drive Athenians to ever greater urgency. Yet, they recognized their vulnerability. Much of their grain came from abroad, including the Black Sea, so should an enemy cut off Athens from Piraeus they might starve the city into submission. So, the Assembly voted to construct two massive Long Walls, one, some three-and-three-quarter miles in length, on a line from Pnyx Hill to Piraeus, the other slightly shorter from just south of the Acropolis to Phalerum. Constructed from brick on poros and limestone bases, these broad, battlemented walls with regularly spaced watchtowers, would provide a secure corridor between Athens' circuit walls and strongly fortified Piraeus, while, at the same time enclosing a vast acreage of useful agricultural land.[40]

When the Spartans learned of this, they acted swiftly. Twenty-one years earlier they had let themselves be duped while Athens built her city wall. This time, they would attack before work was completed. Despite being overstretched—the helot war was dragging on—they reached an understanding with the Thebans, so recently pariahs, now loyal allies, and marched north to Tanagra near the Attic border. Athenians and Argive allies scrambled to meet them, squadrons of Thessalian cavalrymen riding at their side. Then: missiles flying; sword blades flashing; the resounding clash of shield on shield; ground lost and gained; confusion; the sun setting on a field of corpses; and in the morning, although Sparta and Thebes claimed victory (in triumph, Sparta hung a shield emblazoned with Medusa's head above the entrance to Olympia's new Temple of Zeus), the outcome was uncertain. Yet the status quo had shifted. In the heat of battle the Thessalians, like their mythical ancestors, the Centaurs, had proved treacherous, turning on their friends, siding with the enemy, vanishing, as evening fell, renouncing their alliance with Athens. But the Spartans, too, lacked appetite for reengaging. They trudged home, mission unaccomplished, while Athens' Long Walls stretched and soared, and, thanks to its safe corridor, the city effectively became a landlocked island, impregnable so long as her fleet ruled the waves.[41]

Athens seemed irrepressible. Before long, Aegina surrendered. Her city walls were torn down, her warships commandeered, and, swearing oaths of loyalty, her leaders undertook to pay a yearly tax to Athens. Soon after, the Athenians seized Boeotia (except Thebes) and brought Locris and Phocis under their control. But still they wanted more. A year later (in 454 B.C.) they burned Sparta's port, claimed Zacynthus and Cephalonia, and occupied Naupactus on the north coast of the Gulf of Corinth, resettling the town with grateful friends—helots, granted safe passage into exile after eight years' fighting, determined to take vengeance on the Spartans and their allies by helping the Athenians control traffic in the Gulf. The next year Pericles himself led a fleet that torched a string of towns and villages on the Peloponnesian west coast, raided Sicyon and, with a well-judged mix of violence and diplomacy, brought much of the west coast of mainland Greece under Athenian control.[42]

Yet, as Aeschylus had warned in *Persians,* men must not "think too big." "When hubris flowers, it bears rich fruit—blind recklessness, a bumper harvest thick with tears." Five years after it had first set out, the Athenian campaign in Egypt ended in disaster. The Persians relieved the siege of Memphis forcing the Athenians to retreat back up the Nile to an island on the Delta, where they beached their triremes, and built a strong stockade; but the Persians dug canals that drained the river dry, and across the cracking earth launched their attack, burning stranded warships, and forcing the Athenians to sue for terms. A relief force from Athens and her allies racing to the Delta unaware of what had happened made easy pickings for Persia's fleet. Not one trireme escaped, and there were few survivors. The League's losses were enormous: 250 ships and well over 10,000 men.[43]

The reaction back in Athens can only be imagined, but, if blame was levelled against Pericles, he was quick to deflect it, as he pandered to the People and won their vote with a bill subsidizing jury pay to the tune of two obols a day. While barely a living wage, it meant that no citizen performing his civic duty would be out of pocket, while poor and elderly urban dwellers could from time to time receive a form of stipend. Consciously or not, this professionalization of part of the democratic process had profound repercussions. For centuries, men had been free to enrol legitimate children as citizens no matter whether they were born to Athenian or foreign mothers. Thus, Pericles' own grandfather enjoyed full citizenship of Athens despite his mother, Agariste, being from Sicyon. In 451 B.C., however, as the People became more jealous of their privileges and pay, Pericles proposed, and the Assembly confirmed, a law restricting citizenship to those whose parents were both from Attic families. Now to be Athenian was more than ever to belong to an exclusive club, a citizenry boasting of autochthony, of springing from the soil, its lineage traced back to Hephaestus and Erechtheus, all of which gave the body politic a powerful sense of both identity and unity.[44]

On the wider stage, however, the situation was again becoming dangerously unstable. Persia's Great King Artaxerxes lost no time in following up victory in Egypt. Members of the Delian League had suffered badly during the campaign. So, with some now keen to sever ties with Athens, Artaxerxes fanned the flames and planned a new offensive. Already Sparta had accepted his financial backing, though she hesitated to invade Attica. Still, Athens seemed exposed. Not only Athens—Delos, too. With Persia's navy resurgent, the island and its treasury were sitting targets, which was why Athens unilaterally decided she must move the League's reserves to where she could maintain a closer watch on them—out of the island's Temple of Apollo; into the closely guarded zone of the Athenian Acropolis.[45]

A crisis seemed to be approaching, but as luck would have it, in 451 B.C., as Persia's fleet and army were beginning to assemble, Cimon returned from exile. Using his connections with Sparta to broker a five-year peace treaty, he led his triremes out to Cyprus smashing the Great King's fleet, destroying his plans for an invasion. In one afternoon, the pendulum had swung again. Even the most resentful members of the League were quick to reaffirm their loyalty to Athens. Cimon's rare mix of generalship and diplomacy had calmed the turbulence, but the elder statesman could not build on his success. He died on campaign, leaving the Athenian conservatives to search for a new champion. For now, though, in the absence of strong leadership, they were no match for Pericles.[46]

Sidelined and eclipsed by Cimon just months earlier, he cleverly regained control of the political narrative. Events were moving quickly.

Shaken by defeat, Artaxerxes invited Athens to discuss peace terms. Leading the delegation was Cimon's brother-in-law, Callias, whose office of torchbearer at the Eleusinian Mysteries set him at the heart of the Athenian establishment, and it was from him, the richest man in Attica, a shrewd negotiator, that the subsequent peace treaty was named: the Peace of Callias. Its significance was incalculable. Not only did it mark the official end of the Persian Wars, it brought Athens enormous kudos, for while Artaxerxes signed it on behalf of myriad subjects, Athens did so on behalf not only of herself and of her empire but of all Greece. The Great King had effectively confirmed Athens as Greece's hegemon.[47]

Quick to capitalize on this, Pericles invited every Greek city "large or small in Europe or in Asia" to Athens for a Panhellenic Congress to discuss "the peace and common good of Greece," specifically "Greek sanctuaries burned by the barbarians; and sacrifices promised to the gods for Greece during the war with the barbarians; and the sea, so that all might sail on it without fear and preserve the peace." In reality, there was little to discuss. Athens already controlled the sea lanes, while most of the "sanctuaries burned by the barbarians" were in Attica. But that was not the point. Rather, Pericles was mooting the creation of a new world order. Previously Sparta had initiated Panhellenic conferences. Now Athens claimed that right as hers. So, Pericles' proposal was deliberately provocative, and unsurprisingly, Sparta refused to attend; her satellites followed suit; only Athens' colonies and allies accepted the invitation, a clear sign that, even with the Persian threat now neutralized, the empire, which had started as an anti-Persian alliance, would endure. The Congress was cancelled, but Pericles had laid down his combative vision, a future of a Greece united under Athens but on Athens' terms, by "one blood, one language, common sanctuaries and sacrifices, and a common way of life."[48]

The failure of the Congress may have presented other opportunities. If the oath sworn prior to the Battle of Plataea is genuine, one of its clauses declared, "I shall not abandon my leaders." Now, however, since even Persia recognized Athens as hegemon of Greece, and since Sparta and her allies had refused Athens' summons to the Congress, with a little creativity, logic could just about suggest that Sparta and her allies had broken the terms of the Oath—which would in turn have rendered another of its clauses null and void: "I shall not rebuild in their entirety any of the temples burned and flattened by the barbarians, but rather I shall let them remain for future generations as a memorial of the barbarians' impiety." Regardless of whether the Oath played a part in his calculations, it was now, in 449 B.C., that Pericles proposed to transform Athens, the Acropolis and wider Attica. An ambitious building programme had marked the birth of Athenian democracy. Now a similarly ambitious programme would mark the city's rebirth, stronger, more determined than before, the self-proclaimed champion of Greek freedom and values, whose citizens were favourites of the gods. For Pericles the timing could not have been better, drawing focus from the recent Egyptian disaster (airbrushed from the annual funeral orations that kept Athens' history alive) and from Cimon's victories in Cyprus (overshadowed by the peace treaty).[49]

It was surely with these thoughts in mind that Pericles and his associates drew up their plans, framing proposals, calculating costs, estimating schedules, agreeing to the message that they wished the buildings and their sculptures to convey, sounding out architects and artists. By the time the plan was put before to the Council, it was sufficiently well honed that the 500 members were prepared to recommend it for a vote in the Assembly, and opinions already canvassed probably suggested that the vote would pass. Of course, this did not make the speech in question any less significant. Which was why, after the sacrifices and the prayers and curses, once the crier had intoned the well-known formula, "Who wants to speak?," once Pericles had strode onto the Platform, the focal point of all those thousands gathered on Pnyx Hill, the hubbub of anticipation faded to such urgent silence, as the mesmeric orator revealed his vision for the future.

6 EMBRACING PAST, PRESENT, AND FUTURE

I shall start first with our ancestors.

—PERICLES (QUOTED IN THUCYDIDES, 2.26)

The programme outlined by Pericles and passed by a show of hands in the Assembly looked back to a triumphant past and forward to imagined future glories, while embracing a present where—at least for the time being—Athens was stronger than ever. At its heart were Attica's burnt temples. By 449 B.C. many sanctuaries had acquired added layers of significance, as their religious and political identities evolved within already potent landscapes: Rhamnous near the battlefield of Marathon, sacred to Demeter and Nemesis; Sunium, its headland shared by both Athena and Poseidon, where once a Persian warship had been dedicated; Eleusis, home to the Mysteries, beside the Bay of Salamis; and the Athenian Acropolis, the city's hub, of all the holy sites the most remarkable. All would be beneficiaries of the new building programme, yet the first temple was begun at none of them, but rather on Colonus Hill overlooking Athens' Agora.[1]

Heading up the entire operation was Pheidias. Like everyone involved in the project, he was answerable to a special board of commissioners (with an annually rotating membership but a permanent secretary), appointed to keep an eye on progress and be in ultimate charge of budgets. But Pheidias had already proved himself reliable. His artistic vision and skill as project manager had been tried, tested, and approved in recent state-funded projects. While no records of his responsibilities survive, he was later described as the "overseer of everything," which suggests he had responsibility for budgeting, sourcing, buying, and transporting materials, as well as hiring and supervising architects, labourers, and builders, and making sure that operations came in on time. He was also contracted to construct the huge cult statue, the agalma, for the Temple of Athena on the Acropolis. And, since this statue was embellished with sculptural or painted details, whose subject matter recurred elsewhere on the temple and on other buildings which were part of the new project, it is likely that Pheidias intended to forge visual links between them all.[2]

Working alongside Pheidias was a team of architects, some responsible for just one building, while others worked on several, occasionally relocating mid-construction. Many are rightly famous, but the identity of the architect responsible for the first temple is elusive. While the building itself with its one-roomed sekos was unremarkable, its location was conspicuous—in the city's democratic heart, close to the Council House, many key administrative buildings, and the tyrannicides' statue near where they struck their blow for freedom. It was appropriately close, too, to the Cerameicus with its potteries and foundries, since the temple's gods presided over manufacturing: Hephaestus over artisans and craftsmen; Athena over weaving. But, as we have seen, this pairing had another, deeper significance. In their own way both gods shared responsibility for the birth of Erechtheus, the ancestor of every Athenian citizen. As quasi-parents, it was only right that they be honoured first. Appropriately, too, this temple celebrating autochthony was built (even its roof) from 100,000 tons of native marble cut from quarries on Pentelicus, roughly fashioned on site and hauled on ox- or mule-cart down a specially laid road into the city. Only the pediments, friezes, *metopēs,* and acroteria used Parian marble, since this allowed for greater detail in their carving, their subject matter chosen to contribute to the narrative of democratic Athens' unique character.[3]

The theme of family was central to both pediments. The east side above the cella door, the site of greatest impact, showed Athena's birth

6.1 The west face of the Temple of Athena and Hephaestus.

from Zeus' head, or more likely its aftermath, when she stood beside him, fully grown and fully armoured, as Hephaestus, facilitator of her birth, looked on. On the west pediment was Hephaestus' readmittance onto Mount Olympus following his reconciliation with his mother, Hera. (Because she mocked him for being lame, he had bound her to her throne with gossamer-thin chains, but Dionysus and his wine persuaded him to free her, so, with Hephaestus riding unsteadily on mule-back, the two gods swayed home to Olympus, where son liberated mother and harmony was restored.) The sculptures do not survive. Extant vase paintings showing Hephaestus' return to Mount Olympus have an earthy feel (his mule is often shown as ithyphallic), but the pedimental sculptures seem to have been more heroic—surviving cuttings in the marble show that the god rode in a chariot. To have had him ride an ithyphallic mule, however, would not have been entirely inappropriate. It was Hephaestus' rampant lust that resulted in Erechtheus, and through him all Athenians. Moreover, while the east pediment, showing chaste Athena's birth, looked across the Agora, the democratic heart of Athens, and obliquely to the Acropolis, its soul, the temple's west pediment rose above a smoke-wreathed sea of smithies, potters' kilns, and cheap bordellos, the city's throbbing groin.[4]

At the apex of each gable end, two sculptures in the round developed the idea of family. Here Hephaestus' nurses, sea nymphs Thetis and Eurynome, accompanied by Victories, gazed out across the city, watching over the Athenians, Hephaestus' children, as they once guarded the god. The leitmotif of family continued inside, too. Beneath bronze statues of the gods, the work of Pheidias' young protégé, Alcamenes, erected between 421 and 415 B.C., a frieze showing Erechtheus' birth was carved onto the plinth of polished Eleusinian grey limestone. Ionic (or continuous) friezes appeared, too, in both porches. Their hero was Theseus. The west frieze showed the Centauromachy, its outcome hanging in the balance. But while much of its treatment was familiar—flailing hooves and thrashing bodies, centaurs crushing a Lapith beneath a boulder, Lapiths dealing mortal blows to wounded enemies—the portrayal of Theseus himself was revolutionary. Placed in the centre of the melée, the frieze's focal point, his stance was identical to that of Harmodius in the statue group of the tyrannicides a stone's throw from the temple in the Agora. Its significance cannot be understated. Blurring mythology and history, it melded the heroic Theseus, founder of united Attica, with one of the two fathers of democracy. Recent artworks in the Painted Stoa and at Delphi had shown near-contemporary Athenians in the company of gods, but this went even further. It was the first time that a man, a citizen, dead only a few generations, was identified so unequivocally with a demigod. The east frieze repeated the conceit, this time showing Theseus in the same posture as Aristogeiton's statue. We cannot tell which battle is being shown here, but Theseus' enemy is human—perhaps the rebel sons of Pallas, his uncle, who tried to usurp the throne and rule as tyrants. With Theseus, the proto democrat, imagined here as Aristogeiton's doppelgänger, this subject would be appropriate, meaning that together the friezes should be understood as celebrating democratic Athens' triumph over both domestic and foreign threats—the sons of Pallas represented the Peisistratid tyrants; the Centaurs represented the Persians.[5]

6.2 The Centauromachy from the Temple of Athena and Hephaestus.

To identify Theseus with the tyrannicides was daring, but the east frieze went even further. Seated amid the fighting were two sets of gods. Significantly larger than the partially clothed or heroically nude human combatants, they were dressed in flowing robes: on the left, Athena with her shield and aegis, with Zeus holding his sceptre next to Hera; on the right, Hephaestus with a goddess, perhaps Aphrodite, and Apollo, both of whom had nearby sanctuaries. All watched keenly as the battle swirled around them—as they do in Homer's *Iliad,* and on the east frieze of the Siphnian Treasury at Delphi, where they gesticulate with animated zeal like spectators at a sports match while Trojan and Greek heroes clash, sculptures that Pheidias knew well. He had seen them when he stayed in Delphi, installing the Marathon Monument, just 60 yards east of the Siphnian Treasury, and they were almost certainly the inspiration for the east frieze of Athena and Hephaestus' temple. Delphi's Athenian Treasury, where *metopēs* linked Theseus and Heracles, inspired him, too. The heroes appeared, similarly paired, on the new temple. While fifty of its sixty-eight *metopēs* were blank, on the ten beneath the eastern pediment were sculpted some of Heracles' labours, while

6.3 The Assembly of the gods from the Siphnian Treasury at Delphi.

the four closest on the north and south sides showed scenes from Theseus' adventures.[6]

The sculptures of the Temple of Athena and Hephaestus, then, drew heavily on earlier iconic Athenian structures: the tyrannicides' statue; Athens' Treasury at Delphi; the hero-shrine of Theseus with its painting of the Centauromachy; and perhaps also the nearby Painted Stoa. Their carefully curated message was a powerful one, setting the theme of ancestry and family (since Athenians were "descended" from the two gods) alongside Athens' mission to defeat autocracy and barbarism, as Heracles, Theseus and the tyrannicides had done. Begun in 449 B.C., the temple was not completed until 415 B.C., so it is impossible to tell how many of these ideas evolved during construction. But the story that the sculptures tell suggests a focussed mind, and if others subsequently played a part in their design and execution, they likely adhered to Pheidias' original objective.[7]

One reason why the temple took so long to build was that priorities kept changing as new projects came online, among them the construction of a new (middle) Long Wall linking Athens and Piraeus. Running 550 feet east of the existing west wall, its purpose was to render even more impregnable the corridor between sea and city, now an easily defensible roadway between two high protective ramparts. Requiring less expertise than a temple, the wall rose rapidly, and within two years it was sufficiently complete that most of its workforce could be redeployed to other duties. Among them was its architect, Callicrates, reassigned to help work on a far more glamorous project, which had already been two years in the planning: a temple for Athena on the Acropolis.[8]

God-fearing citizens, recalling Athena's instruction to abandon Athens and her temples to the flames, believed that thanks to her the city was being made great again. As Solon wrote a century before,

> *Our city will never fall through Zeus' will*
> *or through the stratagems of blessèd gods who live forever;*
> *for she watches over us with a most powerful spirit. Born of a mighty father,*
> *Pallas Athena stretches out her hands above us.*[9]

Clearly Athena needed to be honoured with a most impressive temple, one to rival if not surpass those celebrated temples at Olympia and Ephesus and Samos, but they faced a huge dilemma. While a temporary shrine to house her xoanon stood in its ruined cella, no one wanted to desecrate the site of the Old Temple or rob Athens of one of her most powerful memorials by building on it. Instead, the Assembly voted to leave the ruins untouched, a poignant centrepiece for the Acropolis, a focal point for many of the sacrifices made there, since the altar of Athena facing them would not be moved. The decision was not without consequences. The need to preserve the site, to avoid interfering with other nearby sanctuaries and to accommodate a route (375 feet long and 26 feet wide) for ritual processions from the Acropolis' gateway to the altar, meant that the only suitable location was the site of the unfinished temple started after Marathon. But in the intervening forty years, ambitions had evolved. With Pheidias' cult statue, the agalma, far larger than anything conceived a generation earlier, the temple needed to be bigger, too. So, before construction could begin, the platform was extended to the north for greater width.[10]

Which reveals the agalma's importance. Previous temples were constructed without consideration for the statues they would house. But in this case the size and proportions of Pheidias' agalma, along with considerations of how it would appear within the context of the cella, dictated the design of the whole building. So, in the two years between the contract's approval and construction work beginning, Pheidias, the "overseer of everything," is likely to have engaged in many project meetings with his team, but chiefly his lead architect, Ictinus, and Callicrates, Ictinus' assistant. Today, little is known of either man, their previous work, or why they were chosen, and the loss of Ictinus' book on the design and building of the temple (perhaps based on notes made for his annual reports before the Council) is frustrating, especially since this building—today called the Parthenon, but known at the time (despite its actual measurements) as the Hekatompedos Naos, or Hundred-Foot Temple—would be unlike any other yet seen on the Acropolis, not simply larger, but more sophisticated, incorporating new discoveries in mathematics, new ideas about proportions and new theories of harmony, a showcase for the intellectual enlightenment that characterized contemporary Athens.[11]

The sekos contained two rooms: the west-facing opisthodomos, used in part as the imperial treasury, its roof supported by four towering columns; and the cella, designed specifically to showcase the agalma. Proportionally this chamber was larger than average, its length increased at the expense of the two porticoes, which in turn became shallower than normal, and, during the construction process, further subtle changes were achieved, as fractions of an inch were shaved off walls to make proportions appear more ideal or add to a subconscious sense of spaciousness, enhanced already by a row of two-tiered Doric columns running down the two sides of the nave and laterally behind the agalma. While their practical purpose was to support the coffered ceiling, by framing the huge statue, they added to a sense of width.[12]

6.4 The Parthenon atop the Acropolis seen from the southwest.

Further to ensure that the agalma could be seen to best advantage, Ictinus modified the structure of the cella in revolutionary new ways, setting tall windows either side of the doorway, to allow light from the rising sun to flood inside and lend the room a brightness uncommon for Greek temples. The doorway, too, he made colossal, while the doors themselves were breathtaking. Made of cedar wood, and reinforced by iron bars, they were faced in gold and ivory, their panels adorned with lions' heads and rams' heads and Medusa's severed head. Thrown open for religious festivals, they framed the statue to perfection.[13]

The proportions of the doorway (2:1) were an exception. To help achieve a sense of unity and harmony throughout the building, Ictinus used another ratio (4:9) for many of its measurements from the proportions of the stylobate to the correspondence between the height of its horizontal cornice and its width, to the relationship between the diameter of columns at their base and the distance between the midpoints of their lowest drums. Not only was each measurement calculated to perfection (the difference between the length of the two long sides is a mere 0.1 inches) but refinements first seen in Corinth's sixth-century-B.C. Temple of Apollo were honed as never before. To trick the eye into seeing straight lines, Ictinus eliminated every genuine straight line in the building. Employing an almost imperceptible upward curvature, the stylobate swelled marginally in the centre (2.66 in. on the short sides; 4.33 in. on the long), a phenomenon repeated in the architrave. Each exterior Doric column showed subtle entasis, swelling 0.7 inches from the vertical at mid height. And because the corner columns, which at certain angles would be seen with sky, not wall behind them, would otherwise seem less substantial, they were made wider than the rest—by 1.57 inches—with slightly less space between them and the next column. Moreover, each of the 46 exterior columns inclined gently inwards, so that, were they to be extended, they would meet high above the stylobate—those on the long sides 1.24 miles and those on the short sides 3.11 miles into the sky.[14]

The quality of design was matched by that of the workmanship. No undertaking on this scale had been seen in Attica since the building programme of the first decades of democracy or the subsequent construction of the fleet, and the diversity of both workforce and raw materials was staggering. As Plutarch wrote,

> The raw materials which would be used were stone, bronze, ivory, gold, ebony and cypress-wood. The skills or crafts which moulded them were those of carpenters, modellers, coppersmiths, stonemasons, dyers, gold-workers, ivory-workers, painters, embroiderers and engravers. Also, the suppliers and hauliers of these materials, people such as merchants, sailors, ships' pilots, wagon makers, handlers of oxen and drivers for everything that was brought in overland. Also rope-makers, weavers, leatherworkers, road builders and miners. Each of these activities (like a general with dedicated troops under his own personal command) could draw on a dedicated battalion of unskilled workers, employed in a junior role in the same way as an instrument is governed by the hand or body or soul. In this way, meeting such demands, Athens' wealth was rolled out far and wide and divided among every generation and class in the city.[15]

Although Plutarch was probably projecting his knowledge of imperial Roman building programmes onto what even for him was a distant past, and even if his inference about the trickle-down effect on the Athenian economy is questionable, his inventory of artisans, tradesmen, overseers, labourers, and raw materials accurately reflects the epic nature of a project designed to build the most expensive temple in the whole Greek world.[16]

With the Middle Wall complete and the Temple of Athena and Hephaestus put on temporary hold, workmen used a mixture of repurposed limestone blocks from the unfinished Marathon temple and newly quarried stone to build the three-stepped platform. At the same time, twelve miles to the northeast on the slopes of Mount Pentelicus, gangs of labourers hewed heavy blocks of marble, iron hammers clanging on iron wedges. It was the start of a long process: the temple needed half a million cubic feet of marble. Once cut, each slab was assessed to see how it might best be used before being roughly shaped—column drums rounded, wall blocks squared to reduce their weight as much as possible before transportation—or occasionally set aside to be appraised by master sculptors looking for the raw materials from which to craft *metopēs* and pediments. Most urgent were the marble blocks for facing the platform, and, with these chosen, the first transport wagons arrived. Summer was the best time for this journey, with the ground baked hard, and mules and oxen, freed from agricultural duties, hired by the state to drag the four-wheeled carts, the heavy marble blocks strapped tight, from the mountain down the specially constructed road across the dry Eridanus into the city, where at the foot of the Acropolis, the cargo was unloaded and dragged on rollers up the ramp through the ruined gateway onto the plateau.[17]

As teams of builders—slaves and freemen working side by side, each paid alike a drachma a day—executed their skilled work, the temple started to take shape. With the stylobate complete, the lowest column drums were hoisted with cranes and set in place with crowbars. Already, sculptors had marked and chiselled out the first few inches of the twenty flutes that would eventually run up each column, their gentle undulations creating a more three-dimensional surface, taking the eye upwards, lending a sense of unity to the composite creation. In the centre of each drum, was a square socket. This housed the *empolion,* a cedar sheath, which, soaked in water, expanded to fit snugly into place encasing round dowels (lead wrapped round iron to stop it rusting and expanding and then fracturing in the salt air), which in turn helped hold the drums together. As each drum was painstakingly manoeuvred into place, stonemasons sprinkled sand onto its flat upper surface and using a stone smoothing-plate rubbed it so true to the horizontal that, when the next drum was set in place above it (lowered gently down onto the metal dowel), the join was so perfect that not even a hair could be inserted between them. So, gradually as columns rose, the temple's exoskeleton took shape. Only now did work begin on the sekos walls: marble blocks winched into place, ropes looped round bosses left protruding from the surface, and later chiselled off; double-T clamps made from purest iron smelted in furnaces at Laurium and coated (like the column dowels) in lead inserted tightly into preformed grooves to fix each block both vertically and horizontally; and, when all was done, the painstaking, backbreaking toil of smoothing down and polishing the marble—workmen poised on wooden scaffolding like an army of rhythmically moving statues, hair, skin, and tunics white with marble dust.[18]

It was now that the first sculptures must be set in place, the triglyphs and *metopēs* embedded as the course above the architrave, before the roof could be installed. For five years in ateliers on the Acropolis, master sculptors—nine men, both citizens and metics, closely supervised by Pheidias—had been working on the *metopēs,* ninety-two marble blocks, each carved in high relief, each roughly four feet square, which would be set, uniquely for a mainland temple, on each of the four sides of the new building. While their subjects were conventional enough, when all the temple's sculptures had been set in place, it would be clear that from the start their composition and arrangement had been planned with great creative genius to contribute to the overarching narrative of the entire building.[19]

Uniting all four sets of *metopēs* was the theme of conflict. On the west side, the first seen by approaching worshippers, was the

Amazonomachy. A familiar subject, it was especially piquant here since Theseus had joined the battle from the Acropolis and fought it on the plain below. There was, of course, an added layer of relevance. The legendary Amazons stood for the Persians. Both had occupied the Areopagus. But behind these apparent parallels lay a darker truth. While the Amazons had been defeated, the Persians had breached the Acropolis and destroyed the temples, which may be why the *metopēs* suggested that the Amazons might win the battle. Many showed their horses trampling dead Greeks. Very few showed an Athenian overpowering an Amazon. This was certainly deliberate. The battle would result in eventual victory for Athens, but at great cost, and it was this cost that these *metopēs*—facing west to the dying sun—suggested.[20]

To reach the altar, worshippers would generally take the processional route skirting the north side of the temple. The *metopēs* here showed the Trojan War (already juxtaposed on the panels of the Painted Stoa with the Amazonomachy and the Battle of Marathon). The sculptures showed the war unfolding: Athena leaping from her chariot to fight at Troy; the Greeks' disembarkation; and (while many of the middle sculptures are now too damaged to interpret) the city's sack—Menelaus and Odysseus storming through the streets of Troy to search for Helen; Helen taking refuge at Athena's statue, protected by Aphrodite and Eros; Theseus' son, Demophon, rescuing his grandmother, Aethra—and then, the final victory, two gods watching, absorbed, as Iris, the messenger goddess, who had once stood tall atop Callimachus' Marathon memorial, brings news to Zeus, and Hebe, goddess of youth, informs Hera, while Selene, the moon goddess, sinks into the sea.[21]

Read from left to right (from east to west) the narrative arc was clear. But this was not how worshippers encountered it. Instead, as they walked west to east towards the altar, they experienced the story in reverse, as if travelling back through time from the conclusion of the war to its beginning. Given the decision to show the action unfolding from start to finish, this was, of course, inevitable, but nothing forced Pheidias and his team to adopt this linear design, and clearly much thought had been put into its implications, not least regarding concepts of time and space. For centuries, these concepts had intrigued epic poets such as Homer (whose *Odyssey* included many abrupt changes of location and broke free of linear narrative) as well as more recent tragedians such as Aeschylus. As will be seen, both concepts were central to the sculptural programme, but what made them especially powerful here was the *metopēs*' location, facing the burnt Old Temple. These ruins, too, forced worshippers to look backwards through time as they contemplated the Persian destruction, part of an ongoing narrative of eastern hubris and Greek vengeance that stretched back to the Trojan Wars and set Athens' contemporary victories in the context of a long and legendary struggle.[22]

This journey back through time, juxtaposing the real space of the Acropolis and the heroic or divine setting of Troy, was in part preparation for the next battle, shown on the east *metopēs*. Again, the subject was familiar: the Gigantomachy, foundation myth for the Panathenaic Games, subject of the Old Temple's east pediment, the image woven every year into Athena's peplos. But here, in pride of place above the cella doors, the composition's layout was both fresh and thought-provoking. As worshippers continued their journey round the temple, the memory of the last of the north *metopēs* still vivid, they encountered on the first of the east *metopēs* the sun god, Helios, his chariot rising from the sea, a shoal of dolphins dancing at his feet. Their journey back through time along the north side of the temple had led them to the dawn of a new day—and a battle fought not just on earth but across the wider cosmos. As the viewer scanned the rest of the east *metopēs* in turn (which again meant reading them from right to left), time continued to reverse. The Gigantomachy was fought over a lengthy night. Only when the gods won did the sun rise. So, the conflict appears to unscroll backwards from victory (sunrise at the northern right-hand side) through scenes of battle, as giants grapple with gods (including from north to south Hephaestus, Aphrodite, Artemis, Apollo, Zeus and Hera, Poseidon and his wife Amphitrite, Ares, Dionysus, and at the far-left side, lithe, leaping Hermes).[23]

Most of these east *metopēs* contain two combatants—one god, one giant—but two include an extra figure. In the fourth *metopē* from

6.5 A replica in situ of the Parthenon's southwesternmost *metopē* showing a scene from the Centauromachy.

the left, Nikē, goddess of victory, stands by Athena as she fights Enceladus (the scene shown on the pediment of the Old Temple), a portent of the battle's outcome; while in the fourth *metopē* from the right, Eros, in his incarnation as a primeval creation god, overcomes his enemy with the aid of not a deity but a human—Heracles, summoned by Zeus, who, counselled by an oracle, plunged the universe into darkness, forbidding sun and moon to shine, as Athena swooped through the ether, forward in time to fetch him. It was only thanks to him that the Olympian gods won, a mortal helping them preserve their power and safeguard harmony and justice, a man, whose worth they recognized by making him a demigod.[24]

Many worshippers, their attention focussed on the altar or agalma, may never have continued round to the south side of the Parthenon, but the *metopēs* installed there could be clearly seen from streets and rooftops south of the Acropolis as well as Muses' Hill. Here the battle was the Centauromachy when drunken violence erupted at a wedding. The subject matter was familiar, but again the composition was extraordinary. Once more, it played with the idea of time, since, rather than unfolding linearly from left to right, the fighting rippled out from central scenes, which showed the wedding preparations *before* conflict broke out—the wedding dress being woven; athletic games; the bride's arrival; the groom presenting gifts; guests dancing; servants making up the marriage bed; two women standing near Athena's statue. To include these episodes in a depiction of the Centauromachy was unusual, and the symmetry of the composition lent them added focus, encouraging the viewer to reflect on what the scenes might signify and by extension on the leitmotifs that wove through all four sets of *metopēs*.[25]

The most obvious linking theme was fighting which resulted in Greek victories over more-or-less barbaric enemies. Three of those conflicts followed the abduction of a woman (the Lapith bride by Centaurs; the Amazonian queen by Theseus; Helen by the Trojan Paris), perhaps a nod to the contemporary belief that the roots of hostility between east and west that climaxed in the recent Persian Wars, lay in legendary kidnappings of princesses (Io, Europa, Medea, and Helen). These abductions spoke in turn to the sanctity of marriage, exemplified by Zeus and Hera, shown sitting side by side as they learned of Troy's capture in the north *metopēs* and fighting side by side in the east *metopēs* (together with Poseidon and *his* wife Amphitrite). But there were further links to contemporary Athens. Like other recent artworks, the *metopēs* foregrounded Theseus and Heracles (Theseus in the Amazon- and Centauromachy; his son, Demophon, at Troy; and Heracles in the Gigantomachy). Both men were believed to have gained immortality thanks to their deeds on earth, including in these battles; and, since these battles paralleled the Persian Wars, the unspoken implication was that, like Theseus and Heracles, the Athenians who fought the Persian Wars were more than human, too.[26]

This much we can extrapolate. The significance of other details remains more elusive, not least the ubiquity of horses in every set of *metopēs*, whether ridden, yoked to chariots, or fused with men as Centaurs. Lending a sense of heroism and variety to each composition, they were creatures of especial interest to Poseidon, so perhaps their prevalence not only on the *metopēs* but on the pediments and frieze was intended as a nod towards the god, a recognition of his importance in Athens' divine panoply. But what of the motif of women standing by Athena's statue, which appears both in the Centauromachy and on the scene of Troy? In each case the statue, slightly less than life-sized, and standing on a plinth, is peplos-clad, her pose stiff and archaic, facing forwards, arms held stiffly by her sides. Despite their stance, it is tempting to see in them a reference to Athena's xoanon, a further link between mythology and contemporary Athens: Athena's statue taken to Salamis was thought to have protected the Athenians; the statues on the *metopēs* are protecting Helen and the Lapith women. Further details of the Lapith wedding scene may have parallelled Athenian experience, but while the weaving of the dress, the dancing, the athletic games all had equivalents in the Panathenaic festival, other than to observe that these activities are seen occurring in the quiet eye of the storm as battle rages round them, it remains hard to see what point they may be trying to make. As for the themes of space and time, their significance would become apparent when the pediments and frieze were set in place.

The *metopēs,* too, were sculpted in the quiet eye of the storm of war. In the six years it took to complete them, Athens was conducting military operations throughout Greece—with varying degrees of success. And the kaleidoscope of international relations kept turning. As Athens' allies old and new chafed at her growing imperialism, pressure mounted for Sparta to intervene. But the Spartans were pious people. Honour-bound by the five-year treaty signed with Cimon in 451 B.C., they refused to invade Attica. But there were other ways to intervene. In 449 B.C., months after Cimon's death, they launched a proxy war ostensibly to liberate Delphi from the control of Athens' Phocian allies, but in fact to drive a wedge through Athens' mainland territories. An early Spartan victory saw Pericles himself lead his Athenians through Phocis and retake the temple, but this "sacred war" was a bellwether. By 447 B.C., as work on the Parthenon began, the treaty was running out. It was the moment for which the oligarchs of neighbouring Boeotia had been waiting. Confident of Spartan help, they overthrew Athenian-backed democrats and began the fight back to reclaim their land. Next spring, 1,000 Athenian hoplites led by one of Pericles' close friends marched into Boeotia and won a resounding victory, but on their homeward march at Coronea, at the entrance to a mountain pass, they were ambushed. Near a temple of Athena, many were slaughtered; survivors were led off as captives; and such was the Athenians' desire to free these hostages that they capitulated to demands, withdrew completely from Boeotia, and shelved their ambitions for a land empire.[27]

Athens' troubles were only just beginning. Within weeks, Euboea announced its secession from the empire. Then, as Pericles led troops east to deal with that uprising, Megara on Attica's western border revolted. Then, still worse news. An army of Sparta and her allies was massing near the Attic border. It was just like that time sixty years before, when Attica was attacked on three fronts simultaneously. At democracy's dawn, everything seemed possible, and Athens surfed the tide of victory. But now, suddenly, and unexpectedly, and with morale already dented by defeat at Coronea, Athenians seemed in danger of being outmanoeuvred. All Pericles could do was leave Euboea, face the Spartan army, and stake everything on one existential battle.[28]

Just as sixty years before, they found the enemy drawn up amid the stubble of the wheat-fields of Eleusis across the bay from Salamis. Just as sixty years before, they waited in the warm sun for the order to advance. And, just as sixty years before, what next happened was extraordinary—the enemy turning, abandoning their tight formations, shouldering their weapons, melting like a mirage into the late summer haze. The men of Athens were incredulous. With renewed vigour, they sailed back to Euboea and returned the island to Athenian control. And the next year (445 B.C.), agreeing formally to renounce Megara and certain other erstwhile allies, they signed a thirty-year peace treaty with Sparta.[29]

Without doubt, Athens had experienced a major setback. The rebellions had exposed her vulnerability, and had the Peloponnesians given battle at Eleusis, they might well have won. Whereas, thanks to the Athenians' invincible navy, they could conceivably impose their will on islands and coastal cities, by land they were no match for the combined armies of Sparta, her Peloponnesian allies, and Boeotia. The best Athens could hope was that her subjects realized rebellion was dangerous, and that her enemies kept out of Attica. This was what the treaty seemed to have achieved, and, if it was not the outcome many had been hoping for, it was by no means a poor substitute.

Moreover, the circumstances of the enemy's refusal to give battle helped boost Athenian self-belief, since, while there could be many explanations for what happened, each could be spun positively. Either the Peloponnesians had experienced a loss of nerve, in which case they were intimidated by Athens' army; or the Spartans had been bribed, which meant they could be paid off in the future. This was, in fact, the Spartan explanation—they condemned the king-commander to exile—and many believed that an entry in Pericles' end-of-year accounts "for miscellaneous needs" was further proof the bribe was paid. Others, however, suggested other reasons for the enemy's retreat: yet again Eleusis' gods had intervened to protect Attica. On 2 September 446 B.C. there was a solar eclipse. If this coincided with the invasion (whose precise date is unknown), it would have sent shockwaves through both armies. God-fearing Spartans would have seen it as an omen forbidding them to fight, while for Athenians it would have been clear evidence of divine support. Legends telling how "the blazing sun god reined in his swift-hooved horses" both while Athena was being born and during the Gigantomachy would have added a still deeper sense of gravity to the eclipse (and heightened the significance of solar darkness in new sculptures showing those mythological events).[30]

So, Athenian ambition shone as bright as ever, and Pericles' determination was undimmed. Six years earlier, his Panhellenic Congress came to nothing. Now, though, in 443 B.C. a proposal for a Panhellenic colony met with success. For four years, refugees from Sybaris in southern Italy, expelled by neighbouring Croton, had been trying to persuade mainland Greeks to help them return home. Sparta had rejected their appeal, but Athens not only saw its potential but convinced other Greeks (including Peloponnesians) to unite in establishing a new city near the former site of Sybaris, a colony which for the first time in Greek history would include settlers from a mix of poleis and ethnicities and would in consequence be truly Panhellenic.[31]

The oracle at Delphi was consulted; Apollo gave his blessing; and, close to ruined Sybaris, Thurii took shape. It was a very modern city, designed by Hippodamus, an innovative urban planner from Miletus, a flamboyant long-haired lover of cheap clothing and expensive jewellery, whose redevelopment of Piraeus with wide boulevards that radiated from its agora had been transformative. At Thurii he imposed a strict grid system: four perfectly straight boulevards (each named from a god) ran lengthwise through the city, intersected at right angles by three straight avenues. Surrounding the central agora were residential blocks, each named from Greek ethnicities or regions—Achaean, Dorian, Ionian, Boeotian, Athenian—to demonstrate the sheer diversity of Greeks who lived there side by side. But its two official founding fathers were Athenian (one, Lampon, was a celebrated soothsayer and oracle-interpreter) and with its democratic constitution and ten tribes, Thurii soon took on the feel of a new Athens transplanted into the rich soil of Italy. Among its settlers were entrepreneurs with a keen business eye, and intellectuals such as the historian Herodotus, and the ruthlessly forensic philosopher Protagoras, who was enlisted to draw up its laws. A more polar opposite of Lampon would have been hard to find.[32]

Thurii's foundation can be seen either as an exercise in cynical manipulation—another step along the road towards conflating panhellenism with Athenian imperialism and defining Athens as de facto hegemon of Greece—or as a visionary's dream, a city where Greeks of every ethnic group could live and work in harmony. But if it was the latter, it failed in its ambition. The colonists quickly became irritated with the repatriated Sybarites. Denouncing them for acting autocratically, for claiming the best land and the key offices of state, and for insisting that their wives take precedence at festivals, they massacred the very people they had come to help. Despite this, Thurii was a remarkable success for Pericles and Athens. A gateway to the wealthy west-Greek poleis of Italy and Sicily and to the wider world beyond, it opened a new chapter for Athenian ambition. Just a few years later, the one-eyed comic poet, Hermippus, could reel off an almost endless list of benefits Athenians enjoyed thanks to their bold expansionism and buccaneering business acumen:

> From Cyrene: spices and ox hide. From the Hellespont: mackerel and salt fish of every kind. . . . The Syracusans send pigs and cheeses. . . . From Egypt: billowing sails; papyrus rope. From Syria comes frankincense. Lovely Crete sends cypress wood for honouring our gods. Libya has ivory for us to trade. Rhodes supplies raisins and sweet, juicy figs. And then there are Euboean pears and juicy apples; captives from Phrygia. . . . Paphlagonia provides the acorns and sleek almonds that enhance our feasts; Phoenicia, fruit and fine bread-flour; and Carthage, carpets and soft, multicoloured pillows.[33]

Athens was thriving. Her economy was booming, her influence increasing. On her Acropolis the most perfect temple ever built was taking shape. Yet recent events had exposed vulnerabilities. While Sparta, her nemesis, had signed a thirty-year peace treaty, this would not stop Spartans probing those weaknesses, waging proxy wars, or stoking discontent in Athens' subject states, many of them already hotbeds of unrest, and ripe for revolution. At home, too, the city was increasingly divided as the implications of a century of change and innovation made themselves felt. Chief among these innovations had been the Lydian invention of coined money. As its impact filtered through society, power and status no longer became the preserve of landowners. Instead, cash-rich traders and businessmen emerged into the public eye. One was Cleaenetus, the owner of a tanning factory, whose wealth forced him to fund a chorus or dramatic trilogy in 460 B.C., and whose daughter married into an old, landed family. Another was Hagnon, a friend of Pericles, who owed his prominence to business, not to ancestry. As for Pericles himself, since the 450s B.C. he had been harnessing the power of money to seduce the voting public, persuading the Assembly to dole out daily payments to the poor as compensation for lost wages on days they served as jurors or attended public festivals.[34]

Now citizens received cash payments, too, for military service, whether they served as oarsmen, hoplites, or cavalrymen. No longer did landed gentry or yeoman farmers fight simply for the honour of protecting homes and country. These payments were important since wars were becoming more frequent. In the sixth century B.C., when networks of marriage ties (such as between the families of Cleisthenes of Sicyon and Megacles of Athens) united city-states, wars were relatively uncommon. It was only under democracy that, fuelled by the People's hunger for new subject lands and politicians' need to gain or maintain power through winning victories, warfare became so commonplace that scarce a year went by without a military campaign.[35]

Now, with the balance of politics shifting towards "new money," with conflict normalized, and with men such as Protagoras introducing new ideas, questioning long-held beliefs, and challenging traditionalists with their inflammatory visions of a world in which the gods played little or no part, new fissures—imperceptible at first—were starting to appear. Within decades they would extend, expand, and deepen to expose disturbing fault lines running through Athenian society and even impact how the citizens of Athens responded to the Parthenon.[36]

7 ATHENS ON THE CUSP

Their souls have not gone down to Hades. I have myself set them to live in heaven and shall bestow on them a glorious name.
—EURIPIDES, *ERECHTHEUS*

In spring 442 B.C., the year after Thurii's foundation, Athens held an ostracism. Tensions were running high between the leaders of two opposing factions, the progressive Pericles, and Thucydides Melesiou, nephew of Cimon, who had inherited the elder statesman's reputation for generosity towards the People and his mantel as champion of Athenian conservatives. Searching for a chink in his opponent's popularity, Thucydides had tried to use the Parthenon as leverage against him. Pericles' building programme, he railed, was both disgraceful and immoral. When the imperial (League) treasury was moved to Athens from Delos, the professed reason was to enhance security from Persian attack. But now that it was relocated, money paid each year by allies to protect them was being squandered on prettifying the city.[1]

"The Greeks must see this as an act of downright tyranny," he thundered in the Assembly. "Using contributions wrung from them by force to fight the Persians, we are gilding our city, tricking her out like some preening woman putting on a pretty face with her expensive jewels and statues and temples costing such vast sums of money." It was a powerfully appropriate image, and the parallels were plain to see: the Parthenon's stepped platform stood for the platformed footwear favoured by the city's courtesans; its creamy marble was their whitened skin; the paintwork was their makeup, and the precious stones inset into its statue were their jewellery. Thanks to Pericles, Thucydides Melesiou was none too subtly suggesting that Athens, city of the virgin goddess, was assuming the appearance of a common whore.[2]

For Pericles such slurs were tiresome. Time and again, he batted them away, albeit sometimes bending the truth. The allies, he claimed falsely, "contribute not one horse, one soldier, or one ship. All they contribute is money, which belongs not to the men who give it but to those who take it, so long as they provide the services for which they receive it." So long as Athens was providing their protection, he argued, she could use the surplus cash however she wished. The building programme would, he said, bring Athens "everlasting honour," while the work itself would "inspire every craft and skill, rouse every hand to action, and bring employment to the city, so that she both beautifies and sustains herself."[3]

Yet Thucydides Melesiou would not let up. Repeatedly, he accused Pericles of squandering public money to the detriment of the economy, chipping away at popular support, until in 443 B.C. the tide seemed to be turning. A veil of truculence descended on the city. When, in a restless Assembly—6,000 hostile faces—Pericles demanded, "Have I spent too much?," a swell of angry voices answered him, "Too much, and more!" A barrage of noise, a moment of great jeopardy. Get it wrong, and not just the building project but Pericles' political career was finished. As the chanting grew in volume, he knew that anything he said would be a gamble. So, in a daring throw of the dice, when the herald had restored sufficient silence, he announced, "In that case, the treasury can keep its money. I shall fund it all myself—and dedicate every building in my name."[4]

It was a high-risk stratagem. Aside from whether Pericles could foot the bill, there was the question of how the People would react to such an audacious proposal. The last person to fund a temple in the city was Themistocles; he had been exiled and condemned to death. Before him Hippias and Hipparchus had begun constructing their Temple of Zeus; one had been exiled; the other assassinated. With Pericles bearing a strong physical resemblance to Peisistratus, there was real danger that people would accuse him now of acting like a tyrant, too. For the tensest moment, his fate hung in the balance. Then pandemonium. Thrilled by his bravado, the Assembly roared its approval. The building project was back on track. The public purse would pay for it. It was the pinnacle of Pericles' political career. And when in spring 442 B.C. the urns were emptied and the ostracism votes counted, it was Thucydides Melesiou who found himself condemned to exile for ten years. With Pericles triumphant, all overt opposition to the building project had been crushed. As another Thucydides, the historian, would later write of Athens' constitution in those years, "On paper it was a democracy; in reality it was rule by the first citizen."[5]

So, work on the Parthenon continued uninterrupted. Much of its structure was already complete. With both marble pediments in place—blank-faced for now—heavy beams of cedar-wood shipped from Carpathus, were winched into position, resting on load-bearing columns in the cella and opisthodomos to span the full width of the sekos. Whether these rooms had ceilings, too, or whether it was possible to look up through their rafters to the roof remains unknown, but the ceiling of the peristyle outside was rich with rows of marble coffers, each delicately moulded and painted vividly with geometric patterns—white eggs, red darts against a blue background; gold stars, palmettes, and lotus blossoms; gold beading; a blue ground with a gilded floral design—and the interior may have been similarly furnished. More probably, however, it was not: in the absence of a ceiling, light could filter through translucent marble pantiles, rows of overlapping ridge tiles vertically ranked and nailed into the gently sloping roof, bathing the interior in a soft golden haze.[6]

Even with the roof in place, much remained to be done: there were the columns to be fluted, their vertical lines marked upwards with a plumbline from the grooves already cut into each lowest drum, five sculptors working on each column for roughly twenty-two days; there were the capitals to carve, the tall wooden grilles to fix between the columns of the porches, the marble blocks to smooth, thin coats of tinted wax or varnish rubbed into the walls and columns to protect them from the elements, reduce the harsh glare of sunlight on the marble, and give the outside of the building its distinctive mellow glow like creamy new-churned butter. There were the *metopēs* to paint (red backgrounds contrasting with the blue trigylphs between them); there were the metal spears and bridles to affix; there was the architrave to decorate with wide gilded meanders, a key pattern alternating with square saltires, set atop a line of gilded lotus blossoms and palmettes against a background of deep blue. And there was the frieze to sculpt and paint.[7]

Work on the frieze began immediately after the *metopēs* were finished, executed by the same small team of master sculptors. But this time they could not work in studios. Because the marble was in place already, part of the fabric of the upper sekos wall, they were obliged to climb scaffolding and work in situ 40 feet above ground level. And while previously they had created discrete *metopēs* to alternate with triglyphs (a Doric frieze), this time they would produce one continuous, uninterrupted band of sculpture (an Ionic frieze) 525 feet long, 3 feet 4 inches high, carved in low relief (at most 3 inches deep) around the top of the sekos's outer wall. The first stage of the process, almost certainly performed by Pheidias himself, was to sketch the scene onto the marble, a precise drawing of every detail of each man and woman, horse and chariot, their wheels marked out with a compass. Then, for six years, armed with chisels, drills, and rasps, the small army of sculptors chipped through these drawings to give them depth and texture.[8]

When the frieze was finished, its position high up behind the colonnade made it more difficult to see than other sculptural elements but at the same time lent a sense of privacy and intimacy. Heads craned at an angle, to perceive what it was showing in its entirety, viewers were forced constantly to move, at first because the outer columns interfered with sightlines, but then, as they engaged with it, because the sheer momentum of the design compelled them onwards with its energy and drive.[9]

Spanning the entire west side were groups of men, most young, some clothed, but others nude (a conventional visual indicator of heroism, even though, as viewers would soon see, these men together with the women who would join them on the east side seemed, in fact,

7.1 A replica of the western section of the Parthenon Frieze in situ.

to be contemporary Athenians, the first and only time that living—albeit anonymized—massed citizens were shown in temple sculptures). All were connected in some way with horses, and, in contrast to the violence of the battle with the Amazons shown on the *metopēs,* behind which this section of the frieze was set, their demeanour indicated that they were preparing for a peacetime cavalcade. Some were mounted, others standing beside horses, others apparently examining them. Since most were moving off or preparing to move off towards the left, they drew the viewer's focus towards the north side of the temple, beside which worshippers must process to reach the altar. But closer inspection revealed intriguing details. On the far right stood a young man facing south, nude but for a cloth draped over his uplifted left arm as he arranged the fabric with his right hand. To his left another young man tied his sandal, his foot resting on a rock. Behind were six unmounted horses, two rearing, flailing their front hooves, while another pair (one reined in by a stable boy with naked buttocks) were examined by a steward, making notes about them on a tablet. Still moving north, men on prancing horses alternated with unmounted colleagues, another young man tying his sandal, others readying to mount and another inspection scene. Meanwhile, among them all stood stewards and a trumpeter, all apparently waiting for the event for which they gathered to begin. The composition's jerky rhythm and its figures' arrangement—some overlapping, others discrete, some horses standing calmly, others trotting, others rearing, most facing north but some turned south—lent an air of expectation, recognizable to anyone familiar with the cavalry pageants, which were staged regularly throughout the city—in the Agora, near the Academy, near the Lyceum, in the Hippodrome.[10]

These events, too, were preceded by inspections, judges armed with styluses and tablets stalking through the throng, the air heavy with the smell of horses whinnying and scratching the dry soil. The judges approved those animals which were fit, well trained, dependable, while "those that cannot keep pace or, being wilful, do not stay in place and are unmanageable, they brand on the jaw with the sign of a wheel, and any horse so treated fails its inspection." Such displays

7.2 The southmost section of the Parthenon's west frieze.

were celebrations of the city's newfound self-sufficiency. Following the Battle of Tanagra, when the Thessalian cavalry betrayed them, Athenians had expanded their own squadrons of elite horsemen until they were 1,000 strong, a source of civic pride. Describing them, divided into their ten tribal units, performing dressage and manoeuvres, an "eye-catching spectacle," Xenophon, a near-contemporary, advised divisional commanders:

> If you spur your horse on and lead at a moderate pace, which shows a spirited horse at its liveliest and best, there will be such a constant clattering of hooves behind you, and such regular neighing and snorting, that the entire division (not just you) will make a magnificent display.[11]

Elsewhere, Xenophon described what for him would constitute an ideal cavalry pageant held in the Agora:

> For gods and mortals, who are watching, the best thing is for the cavalry to ride around the Agora, beginning at the statues of

> Hermes [on the north side] and paying homage to all the gods and shrines they meet. Once they have completed a full circuit and are back at the statues of Hermes, it would be good if they galloped by squadron across [the Agora] to the Eleusinium [the shrine to the Eleusinian gods at the south of the Agora]. . . . After this gallop, they should retrace their steps, riding back to the statues at a walk. Such a display will enable gods and men alike to take pleasure, seeing all the agreeable sights provided by men on horseback.[12]

Such preparations were shown, too, at the western end of the north frieze, where another young bare-buttocked boy was belting a friend's tunic. But soon the cavalry arranged in tribal groups was mounted, trotting, and then galloping in tight formation, before a marshal reined them in again. The dynamism of the sculptures was astounding: the sense of motion flowing through the horses' hooves; the rhythm created by the rise and fall of horses' heads; how the beasts' postures in each sequence were arranged—like frames in an animation film—conveying the impression of fast-forward movement. Similarly impressive was the sense of three-dimensional perspective created in a sculpture a mere 3 inches deep by overlapping up to eight horses and riders, whose arrangement, fanning forward, added to the sense of propulsion. To enhance the sense still further, each foregrounded section leader was set slightly ahead of his unit, some twisting round to look behind them, lending the composition a sense of unity, which was further reinforced by a technique known as isocephaly—which meant that that all the riders' heads were set at the same level. Meanwhile, their detached, dispassionate expression, and the striking similarity of their features, suggested a cool anonymity in vivid contrast to the energetic individualism of their mounts, creating a strong visual tension between the riders and their horses with their nodding heads and prancing hooves, enhancing the vivid sense of pace and tempo.[13]

Not quite halfway along the north side, the horsemen were replaced by a procession of chariots, each with a driver and a rider,

7.3 The westernmost section of the Parthenon's north frieze.

helmeted and tunicked, carrying a large round shield. Like the cavalry, the first chariots were shown at rest, but as the frieze progressed the horses gained momentum, until, the teams spaced out, they galloped at speed before reining in—at which moment the hoplite in the leading chariot was shown leaping out, preparing to run next to it on foot. With its prominent stewards and marshals, there was just one thing the scene could represent: the *apobatēs* race, part of the Panathenaic Games, specifically for Athenian participants, where armoured hoplites jumped from moving chariots before racing for the finishing line, the event commemorating Athena's victory in the Gigantomachy. Here, too, the composition exuded energy and motion, hazard, too—the leading chariot skidding to a halt, its driver throwing his weight back, pulling in the reins, his team's hooves dangerously close to the legs of a marshal, who leaps back to avoid them.

In the final section of the north frieze, the tempo changed dramatically. There were no longer any horses. Instead, bearded men bunched close walked in procession with, ahead of them, musicians playing the kithara (a large lyre) or aulos (an oboe-type wind instrument), men picking up and carrying large jugs on their left shoulders, others bearing trays of sacred cakes, and herdsmen leading sheep and heifers to be sacrificed. The tripartite arrangement of the north frieze was repeated on the south side, too, with a similar dynamic: the cavalcade of horsemen walking, galloping, then slowing down; the chariots at rest, in motion, slowing down again; the slow, stately procession with musicians, pot bearers, tray bearers, and animal handlers—although here there were no sheep, just heifers.

At the east side of the temple, the frieze showed both processions, north and south, turning in towards the centre, and as they did the tempo slowed yet further. For the first time women and girls appeared, unprecedented in Greek art for their sheer number, each bearing sacred objects—libation bowls and jugs and incense burners, the essential paraphernalia of sacrifice. In front of them, small knots of men stood talking, some leaning on walking sticks, one with his arms draped round a comrade's shoulders, many but not all facing the oncoming procession, and all apparently relaxed. Whether the fifth-century onlooker could have

7.4 The central eastern section of the Parthenon Frieze.

determined who they represented from their dress and stance is deeply uncertain. If, as is possible, they represented the ten tribal heroes, their poses may have reflected their statues in the Agora.[14]

But the identities of the seated figures occupying much of the central part of the east frieze were in no doubt. Most were immediately recognizable through iconography. Shown twice the scale of their human counterparts, they were the twelve gods of Olympus. Their postures and grouping were intriguing. First to be seen by the viewer approaching from the north was Aphrodite, holding a sunshade and pointing to the approaching procession, her son, Eros, at her knee. To her left was Artemis; then Apollo turning to address Poseidon, who tapped him lightly on the shoulder; and finally in this section, closest to the centre, muscly Hephaestus, a crutch beneath his right arm, twisted round to talk with Athena, who was clad in a flowing peplos, her spear resting on her shoulder, her aegis draped across her lap, the warlike goddess, unhelmeted, at peace.

Beyond a central scene (to which we shall return) were shown the other six Olympians. Reading inwards from the left were: Hermes with his wide-brimmed sunhat and winged sandals; Dionysus, grasping his thyrsus in his left hand, his right arm leaning on Hermes' back, as he twisted round to watch the oncoming procession; Demeter, her chin resting on her right hand, a burning torch in her left, her legs overlapping with Dionysus'; Ares, unusually unarmoured, leaning back, impatiently clutching his right knee; Hera, veiling her head, with a goddess—perhaps Hebe, wife of Heracles, or Iris—standing by her shoulder, as she turned her head around to look at Zeus, seated in majesty beside her, his left wrist resting on the low back of his throne.[15]

Separating the two groups of gods was another discrete scene involving five human figures: two young girls approaching an older woman, who occupied the midpoint of the composition, standing back-to-back with a bearded man, busying himself with a folded length of fabric and assisted by a bare-buttocked boy. The focus of the entire frieze, sited directly above the doorway to the cella, this central scene clearly carried great significance. Almost certainly, the woman at its heart was the priestess of Athena, and the girls were most likely the Arrhephoroi. Each carried a cushioned stool on her head, while one also carried a footstool. While it is unclear for whom these are intended, it is probably the two adults. As for the bearded male, his costume—a short-sleeved, ankle length, unbelted chiton—shows he is a priest, most likely the Archon Basileus, the magistrate who oversaw state religion, its festivals and ritual. The boy's identity is less certain, but he may be the temple boy, whose tasks included feeding the sacred snake with honey cakes, and whose role was celebrated in a statue near the Arrhephorion.[16]

But what are these characters doing? It is generally agreed that the fabric held by the two males is Athena's sacred peplos, woven for her close to the Old Temple on a loom erected in the presence of the Arrhephoroi. Its original paintwork would have made its identification easier: the robe was saffron yellow. Since it is apparently being folded, this is the old peplos, ready to be put away in storage, preserved with all the others from past years. The peplos which Athena is shown wearing on the frieze (immediately to the right) is, then, her newly consecrated robe. For added realism, both garments may have been painted to suggest that (like the actual peplos) woven into them in blue were scenes from the Gigantomachy, the battle shown in high relief still raging on the *metopēs* immediately in front of the east frieze. The contrast between the two representations could scarcely have been greater and was probably deliberately intended to stress that the bloody, existential battle was over, its threat so neutered that its fighting could be woven into fabric, folded and put away—a neat parallel for the Persian Wars, now won and celebrated on the temple sculptures.[17]

Keen-eyed observers may have noticed that the postures of these two male characters approximately paralleled those of the two figures occupying key positions at the extreme right of the north and west friezes respectively: the adult arranging his robes; the bare-buttocked boy belting his friend's tunic. Greek literature sometimes used a technique known as "ring composition," where ideas introduced at the beginning reappeared at the end, transformed by what had gone on in between. This is what happens here: everyday acts of handling or belting garments seen at the beginning of the frieze's narrative are transformed at its conclusion through ritual and context into a service for the goddess, performed by representatives of Athens, whose ages span the generations. But, while this episode has rightly been the focus of much modern debate, it was not the only action being performed in this key central scene. It is not even the focus of Athena or her priestess, who instead busies herself with removing what seems to be a footstool from the head of one of the Arrhephoroi. The actions of these three figures, priestess and Arrhephoroi, are independent of and unrelated to that of the priest and boy, and, while we may never know the significance of the stools and footstool, the girls' act of bringing objects to the priestess—carried on their heads, where they cannot see them—brings to mind the annual ritual of the Arrhephoria, when they carried objects from Aphrodite's Garden through the rock, to give the priestess for safe keeping.[18]

So, the five human figures of the central scene remind viewers of two major rituals performed on the Acropolis: the journey of the Arrhephoroi celebrating annual cycles of death and rebirth; and the presentation of the sacred woollen peplos with its scenes of order trumping chaos woven in the Arrhephorion near the entrance to the cleft through which Erechtheus and from him all Athenians were born. Reading from left to right, the "mission" of the Arrhephoroi is on the brink of being accomplished (the priestess has still to take the stools), while the presentation of the peplos, the fruit of their loom, is over. This scene, then, heady with ideas of death, birth, transfiguration, and cultural development, shows a transition from something still being done to something already completed with at its fulcrum the quiet yet powerful figure of the priestess—an idea which the gods on either side develop further.

On a basic level, their grouping largely mirrors their arrangement on the east *metopēs* (and perhaps the largely lost east pediment) with Hermes, Dionysus, and Ares on the left and Apollo, Artemis, Eros, and Aphrodite on the right. On a slightly more esoteric level, Athenians would know that the gods at each extremity (Hermes and Aphrodite) shared as their specific holy days the fourth of every month, while, reading from the right towards the centre of the frieze, the next three gods sat in the precise order of *their* holy days: Artemis (the sixth); Apollo (the seventh); Poseidon (the eighth). Only Athena (celebrated on the third) and Hephaestus were out of sequence. But Athens being Athena's city, and this her temple, and since she and Hephaestus ultimately parented every Athenian citizen, it was right that this couple should enjoy a prime central position, which mirrored that of Zeus, Athena's father, and Hera, his bride, Hephaestus' mother, on the left. On a wider, deeper level, however, combined with the central scene above the cella door, the arrangement of the twelve Olympians conveyed the idea familiar from other Athenian buildings and artworks, that Athenians enjoyed a special place in the gods' affections, achieving through their sacrifices and their democratic constitution heroic status close to the divine. Pheidias had explored this radical idea in his Marathon Monument at Delphi, where he set Miltiades among the gods and heroes of Attica, but here on the Parthenon frieze, thanks to the composition's scale, he had more scope for greater subtlety, and he used the iconography, positioning, and posture of his characters to brilliant effect.[19]

Pheidias may have imagined the gods sitting in a semicircle (their arrangement seems to suggest this), but viewers see the composition as linear, and when they read it from left to right the underlying ideas become increasingly clear. One of the most important duties of Hermes (on the far left) was to conduct dead souls to the Underworld; Dionysus and Demeter were two of the great figures of the Eleusinian Mysteries, with their promises of a blessed, heroic afterlife; and more than any other, Ares, god of war, was responsible for violent deaths and endings. Each of these gods overlaps the next, establishing them as a coherent grouping, and the posture of each of the quartet's members, staring fixedly towards the procession, suggests rapt anticipation. Dionysus twists round to view it. Ares clutches his knee—a visual indicator of impatience. Like them, Zeus watches as the human ritual unfolds, but unlike them he is impassive, magisterial. Unlike them, too, he sits not on a stool but on a throne, into whose front arm support is carved a sphinx, a creature associated with death and often seen in cemeteries on funerary sculptures. A small detail, it is significant, since it connects Zeus, too, albeit obliquely to the Underworld. With Hebe, wife of Heracles (bridging mortal, heroic, and divine), beside her, Hera is the first so far to turn her head away from the procession, which makes her gesture even more noteworthy: she is veiling her head, apparently abruptly, an action associated in Greek iconography with profound emotions such as grief.[20]

If passions run high among the six seated gods on the composition's left, the mood among those on the right is curiously relaxed. Two pairs of gods—Athena and Hephaestus; Poseidon and Apollo—are deep in conversation. Hephaestus and Apollo do not even look at the procession but turn to face their interlocutors, and, while Artemis, goddess of childbirth, and Aphrodite, goddess of reproduction and fecundity, so crucial to the city, do watch the approaching mortals, their attitude is casual. One hand linked through Aphrodite's arm, Artemis adjusts her clothing, while Aphrodite half reclines as she points languidly ahead, gently resting her left wrist on Eros' shoulder, as her son leans back against her knee. The apparent lack of engagement shown by many of these gods can seem perplexing, especially given their central role in Athenian life: Athena was the city's patron goddess, Hephaestus the progenitor of every citizen; Poseidon, ruled the sea, upon which Athens' military and economic power depended, while Apollo, god of Delos, father of the Ionians, and patron of the arts, was arguably the central deity of Athens' empire. But when the composition is regarded as a whole, their attitudes make perfect sense.[21]

Pythagorean philosophers, whose teachings were prevalent in Athens, associated the right hand with the good, considering a journey made from left to right to be a passage (like that made by Eleusinian initiates) out of darkness into light. Seen in the context of the intervening panel, this bipartite assembly of Olympian divinities can be understood to show a similarly evolving sequence. On the far left are four gods, each connected in some way to the Underworld and the transformative Eleusinian Mysteries, all eager for the arrival of procession and sacrifice; then comes the pivotal scene introduced by Hera turning emotionally to adamantine Zeus: the Arrhephoroi approaching Athena's priestess, the archon and boy whose actions denote a rite completed, with this sense of relaxation following the climax of the ritual imbuing, too, the grouping on the right, where gods central to Athenian civilization, its commerce, empire, and regeneration converse, perhaps about the city's future. From death comes life. Out of the heroic past emerges the heroic future.

Beginning with Hermes, Dionysus, and Demeter, gods of death and Eleusinian transfiguration, the sequence climaxes with Aphrodite and Eros, each of whom has an interest in new life and plays a key role in the rituals of the central panel—Aphrodite's Gardens were the turning point of the Arrhephoroi's journey, while runners brought the torch flame from Eros' altar at the Grove of Academus onto the Acropolis to light the altar fire for sacrifices prior to the presentation of the peplos to Athena. The frieze, then, culminates in scenes that must be read as speaking to the death and rebirth or transfiguration of the city, and the arrangement of the figures of the east frieze works at many levels to convey a patriotic message: about Athens, her temples destroyed in the Persian Wars but now rebuilt, her power demolished but now greater than before; about her destiny, favoured by the gods, who have accepted and delighted in her sacrifices, and in consequence cooperate to ensure her future greatness; about Athenians themselves, the children of gods, who through deeds and devotion can (like Heracles and Theseus) enter into the gods' presence and achieve heroic status.[22]

Familiar from other contemporary artworks, this controversial notion was embedded in the central scene with its human protagonists flanked by Athena on the right and Zeus, the only male god with an exclusive sanctuary on the Acropolis, on the left. The journey of the Arrhephoroi embodies the idea of death and rebirth, their annual Athenian ritual on behalf of the entire polis mirroring Eleusinian rites promising personal salvation, and—reading left to right—the entire central composition echoes their descent into darkness as if to death (a journey associated with Hermes), and back into the light from the Gardens of Aphrodite, through the vulvar cleft of the Acropolis. On the frieze they carry not "unspeakable" objects, but footstools, intended for Athena's priestess and the Archon Basileus, the Athenians' representatives, whose pose, if they were to sit on them, would resemble that of the twelve gods, transcending their human status like Heracles on entering Olympus.[23]

Other details add to the suggestion that the Athenians are imagined not simply as worshipping the gods or even just approaching them on earth. We have seen how the *metopēs* took the viewer on a journey from the physical setting of the Acropolis (the Amazonomachy) through time (the backward-moving Trojan War) towards the otherworldly setting of the Gigantomachy. When the pediments were installed, six years later, they too would show the action of the west side rooted physically on the Acropolis (the contest of Athena and Poseidon appearing for the first time in sculptural art), and the east side (Athena's birth) set in the celestial world of gods. So, it is more than probable that the frieze embraced the same concept, in which case, the procession, too, should be imagined moving from a physical to metaphysical realm, where Athenians can share the same space as the gods (as initiates believed they did at Eleusis). Each morning the deep shadows of the building's west side contrasting with the dazzling sun-washed east confirmed the nature of that journey from darkness into

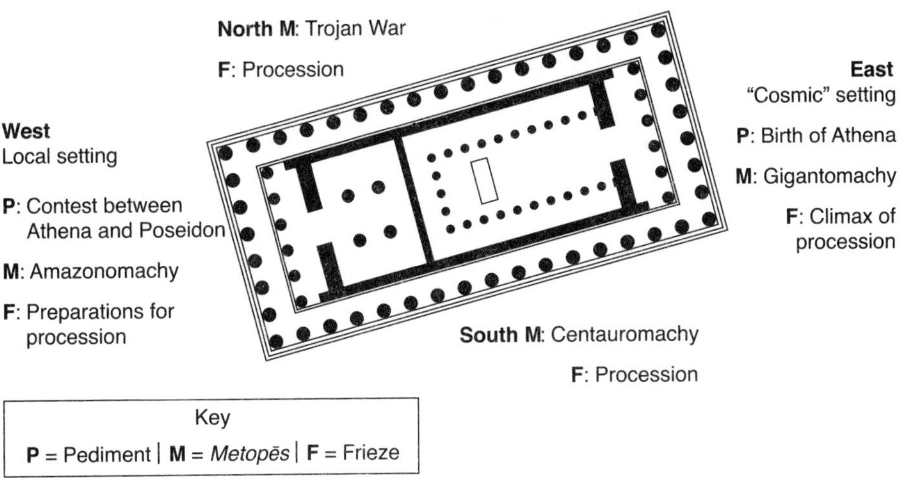

7.5 The "Sacred Journey" from the west to east of the Parthenon.

light, familiar not only to the Arrhephoroi and the many followers of Pythagorean teaching but to all Eleusinian initiates, as they recalled the blinding climax of the Mysteries with their promise of a better life to come.[24]

Citizens transformed into heroes: never before had temple sculptures carried such a revolutionary message. Earlier buildings had shown sculptural processions. Carved on the columns of the Temple of Artemis at Ephesus were men and women in procession with cattle taken to an altar to be sacrificed. That temple's frieze, too, showed parading horsemen, chariots, and riders interspersed with seated figures, as well as wars with Amazons and centaurs. Processing figures once adorned the outer sekos walls of the Temple of Cybele at Sardis. And, in Persia at the palace of Persepolis, carved files of subject peoples approached the presence of the Great King, bearing the tribute that was evidence of their oppression. Had the outcome of the Persian Wars been different, these subject peoples would have included the Athenians. Instead, by contrast, on the Parthenon frieze, a free people, transfigured and heroic, they were entering the presence of their gods.[25]

The frieze, then, was intended not simply to replicate or represent the Panathenaic procession (though it, too, took worshippers from the

Cermeicus Cemetery's dead zone to the divine precinct of the Acropolis), but to transcend it. The cavalcade and *apobatēs* race were certainly both features of the Panathenaic Games, and the eastern sections of the frieze did show processing worshippers. But metics took part in the Panathenaic procession, their daughters carrying large water jars—on the frieze it is Athenian male citizens who carry them, and when painted it could probably be seen that metics, who marched in purple tunics, were not included in the sculptures of this most Athenian of temples, only Athenians. Even more significantly, while the Panathenaic procession was held in honour of Athena alone, the procession on the frieze showed Athenians being welcomed by all twelve Olympian gods. "Throughout the year," Pericles would later say, "we hold games and sacrifices," and rather than being simply a snapshot of the Panathenaic procession, the frieze imagined an idealized parade in honour of all Athens' gods, a distillation of an entire year's worship, an expression of the city's piety, and of its sacrifice not just of cows and sheep but of its land and men over so many decades. While here the worshippers are bringing beasts to slaughter, it implies that they are equally prepared to sacrifice themselves for Athens—which is perhaps why Pheidias showed them to be impassive and anonymous. The sacrificial victim needed to approach the altar willingly, without emotion. Nonetheless, the frieze did include some elements from the Panathenaic procession, not least the presentation of the peplos and the inclusion of the sheep on the north frieze. Whenever heifers were sacrificed to Athena, religious law demanded sheep be sacrificed to Pandrosus/Pandora, the faithful princess, role model for the Arrhephoroi, who obeyed the goddess by not opening the casket that contained Erechtheus. "Whoever sacrifices a cow to Athena," the law stated, "must sacrifice a ewe to Pandrosus/Pandora." This was the sacrifice suggested by the sheep shown on the north frieze, included not simply for ritual accuracy, but highlighting Pandrosus/Pandora's importance on the Acropolis and throughout Athens. And, while their position on the north frieze reflected the geographical reality of the Acropolis (sacrifices to Pandrosus/Pandora were made north of the Parthenon), the siting of these sculptures beside the Sacred Way along which worshippers processed towards Athena's altar lent them greater visibility. At the same time, at the climax of the frieze above the cella doors, the juxtaposition of the peplos ritual in honour of Athena and a ritual performed by the Arrhephoroi, devotees of Pandrosus/Pandora, showed how closely goddess and heroine were linked in the life of the Acropolis.[26]

Pandrosus/Pandora would be further honoured on another major sculpture. As the frieze neared completion, in the cella, the huge statue, the agalma, of Athena was being constructed. Years of highly skilled, painstaking work had gone into its preparation, but not in the building site that was the Parthenon. In a specially built studio, perhaps on the Acropolis, Pheidias had supervised and personally worked on its construction in such a way that, once completed, it could be dismantled, transported to the cella, and reassembled there. At its core was an immense beam of cypress wood, 2 by 2.5 feet wide, which like the mast of an outsized trireme ran the full height of the statue and was sunk through the plinth (itself faced with Pentelic marble—and Eleusinian limestone) some 14 inches down into the temple floor. Attached to this was a massive hollow framework, an armature of cypress and citrus woods, specifically chosen to resist insect infestation and withstand decay, a network of poles and battens, beams and wedges, which once in situ were coated with tar and clay to ensure stability and form. On top of this substructure the statue's wooden shell was set in place, and over this a thin veneer of gold and ivory.[27]

Towering 40 feet tall, it showed Athena not as she appeared outside in the bronze Athena Promachus, helmet down, spear brandished, ready for the fight, gazing to the pale-blue hills of Salamis, but at rest. She was still dressed for battle—her aegis slung over her peplos, the severed Gorgon's head hung round her neck, her left hand resting on her great round shield, her spear propped by her shoulder—but that battle was now won. Details on Athena's triple-crested helmet spoke of triumph and sacrifice. Its cheek pieces were folded back, no need now to protect her face, while its triple horsehair crests were secured by fixings in the shape of three totemic creatures: a sphinx (symbol of death, linking the helmet to the front arm support

7.6 Conjectured replica of Pheidias' statue of Athena Parthenos in Nashville, Tennessee.

of Zeus' throne on the east frieze), flanked on either side by griffins (appropriate for a priceless statue and a building doubling as the imperial treasury, since griffins were believed to be the fiercest guardians of gold). And to underscore the message of a battle won, Athena stretched her right hand out towards the temple doors, while dancing on her palm was Nike, winged goddess of victory, 6 feet tall, holding a victor's garland.[28]

The agalma embodied the triumph of Athena, her city, and her people, and its cost was staggering: some 700 talents, enough to pay for 200 new triremes, and half as much again as the 450 to 500 talents spent on constructing the temple. Around 40 talents (10,000 times a craftsman's annual salary) went on the ton of gold, which, hammered into thin strips, was moulded round the wooden shell, attached by tiny nails to gild Athena's peplos, aegis, sandals, shield-face, spear, and helmet, all polished to such glittering intensity that its curving, folded surface shimmered with myriad reflections. This gold was not just for display. As easily as it was attached, in an emergency it could be removed, "borrowed," and melted into coinage, on the proviso that when times improved it would be all replaced.[29]

Athena's flesh—her face, arms, hands, and feet—was rendered in an ivory veneer. Greek craftsmen had worked ivory for centuries, but the process of making it malleable was complex. Elephants' tusks are formed from thin layers of dentine, which could be unrolled into sheets up to 45 feet long, and a mere thirtieth of an inch thick, before, softened by heating them, soaking them in beer, or boiling them with mandrake root, they took on the pliability of wax. Then they could be moulded, glued onto a statue, fixed in place with dowels, and coloured to achieve the smooth effect of skin. Thus, the agalma's cheeks and lips glowed rosy pink while olive-grey-green glass fixed into its eye sockets made the goddess seem to gaze, unblinking, at her worshippers, her benign expression the antithesis of the petrifying stare of the Gorgon, whose severed head (likewise in ivory) warded off evil. To see the statue standing in the cella's half-light, gleaming, radiating back the morning sunlight streaming through the open door and windows, it must have seemed to worshippers as if they had come into the presence of Athena herself.[30]

The concept and design belonged to Pheidias, but its execution involved teams of expert artisans and craftsmen: merchants and suppliers to source and acquire raw materials; carpenters and metalworkers; modellers and mould-makers; engineers and logisticians to consult on structural stability and transport. All had to be coordinated, supervised, consulted; anxious egos needed to be massaged, artistic temperaments placated; problems needed to be solved. For Pheidias, not only working on the statue but masterminding the entire new building project, the stress must have been almost unimaginable. But by 438 B.C., when the albeit still-unfinished temple was consecrated at the Great Panathenaic Festival, the agalma was already installed, with, in front of it a shallow rectangular pool of water, both to prevent the wood and ivory from drying out and cracking in the salty air, and to reflect light up onto its gleaming robes, where ripples would imbue the statue with astonishing vitality.[31]

The glimmer of gold, the glow of ivory, the flash of inlaid silver, copper, bronze and glass and coloured stones—all emphasized the opulence of this towering Athena. But further refinements added to its sophistication. For the first time in Greek art, Pheidias had made visual links between a statue and its temple's *metopēs*. Thus, the Centauromachy was sculpted on the rim of Athena's sandals; the Amazonomachy was sculpted on the outside of her shield (the composition of at least one grouping identical to the *metopēs*); and the Gigantomachy was painted on the inside of her shield. Only the Trojan War was not replicated on the statue. This was the third time the Gigantomachy appeared on or in the temple, and each time it was presented differently—on the *metopēs* in high relief; on the frieze imagined woven into the peplos; and here, painted in two dimensions—a reminder of the myth's pervasive significance. But equally striking was how the Gigantomachy and Amazonomachy were placed on both temple and shield. The side first facing the viewer (the front of the shield, the temple's west façade) showed the Amazonomachy; the side closer to the goddess (the shield's back; the east *metopēs* above the cella door) showed the Gigantomachy, suggesting an equivalence between temple and shield, both in their own way a bulwark for the city.[32]

Another myth was carved on the agalma's plinth—white marble, gold or gilt bronze figures set into dark Eleusinian limestone. In the second century A.D., guides told the traveller, Pausanias, that they showed the birth of Pandora, prompting him to gloss: "Hesiod and other poets tell how this Pandora was the first woman; before Pandora was born, the race of womankind did not exist." If Pausanias understood his guide correctly, it was a curious subject for the plinth. Not simply the first woman, but a "savage beauty," this Pandora wilfully disobeyed orders, opened a storage jar, unleashing pain and pestilence on humankind. Unless it was intended as a warning against hubris, hers was not a story that sat easily with images of victory so carefully curated elsewhere on the temple. Instead, it is more likely that Pausanias mistook his guide (or that the guide was himself confused). He meant, of course, Pandrosus/Pandora, the archetypal Arrhephoros, her identity confirmed by the coiling serpent that reared above the plinth, the embodiment of Athens' King Erechtheus, entrusted by Athena to Pandrosus/Pandora's care.[33]

The correct identification of Pandrosus/Pandora makes the plinth's significance clear. The east pediment would show another birth, Athena's, so together these east-facing sculptures (pediment and plinth) celebrated births of two key figures, goddess and heroine, linked through real-life sacrifices on the Acropolis, which were replicated on the temple's frieze. The plinth's loss and the lack of a proper description prevent proper understanding of other potential links, but, viewing it in the first century A.D., Pliny the Elder recorded that the birth was accompanied by more than twenty gods. This suggests a composition similar to that of the east pediment, where groups of gods flanked Athena's birth, and also the east frieze, where groups of gods flanked central scenes showing the Arrhephoroi (Pandrosus/Pandora's "successors") with footstools together with the folding of the peplos, woven in their house. Foregrounding Pandrosus/Pandora and her Arrhephoroi in such key locations highlights their importance. With the agalma erected and the temple consecrated, this would have been even more apparent. Originally positioned next to Athena's chryselephantine statue was her ancient xoanon, on which the priestess and Arrhephoroi lavished such care, two contrasting incarnations of the goddess standing side by side—the one, ancient and venerated, expressing religious devotion; the other, extravagant and lavish, projecting imperial power.[34]

With agalma and xoanon in place, the same basic team of nine who carved the frieze and *metopēs* (perhaps now joined by Pheidias' star pupil, Agoracritus) began work on the pedimental sculptures. Again, their design was likely planned and drawn by Pheidias himself, but he did not supervise their execution. Now that the Parthenon was largely finished, and the sculptural programme for the other temples worked out, he left Athens for Olympia to build another statue. Like the agalma of Athena, it would be 40 feet tall, faced in gold and ivory, inlaid with glass and precious jewels, and holding a dancing Victory in its outstretched right hand. But this time its subject would be Zeus, the god seated in majesty, dominating the cella of the temple built two decades earlier, so impressive that in centuries to come it would be thought a wonder of the world.[35]

The Parthenon's pedimental sculptures were equally impressive, carved in the round with such perfection that even the backs of figures, which, once placed, no human eye would ever see, were rendered in painstaking detail. Sculpted in workshops on the Acropolis, they were painted and perhaps placed on temporary exhibition, before being winched delicately and precisely into place with massive cranes and fastened to the gable ends with metal dowels and spikes, or L-shaped clamps. Huge, heavy, and imposing, with some elements breaking out from their triangular frame to add energy and vigour, like the *metopēs* and frieze their subject matter underlined the differences between the thought worlds of the temple's west and east façades. The west pediment celebrated Athena's contest with Poseidon for the control of Attica. Like the Amazonomachy *metopēs* below it, the episode took place in Athens on the Acropolis itself, as nearby tokens (Athena's olive tree; the marks of Poseidon's trident) proved. Its vivid composition anchored the scene in space. Flanked by anthropomorphised local river gods (Ilissus to the south, Cephisus or perhaps Eridanus to the north, reflecting their real geography), the two gods leapt from chariots, whose horses reared beside them, Poseidon with his trident striking the rock as water bubbled up, Athena showing off her olive tree, fresh-planted, and already heavy with fruit. Between them, Zeus wielded his thunderbolt, poised to intervene to prevent violence and enlist King Cecrops as arbitrator. The outcome hung in the balance, but visual clues showed how it would end. Battle scenes in art traditionally placed victors on the left, which is where Athena was located on the pediment, while accompanying her as charioteer was Nike, goddess of victory.[36]

On either side of the two gods cowered mortal or heroic onlookers. Among those on Athena's side were Cecrops (complete with snaky tail), Pandrosus/Pandora, other members of his family (including, perhaps, Ion and Creusa), and early kings of Athens, while behind Poseidon, mirroring them, was the royal family of his power base, Eleusis. The subsequent destruction of many of the sculptures means that there can be little certainty, and we cannot tell with what degree of confidence first viewers could identify specific figures. However, like the other Parthenonic artworks, it is likely that the composition conveyed layers of meaning. Superficially, it commemorated Athena's legendary rivalry with Poseidon, whose resolution united their two cities and strengthened Attica. But on a deeper level, it resonated with other themes: the concept of a mortal—here her father, Cecrops; Heracles on the east *metopēs*—being enlisted by the gods, when problems threatened to upset their harmony; and the close links between Athens and Eleusis, not least between the rituals of Pandrosus/Pandora and the Eleusinian Mysteries.[37]

In keeping with the *metopēs* and frieze, the location of the scene shown on the east pediment shifted to the realm of the divine, with the action flanked not by river gods, suggesting place, but the sun and moon, drawing attention to the concept of time. It focussed on the moment immediately following Athena's birth after what mythographers called the night of the "dark moon," the first time the scene appeared on temple sculpture (the east pediment of the Temple of Athena and Hephaestus in the Agora was sculpted slightly later). The goddess took centre stage, where, although they, too, are badly damaged, it is likely that the figures showed Athena, newly born but fully adult, fully armed, having just emerged from Zeus' head, with Zeus enthroned beside her, and on his other side Hephaestus clutching the axe with which he had delivered her. Surrounding them were other gods—Dionysus to the left, luxuriating on a panther skin, with Demeter and Persephone close by, and Artemis and Aphrodite on the right, mirroring their positions on the east frieze. Like the west pediment, the scene could be interpreted on different levels. Athena's birth was, of course, central to her worship, celebrated in festivals and hymns, where (as we have seen) the choreography of the nativity was sometimes stressed:

> *For long, long hours the blazing sun god*
> *reined in his swift-hooved horses until from her deathless shoulders*
> *the maiden, Pallas Athena, removed her divine armour.*[38]

The composition emphasised this timing: on the left the sun god urged his eager chariot team up into the sky, while on the right the horses of the moon, exhausted, sank beneath the waves. Meanwhile, the pediment itself was primed to interact with the real rising sun. Drill holes reveal how horses' manes were enhanced with metal extensions, and other elements, too, were cast in metal and fixed onto the marble, so that at dawn they flashed and shimmered.[39]

Furthermore, this emphasis on daybreak underscored the links between the birth scenes of the pediment and statue base (where Pandrosus/Pandora's birth was also flanked by the rising sun and setting moon and attended by a multitude of gods) as well as between the pediment and east *metopēs,* showing the sun god in his chariot. There his rising marked the end of a long battle, when time had again been temporarily frozen. The vision of a longed-for dawn, a victory, and a new birth had surely resonated with Athenians for decades following the Persian Wars. So, Athena's rebirth on the sculptures every morning mirrored her city's rebirth, an idea suggested in the culmination of the frieze, the arrangement of whose gods—Eleusinian deities on the left, others including Aphrodite on the right—may have been largely replicated on the pediment.[40]

Even in their ruined state the sculptures' brilliance shines through: the energy rippling outwards from the central scene; the liquid flow of drapery, the plasticity of form, the stylised and geometric, almost cubist, rendering of the heads of the moon goddess's exhausted horses with their bulging eyes, their flaring nostrils, and their flapping lips. Yet, masterpieces though they are, they were designed to convey a political message, telling of Athens' unique place in the gods' affections and of her citizens' status equal to that of heroes. The subject and positioning of each sculptural element were carefully curated to underline this message: the *metopēs* highlighting the triumph of human demigods (Theseus over centaurs and Amazons, Heracles over Giants); the procession on the frieze, its iconography suggestive of the concept of the hero, since in Greek art heroes were invariably represented in the company of horses as athletic young men, purged of emotion; the journey from the west side of the temple, showing myths embedded in the soil of Athens via the north *metopēs* through time and space to the east façade with its visions of Athena's birth, the Gigantomachy and Athens' citizens interacting with their gods, a transcendental journey to the realm of the divine otherwise reserved for demigods and heroes.[41]

Also lost are other known or conjectured sculptural details, chief among which is the chryselephantine Ionic frieze which some suggest ran round the cella's interior, holes for whose fittings may survive in the marble. No source mentions this frieze, and, while there is evidence for more ivory being sourced than was needed for the statue, this could have been used to decorate the cella doors. It is, however, an intriguing thought, and if this frieze did exist its subject matter almost certainly tied in with themes shown elsewhere in the temple. It will probably remain forever an unknown. Regarding the acroteria we can be more certain: stylized marble renditions of interweaving palm branches sprouted from the apex of each pediment, while to the lower corners golden statues of winged victories were fixed, as if they were about to launch themselves into the skies of Attica.[42]

The most decorated temple in the entire Greek world, the Parthenon was a work of enormous complexity: part offering to the city's goddess and home for two iconic statues, the xoanon and the agalma; part statement of Athenian hegemony; part treasury; part testament to the brilliance of Athens' craftsmen; part celebration of victories past, present and future; and, through the medium of sculpture, part declaration of Athenians' unique identity as a people who, thanks to their sacrifice and efforts, had (as they would have it) achieved superhuman status. Speaking at the end of Euripides' now fragmentary tragedy, *Erechtheus,* performed a decade or so after the completion of the Parthenon, Athena says of Erechtheus' daughters, who gave their lives for Athens: "Their souls have not gone down to Hades. I have myself set them to live in the heavens and shall bestow on them a glorious name." Like Aeschylus' verses a generation earlier, defining heroes as "those close in birth to gods, those close to Zeus, in whom divine blood is not extinct," they were lines that might encapsulate the spirit of the Parthenon.[43]

So, too, might lines from Homer's *Iliad,* the poem that gave Greeks their identity. To protect Achilles as he went to battle, Hephaestus made a shield, which the poet describes in detail. At its centre were engraved the sun and moon and stars, with, moving outwards, "two lovely cities of mortal men. In one were marriages and feasting. . . . But around the other lay two armies clad in shining armour." And around it all, on its outer rim appeared the River Oceanus, which Greeks believed encircled the whole earth. The parallels between this shield and the sculptures of the Parthenon were striking. The action of the temple's pediments, too, was bounded by on one side rivers and the other heavenly bodies, while in its *metopēs* and frieze it, too, showed scenes of war contrasted with a city and its gods at peace. Moreover, as we saw earlier, Pheidias, a man who spoke of finding inspiration in the *Iliad,* had taken pains to draw attention to the idea of the temple as a shield by repeating themes shown on the temple's *metopēs* on the outside and interior of the agalma's shield. So, it is not unlikely that Athenians, familiar with Homer's set piece description, drew parallels between their own new temple and Achilles' shield, forged by their divine ancestor, Hephaestus, for a fighter destined to become a demigod.[44]

For most Greeks, the temple, with its high security, its wooden grilles, its fabulously costly statue, and its opisthodomus crammed with priceless treasures, was evidence of Athens' power and wealth. In 422 B.C., around the time Euripides staged his *Erechtheus,* an inventory of its treasury included gold libation bowls, gold wreaths, a gilt mask, silver libation bowls, incense burners, helmets, breastplates, swords and shields, two styles of couches, ivory-inlaid tables, a gilt-and-ivory-inlaid flute case, Persian daggers, coins and uncoined gold. Fusing high art with flagrant grandstanding, the Parthenon, like the rest of the ongoing building programme, reflected the increasing bipolarity of Athens, a beacon of democracy that ruled an empire like a tyrant with an iron fist. By 432 B.C., when the last sculptures were craned in place and the temple stood, completed, fissures already cobwebbing a decade earlier throughout the city's fabric had split still wider. In contrast to the harmony imagined on the temple's frieze, Athens was becoming dangerously fractured. A new generation was emerging, which had not experienced the Persian invasions. New values were challenging old moral standards. New ways of thinking were confronting long-held certainties. The city was mutating, and in the vanguard of its metamorphosis was Pericles.[45]

8 FRACTURES AND FISSURES

Man born of mortal woman cannot discover the gods' plans with his merely mortal mind.

—PINDAR, FRAGMENT 61

In 449 B.C., as work on the Temple of Athena and Hephaestus began in Athens' Agora, a team at Eleusis led by Ictinus began an ambitious project to enlarge the capacity of the Telesterion (Initiation Hall) for up to 3,000 initiates. Twice the width of its unfinished predecessor, at 167 feet square and over 50 feet high, with a central lantern window set above the inner sanctum, it would be the largest indoor space on the Greek mainland, its west side cut into the living rock of the adjacent hill, its roof supported by twenty internal columns. But almost immediately Ictinus was recalled, reassigned to focus on the Parthenon. His replacement, Coroebus, amended the design. Two storeys high, his Telesterion would still be built out of iconic, spiritually potent, Eleusinian limestone, but now seven rows of six internal columns would support the roof. For initiates thronging the eight shallow steps that ran around the walls, sightlines were of secondary importance. Disorientated in the darkness, bewildered by the jostling and din that had accompanied their entrance to the hall, awestruck by the performance of the sacred drama, and dazzled by the climactic blaze of light, their senses altered by a psychoactive drink, they were probably aware of the great crowds, but little else. The experience was intensely personal. No one emerged unchanged,

8.1 Steps and column bases of the Telesterion at Eleusis.

which was why the iconography of Eleusis pervaded so much of the Attic building programme.[1]

Hosting the annual enactment of a sacred drama, the Telesterion was not the only new performance venue with a complicated roof. Also begun in 449 B.C., the Odeon was sited on the south slope of the Athenian Acropolis on a terrace east of the Theatre of Dionysus (also perhaps renovated at this time). It would be Athens' largest indoor concert hall, home to the music competitions which Pericles added to the Panathenaic Festival (with himself as judge). Surrounded by a colonnade, its roof rising sharply to a central apex, the building was almost square, and, like the Telesterion, its huge dimensions demanded a profusion of internal columns. To enhance acoustics, the entire Odeon was built of wood. Its materials and design had political resonance, too. Said to have been modelled on a huge Persian tent, reputedly belonging to the Great King himself, abandoned at Plataea, its ninety internal columns were supposed to have been made from masts of Persian warships captured at the Battle of Salamis. No matter whether this was true, like the Parthenon the Odeon proved how victory in war could lead to cultural renaissance, an arts venue on whose raised stage surrounded by many rows of seats beneath a smoothly sanded roof virtuosi on the lyre and aulos competed for amphoras of sacred oil, and rhapsodes sang Homeric poems of Greeks triumphing over Asiatic Troy.[2]

Victory over Persia was the gift that kept on giving. With a view over the tyrants' unfinished Temple of Zeus to the Acropolis, on a hill-side above the River Ilissus, where plane trees cast their shade, cicadas chirring in their branches, a temple was erected in the early 430s to Artemis Agrotera (the Huntress), to whom Athenians had vowed to sacrifice a goat for every Persian killed at Marathon. On the anniversary of victory each September, worshippers accompanied by young men in armour drove fifty goats to slaughter in the sanctuary, the statue of the goddess with her bow, now housed in an exquisite temple, a tiny jewel-like building with a deep porch and an almost square cella. Designed by Callicrates, with four slim Ionic columns front and rear, its long uncolonnaded side walls were enhanced with decorative mouldings. Above these an Ionic frieze ran round the building but surviving fragments, which show men seated on rocks along with scenes of violence—running hoplites, a woman clinging to an altar for protection, the abduction of women and children—are too scanty to interpret.[3]

Meanwhile, throughout Attica, temples were being built at such a rate that, rather than design each individually, architects followed the same basic blueprint as the Temple of Athena and Hephaestus in the Agora. The first was on the clifftop at Cape Sunium, whose early democratic temple to Poseidon had still been incomplete when Persia's army torched it. It was near these ruins that the Greeks set up a captured trireme after Salamis and, following the war, Athenians erected a temporary shrine for Poseidon close to the cliff edge, together with a stone Temple of Athena on a low hilltop nearby. Surrounded on two sides by a colonnade, and furnished with unfluted columns and a simple, packed earth floor, it was a curiously modest building, perhaps deliberately calculated not to provoke the sea god's jealousy. Considerably more impressive was the new Temple of Poseidon begun in 444 B.C. Built from relatively soft but dazzling white marble from

8.2 The Acropolis and retaining wall of the Sanctuary of Olympian Zeus from the Temple of Artemis Agrotera.

local quarries, the temple and its setting high above the sea were as commanding as the Parthenon on the Athenian Acropolis. Running round all four internal walls of its east portico were Ionic friezes, carved, like the pedimental sculptures, from Parian marble. Not completed until after 421 B.C., they showed familiar scenes: facing east above the cella door, the Gigantomachy; opposite, the Centauromachy; and along both shorter side walls, the deeds of Theseus, Poseidon's son. Linked thematically to sculptures already seen on other temples paralleling the Persian Wars and celebrating humans heroized for bravery, the frieze conveyed a message of Athenian exceptionalism and divine approval. Perhaps this was communicated on the pedimental sculpture, too, but all that remains of these is one fragment of a seated woman.[4]

The next temple to join the matrix of those modelled on the Temple of Athena and Hephaestus was dedicated at Pallene east of Athens to Athena and Apollo, together patrons of Ionians, the Delian League, and Athens' empire. Built in Pentelic marble and aligned with Delos, thanks to its unusual history (the entire building was relocated to

Athens by the Roman Emperor, Augustus, reconsecrated to Ares, and later destroyed), only fragments of its sculptures survive. But reconstructions suggest that the east pediment showed Athena, wearing the triple-crested helmet familiar from her statue in the Parthenon, sending Theseus to fight the sons of Pallas, when they tried to depose him (a further link with the Temple of Athena and Hephaestus). The west pediment, too, may have shown the goddess (wearing the single-crested helmet identifying her in her role of Polias) dispatching Theseus on another mission, but there is too little evidence to suggest which one. In addition, two sets of *metopēs* foregrounded Theseus, one showing him fighting the sons of Pallas, the other the ubiquitous Amazonomachy, both celebrating Theseus' (and by extension Athens') triumph over wrongdoers.[5]

The third temple modelled on the Temple of Athena and Hephaestus was built for Nemesis, goddess of retribution. Shared with Themis, goddess of justice, its site, a hilltop above Attica's east coast at Rhamnous, seven miles north of Marathon, was of deep mythological significance. Legend told how, as Nemesis tried to escape the lustful Zeus, both changed into swans, skimming the Aegean, until at Rhamnous the exhausted goddess could resist no longer, and from her resulting swan's egg was born Helen, whose abduction sparked the Trojan War. The war's end was shown inside the temple. Faced with Pentelic marble and crowned with a grey slab of Eleusinian limestone, low-relief sculptures on the front and sides of the cult statue's plinth showed Helen being led home to Nemesis by her foster mother, Leda, accompanied by Greek heroes, through whose courage the goddess of retribution had punished Asiatic Trojans, an outcome paralleling Persia's defeat at nearby Marathon.[6]

Perhaps there was a still more potent link between the temple and the battle. The statue of Nemesis was noteworthy enough—almost 12 feet tall, her robes flowed loose; she held an apple branch in her left hand, and in her right a cup, carved with barbarians; and on her head she wore a crown picked out with figures of winged Victory and deer. But even more noteworthy may have been the marble from which it was carved. According to later tradition, the Persians, "convinced that nothing would stand in the way of their overrunning Attica, brought with them a block of Parian marble, to raise a trophy to commemorate their deeds." It was from this very block, a Roman-era tour guide swore, that Pheidias had made the statue. He was wrong about the sculptor. It was Pheidias' pupil, Agoracritus. Carried away by the neat idea of how the stone so redolent of Persian hubris was carved into the goddess of revenge, he was probably wrong about the marble, too. But the story is a reminder of the importance of provenance. The guide invested the marble with a similar significance and potency to that which Eleusinian limestone apparently possessed. At Rhamnous on the statue base as well as in the Parthenon and many other Attic temples this limestone was redolent of Eleusis' promise of rebirth. And now it was being built into the very portal to the Acropolis itself.[7]

In 437 B.C. with the Parthenon structurally complete, work shifted to the Propylaea, the monumental entrance complex, built in Pentelic marble and intended both to give security and, by reflecting the Parthenon's proportions and design, to add beauty and coherence to the entire Acropolis. In charge of the project was Mnesicles, an architect of whom we know too little. His brief to design a composite but coherent arrangement of gateways and side chambers on unforgivingly uneven ground was demanding. He rose to it with aplomb. His first decision was to shift it off its predecessor's axis, so that it not only aligned precisely with the Parthenon, but, looking outwards through its open doors, framed perfectly the distant hills and bay of Salamis. Like the Parthenon, the Propylaea was a monument to victory.[8]

So, covering the west face of the Acropolis, the Propylaea reflected the Parthenon, but it was not slavishly identical. Approached by a ramp that zigzagged up the steep incline, the Propylaea's façade was in effect a narrower version of the temple's west one with six Doric columns, an entablature with subtle upward curvature, blank *metopēs*, and triglyphs, and a pedimented roof. A central ramp led through a hall—six Ionic columns supporting a coffered marble ceiling, painted a deep azure blue and inlaid with golden stars—to the towering portal, a massive central gateway with heavy wooden doors, flanked on each side by two more doorways, each decreasing

8.3 The Propylaea.

incrementally in height, approached by low flights of steps, which led out through a shallow porch, a mirror image of the west façade, onto the rock itself. Mnesicles' original design was for the Propylaea complex to span the entire width of the rock with two large halls to the northeast and two smaller rooms projecting a short way to the southwest.[9]

But as work progressed, plans changed. To construct the southwest rooms would have meant destroying remains of Bronze Age walls, and, while Mnesicles and his contemporaries did not know their precise age, they recognized their antiquity, so old, that they must date back to the time of Theseus, Cecrops and Erechtheus. Like the Old Temple's foundations, these relics of a past heroic age possessed such deeply spiritual associations for fifth-century Athenians that they agreed to leave them undisturbed. So, Mnesicles modifed his plans, scrapped the southwest extension, and left the stones exposed, nestling against his modern marble walls, a visual reminder of the city's continuity. Meanwhile, into the south bastion's new facing he set an opening through which its Bronze Age predecessor could be seen, fusing past and present, melding the world of contemporary citizens

8.4 The Nikē Bastion with "windows" revealing the earlier Bronze Age walls.

8.5 The course of Eleusinian limestone built into the Propylaea, with (*below*) blocks whose lifting bosses have not been removed.

with that of the heroic ancestors, in whose footsteps they were following.[10]

The bastions were faced in polished white Pentelic marble, except for their topmost course, where Mnesicles set a band of Eleusinian limestone. A second band ribboned round the lowest course of the great central hall and formed the top step of its flight of stairs. Embedded at the entrance to the Acropolis, it created a potent boundary which all must cross, dividing the secular world of humankind from the sanctified domain of the divine. Just as to walk from the west end of the Parthenon, where sculptures showed scenes set in the physical geography of Athens, to the east end, where sculptures showed episodes set in the cosmic world of the divine, was to undertake a spiritual journey, so to cross the threshold of the Propylaea was to pass, as it were, through a forcefield of Eleusinian energy, alive with its promise of transfiguration and regeneration. Like the worshippers shown in procession on the Parthenon frieze, Athenians who stepped onto the rock to commune with their gods would somehow be themselves transformed.[11]

But in 432 B.C., five years after it was started, work on the Propylaea was permanently suspended. The bastions, the central and northeast halls, and two walls of the southwest hall were all completed, but many of the lifting bosses still remained in place, and they would never be removed. The Periclean building programme had ground to an abrupt halt. Events of the past decade had caught up with it.[12]

~ ~ ~

Athens' empire was a constant tinderbox. In 440 B.C. a dispute flared between Samos and resettled Miletus over Priene, a city on the north coast of the great Bay of Miletus in the shadow of the cliffs of Mount Mycale, which both claimed as their own. Negotiations failed. War broke out and when Samos, an oligarchy allied with Athens but not a tax-paying member of her empire, defeated Miletus, a member state, democratic Milesians sent delegates to Athens, demanding that the People take their side. Since the alternative (to let quasi-independent oligarchs prevail over Athens' democratic "colony") was unthinkable, they did. Pericles sailed east, removed the oligarchs from power, established a democracy on Samos, installed a garrison, sent fifty hostages to Lemnos, and cruised back home to Athens. But the Samians were playing a longer game. Some had already slipped across the sea to Sardis where the Persian satrap seized the opportunity to make mischief. Bound by the Peace of Callias, he could not engage with the Athenians, but nothing prevented him paying mercenaries to liberate the hostages and help the rebels. So, the oligarchs retook Samos and sought help from Sparta. Meanwhile, emboldened on the Bosporus, the citizens of Byzantium, declared that they, too, were leaving Athens' empire.[13]

Events were spiralling out of control. Speed was of the essence. Again, Pericles headed east but an initial victory was squandered, since many of the enemy escaped to fight another day. Had the Spartans and their allies mobilized, and further subject states rebelled, the situation for Athens would have been dire, but the Corinthians refused to get involved. The tide seemed to be turning. But there was no time for complacency. Reports suggested that in Caria a Persian fleet was readying to sail to Samos' rescue. It was a false alarm, but slicing back to Samos, Pericles discovered to his horror that the general, whom he had left to besiege the city and blockade the island, had bungled his command. The enemy had won a daring victory, confining the Athenians to camp, and making the besiegers the besieged. Pericles' arrival turned the tables. Sheer numbers were on his side. He reestablished the blockade and dug in for a siege. Nine months later it was over. Accepting the Samians' surrender, Pericles demanded hostages and hefty reparations, and watched as starving islanders tore down their city walls. Days later, the shrewd burghers of Byzantium, too, ended their rebellion.[14]

But Pericles had one last punishment in store. Transporting the surviving Samian ships' captains and marines across the straits to Miletus, he nailed them to crosses in that city's agora, where they were kept alive for ten long, agonizing days. At last, they were hauled down and, barely conscious, clubbed to death. But this was not the end. Greeks believed that without proper burial, souls of the dead could not enter the Underworld, condemned to haunt the earth forever like homeless refugees. Even after battle, the winning side returned enemy dead for burial. But for Pericles politics trumped religion. He ordered the rebels' corpses to be dumped outside the city and left to rot, unburied, carrion for dogs and birds to feed on. Like his father, Xanthippus, who crucified Persia's governor of Sestus, Pericles was adamant that Athens' enemies be seen to have been punished without mercy, a warning to those contemplating revolution.[15]

Back home, chosen to deliver the funeral oration at the late winter ceremony of remembrance, Pericles eulogized those Athenians who died on campaign, appropriating an image first used by a Syracusan tyrant forty years before, with such commitment that his audience believed it was his own. "For Athens to lose her young men," he said, was "like the year being robbed of its spring," and he went on to draw parallels between the fallen and the gods: "We cannot see those [gods] themselves, but nonetheless we take the honours they receive and the benefits which they apportion as evidence of their immortality." Many found comfort in these words, but not everyone. As he descended from the platform in the public cemetery, an elderly woman accosted Pericles, pressed flowers into his hand, and said with biting sarcasm, "Bravo, Pericles. You deserve this garland, since you have lost so many gallant citizens not, like my brother Cimon, fighting the Phoenicians or Persians, but destroying a city that was our ally and our sister." She was Elpinice, the grande dame of the Philaids, sister of Pericles' late rival, Cimon—but in this context, even more significantly the wife (or widow) of the statesman, Callias, who ten years earlier made peace with Persia.[16]

A more public reprimand soon followed. While on campaign in Samos, Pericles had made a powerful enemy—the general he left in charge while he sailed south to Caria. In personality and outlook, the two men were polar opposites, and Pericles had little time for his less experienced colleague. He had been overheard rebuking him for voicing his approval of a young man's beauty. "Generals," he snarled, "should have not just clean hands, but clean eyes, too." And, following the setback at Samos, he snapped, "You may be a good poet, but you're a useless general." He was, in fact, an outstanding poet: for the general was Sophocles, now one of Athens' leading playwrights.[17]

Sophocles had come a long way since he led the chorus celebrating victory at Salamis. With his debut theatrical production, Sophocles, not yet thirty years old, had defeated Aeschylus, and his experiments with staging—increasing the number of actors from two to three, enlarging the chorus from twelve to fifteen, and introducing painted scenery—made him the most innovative dramatist of his age. But politics were in his blood. Two years before the Samian War, he had served as one of the ten Hellenotamiae, the treasurers who oversaw the empire's finances, and his subsequent election as general showed the respect in which his fellow tribesmen held him. He may have been exuberant and sexually promiscuous, but he was also a deeply religious intellectual, whose profound beliefs were rooted in an ancient past. For Sophocles the gods were real, and their laws adamantine. Outraged at Pericles' unholy punishment of the Samian rebels and refusal to allow their corpses burial, Sophocles channelled his anger into writing a new tragedy, *Antigone.*[18]

Sophocles set *Antigone* in the aftermath of civil conflict, the legendary Theban War, where Polyneices, exiled by his brother, Eteocles, led an army against his city to regain the throne. When the brothers killed one another in combat, their uncle, Creon, Thebes' new king, while granting Eteocles full military honours, refused Polyneices burial, leaving his corpse on the battlefield to rot. So far, the myth was familiar to Athenians. As funeral orations reminded them each year, their own hero Theseus, horrified by such impiety, invaded Thebes and forced Creon to back down. But in *Antigone,* Sophocles made no mention of either Theseus or Athens. Instead, in the claustrophobic, tightly knit royal family of Thebes, the dead brothers' sister, Creon's niece, Antigone, defies his edict and buries Polyneices, while the gods display such anger that the king is forced to change his mind—too late. As the play ends, the broken ruler mourns his own dead son and wife, and the destruction of his household. For those with eyes to see them, parallels with events on Samos (in Elpinice's description, an "ally" and a "sister") were crystal clear. Like Creon, Pericles had eulogized his own side's dead, but by denying burial to the defeated enemy, he behaved like a tyrant and diminished his city. In one scene in particular, Sophocles allowed his anger to blaze through. As Creon announces petulantly that to defy his edicts means her death, Antigone responds:

> To my mind, "edicts" that a mortal man like you impose have no authority to supersede the gods' unwritten and established laws. No! They are eternal—not just for today or yesterday—and no one knows when they were first laid down. Me, I had no intention of failing in my obligations to the gods, just because I was afraid of some *man*'s whim![19]

The deep sense of injustice felt by Sophocles on Samos is palpable, and elsewhere in his play, he challenges the modern values of those—including self-styled intellectuals such as Pericles and his philosopher friends—who eulogized man's ingenuity and technological development. In one choral song, conceding that humankind had learned to cross seas, hunt every kind of species, exploit the earth's resources for his needs, and, thanks to "speech and rapid thought," rule cities well, he warned:

> Man's innovation exceeds the bounds of hope, but it brings with it the power for bad as well as good. When a man respects his country's laws and laws of gods, to whom he's bound by oath, his city prospers. But there's no place in any city, for a man, who thanks to his own recklessness does wrong. A man like that's not welcome in my house, and I could never sympathize with him.[20]

Moreover, there was still one force of nature that humanity could never conquer. Death, argued Sophocles, is stronger than any human power, and it matters how we treat the dead—not just our own dead, but our enemy's. In the context of its time, this was a provocative political statement. Even as the tragedy was being performed, sculptors were working on the Parthenon frieze where Athenians were imagined, upholders of Greek values, transcending their mortality, aspiring to be heroes, and entering the presence of the gods. In *Antigone,* however, death is final, and, while in other versions of the story Athenians and Theseus ride to the rescue, championing the gods' laws, here they do not even merit a mention. How could they, when their leading politician, Pericles, had acted in precisely the same way as Creon?[21]

Another surviving tragedy, which may have been produced around this time, might also reflect a growing criticism of Pericles' high-handed behaviour. *Prometheus* was for a long time attributed wrongly to Aeschylus, but may instead have been written by his son, Euphorion. Part of an otherwise lost trilogy, it showed Prometheus subjected to cruel punishment for defying Zeus' will. But, unlike in *Antigone* (with which it shares some tropes—there is even a speech tracing humankind's growing ingenuity and technical development), here Zeus is a tyrant, who uses his servants, Violence (Bia) and Power (Kratos, perhaps not coincidentally part of the word *demokratia*), to force an unwilling Hephaestus to shackle Prometheus to a rock to be "roasted by the sun's blazing rays"—a powerful visual image reminiscent of crucifixion. "The will of Zeus is harsh, like that of anyone whose power (*kratē*) is new," complains Hephaestus; "Zeus wields power with illegitimate laws," the Chorus of sea nymphs complains; while Prometheus himself contends that "Zeus is harsh, maintaining his own form of justice." And, since the supreme god has seized total power, "no one is free except Zeus" (a shocking idea for a democratic audience, who much preferred Aeschylus' sentiment in *Persians,* that Athenians "are not slaves of any man—nor vassals either"). While later in the trilogy Zeus and Prometheus appear to have been reconciled, and while dramatists had license to explore unpalatable ideas, such criticisms of their most powerful god must have shocked many in the theatre. Regardless of whether the play was performed in the wake of Samos, as the "crucifixion" scene suggests, or another time during the 440s or 430s, consciously or not some in the audience likely drew parallels between the tyrant god and their own "first man," Pericles, known to many by the nickname, "Zeus." It worked on many levels. For some it signified a grudging respect; for others a disdain of his authority; but few can have been unaware of its irony—for, while most Athenians believed in the traditional gods of Greece, Pericles and his intellectual circle were starting to question them.[22]

Pericles knew some of the most controversial thinkers of his age, who were reshaping how people viewed the world. They were heirs to the great philosophers of early sixth-century-B.C. Ionia, daring intellectuals, who filtered and repurposed earlier ideas from Greece, Egypt, and the Near East in an attempt to find rational explanations for the physical universe, men such as Thales, who, believing that a universal soul pervades both living beings and seemingly inanimate objects, proposed the idea of a "first principle," from which all things were formed and to which they would ultimately revert. For Thales that first principle was water. For his friend, Anaximander, the first Greek to try to map the world, it was fire. Moreover, he said, celestial bodies were not gods but physical phenomena, the sun and earth were both cylindrical, of equal size, and stars were firelight seen through channels in an all-encompassing vapour. Anaximenes, who like Thales and Anaximander lived in Miletus, disagreed, proposing air as his first principle, with everything created by a combination of its motion and compression.[23]

In the next generation, Xenophanes from nearby Colophon was more outspoken. A keen observer of fossils, he suggested that earth and water are in constant flux, insisting that, while absolute knowledge was impossible, Greeks' view of their gods was woefully wrongheaded. Not only was Homer wrong to attribute vices—theft, adultery, deception—to gods, but to imagine them being born or wearing clothes or even having human form was patently absurd since, "if oxen, horses or lions had hands and the ability to use those hands to draw and fashion things as men can, horses would draw their gods like horses, oxen would draw their gods like oxen, and each creature would make the bodies of their gods identical to their own." Instead, there was one supreme god, unlike humans in brain and body, complete in itself and motionless, directing the universe through thought alone, while the souls of living beings migrated after death from one body (or, indeed, one species) to another.[24]

This belief in metempsychosis, the transmigration of souls, probably originated in Egypt, and it inspired other influential thinkers, too, not least Pythagoras, an Ionian mystic from Samos, born in the first half of the sixth century B.C., a political refugee, who moved to Croton in Italy, where he set up an influential school, the first man to call himself a "philosopher" ("lover of wisdom"). The soul, he taught, was on a journey to acquire wisdom, part of which involved rebirth into new bodies, human or animal, with privileged treatment given to those who led pure lives. Partly for this reason he and his followers were vegetarians, whose lifestyle was both abstemious and communal, since "friendship means equality," and "friends have all things in common."[25]

Central to Pythagoras' teachings was the belief that numbers were fundamental to the structure and behaviour of the universe, and that "the principles of mathematics are the principles of everything."

He found proof in music, discovering the mathematics behind musical intervals, and his ideas proved highly popular in democratic Athens. Aeschylus was a devotee, and Pythagorean doctrine informs many of his tragedies, from the idea behind *Oresteia* that vengeance should give way to justice, to the concept that the world is made up of ten fundamental opposites (limit/limitlessness, odd/even, one/many, right/left, male/female, still/moving, straight/bent, light/darkness, good/bad, square/oblong), the first element in each pair being positive, the second negative, and the ideal situation being the stable subordination of the latter to the former. Pythagoreanism informed the visual arts, too. In its discussions of mathematics and ideal proportion in sculpture, Polycleitus' *Canon* owed much to the philosopher's teachings. As we have seen, Pheidias' design for the sculptures of the Parthenon may have owed them a similar debt.[26]

Pythagoreanism almost certainly influenced another of Pericles' inner circle, Damon. A controversial musicologist, his main interest lay not in music's abstract, cosmic qualities, or even in its technicalities, but in how melody, harmony and rhythm might influence a person's mood, behaviour, and character and, by extension, the mood and life of an entire city. "Music is of use for all the virtues," he maintained, "and in singing or playing the lyre a pupil learns not merely discipline and moderation, but justice, too." Employed properly, Damon believed, music and the arts could help turn citizens towards the good. Already the poet, Simonides, had linked the visual and literary arts, writing that "poetry is spoken painting, and painting silent poetry," but for Damon the practical potential of the arts was nothing short of revolutionary. Certain harmonies and rhythms, he argued, encouraged slavishness, insanity, and hubris, so for society to prosper these should be shunned in favour of those inspiring nobility and grace. It was a theory (as Simonides would no doubt have agreed) that could apply equally to visual art, but also, maintained Damon, to rhetoric: if a public speaker crafted speeches following his tenets, and delivered them with suitable finesse, the positive effect that he might have upon his city was incalculable.[27]

It was small wonder, then, that, after marrying an Alcmaeonid heiress, Damon tried influence the head of the Alcmaeonid family, Pericles. From the 460s B.C. onwards, the two men's relationship became the subject of suspicious gossip. Enemies accused Damon of being the intellectual powerhouse behind most of Pericles' proposals, a puppet master pulling his less able pupil's strings, the originator of the idea of jury pay. But supporters praised him. Thanks to "the songs he learned from Damon," they said, "Pericles harmonized the city."[28]

Damon was not the only intellectual to cast his spell on Pericles. Another member of his circle, Anaxagoras, now in his fifth decade, had come to Athens from Ionia, and like philosophers from that region his quest for knowledge was all consuming, his ideas revolutionary. Like Anaximander, he held that the sun was not a god but a huge lump of molten metal "bigger than the Peloponnese" and the moon an inhabited satellite complete with hills and valleys, while the entire universe was formed of minute particles, which had existed for all time and contained the seeds of all things. Life, he said, was generated by not gods (Hephaestus' semen, for example, impregnating the Acropolis to create Erechtheus and the Athenians) but moisture, heat, and minerals combining to produce the first life-forms. Thunder came from not Zeus but colliding clouds, with lightning flaring from the sparks thrown out by these collisions; eclipses occurred when other heavenly bodies temporarily intervened between the earth and sun or moon; and far from being the work of earth-shaking Poseidon, earthquakes were triggered when a sudden rush of air slammed hard onto the land. Instead of gods, "Nous" ("Mind" or "Reason," a word that became Anaxagoras' own nickname) animated everything, and while myths such as those in Homer's epics were useful allegories, they contained no religious truths.[29]

Neither did freaks of nature. An anecdote finds him debating with Lampon, the dyed-in-the-wool soothsayer who helped found Thurii. At the height of Pericles' political war with Thucydides Melesiou, a deformed ram was found on his estates in southeast Attica, with one single horn that sprouted, strong and vigorous, from the middle of its forehead. According to Lampon, it was a divine sign from the gods that power would pass into the hands of one man: Pericles. To Anaxagoras, however, the creature was simply an aberration, which he demonstrated by dissecting its malformed skull. It was not the only omen he dismissed. When a meteor "about the size of a wagon load" crashed to earth at Aegospotami on the Hellespont's European coast in 467 B.C., it caused great consternation, since many thought that it foretold disaster. Not Anaxagoras. For him it was an opportunity for close scientific study, allowing him to postulate that "if heavenly bodies are shaken from their path by vibrations, one might be torn away and so crash down to earth."[30]

Anaxagoras' teachings mirrored those of an earlier Ionian philosopher, Heraclitus, who called *his* all-motivating force (a never-changing presence in a world of constant flux), not "Nous" but "Logos" ("Reason"), insisting that this "one and only wise thing is and is not willing to be called by the name of Zeus." It was not his only radical conclusion. Like Anaxagoras, Heraclitus was scornful of those who trust "the people's poets," but he went further. Although writing at the time of the Ionian Revolt, and familiar with the concept of democracy, he was contemptuous of those who take their guidance from "the mob, not understanding that most men are useless, and only a very few are good." It was not a view which, for all his intellectual pretentions, Pericles could espouse in public. Nor, given the amount that the Assembly had spent on the agalma of Athena could he repeat Heraclitus' observation that "praying to statues is as useful as conversing with a house."[31]

Another friend of Pericles was the Ionian philosopher, Protagoras, an immigrant from northern Greece. His interests were exceptionally wide ranging. Titles of his (now lost) books included not just *On Virtues* and *On Mathematics* but *On Those Who Dwell in Hades* and *On Wrestling*. Like Damon, Protagoras was interested in how philosophy could be applied to statesmanship. His chief desire, he wrote, was to instil "sound judgement both in private affairs (how best to govern one's own home) and in politics (how to wield most influence within the city in both words and deeds)," adding that "speakers who are wise and good persuade their city that the proper thing to do is what is beneficial, and not harmful." But on one subject he felt unable to pronounce. His treatise, *On the Gods,* began: "I cannot tell whether or not the gods exist or what they might be like because the issue is opaque and human life is short." Xenophanes had written much the same some generations earlier, but it was still a controversial standpoint.[32]

Ruthlessly forensic, Protagoras insisted that all knowledge must be based on reason. Even then, it would be limited by human understanding, since "mankind is the measure of all things: of those which are, that they are, and of those which are not, that they are not." It was, however, possible, he argued, to advance intellectually with the help of a good teacher by balancing conflicting arguments and employing precise language, honing linguistic expertise, and polishing rhetorical skills. If Protagoras was the good teacher, his star pupil was Pericles. Following a fatal sporting accident involving a young man and a javelin, Protagoras and Pericles spent an entire day debating whether "in the strictest sense" the blame lay with the javelin, the man who threw it, or the officials presiding over the games, who should have kept a tighter grip on health and safety. It was a familiar dispute. Immediately after the annual Buphonia festival when an ox was sacrificed to Zeus on the Acropolis, the priest fled, throwing away his knife; a ritual trial was held to determine who bore responsibility for the ox's killing; all those involved passed on the blame, "those who provided water blaming those who sharpened the axe and knife . . . who blamed the man who gave the axe, who blamed the man who cut the creature's throat, who in turn blamed the knife, and since the knife was unable to speak, they found it guilty" and threw it into the sea. What made the discussion between Protagoras and Pericles different was that it was purely secular.[33]

Damon, Protagoras, and Anaxagoras were influential members of Pericles' innermost circle but eclipsing all of them was another Ionian immigrant. Young, poised, and beautiful, Aspasia was quick-witted, well educated, and not at all content to play the role of a demure Athenian woman, expected (as Pericles himself once put it) "not to be spoken of for either good or ill." She came to Athens almost by accident. In 460 B.C., another Alcmaeonid grandee, Alcibiades the Elder, had been ostracised; during his exile in Miletus, he married Aspasia's sister; on her father's death, he became her legal guardian; and when he returned to Athens with his wife in 450, he brought Aspasia with him.[34]

Perhaps he had already promised her dying father to find Aspasia a husband, but in the light of Pericles' citizenship law passed just the year before, the prospects of arranging a good match were slim: even if he could cope with her intellect, her energy, her character, her conversation, her vitality, no Athenian man wishing for a son and heir would marry her. But as luck would have it, Pericles already had two sons and, when Alcibiades the Elder introduced him to Aspasia (perhaps—despite Pericles' aversion to parties—at an event to celebrate his homecoming), Pericles realised that he had met his match. He must have known that for the sake of his reputation and political ambition he would be well advised to steer well clear of such a dazzling woman. But it seems that Pericles, who prized reason above all else and did his best to master his emotions, quite simply fell in love. Luckily, he had recently divorced his wife, arranging that she should marry Alcibiades the Elder's own son, Cleinias. Indeed, when Cleinias died in battle, Pericles became guardian to their two sons.[35]

Soon Pericles and Aspasia were living as husband and wife, rumoured to kiss passionately whenever he left home, and before long they became parents to a son, who, though not a citizen, was named after his father, Pericles. But motherhood could not satisfy Aspasia, and the responsibility of looking after Cleinias' sons—the wilful Alcibiades and his headstrong younger brother—was unlikely to be something that she relished. Among Athenian intellectuals she was fast becoming a celebrity, a social revolutionary, a woman who could hold her own with any man, a brilliant speaker, steeped in the latest theories of rhetoric, whose words could mesmerize and whose reasoning could spellbind, whether she was discussing the most erudite of topics, advising husbands on how best to educate their wives, or opining about love and Aphrodite. For Pericles' rivals, Aspasia exposed a welcome weakness in his armour. Thucydides Melesiou's ostracism had left conservatives without a leader at a time when Pericles was winning popular support through his generous domestic programme and hardline foreign policy. Which left opponents only one effective option: ad hominem attacks backed by denunciations of his circle's radical new doctrines.[36]

Despite the bold ideas of visionary and revisionary philosophers, most Greeks still cherished traditional beliefs. Most Athenians who backed Pericles' proposals in the Assembly accepted the existence of the gods. They still made sacrifice to win divine approval and ward off anger. They still wrote curses on lead tablets and dropped them into wells or buried them for the avenging spirits of the Underworld to read and act on. And they still devoutly celebrated the myriad religious festivals which defined the year, the great state festivals, the local festivals, the urban festivals and festivals in isolated caves and villages to honour gods and demigods whom few outside their deme had even heard of. To worship "in the ancestral way" was to ensure stability, and rituals were vital for protecting the state's spiritual and social integrity, be they performed by throngs of citizens and metics of both sexes at the Panathenaea, or by crowds of women at fertility festivals, or by chosen office holders such as the Arrhephoroi.[37]

Observing these unchanging calendars of ritual and sacrifice, many Athenians considered the new rationalism of Pericles and his circle to be anathema. For political conservatives it was a weapon ripe to be unleashed—and not least in the theatre, where tragedy was a powerful forum for debating social issues, encouraging debate by using the scenarios and characters of myth to view pressing moral questions in a wider human context. But it was not the only dramatic genre. Comedy, too, was intensely political, but unlike tragedy its action generally took place in an absurd, surrealist world, where politicians, generals, and other living personalities became characters in a parallel universe, a farcical but immediately recognizable Athens. While no complete comedy survives from the 440s or 430s, fragments do—and many savage Pericles.[38]

The year after Thucydides Melesiou was ostracized, they launched an attack on Damon, labelling him a dangerous power broker, an enemy of democracy, an éminence grise promoting subversive, revolutionary ideas, shaping his protégé, Pericles, as a trainer shapes an athlete, or as the centaur Chiron shaped Achilles. In *Cheirones* (Chirons), the comic playwright Cratinus called Pericles "the greatest tyrant, born from civil strife," while in another of his plays he wrote, "Here comes squill-headed Zeus, wearing the Odeon like a crown now that the ostracism's over." It was not just a jibe at the expense of Pericles' large head and nickname, "the Olympian," but a barb combining references to Thucydides' ostracism and the newly finished Odeon, the concert hall associated with Damon, the musician and, modelled on the Great King's tent, a symbol of tyranny. The idea that Damon was wielding power behind the scenes, manipulating the democratic process to suit his will, played on the People's fears. In 442 B.C., they ostracized him. But then, just three years later, in 439 B.C., they banned comic playwrights from targeting named characters. There is no evidence for Pericles' involvement in this censorship, but it was in his interests. He knew the importance of controlling the narrative and now, following his victory at Samos, he enjoyed enormous political capital. But not for long. Just two years later the legislation was repealed. It had been of little effect anyway. In the absence of comedy, rumour had run riot. Outrageous stories circulated. Some imagined Pericles seducing virtuous women with gifts of peacocks, diplomatic gifts from Persia, symbols of barbarian degeneracy. Others cast Pheidias in the role of pimp, bringing freeborn women (who pretended to their husbands they were going to view the sculptures) onto the Acropolis for sexual trysts with Pericles, thus sullying the precinct of the virgin goddess.[39]

They were not the only charges levelled against Pheidias. No sooner was Athena's agalma unveiled, than creative conservatives persuaded one of his assistants, to crouch, a frightened suppliant, beside the Altar of the Twelve Gods in the Agora, beg for immunity from prosecution, and accuse Pheidias of misappropriating gold meant for the statue. On the Assembly's orders, the agalma was deconstructed, its gold sheets set onto the scales. Their weight tallied precisely with the purchase records. Pheidias had won, but Pericles' enemies had

8.6 The Strangford Shield, a copy of the shield of Athena's statue in the Parthenon, with figures said to represent Pericles and Pheidias.

made their point. They would probe everything he did, chip at his reputation, and make his life as difficult as possible. And sometimes the People would support them. Even now, as Pheidias began the tiresome task of replacing all the gold, they voted to exempt the false accuser from taxation for life and charged the generals with protecting him.[40]

Then came a lawsuit accusing Pheidias of falsifying accounts for purchases of ivory, and then a further accusation, harder to disprove, that he had carved portraits of himself and Pericles on the agalma's shield—a sacrilege, since by convention no living person should be portrayed on temple sculptures. A later copy of the shield shows two fighters battling the Amazons: a helmeted warrior, his face hidden by his raised sword arm (but "plain to see from side on"), and a burly, squat, bald-headed man "holding up a stone in his raised hands." Side by side like the tyrannicides and flanked on their right by a composition mirroring the temple's southernmost west *metopē,* they make for a striking pairing, and it is entirely possible that some contemporaries did recognize Pericles in the armoured warrior and Pheidias in the bald man with the stone (symbolic of his role as sculptor and overseer of the building project). It is possible, too, that, given the tenor of other sculptures suggesting Athenians' elevation to heroic status, they were scandalized to see this idea applied specifically to Pheidias and Pericles, transported through the medium of art to take part in a legendary battle for the liberty of Athens. The case may have gone to trial, but, if it did, its outcome is unknown. So is Pheidias' fate. Some sources suggest that having finished his statue of Zeus at Olympia (where he allegedly carved his lover's name on one of the god's fingers, an act as blasphemous as showing himself and Pericles on Athena's shield), Pheidias was found guilty and condemned to death.[41]

Back in Athens, Pericles' opponents circled closer, probing weaknesses. In the Assembly, a fanatical soothsayer, Diopeithes, proposed impeaching anyone suspected of *asebeia* (impiety) by questioning the gods' existence or teaching new scientific theories about astronomy—essentially, thought-crime. Freedom of speech was central to Athenian democracy, but it was (and remains) fragile. The suppression of ideas is dangerously alluring to those not eloquent enough to counter them in other ways. Years of poring over entrails or interpreting the flights of birds meant that Diopeithes understood Athenians' ingrained conservatism and suspicion of the iconoclastic rational ideas embraced by some of the elite. Appealing to both religious traditionalism and social prejudice, his bill passed easily, and the mood in Athens darkened. Anaxagoras had already fled the city; so had Diagoras; now it was the turn of Protagoras, an angry mob seizing his writings, heaping up a bonfire in the Agora and cheering as its flames engulfed his manuscripts. Distancing himself from old friends, Pericles announced in the Assembly that Athena herself had communed with him. A builder had fallen from scaffolding high on the Propylaea and suffered serious injuries. Immobile, he lay in agony, and there was nothing anyone could do, not even leading doctors . . . until (said Pericles) Athena spoke to him in a dream and personally prescribed the necessary treatment; at which (said Pericles) he visited the patient, whom he quickly, easily restored to health; as a record of which miracle and proof of his own piety, Pericles set up a bronze thanks offering, a statue of Athena Hygieia (Athena, Goddess of Health) beside the Propylaea, near an existing altar of the goddess.[42]

It was a small if cynical victory. But Pericles' enemies remained merciless. They knew his greatest weakness was Aspasia, and repeatedly they targeted this clever, independent-minded woman, both for her alleged influence over Pericles—it was because of her, they said, that Pericles had sided with Miletus, her native city, in the Samian War—and for her entirely fabricated immorality. In attack after mean-spirited attack, they dismissed her as Pericles' "cheap whore," a madam who ran a brothel from the house she shared with him, an emasculating virago like the mythical Queen Omphale, who enslaved Heracles, or like Deianira, who engineered the same hero's death. The comic playwright, Cratinus, was in his element. Audiences wept with laughter as he riffed on Pericles' nickname, "Olympian," and his reputation as the city's Zeus in coarse, misogynistic lines: "The goddess of buggery gave birth to bitch-faced Aspasia to be his Hera." Later (albeit questionable) tradition suggested that another comic, Hermippus, went further. Trusting that Athenians believed the slanders, he is said to have taken Aspasia to court, accusing her of procuring freeborn women for Pericles' sexual pleasure. According to Plutarch, when Pericles stood up to speak in her defence, the strain became apparent. He broke down and wept, begging jurors to acquit her. Against all expectation, they did.[43]

Still charges kept coming. At the usual euthyna, where at the end of every year officials and their accounts were painstakingly examined, one of his enemies demanded that, if irregularities were found, and Pericles was put on trial, the jurors' ballots must be laid atop Athena's altar on the Acropolis. It was a double-pronged attack not only questioning Pericles' hard-cultivated reputation for honesty but suggesting that Athena's intervention might cause the votes to go against him. The motion failed, but Pericles could not relax. Locking himself in his office, he spent tedious, long hours preparing his accounts. Even his ward, young Alcibiades, was not permitted to disturb him. Turned away, he muttered, "Wouldn't it be better if he worked out how he could *avoid* presenting his accounts in the first place?" For Pericles, however, due process mattered. Despite their best endeavours, his opponents could find no evidence of misconduct.[44]

Which frustrated them still further. So much authority lay in the hands of just one man, whose standing seemed impervious to all attack, an aristocrat, who could manipulate a crowd, a populist, behaving (in their view) like a despot. But there was nothing they could do. In the theatre, he and his circle could be called "the New Peisistratids," and comic characters could call on him to swear an oath that he would never make himself a tyrant, but when it came to votes in the Assembly, comparisons to Hippias went unheeded. Every year he was elected general, a uniquely powerful role, since on campaign a general's word was law, and as new generations became used to following his orders on the battlefield, they became accustomed to accepting his political authority as well. So long as he continued to lead Athens to victory and prosperity, Pericles' position was unassailable. As another comic playwright wrote,

He has the power to tighten or relax the screws on cities and their taxes,
to build them their stone walls and pull them down again.
He controls their treaties, their armed forces, their authority, their peace, their wealth, their happiness.

But he could not control the Spartans or their allies. Fearing his ambition, at first they tried to undermine him. Then they went to war.[45]

9 THE ROAD TO WAR

They knew the men they sent away,
but now, in place of men,
there comes to every house
an urn and ashes
—AESCHYLUS, *AGAMEMNON,* 433–436

The Thirty Years Peace treaty signed with Sparta in 445 B.C. had offered Pericles countless opportunities—especially since he could rely on pious Spartans not to break it. Yet it would not last forever. One day war would come again, but meanwhile the stronger Athens made herself the more likely she would be to win it. But she must be audacious. The Greek world stretched from Spain to the Black Sea, and for an enterprising city ready to trade and conquer, the pickings could be rich. However, there were great risks, too. The Samian War had demonstrated the fragility of Athens' empire, the ongoing threat of Persia, and the danger posed by Sparta's League. Byzantium's secession, too, threatening Athenian control over the Bosporus, had highlighted the urgency of safeguarding grain shipments from Crimea on which Athenians depended.

So, following the Samian War, Pericles led a fleet, its magnificence and size well calculated to intimidate and impress, east to the Hellespont, out through the Bosporus, and into the Black Sea. As it hugged the fertile coastline, following the fabled route of Jason and his Argonauts in their search for the Golden Fleece, kings and potentates met him with promises of friendship and cooperation. They were wise to do so. When one tyrant refused to entertain him, Pericles deposed him and left behind 600 armed Athenians to guarantee the city's loyalty. North to the Sea of Azov, too, he sailed, where he established an Athenian colony and made treaties with the local king. By the time he sailed home, Pericles was confident that crucial trade routes would stay open. Neither Persia nor any other foreign state would interfere with Athens' food supply.[1]

Meanwhile, Athens was tightening her control of the resource-rich north Aegean with its gold and silver mines and forests by establishing new settlements east of the Chalcidice. Already in the 440s B.C., Pericles had persuaded the Assembly to send a thousand colonists to Brea (its location now unknown but probably on the Strymonian Gulf) as a bulwark against Thracian attack. In 437 B.C. these were followed by a further wave of settlers led by Hagnon, who had recently served with Pericles at Samos. Their destination were the ruins of Ennea Hodoi, where Athenians were massacred a generation earlier when they tried to plant a settlement at the crossroads of key trading routes that led deep into Thrace and east towards the Hellespont. Now, combining force with diplomacy, they drove out some local warlords, cut deals with others, and constructed strong defensive walls to fortify a settlement atop a spit of land where the River Strymon formed a lazy loop: Amphipolis.[2]

But storm clouds were already brewing. Far off on the east Adriatic coast, other colonists were waging civil war whose fallout would engulf the whole of Greece. The town of Epidamnus had little contact with Corcyra, its metropolis, which in turn remained aloof from almost everyone. Wealthy, and possessed of a strong navy, the Corcyreans saw no need for membership of any league or empire, be it Spartan or Athenian, and they had long since shunned their own metropolis of Corinth. So, in 435 B.C., when besieged by local oligarchs following a popular uprising, Epidamnus' democrats demanded help from the Corcyreans, Corcyra, true to form, refused to get involved. Corinth was cannier. She sent military aid to Epidamnus, installed new settlers, and, leapfrogging Corcyra, claimed the city as her colony. The Corcyreans were incandescent; the situation spiralled into war; Corinth's fleet was routed; and Epidamnus fell to the

Corcyreans. Now it was Corinth's turn to be enraged. She constructed a new fleet, recruited rowers from across all Southern Greece, enlisted the support of her Peloponnesian League allies, and prepared to attack Corcyra.[3]

For Pericles and Athens, this quarrel in a faraway country must at first have seemed of little real significance. But one early summer morning in 433 B.C., with scaffolding still on the Propylaea and the almost-finished Parthenon, two groups of diplomats—one from Corcyra, and one from Corinth—were ushered onto the Pnyx. The Corcyreans spoke first. They had, they said, no interest in war, which was why they made no military alliances. But now, as victims of aggression, they called on the Athenians—so famous for supporting the oppressed—to help. This would not, they said, breach Athens' treaty with the Spartans, which allowed both sides to make alliances with neutral states. Rather, it would be in Athens' interest. Aside from Athens, Greece's strongest fleets belonged to Corinth and Corcyra. If Corinth won this war, she would assimilate Corcyra's fleet, becoming more than a match for Athens. If the Peloponnesian League then went to war with Athens, Athens' ships would be outnumbered. Whereas, united, Athens' and Corcyra's fleets would be invincible.[4]

In response, the Corinthians urged Athens not to get embroiled in a private dispute between metropolis and rebel colony. Corinth, they maintained, had every right to punish Corcyra, just as Athens punished Samos seven years before—at which time, as Athenians should recall, it was thanks only to Corinth's intervention that the Peloponnesian League had not sailed to Samos' aid, one of many services that she had rendered Athens over time. An alliance with Corcyra would bring Athens into conflict with both Corinth and the entire Peloponnesian League and so break the terms of the peace treaty. Corinthians were Athens' friends. But if Athens sided with Corcyra, all bets were off.[5]

The Assembly was faced with a stark choice, and the grave debate stretched over two long days. On one side was surely Thucydides Melesiou. Newly back from ostracism, he shared Cimon's views, that Athens and the Peloponnese should act in concert for the good of all and that Sparta should be cultivated as a friend. Moreover, he would argue, to form an aggressive alliance with Corcyra would break the treaty—and more importantly the oaths they swore before the gods, when it was ratified. As dusk bathed the Acropolis, Thucydides Melesiou seemed likely to prevail, but next morning opinions shifted. From childhood, Athenians were used to hearing stories of how since the time of Theseus they had helped those in need: it would be shameful to refuse this current plea for aid. They were used to conflict, too. If war was inevitable, it made no sense to let Corinth profit from Corcyra's fleet and key location on the sea lanes west to Italy, so crucial for Athenian trade.

It was then that Pericles suggested what seemed to be a middle course; a third way; a purely defensive alliance. Athens would send triremes to Corcyra but not intervene unless Corinth attacked the island, in which case Corinth, not Athens, would be breaking the treaty. It seemed a clever compromise. Threatened by Athens' fleet, Corinth might back down, in which case Athens' claim to be the arbiter of Greek disputes and rightful hegemon of Greece would be enhanced. But if fighting did break out, Pericles was confident of victory. And if it then meant war with Sparta and the Peloponnesian League, so be it. Athenians were well prepared. They did not fear an enemy that fought mostly on land. With her Long Walls to Piraeus and supremacy at sea, Athens could withstand the most protracted siege. Her enemies would tire of war before she did.[6]

Pericles' motion passed. So did his suggestion that Athens send ten triremes commanded by three generals, none of whom was Pericles. He knew the risks, how easily they might become embroiled in fighting. He knew that fingers would be pointed if they did, and he did not want them to be pointing at him. Instead (in a characteristically Machiavellian manoeuvre), as one of the generals he sent Thucydides Melesiou's nephew, the dashing Lacedaemonius (whose name, of course, meant "Spartan"), the son of his old, dead adversary Cimon. So fully did Pericles entangled rivals in the mission that he neutralized their opposition, even as he had wrong-footed his enemies abroad.[7]

If anyone believed it was a workable solution, he was soon proved wrong. Rules of engagement allowing contact only if the enemy attacked Corcyra did not survive the heat of battle. Despite the brooding presence of Athenian triremes, the Corinthians and Corcyreans clashed near the islands of Sybota, east of Corcyra near the mountainous mainland. As the Corcyreans backed water, no match for the Corinthians, the Athenians rowed to their rescue. At sunset both sides claimed victory, but the outcome of the battle was irrelevant. What mattered was that by attacking Corinth's fleet, Athens had come dangerously close to breaking the peace treaty. The threat of full-scale war was suddenly more real.[8]

Pericles seemed unconcerned. Rather than diffuse the situation, he aggravated it. Ramping up his rhetoric, he turned his sights on Corinth's ally, Megara. Because of the peace treaty, Athens could not attack the city militarily, but it *could* destroy its economy. Carefully Pericles' hawkish lieutenants prepared the ground, inventing or inflaming aggravations. As tensions rose, Pericles persuaded the Assembly to adopt a new, artful strategy: an economic embargo, the first in history, a series of increasingly punitive decrees, exclusion orders, banning Megarians on pain of death not just from trade with Athens and any member of her empire, but from even setting foot in Attica or sailing on "the sea or to the continent." There are always ways round sanctions, and Athenians may have been exaggerated their effect, but their chief purpose was clear: to let Greece know that Athens would not be cowed.[9]

Such provocations continued. Built on Chalcidice's western promontory, Potidaea was a Corinthian foundation, which following the Persian Wars had joined the Delian League. Now part of Athens' empire, it maintained loose ties with its metropolis, letting Corinth appoint its magistrates, but in 432 B.C. Pericles demanded that this anomaly should end, that Potidaea cut all ties with Corinth, send hostages to Athens, and tear down its city walls. As he anticipated, not only did Potidaea refuse, but Corinth responded by dispatching troops to Potidaea—though, to avoid breaking the peace treaty, these were volunteers and mercenaries, not her official army. As other regional cities were sucked into the conflict, Athens sent forces of her own, and, following an early victory, dug in for a long siege.[10]

Individually, each of these three confrontations—Corcyra, Megara, and Potidaea—was provocative. Cumulatively, they signposted Athens' readiness for all-out war. Their timing was not accidental. Pericles, wily general and veteran statesman as he was, knew well the importance of morale and public sentiment. No matter his own beliefs, or lack of them, he understood that most Athenians still clung to their traditional religious views. He still heard stories of the Persian Wars, how gods and heroes intervened to protect Attica, and such tales likely circulated about recent conflicts, too. Moreover, he had overseen the process of enshrining these beliefs in marble, in temple sculptures he had helped commission. And now at last in 432 B.C. the Parthenon was finished—for pious Athenians a perfect gift to their patron goddess, a payment of honour to ensure that in return she would forever "shield her people as they march to battle and come home again." There could be no better symbol of the People's trust in their divine protection. There could be no better time to go to war.

In Sparta, too, the urgency for war was building. For long years her proud warriors, their hands tied by the treaty, had watched as Athens strutted unchecked on the Greek stage. But now Athens was pushing that treaty to breaking point. Frustrated young Spartans increasingly backed calls to reassert their city's leadership and fight beside their allies, Corinth and Megara. As war drums beat louder, ephors sent ambassadors to Delphi to ask the oracle what they should do. The god's response was startling: if they fought with every sinew of their bodies, they would win. Apollo would himself support them, whether they requested his support or not. That the father of the Ionians, patron deity of Athens' empire, made such promises gave Spartans a real cause for hope. But still they temporised.[11]

When Athenians heard the oracle, they must have been bewildered, if not terrified. Not everyone in Athens was as keen on war as Pericles. Thucydides Melesiou almost certainly counselled caution, while dramatists challenged citizens to weigh up the situation and potential consequences—albeit subtly. In spring 432 B.C., with the final

9.1 The Theatre of Dionysus from the Acropolis with (*left*) the Temple of Olympian Zeus in the distance.

pedimental sculptures of the Parthenon just recently in place, Euripides staged *Medea*. Set in the mythological world of Athens' current adversary, Corinth, the play was shockingly modern, combining a new style of music with revolutionary stage effects, and bristling with contemporary allusion: sailing, like Pericles, to the ends of the Black Sea in search of gain (the Golden Fleece), Jason had brought home a foreign princess, Medea; exiled, the couple fled to Corinth, where Jason betrayed Medea by marrying the king's daughter; but Medea wreaked revenge, killing the princess, her father, and her own children by Jason, before effecting her escape.[12]

Euripides' treatment of the myth diverged from other versions. Medea's killing of her children was his invention. But more shocking still was the central scene of his dark tragedy: as Medea plots revenge, a solitary figure wanders onto the stage; he is Athens' king, Aegeus, en route from Delphi, and in a strangely comedic episode his sympathy for the abandoned foreigner becomes so great that (ignorant of her intentions) he offers her asylum. So, in the final tableau, it is to Athens that the blood-drenched filicide is fleeing—in a chariot lent her by her grandfather, the sun god Helios. The staging added to the drama: adapting technology used in the recent building programme, the production team arranged for Medea and her chariot to be hoisted high above the stage on a crane—just as the sculptures of Helios, his chariot and horses had been craned into place on the Parthenon's east pediment some months earlier, a shocking visual parallel. Still more disturbingly, the audience all knew what happened next. While the play ends with her escape, myth told how, once in Athens, Medea seduced Aegeus, before years later, she tried to kill his son, fled east, and founded a new race that bore her name, the Medes (another term for Persians). As for Aegeus' son, who narrowly escaped, he was none other than Theseus.[13]

How Athenians interpreted the play we cannot know, but some may have seen it as a powerful warning: Aegeus' involvement with Corinth resulted in bad things for Athens, near-death for Theseus, the spawning of her enemies, the Persians, while in child-killing Medea they may have seen an allegory for war. Like the looming conflict, Medea, too, came to Athens from Corinth, invited willingly into the city by an unwitting leader, blind to potential lethal consequences. "In peace time," Herodotus was writing around now, "sons bury their fathers; in war, fathers bury their sons." If they had already heard the historian recite these chilling words at one of his celebrated readings, the audience may have recalled them as they watched Jason, begging for the corpses of his own dead sons, their burial denied by pitiless Medea—as Pericles denied parents of Samian rebels the right to bury their crucified sons just seven years earlier.[14]

A clever craftsman, Euripides had prepared his audience for such a reading. Following Aegeus' exit, with Athens committed to receive Medea, his chorus sang:

Since time began, the citizens of Athens have been rich indeed,
the children of Erechtheus, the children of the blessed gods,
born from a holy land that's never been defeated.
And so, they grew strong in the shining light of wisdom,
stepping lightly in the clear pellucid air,

where once they say that golden-headed Harmony
gave birth to the nine sacred Muses—
and the clear flowing waters of Cephisus nurtures them.

They say that Aphrodite, goddess of desire,
drinks deep of the Cephisus,
sailing in her barge to Athens,
fanned by breezes scented in the honeyed air;
and setting on her hair a scented garland twined with roses,
she sends her sons, the Erotes,
to sit at Wisdom's side,
collaborators in all kinds of excellence.

And so, I ask: how will the city welcome you, Medea?
How will Cephisus with his sacred streams,
how will the soil of Athens receive you,
stained by the bloodguilt of your sacrilege,
your own sons' murderess?[15]

Familiar from motifs shown on temples and repeated in the annual Funeral Oration, the imagery is electrifying: Athenian autochthony; descent from Hephaestus and Athena; Athenian invincibility; the landscape of Athens (established, as on the Parthenon's west pediment, by reference to its rivers); Aphrodite and Eros—or, here, twin Erotes—joining with Wisdom to produce "all kinds of excellence" (perhaps a nod to the arrangement of the gods on the Parthenon's east frieze). Euripides, whose dramas—despite Aristophanes' accusations that "he has persuaded everyone there are no gods"—were deeply religious, has taken all these tropes, each of them used by Pericles in speech or sculpture, to warn against a war that Pericles seemed all too happy to embrace.[16]

The audience may also have detected personal attacks. Like Medea, Pericles' wife, Aspasia, was also a single-minded, independent, clever easterner. Critics had already blamed her for the Samian War, and a few years after *Medea*'s first performance, when a comedian accused her of being (indirectly) responsible for conflict with Sparta, too, he was probably repeating a well-worn idea. Rehashing slanders that Aspasia was a brothel keeper, and parodying Herodotus (who traced Greek enmity with Persia to a series of mythological abductions), Aristophanes wrote how

Some drunk young players went to Megara
and carried off the tart, Simaetha.
At which Megarian garlic-munchers, noses out of joint,
made off with Aspasia's working girls, a lovely pair,
and this was the beginning of a Greece-wide war—
all for the sake of three trollops.
Then, Pericles the Olympian, in fury
hurled lightning bolts, let thunder roll, and discombobulated Greece.[17]

Still more resonant for the first audience of *Medea* was the line questioning how the soil of Athens would accept the killer, "stained by the bloodguilt of your sacrilege?" Even as the play was staged, the "Alcmaeonid Curse," dormant for eighty years, was being revived and weaponized by Pericles' enemies. Perhaps it was Thucydides Melesiou who resurrected it, but, as momentum for war increased, it was picked up by the Spartans, who demanded that Athens "drive out the curse of the goddess," meaning the Alcmaeonidae in general, and Pericles in particular. They knew that such demands would sow dissent, encouraging Athenians to question Athena's attitude towards the impious family, and their own allegiances. But Athens responded tit for tat, suggesting that Sparta drive out her own curses, stemming from when she starved Pausanias almost to death inside her Temple of Athena and slaughtered helots taking refuge at an altar—because of which some Spartans thought Poseidon sent the earthquake of 464 B.C.[18]

Spartan ultimata—they also called for Athens to lift sanctions on Megara, to end the siege of Potidaea, and restore Aegina's independence—entrenched Athenian determination. Yet, as the two Greek mainland superpowers stared one another down, it was Thebans who launched the first strike—an unexpected nighttime raid on neighbouring Plataea, one of Athens' oldest allies. Rain-lashed, they met determined opposition, and within hours nearly 200 were trapped inside the city. Athens' response was speedy: to send a task force to support Plataea; to grant asylum to Plataean women and children; to hold the Theban prisoners as hostages. Too late. By the time that the Athenian relief force reached Plataea, every Theban had been slaughtered. Now there was no going back. All Greece was at war.[19]

As both sides finessed preparations—sending diplomats to Persia to seek the Great King's backing, a miraculous volte face—rumours circulated of an earthquake striking Delos. The historian, Thucydides, makes mention of it. As a rationalist, a pupil, it was said, of Anaxagoras, his report is scant: "A short while before [the war began], Delos was shaken by tremors, though no Greek could remember it being previously subject to seismic activity." This was because it never had been. Nor was there an earthquake now. But the fake news of an earthquake was sufficient to cause Spartans joy and Athenians alarm. Delos was Apollo's island. The god had promised Sparta his support. It did not take much for god-fearing Greeks to jump to conclusions and, years later, once the war was over and Athens defeated, they remembered how even at the time the bogus earthquake "was said and believed to be a portent of what did eventually happen."[20]

It was not the only portent. As Greece ramped up for conflict, all unusual phenomena were thought to be a message from the gods and rigorously examined by religious experts. Seers and oracles went into overdrive as men tried to second guess the war's outcome. For Pericles, an "accursed" Alcmaeonid and religious sceptic, this must have been especially vexing, since signs of divine disfavour could be seized on by opponents to sideline him or argue against war. His reaction just a few months later shows his frustration. Thucydides writes how, "on the day of the new moon, which is the only time it seems that this can happen, there was an eclipse of the sun just after noon. It formed a crescent shape, and some stars became visible, but then it returned to normal." It so happened Pericles was on his flagship, set to launch the fleet, when the eclipse took place. According to Plutarch, "as darkness descended, everyone was struck with terror, thinking it a portent. So, when Pericles saw how frightened and confused his helmsman was, he held his cape in front of the man's eyes, covering his head, and asking if this made him frightened or if it foretold anything frightening. When the helmsman said it didn't, Pericles asked, 'So, where's the difference between this and the eclipse, except that something bigger than my cape has blotted out the sun?'"[21]

For Pericles, pupil of Protagoras and Anaxagoras, cold logic and science trumped religion, but he was very much in the minority. Athenians trusted his political and military nous, but most disagreed with his beliefs. Still, with the enemy preparing to invade, they followed his advice: that, instead of marching out to battle at Eleusis and relying on its gods as they had done before, anyone who lived outside the city must leave his home and move to Athens. Pericles' strategy was at last being put to the test: taking refuge behind their walls and turning their city into an "island" fortress, Athenians would sacrifice the land of Attica because, so long as they controlled the sea, they would prevail. Not since the Persian invasions had such wholescale evacuation taken place, and only then because the policy was sanctioned by Apollo's oracle. Now, though, it was on Pericles' say-so that reluctant farmers and smallholders shipped their livestock overseas, and—along with villagers and townsfolk from all the outlying demes—loaded their belongings onto donkeys or in carts, some taking even doors and window frames from their abandoned homes as they clogged the roads that snaked into the city. Wrapping such cult statues as could reasonably be moved, transporting votive treasures for safekeeping, they left behind their sanctuaries and rural temples, too.[22]

Once inside the city, a further problem faced them: where to live? The wealthy had townhouses. Some could stay with family or friends, but they were a small proportion. The rest were forced to camp wherever they could find a space: between the Long Walls, and in squares, in hero-shrines—and temples. Only a few places were off limits. Thucydides names the Acropolis and the Temple of Eleusinian Demeter, and the pairing is not accidental. The cults of Eleusis and the Athenian Acropolis formed the backbone of Athenian religion.

They could not be compromised. But the pressure of numbers meant that other sanctuaries were commandeered by homeless refugees. None are specifically identified, but it is likely that families now settled in or round the Temple of Athena and Hephaestus and the Shrine of Theseus to name but two. They even took up residence on one piece of sacred land beneath the cliffs of the Acropolis, which was believed to have been cursed, in direct contravention of an oracle, and when the city fell the pious saw this as yet another cause of the catastrophe.[23]

So, claiming to be liberating Greece from Athens' tyranny, the Spartans and their allies poured into Attica. For a while they waited at Eleusis, willing the Athenians to meet them, but no army came. Many in the city thought the enemy would come no further, since twice previously the Spartans had turned back at Eleusis, rebuffed, perhaps, by its gods. But they were wrong. Soon the huge army was on the march again, this time to the township of Acharnae, just seven miles north of Athens, whose fighters watched from Athens' walls, frustrated, itching to run out and fight, as for the second time in fifty years smoke drifted over Attica. The crowded city grew more febrile by the day. Prophets and soothsayers added to the sense of instability, calling into question hyperrational, cursed Pericles and his strategy of doing nothing, whipping up opinion against him. Yet, still he held firm, maintaining enough discipline to check hotheaded hoplites, while sanctioning occasional cavalry raids on enemy positions, a naval expedition against coastal regions of the Peloponnese (at the time of the solar eclipse), and the removal from Aegina of all its native population, an act of vengeance which for many must have seemed as sweet as the late-summer orgy of destruction, which Pericles himself led when at last the enemy left Attica, and its refugees streamed home. At the head of the largest Athenian army ever seen, he swarmed into the fields of Megara, sating pent-up fury on the already economically crippled state.[24]

That winter, Athens held her traditional ceremony for the war dead. Few cared about its origins. For them it was simply an "ancestral custom," practised from time immemorial, though some Athenians

9.2 The Acropolis from the road to the Academy.

could possibly remember the first time its rituals had been observed in years following the Persian invasions. But all knew its format: ten tents erected in the Agora, one for each tribe, in each of which remains (cremated on the battlefield) were placed, and an eleventh tent for the burnt bones of those who could not be identified; two days of mourning—family members making a sad pilgrimage to these soldiers' last encampment, bringing offerings and garlands to lost loved ones; women wailing for their fathers, husbands, brothers, sons; the city grieving its own sacrifice. On the third day, the remains were transferred reverentially into eleven cedar coffins, each loaded on a wagon, before in solemnly reflective procession the citizens of Athens filed through the streets, past the Temple of Athena and Hephaestus on their left, out through the Twin Towers Gate, a little way along the road that led towards the Grove of Academus, until they reached the public cemetery, where graves had been prepared. A service of committal; hymns and prayers and sacrifice; and then the People's representative, "chosen by the city for his wisdom and repute," climbed onto a high wooden platform and addressed the gathered mourners. This year that man was Pericles.[25]

He had already delivered at least one such speech (following the Samian War), and there had probably been more. But just one fragment of these remains. Of this speech of 430 B.C., however, a full text does survive, recorded by the historian Thucydides, who may have heard it—although this does not guarantee its accuracy. As he admits, "It was difficult for me to remember word for word the speeches that I heard with my own ears, and those who reported other speeches to me found the same. So, I have set out what I thought that each man in the circumstances would have said about the situation at hand, keeping as closely as I could to the overall thrust and tenor of what was actually said." The reliability of speeches recorded in Thucydides' *History* is thus notoriously problematic, though, because some of his first readers would have heard them being delivered, it is supposed they cannot be inventions, tout court. Even so, Thucydides' version of this speech by Pericles is unlike any other Funeral Oration that survives.[26]

There are four other examples, either genuine or literary exercises, but, while each has its own character, all follow a similar structure, and cover similar ground. Plato, who includes one in his dialogue *Menexenus,* explains, "The speech must adequately praise the dead and sympathetically encourage the living by appealing to their sons and brothers to imitate their bravery, while providing support for fathers, mothers and grandparents (if still alive)." So far, so predictable. But, he continues, saying that it should "first praise their nobility of birth, and second their upbringing," meaning, he explains, Athenians' autochthony and the nurturing they have received from Attica, a land "loved by the gods" and "fought over" by them, the first place on earth where people learned to cultivate grain and olives (at Eleusis and on the Athenian Acropolis—another pairing of these crucial sites). He then traces Athens' history, constitution, and military prowess (Athenians, he says, "considered it their duty to go to war with Greeks on behalf of Greeks and with barbarians on behalf of all the Greeks"), merging mythology and history to include familiar legends—the Amazonomachy, Theseus' intervention to bury the war dead at Thebes, protecting the children of Heracles—before moving on to recent wars.[27]

Such was the power of these funeral orations, Plato maintains, that they enflamed their audience. As his Socrates playfully maintains, "they bewitch our souls" so that "I myself feel utterly ennobled, and whenever I hear them, I am entranced, and immediately think myself taller and nobler and more handsome than I really am. . . . And this feeling of blessedness stays with me three days or more. Indeed, so embedded in my ears are the message and delivery of the orator that it's only on day four or five that I remember who I am and realise I'm here on earth, since until then I thought that I was almost living in the Islands of the Blest [the home of heroes]." While Plato is exaggerating their impact on their listeners, there can be no doubt that both the speeches and the games that followed (a structure deliberately mirroring heroic funerals of epic) had a profound impact. This was only occasion when everyone in Attica—male, female, citizens, and metics, perhaps even slaves—gathered as one body, so the funeral oration served a vital civic function, bolstering a sense of history and communal identity. Hence the formulaic structure of most surviving speeches. Which makes Thucydides' record of Pericles' speech of 430 B.C. all the more surprising.[28]

It reads like a political manifesto. After a conventional enough preamble, outlining difficulties inherent in according to the dead the due that they deserve, Pericles skates quickly over early history, omitting any mention of religion, and quickly focussing on what makes Athens unique:

> I shall start first with our ancestors, for it is right and fitting at such a time to pay honour to their memory. They lived forever in this land, and through their bravery bequeathed this freedom to each successive generation until the present day. They are deserving of our praise, especially our father's generation, since—in addition to what they themselves inherited—with great effort they acquired the Empire which we have today and passed it on to us.[29]

No mention here of autochthony, or of Athena's contest with Poseidon. This is Attic history stripped bare of mythology and gods, as

Pericles paints a picture of an ideal city, the antithesis of Sparta, where happy, harmonious citizens, enjoying *isonomia,* play an equal part in their democracy regardless of class or wealth, treat peers with liberal tolerance, and never break the rules, "especially regarding the protection of the oppressed, and those unwritten laws that all people recognize cannot be broken without causing shame" (normally, but not here, this is a cue to mention Athens intervention at Thebes and protection of Heracles' children). And Pericles goes on, "Taking the city as a whole, I say that Athens is the educator of all Greece, and that every single one of us can turn his hand to almost anything, with grace and self-sufficiency."[30]

Thanks to their efforts and their empire, Pericles' Athenians enjoy an enviable lifestyle, both public and private. "With our hard work completed," he assures his audience, "we have at hand so many ways to reinvigorate our spirits: the athletic games and sacrifices that we celebrate throughout the year; our elegant and well-appointed homes, in which we take such pleasure every day and banish cares. And then, thanks to the greatness of our city, all things flow in from every land, and we are as familiar with foreign produce as our own."[31]

It is not only in the political or socioeconomic aspects of Athenian life that Pericles is interested. As he returns to address the memory of the war dead, he conjures a euphoric, indeed erotic image of the relationship between citizen and city:

> Gaze every day on the reality of Athens' power. Become her lover. And when you are consumed by the immensity of her achievements, reflect that it was by their daring, and their knowledge of what must be done, and their determination never to be found to fail that these men built it all. No setback was so great that they would ever think of not devoting every ounce of courage to their city. Rather, they bestowed on her the most exquisite offering that they could ever make. They gave their lives, each one, to all of us, and so received a golden reputation that will not grow old, and the most preeminent memorial of all, not here, where they are laid

> to rest, but where their glory will remain forever—in the memory—the inspiration for our words and actions when we need it most. For men blessed by the gods the whole earth is their holy sepulchre, and their good name will be proclaimed, not just inscribed upon their headstones in their homeland, but preserved, unwritten, in the mind, where it will live forever, more permanent than any physical memorial.[32]

Laying down their lives for Athens has turned the war dead into heroes: "Even if they fell short in every other aspect of their life, it is right and proper that by fighting for their fatherland their bravery in battle should blot this out. This virtue has erased all failings. The service they bestowed on the community has trumped all private vices. . . . They turned their backs on bad repute and in the twinkling of an eye, at fortune's pivot, experiencing not fear but glory, they passed from life to death." By dying fighting for Athens, each citizen, regardless of his character or class, has earned eternal fame, an afterlife as glorious as any Homeric warrior.[33]

This idea that through their sacrifice, which has "erased all failings," Athenians, "blessed by the gods" and equal in death, have not simply made their city great but achieved some kind of immortality, mirrors our reading of the Parthenon and its frieze with its representation of Athenians regardless of their social status, being admitted to the presence of the gods. In fact, a short while earlier, the speech has referenced the new temples: "We have provided witnesses to our great power, impressive monuments that those alive today look on with wonder, as those in generations still to come will wonder, too. We do not need a Homer to sing our praises, or any other man like him whose words delight the senses for the moment and then vanish when confronted with the facts." Eternal monuments designed for both his own and future ages to gaze on in awe and recognize the power of Athens' empire: these words reveal much about the Periclean building programme. But no mention of the gods for whom (at least in theory) the temples were erected.[34]

9.3 "Mourning Athena," a marble relief dating from ca. 460 B.C.

Perhaps the text, ideas, and shape of the speech as we possess it owes more to Thucydides than to Pericles. Twice already in his *History* he had used speeches to contrast Athens and Sparta. In the first, Corinthians goad Spartans, accusing them of having no interest in foreign affairs, waiting until the last minute before responding to aggression, allowing proactive, energetic Athens to take over much of Greece. One section of this speech is worth quoting in full, since it encapsulates the image that Athens did project (or wanted to project) at this time:

> They [the Athenians] are always doing something new. They're quick to come up with new ideas and act on whatever they decide. But the most you [Spartans] aim for is to hold onto what you have. You're unimaginative. When you *are* forced into action, you never see things through to their conclusion. *They* dare to overstretch, run massive risks, are confident in danger. Not you. You pull your punches, never trust your judgement, think that danger's going to trap you. *They*'re quick to act; you're slow. *They*'re never home; you never go abroad. *They* go into the world expecting to increase their assets; you're terrified that, if you go too far from home, you'll lose them. When *they* defeat their enemies, they advance as far as possible; when they're beaten, they retreat as short a distance as they can. They dedicate their bodies to their city. Their minds they focus on their city's good. If they don't immediately achieve their goal, they think that they've been cheated, and if they *are* successful, they think it's nothing in comparison to what they will do next. If they fail in something, they're already onto the next thing. So quickly does thought follow action, that it can be said of them alone that no sooner do they want something than they get it. Throughout their lives they work hard and run risks, not stopping to enjoy what they do have, because they're always wanting more. Their idea of a holiday is doing only what's strictly necessary; they'd rather work than rest. In short, it's fair to say that it is not their nature to enjoy peace and quiet—or to let others enjoy it either.[35]

Whether any Corinthian actually said these words or they are simply what Thucydides believed that "in the circumstances" they "would have said about the situation at hand," they so perfectly reflect the can-do optimistic spirit of the sculptures of the Parthenon and its related buildings that they might almost serve them as a commentary, their sentiment rendered more powerful for being placed in the mouth of an enemy. Less generous is the Corinthians' next speech where, describing Athens as "a tyrant city that has taken root in Greece," picking off other poleis one by one, not resting until she has imposed "slavery pure and simple," they try to prod the Spartans into action. Again, they may have said such things, but problematically some of their arguments here are closely countered in later speeches by Pericles, suggesting that Thucydides is pairing them, setting up the kind of debate with which readers were familiar from the Assembly, law-courts, and drama. Which may suggest that they are literary constructs, more Thucydides than the Corinthians or Pericles. So, if this is true of these speeches, is it likely to be true, too, of the Funeral Oration?[36]

Almost certainly it is not a verbatim record. However, unlike the Corinthians at Sparta, Pericles made his speech before a vast audience—so large that some were so far distant that they could hear him barely if at all. Some of Thucydides' first readers would remember attending the ceremony. So, it is unlikely that that he diverged too drastically from Pericles' original. Moreover, what makes this speech stand out is how dissimilar it is to other extant funeral orations: Thucydides' choice not to write a "stock" speech may lend it more credence. So may a detail in Plato's *Menexenus,* where, before embarking on his own version of a funeral oration, Socrates is made to say that he has been instructed by one who was "well versed in the art of rhetoric, having turned out many excellent orators, including the best in all Greece—Pericles, son of Xanthippus." To which Menexenus replies, "You mean Aspasia." Indeed, continues Socrates, Aspasia herself composed a funeral oration purely for his benefit, "improvising part of it, but also drawing on parts she had prepared already (I imagine) when she wrote the funeral speech that Pericles delivered."[37]

Plato's *Menexenus* is problematic. For one thing, it is wildly anachronistic, set years after the real Socrates and Aspasia were dead; for another, the version of Pericles' funeral speech to which it refers, and which to some degree it parodies, is probably the one contained in Thucydides' *History* (already popular in the fourth century B.C.) and not the one which Pericles actually made (before Plato was even born). But the notion that Aspasia authored Pericles' oration, too readily dismissed as whimsy, is instructive. With both Plato and another of Socrates' adherents, Xenophon, portraying Aspasia as a formidable intellectual, and with populist dramatists such as Aristophanes, Cratinus, and Hermippus making much of her alleged hold over Pericles, it is more than possible that some of those braving the cold of the public cemetery in 430 B.C. believed they could detect her influence on the funeral oration. Plato's may be echoing a genuine contemporary view, making it more likely that the speech in Thucydides' *History* reflects what Pericles did say.[38]

One reason why this is important is that it may suggest that Pericles used it to steer his audience away from the traditional fare of Athenian mythology and history towards a more rational view of their world. Perhaps he was inspired to do so by the fact that, unlike when Spartans and their allies had previously invaded Attica, this time they had not been turned back at Eleusis. Until the previous year, the People had possessed firm faith in the protection of the Eleusinian gods, but now this had been exposed as fantasy (thanks to Pericles' own strategy). Still, to omit all mention of gods and heroes would be to go too far. Just two years earlier, the Parthenon had been completed, its sculptures showing many of those episodes from myth which peppered standard funeral orations and tying them closely to the Persian Wars. Perhaps Pericles believed their message required no repetition. According to Thucydides he said he did not wish to talk at length on "well-known subjects." Perhaps he preferred to focus on the frieze's theme of the Athenians' unique heroism.[39]

But, if Pericles did mean to excise religion and mythology from his speech, he was taking a great risk. As we have seen, belief in gods and heroes played a central role in every aspect of Greek life. For two centuries cities had projected that belief through ritual and sacrifice and temples, and, while it is impossible to know how truly every Greek held those beliefs, no politician was so reckless as to question them or sideline them in public. Although we cannot know if Pericles did really downplay gods in this momentous speech, it does speak volumes that Thucydides omits them, confirming what we might anyway believe, that for Pericles the motivation behind temple building was not primarily religious but political. And the danger was that others saw this, too.

In Thucydides' *History,* this funeral oration at the end of the war's first year comes as a high-water mark, with Pericles and Athens still buoyed by a belief in their invincibility. The conflict, they think, will last only a few years. The Spartans and their allies will soon tire. When peace comes, Athens will have shown her enemies that there is no point trying to curb her growth and constantly evolving ambitions. For fifty years, Athenians have found themselves on a remarkable trajectory, seeing their destroyed city rise again, a phoenix from the ashes, acquiring a rich empire, becoming the most powerful force on mainland Greece. She seems invincible. But cautious citizens remembered words inscribed at Delphi: "Nothing in Excess." Too much self-confidence, the pious Greek believed, could lead to hubris, transgression, an overstepping of the line which would attract the anger of the gods. For hubris led to nemesis, gods' punishment.

And so it came to pass.

10 CONVULSIONS

The gods are powerful,
and the law that governs them is strong.
It is by this law that we believe the gods exist; it sets the rules
for what is right and wrong in our own lives.
If, faced with it, you disregard it . . .
there will be no more fairness in the business of humanity.
—EURIPIDES, *HEKABE*, 799–805

The plague stole, undetected, into Athens, a stowaway on ships arriving at Piraeus. Clinging close to sailors, it disembarked, unnoticed, onto busy wharves to mingle with stevedores from nearby warehouses, merchants at their market stalls, fishermen in crowded bars and slave girls in the cubicles of backstreet brothels. From grid-planned boulevards it turned to trail in traders' wakes along the swarming street between the high Long Walls, where Attic refugees encamped in their cramped shanty town, cooking, eating, sleeping, defecating in uncomfortable proximity. And so, it came to Athens, the city packed again to overflowing, the population swollen many times its normal size, 300,000 people crushed inside the walls as late spring turned to summer, the heat grew more intense, and the stench of sewage drifted in the scorching air around the baking cliffs of the Acropolis.[1]

For the second year Attica had been evacuated. The arrival of the Spartans and their allies at the start of the campaigning season had been predictable, their vast army moving at a leisurely pace past Eleusis, across the saddle of Mount Aegaleus, down into the empty, olive-studded plain so clearly seen from Athens, hacking down trees, burning early crops, destroying farms and villages. But no one could predict the plague, gliding up along the Nile from Ethiopia to Egypt, infecting sailors, fanning out across the sea until it came to Greece. The first signs were headaches, inflamed eyes, ulcerated throats and tongues; then sneezing, breathlessness, constricted chests; vomiting until there was no more to vomit; pustules; raging thirst; insomnia; the body seeming to burn up. For seven days these symptoms worsened. Many died, but, for survivors, things got even worse: uncontrollable diarrhoea; loss of sensation in extremities, sometimes lasting even after patients regained health; amnesia; and blindness.[2]

In the sweltering, unsanitary, overcrowded city, there was no thought of hygiene. Flushed with fever, people immersed themselves in reservoirs and water tanks, others swarmed round fountains, and bodies lay unburied in the streets, their decaying presence a pollution and a curse. Staggering through suffocating lanes Athenians, too weak to act, could only watch in horror, as dogs sniffed bloated corpses and carrion birds flapped down, though few tried to feed, and those that did became infected and soon died. So prevalent was the belief that only a proper funeral could release dead souls to make their journey to the Underworld that relatives of the deceased adopted extreme measures. Some appropriated makeshift pyres set up by other families, others dragged off half-burned corpses and threw their own dead into the already raging fires.[3]

Society was breaking down. Law, order, and morality were fracturing. Remembering these dark days, the historian Thucydides, who was infected but survived, recalled:

> When they saw how quickly fortunes changed, people started to indulge those appetites they previously kept hidden. . . . Nothing kept anyone in check: no fear of gods, and no fear of the law. As for the gods, it seemed to make no difference whether people worshipped them or not, since the good and bad were dying indiscriminately. And as far as the law went, no one thought they would live long enough to be put on trial and sentenced.[4]

10.1 Tombstone of Ampharete, early 420s B.C.

Perhaps it made no difference to the rational historian whether people worshipped gods or not, but for most Athenians the sacrilege they saw around them every day must have been terrifying—not only in respect to funerals. In one almost throwaway sentence, Thucydides reveals, "the sanctuaries in which they had encamped were filled with the corpses of those who died there." It is a shocking image. When the starving Pausanias was nearing death, the Spartans had dragged him from their Temple of Athena so that his passing would not pollute the building. Now in sanctuaries across Athens, corpses were "piled high on top of one another." As the pall of oily smoke hung heavier each day, many must have felt that they were living in a city of the damned, abandoned by the gods, victims of divine punishment. Searching for explanations, they remembered an old oracle which warned how "war with Dorians will come, accompanied by plague"; they recalled, too, how Apollo promised to support Sparta; and they all knew Apollo was the god of plague. Almost the first lines of the *Iliad* describe how, angered, he rains sickness down on the Greek army,

> *stalking the high peaks of Olympus, fury in his heart,*
> *his bow and covered quiver slung across his shoulders,*
> *his arrows clattering at his shoulder as he strode*
> *in anger. He came down like the night.*
> *A little distance from the ships he knelt and loosed an arrow*
> *and the clatter of his silver bow struck terror in men's hearts.*
> *First, he attacked the mules and hunting dogs,*
> *then he loosed off his whetted arrows at the men themselves and*
> *struck them*
> *down. And for nine days pyres of the dead, close set, kept burning.*[5]

In the *Iliad,* the cause of Apollo's anger is the impiety of the Greeks' commander-in-chief, Agamemnon, who has taken the daughter of one of the god's priests to be his sex slave, and it is only when she is returned to her father, and lavish sacrifice is made, that Apollo is appeased and ends the plague. For most Greeks, this was not simply a story, but evidence of how religion worked. Small wonder, then, that by summer's end, when the Spartans withdrew, leaving parts of Attica scorched in their wake, Athenians questioned whether their own commander, Pericles, was somehow responsible for both the war (engineered, some said, to deflect attacks on his domestic life) and "all the other disasters," by which they meant the plague. They imagined him, like Zeus, brooding on the Acropolis, "head heavy with the burden of his cares, singlehandedly unleashing havoc from his enormous mega-brain." So, they disregarded his authority and sent ambassadors to Sparta to sue for peace.[6]

When the Spartans rejected these overtures, Pericles convened the Assembly. Citizens were used to his occasional excoriating speeches, and this time he pulled no punches. There was, he said, no going back. At stake was not just victory or defeat, but loss of empire and the danger of recriminations from subject states angry how they had been treated. According to Thucydides, Pericles went on to warn: "To anyone so frightened by what we're facing that he thinks the best and noblest thing would the dissolution of our empire, I say this: it's too late; we can't go back. Your empire is like a tyranny. Maybe it was wrong to set it up, but it would be too dangerous to let it go."[7]

The People, insisted Pericles, must follow him, a man "second to none in the knowledge of what must be done or in the power to express it, a man who loves his city and is above being bribed." It was a messianic statement, whose hubris was compounded in his peroration. The only thing that he had not foreseen, he said, had been the plague, but "to accept phlegmatically whatever the divine might throw at us, and bravely to resist the enemy: this was our city's character in former times; do not resile from it today." Impassioned though this sentiment might be, it did contain one startling admission: that the plague might have been sent if not by gods then at least by the divine. The term Pericles uses ("ta daimonia") is more nebulous than "hoi theoi" ("the gods"), but, while in keeping with the teachings of men such as Anaxagoras, it is nonetheless a nod to popular belief. At the same time, it conveniently glosses over the more dangerous idea, suggested by the Spartans, that the cause of the gods' anger was the centuries-old curse on the Alcmaeonids, embodied in Pericles himself.[8]

But, if Pericles believed he could play down the curse, others disagreed. It was probably at the next year's City Dionysia, still celebrated despite the ongoing plague, that his bitter critic Sophocles produced a tragedy which challenged Pericles and everything he stood for. From its first scene, *Oedipus,* albeit set in legendary Thebes, was devastatingly contemporary. It opens in a plague-wracked city. Perhaps gesturing to the audience, a priest of Zeus describes how throngs of men—young, old, and priests—are gathered round the altars, while "other crowds are sitting in the agora, wreathed as suppliants, and in front of the two temples of Athena." For Athenians, the image could not have been more resonant, its implications clear: though set in Thebes, the drama was about them—and Athens.[9]

There are early hints that Oedipus is meant to represent a familiar contemporary figure. The priest calls him "the first of men," a striking phrase that echoes Thucydides' description of Pericles' government as "the rule of the first man." Like Pericles (who had so recently claimed to be "second to none in the knowledge of what must be done or in the power to express it"), Oedipus is clever. He alone has solved the riddle of the Sphinx, thanks to which he has saved Thebes, marrying its queen, a woman, whom the audience knew from myth (though Oedipus does not) was also his mother, and whom Sophocles chose to call not Epicaste, as she appears in earlier versions, but Jocasta—in Greek Iokaste, "violet garlanded," a nod to Pindar's celebrated epithet for Athens, "violet crowned." Like Pericles ("a man who loves his city and is above being bribed"), Oedipus rails against bribery, saying that he will use his intellect for his city's good.[10]

But the gods intervene. Asked how the plague might be lifted, Apollo's oracle tells Thebes to "drive out the pollution" which blights the land since it harbours the killer of its former king, Laius. Again, parallels were inescapable. "Drive out the curse of the goddess," the Spartans had insisted only three years earlier, when war (and maybe plague) could be averted. Oedipus launches an investigation, but soon comes up against another religious figure, Teiresias, the blind prophet, who accuses Oedipus himself of being the killer. Oedipus' furious reaction, accusing both Teiresias and his own brother-in-law, Creon, of bribery, sets up the tension permeating the remainder of the play between the intellectual's cold logic (Oedipus says he solved the riddle of the Sphinx "thanks to reasoning alone, not learning it from birds [i.e., omens]") and the believer's faith in gods, which turns out to be entirely justified.[11]

Key to the drama is Oedipus' relationship with religion, not just when he rebuffs Teiresias, but when he misinterprets Apollo's oracle that he will kill his father and marry his mother. Relying on only partial knowledge he wrongly assumes the oracle to mean the king and queen of Corinth, by whom he was adopted as a baby, and his excitement when he learns that his supposed father has died naturally sees him dismiss the oracle as superstitious nonsense, a view shared by Jocasta, but considered dangerous by the chorus, the voice of the people, who usually reflect the feelings of the audience. Halfway through the play, they sing a lengthy ode, of which it is worth quoting three stanzas:

Hubris breeds tyranny.
Hubris, crammed with too much empty wealth—
won at the wrong time, in the wrong conditions—
climbs to the highest height,
before being toppled down to absolute destruction,
and there's no way to get back up again.
But dissent is good for the city. I pray
the god will never let that end.
I will always call the god "protector."

If a man walks, arrogant in word or deed,
not fearing justice, not venerating images of gods,
may a cruel fate overwhelm him
for all his ill-starred insolence,
the profiteer who profits without care for justice,
who behaves irreligiously,
who pollutes the sacred with his sacrilegious touch.
What man who acts like this
shall boast he can deflect gods' arrows from his soul?
If such behaviour wins respect
why should I ever dance in honour of the gods again?

I shall not go, a pilgrim, to [Delphi's] sacred shrine, the centre of the earth,
or to the sanctuary at Abae or Olympia,
if men cannot show that oracles are true.
No, most powerful Zeus, if I address you rightly,
most powerful ruler of them all, may this not
escape you or your deathless, everlasting, and imperial command.
The ancient oracles are withering,
already held in disregard.
Nowhere is Apollo honoured.
Religion and religious faith are dying.[12]

Religious scepticism, intellectual arrogance, plague, tyranny, and hubris: it is not just legendary Thebes of which the chorus sings. Many must have worried that these verses applied equally to Athens. The choral ode comes at a turning point. From now, the drama pivots; Oedipus' true ignorance is revealed. Relying on his intelligence, he has committed the worst crimes imaginable: a parricide, he has slept with his own mother. Appalled, he punches out his eyes, declares himself "shunned by the gods" (*atheos,* a word which audiences could also hear as "atheist"), and admits, too late, "it was Apollo, friends, Apollo, who engineered my hideous, horrendous suffering." But his actions have had wider consequences, impacting future and even past generations. "Violet garlanded" Jocasta, who like him dismissed Apollo's prophecies ("From now on I'd not trust an oracle, not even if it only told me to look right or left"), has hanged herself, their young children are orphaned, and the audience, familiar with myth, knew there would soon be civil war. No record of their reaction to *Oedipus* survives, but the tetralogy containing it failed to win first prize. Perhaps it was too political. Perhaps, it alienated Pericles' supporters. Perhaps like *The Capture of Miletus* two generations earlier, it reminded the Athenians too vividly of their own troubles.[13]

Yet Sophocles was still in a minority. Pericles' fellow demesmen still supported him, electing him general for the twenty-ninth consecutive year. Likewise, the Athenians still backed his strategy, evacuating Attica next spring and letting the enemy rampage at will throughout the summer. Less supportive was Pericles' own family. Perhaps frustrated that Alcibiades, his father's ward, praised for his role in the Potidaea campaign, was flaunting his inherited wealth, Pericles' elder son, Xanthippus, began to borrow money to fund his own lavish lifestyle. Recklessly, he named his father as guarantor, but when creditors demanded repayment, far from settling his son's debts, the notoriously parsimonious and scrupulously evenhanded Pericles took him to court. The rift was never mended. Within months, Xanthippus succumbed to plague. Soon Pericles' sister, then other close relations, then his younger son were dead. As he laid a wreath of flowers on the corpse of his last heir, Pericles broke down and wept.[14]

Gripped by depression, he refused to leave home until Alcibiades, whom few men could refuse, persuaded him to return to the arena he once dominated. On Pnyx Hill, a majority of Athenians showed their sympathy, voting to bend Pericles' law of 451 B.C., so that his teenaged son by the Milesian, Aspasia, might be enrolled as a citizen. But not everyone was generous. On stage the comic playwright Eupolis raised a cheap laugh, as he imagined Pericles enquiring, "Is my bastard still alive?" To which the answer comes, "Yes, and he'd long since have been a man [i.e., a citizen], if his mother had not been a whore."[15]

By late summer 429 B.C., Pericles himself contracted the plague. As it tightened its grip, he took to bed. Throughout his life, he had recoiled from superstition, paying only lip service at religious festivals and sacrifices. Now, faced with his own mortality, he put up no resistance when the women of his household (though surely not Aspasia) hung a lucky charm around his neck, even showing it off to well-wishers who crowded his sickroom. But soon he was too weak even for that. Thinking him unconscious, his friends discussed his exploits and achievements, but Pericles could hear. His voice, which once commanded the Assembly, now little but a whisper, he chided them. He owed it all to chance, he said, as much as to his own abilities. Already Greeks regarded Chance to be a goddess (Tychē). So, did Pericles experience a deathbed conversion? Certainly, his mind seemed to be wandering. Despite the death toll from war and plague which had resulted from his policies, with his last breath he boasted, "No Athenian alive has dressed in mourning thanks to me."[16]

There is no reason to doubt the historicity of these words, this scene, reported by Plutarch some five centuries later. Even moderately successful politicians can lose touch with reality, and it would be unsurprising if wealthy Pericles, in power for half a lifetime, surrounded by Greece's intellectual elite, inspired by the latest advances in science and philosophy, saw the world differently from most fellow Athenians. In his building programme, he was ready to exploit religion for the sake of politics, crafting a narrative to suit his vision of the city and its citizens, but at the very least he was likely sceptical about gods, heroes, and oracles. If Sophocles did base his Oedipus on him, it suggests that many if not most in Athens knew this. They certainly knew about the family curse. In times of peace and prosperity, this clearly did not matter much. If it did, Pericles would have been ostracised or at the very least not voted into office. But faced with plague and an expensive war—the Potidaea campaign had racked up an eye-watering bill, 420 talents (almost equal to the cost of building the Parthenon) per annum—public sentiment began to shift, and in the ensuing years concern that Athens had misunderstood or angered her protecting gods became more palpable.[17]

Just months after Pericles' death, another tragedy explored this very theme, its plot constructed as symmetrically as the Parthenon, with mirroring episodes rippling outwards from a pivotal central scene. Like his *Medea,* Euripides' *Hippolytus* ends with a father forced to bury his son, but this time the father is Theseus, Athens' superhero, living in Troezen in temporary banishment, working out a curse he has incurred for killing the sons of Pallas. In Troezen, too, is Hippolytus, his bastard son by the late Amazon queen (whose abduction provoked the Amazonomachy). An avid huntsman, who worships Artemis to the exclusion of all other gods, Hippolytus has vowed to live a life of chastity—setting him at odds with Aphrodite, goddess of sex, who takes revenge by making Theseus' new wife, Phaedra, fall in love with Hippolytus. When, despite her best efforts, Hippolytus discovers this and violently rejects her, Phaedra kills herself but leaves a note accusing him of rape. Returning from Delphi, Theseus discovers it, believes the accusation and, with one of three curses gifted him by Poseidon, demands that the god "kill my son." In response, a bull erupting from the sea spooks Hippolytus' chariot team, which drags him to his death. But before he dies, he is reunited with his father. Artemis (vowing vengeance on Aphrodite) reveals the truth, and (unusually for the time) Hippolytus absolves Theseus of bloodguilt.[18]

For believers in traditional religion, much about the drama resonated with Athens: Theseus' bloodguilt foregrounded in the opening speech, mirroring the curse on the Alcmaeonids; Hippolytus' fanaticism, causing him to ignore basic tenets of Greek religion, and pay no heed to the entire panoply of gods; Hippolytus' wrongheaded certainty causing discord—even between Artemis and Aphrodite, two goddesses whose harmonious relationship and love of Athens are shown so strikingly on the Parthenon sculptures; Theseus, wrongly convinced *he* knows the truth, forcing Poseidon to kill Hippolytus, the god's grandson, despite his innocence. Each of these spoke to a concern that, by abusing her relationship with the gods, Athens, embodied here in Theseus, was spiralling to disaster, destroying her future, just as Theseus destroyed his son, through the agency of Poseidon, the sea on which Athenians depended for their power.

Yet hope remains. While Artemis' promise to kill one of Aphrodite's favourites despite his innocence might chime with the nihilism of the topsy-turvy plague years, where good and bad appeared to suffer equally, Hippolytus' extraordinary death scene (a rare occurrence on the Greek stage) suggests that Athenians might still achieve redemption. Although initially reacting with outrageous blasphemy when he discovers Aphrodite's role in his demise ("If only humankind could curse the gods!"), Hippolytus, reassured by Artemis that he will henceforth be worshipped as a hero, forgives his father, and when Theseus praises his "good, religious attitude," he retorts, "Pray that your legitimate sons might have the same." Since those watching in the audience believed themselves to be Theseus' legitimate descendants, this was a doubly powerful plea, while the closing lines of the chorus might have been a threnody for war-torn Athens: "This misery is shared by every citizen. It came unlooked for. Our tears will sound a steady oar beat. Fates of noble men deserve more share of sorrow."[19]

But the oar beat of tears was drowned out by the ever-louder oar beat of war. Euripides' warning went unheeded as Athens, desensitized by plague and conflict, seemed to turn her back on many of those ancient values by which she once defined herself. Already in 430 B.C., Athenians had broken Panhellenic law by killing enemy ambassadors caught trying to drum up help from Persia; when Potidaea fell in 429 B.C., many were incensed at how leniently the city's starving, dazed survivors were treated (they were permitted to resettle in the nearby countryside). And by 427 B.C., attitudes were hardening. As the Assembly debated how to punish Mytilene on Lesbos following a quashed rebellion, Cleon, son of Cleaenetus, the tanning mogul, stepped onto the platform. One of the new cadre of politicians vying to fill the vacuum left by Pericles, his was a new style of oratory. Pacing restlessly, his tunic hitched over his belt, gesticulating wildly, he accused the Mytileneans of being the worst kind of traitors, who deserved the harshest punishment, their women and children sold as slaves, their men massacred. Mesmerized by his rhetoric, the People sent a ship that very day to see that the sentence was executed immediately.[20]

But some vestige of humanity—or expediency—remained. The next morning, the Assembly was reconvened. Cleon rehashed his arguments: "Your empire is a tyranny imposed upon unwilling subjects, who constantly conspire against you. It's not because you cosset them to your own disadvantage that they obey you. They have no love for you. They are subdued by force." But more pragmatic voices prevailed: it was not in Athens' interests to mete out death so indiscriminately. The first vote was overturned: only the ringleaders would face execution. Another ship was launched, its crew rowing with such determination that it reached Lesbos as the herald from the first was reading the decree. Athenians were proud of their leniency. But it was relative: 1,000 "ringleaders" were killed; Mytilene's walls were dismantled; its fleet was confiscated; and its land was seized to be divided among settlers from Athens. Even for some Athenians the trauma of the episode was inescapable. Criticized at his euthyna for how he had conducted the campaign, the general in charge drew his sword and stabbed himself. A man of principle, he preferred suicide to shame. Not for him the harsh new world of Athens.[21]

Mytilene was not the only city where violence erupted that year. Corcyra witnessed vicious civil war between Athenian-backed democrats and Spartan-backed oligarchs. When the democrats prevailed, they embarked on an orgy of revenge. Watched by an Athenian general,

> they went to the Temple of Hera and persuaded fifty men, seeking sanctuary there, to submit to trial. They condemned them all to

> death. When they saw this, most of those still in the temple, who had not been removed for trial, slaughtered one another—right there in the temple. Some hanged themselves from trees. But in whatever way they could they killed themselves. For the next seven days, while [the Athenian commander] stayed on with his sixty ships, the Corcyrians continued massacring whoever they decided was their enemy. . . . Every form of death was seen, not just the type of thing that often happens in such circumstances, but so much worse: a father butchering his son; men dragged from temples and slaughtered next to them; still others dying, walled up in the Temple of Dionysus.[22]

As Thucydides observed, "the moment that constraints, which keep us civilized, were shaken free, human nature (quick to do wrong even when laws exist to stop it) readily revealed itself to be the slave of its emotions, the oppressor of justice, the enemy of anything that would control it."[23]

Athens watched on as shameful deeds were done, too, at Plataea. Since 519 B.C. when Spartans, reluctant to help Plataea against its neighbour, Thebes, suggested that it "hand itself over" to Athens, "its closest neighbour, and not bad at righting wrongs," the city had been Athens' staunchest ally. Only her men had fought beside Athenians at Marathon. But now, Athens was found wanting, her reputation for protecting the oppressed exposed as an empty sham. Although they gave sanctuary to Plataea's women and children, and sent a garrison to the city, when Sparta besieged it in 429 B.C., on Pericles' orders the Athenians did nothing. Instead, they looked on as for two years Plataea's men were starved into submission. When, following a mock trial, the Spartans executed all survivors, even the most patriotic Athenian agreed that the stain on Athens' reputation was indelible.[24]

And so, the war dragged on. So did the plague, mutating and returning with new virulence that winter, while that summer and the next the plains of Attica were thick with Spartans and their allies, vandalizing towns and villages and vineyards, orchards, olive groves and crops, because—even if it took great time and effort to cut down a tree or grub up vines—they understood the psychological impact it would have on residents of wider Attica. Conflict was expanding into other theatres, too. With Pericles gone, his policy of sitting tight and not engaging in land warfare was forgotten, as Athens, eager to expand her influence, sent expeditions to the west of mainland Greece and further still to Sicily. They had begun the war intending to wear down the enemy and force them to acknowledge their hegemony. But now their strategy had changed, though exactly what they hoped they might achieve was arguably becoming less clear by the day.[25]

And still divisions deepened in the city between the old conservative majority and a new breed of intellectuals, many of them incomers to Athens, typified by one controversial Sicilian who had already persuaded Athens to make war on his island. Now in his mid-fifties, the wealthy, charismatic Gorgias was a silver-tongued philosopher, a compelling rhetorician, who weaponized language and earned a reputation for prioritizing style over substance, persuading listeners that false was true through the sheer bravura of his expression and delivery. Equally worrying for democrats, Gorgias and men like him, soon known collectively as sophists, were willing to pass on their skills—but only to those who could afford them. Before long, young aristocrats, many of whom, like Alcibiades, had come of age in the war years, were paying high fees to hear these sophists' seminars on subjects ranging from morality to science, taught from a distinctly rationalizing standpoint. For Athenian traditionalists, repeating rituals, performing sacrifices, observing the unchanging calendar of festivals, the danger their ideas posed seemed palpable.[26]

So, when the earthquakes came, they thought they were the work of gods.

Thucydides describes them in one tantalizing sentence. Having listed the number of (male) citizens who had died from plague by the end of winter 426–425 B.C., the last year that it struck ("more than 4,400 hoplites, 300 cavalry and an undiscoverable number of the poor") he writes, "There occurred, also, many earthquakes in Attica, Euboea and Boeotia, and especially Orchomenus in Boeotia." Two paragraphs later, he reveals that since there were "many earthquakes" the same summer, the Spartans chose not to invade Attica that year but turned back at the Isthmus of Corinth. He continues:

> Around the same time as these earthquakes were going on, at Orobiae in Euboea the sea withdrew from what was then the coastline before returning to swamp part of the city, inundating some parts, and leaving others permanently under water so that where there was once land there is now sea. All who could not save themselves by running quickly onto high ground were drowned. A similar tidal wave struck Atalante, an island off the coast of Opuntian Locris. It washed away part of the Athenian encampment and wrecked one of two ships, which had been dragged onto the beach.[27]

For Thucydides, influenced by philosophers such as Protagoras and sophists such as Gorgias, these phenomena could be explained by science: "In my opinion, the cause of such events lies in the earthquake. Where the tremors are strongest, the sea is forced back from shore, before suddenly pouring in again with increased violence, thus causing the flooding. Without the earthquake, I cannot see how this would happen."[28]

Of course, he was right, but this was not how most Athenians saw it. For them it had been sent by gods. Even without plague and earthquakes and tsunamis it had been a loathsome year. It had begun with battering, torrential rains that left much of low-lying Attica for long weeks under fetid pools of stagnant water. Then, in mid-May, the Etesian winds, which normally helped cool the city, failed. The heat became unbearable. Crops failed. Plague blossomed. Just as in *Oedipus,* it seemed as if Apollo was scarifying the people and their land, pouring all the acid of his anger over Attica. As for the earthquakes and tsunamis, most Greeks believed they were the work of Poseidon. And then Athena, too, showed her displeasure. As Athens was rocked by yet another tremor, the two northmost columns at the east side of the Parthenon shifted. The entablature above them fractured. And part of the pedimental sculptures showing the mystic moment of Athena's birth dislodged and crashed down to the ground. The implications seemed catastrophic. "Give so that you might receive" was the watchword of Greek religion. If this was how the gods were treating Attica, then surely Athens' gifts—among which was the Parthenon—were unacceptable. Surely Athena had rejected her temple.[29]

With their world collapsing round them, the Athenians asked the Delphic oracle what must be done. The reply does not survive but it provoked an immediate flurry of activity: almost at once, construction work got underway on three new temples, expenditure on which, while fiscally imprudent at a time when war was sapping funds, was more than justified by hope that they would change the city's fortunes. One was on Delos for Apollo himself. Work on the post–Persian War temple had been suspended when the Delian League's treasury was moved to Athens, and the building had been left half finished. Simply to complete it now might seem a hasty afterthought, and risk offending the god further. Led by Cleon, the Athenians took no chances, lavishing Apollo's island with an extravagance of worship. First, they performed rituals of purification, reverentially exhuming burials from the island's graveyard, and relocating them to nearby Rheneia, forbidding anyone thenceforth from dying or giving birth on Delos. Then they revived the old four-yearly Delian Games (whose kudos had been overshadowed by the Panathenaea), adding a horse race to the programme to attract more prominent participants. And then they began work on the temple.[30]

Squeezed between Peisistratus' temple dedicated over a century earlier and the more recent half-finished temple, it was architecturally unambitious, similar in structure to the Temple of Artemis Agrotera in Athens—perhaps deliberately, since Artemis was Apollo's twin and that temple was a reminder of how negotiations with the gods had resulted in success. Like the Temple of Artemis Agrotera, the new Temple of Apollo may have been designed by Callicrates, but what made it remarkable were the contents of its tiny cella, lit (like the Parthenon) by windows either side of the great door. Standing on a gleaming curving plinth combining marble and Eleusinian limestone were seven bronze statues: six gods and heroes flanking Apollo, among them his sister, Artemis; his mother, Leto; and his Athenian-born son, Ion. Originally cast for Peisistratus' adjacent temple, they were transferred to the new building, reconsecrated as a wholly democratic offering.[31]

Democratic Athenian mythology played a major role, too, in the acroteria. Both featured statues showing mortals carried off to Mount Olympus: on one side was Cephalus, King Cecrops' son, abducted by Eos, goddess of the dawn; on the other Oreithyia, daughter of Erechtheus, snatched up by Boreas, the wind god, who had intervened to help the Greeks before the Battle of Artemisium. Both mortals were Athenian, and the choice of subject matter (reinforced through the use of Eleusinian limestone on the statue base and running in a band above the frieze) proclaimed a now-familiar message: the gods' love of Athens and her citizens; the gods' elevation of Athenians to a status greater than mortal. Despite plague, earthquake, and crop failure, Athenians could still not recognize such claims as hubris.[32]

Eight years the temple took to finish, by which time Cleon was dead. So, in 417 B.C., it was his rival, Nicias, who oversaw its dedication. Desperate to fill the vacuum left by Pericles, Nicias, a successful general but nervous speaker, had won the backing of Athenian conservatives in part because, the owner of 1,000 slaves who toiled for his enrichment in the silver mines at Laurium, he basked in his good works. Deeply religious, indeed superstitious—his personal soothsayer accompanied him everywhere—Nicias was famous for the extravagance with which he funded dramas, choruses, and games, and for the statues which he dedicated on the Acropolis and at other sanctuaries in Athens. So, appointed to officiate at the consecration of Apollo's temple, he was determined that it should be done in style and with the greatest show of reverence imaginable.[33]

Previously, choruses arriving on Delos had disembarked dishevelled and disorganized from their sea voyage. For Nicias, however, determined to show Apollo the greatest honour possible, this would not do at all. Instead, he first landed his worshippers and herds of sacrificial beasts on Rheneia, and set his slaves to work constructing a pontoon of boats, painted, gilded, draped with tapestries, festooned with fragrant garlands, across the straits to Delos, and, with Apollo's sunlight sparkling on the waves, he led his chorus, sumptuously robed, all singing to Apollo's lyre and marking out their well-rehearsed, well-choreographed dance steps onto the sacred island. In drifts of incense, their hymns and sacrifice gave way to banquets in Apollo's honour. But even this was not enough. The ceremony over, Nicias made his own dedication—a life-sized bronze palm tree, sister to the sacred tree that grew on Delos and the bronze palm tree at Delphi—and before he left, he bequeathed Apollo one last gift, a plot of land, the revenue from which would pay for sacrificial banquets and prayers to all the gods . . . for his own, personal salvation.[34]

More ambitious than this Temple of Apollo—and considerably more architecturally challenging—was another temple started in 425 B.C. and located on the Athenian Acropolis. Steered through the Assembly by one of Cleon's closest acolytes, it was a brand new Temple of Athena Polias, built to supersede the Parthenon, to give the goddess's ancient xoanon its own home, and to honour the pantheon of gods and heroes who had once shared chapels in the Old Temple but who currently had no proper sanctuaries of their own. But because the Old Temple's ruins were too sacred and symbolic to be built on, the only possible location for the new construction was between them and the north wall of the Acropolis, an awkward piece of land, which sloped so steeply that the eastern side was 10 feet higher than the northwest. To complicate matters further, the site, straddling the remains of the Bronze Age palace, was crowded with religious landmarks.[35]

The project called for an architect with sensitivity and flair. Following the success of his Propylaea, the commission was awarded to Mnesicles. He chose to replicate the basic structure of the Old Temple—one large cella and a tripartite opisthodomos—but topography forced him to arrange the cella and opisthodomos on different levels, with the cella floor 10 feet above the opisthodomos. Also, owing to the lack of access from the west—abutted by the Garden of Pandrosus, there was no space for the usual porch and doorway—the layout of the building was perforce eccentric. While the cella was conventional enough, its narrow porch supported by six graceful

10.2 The Temple of Athena Polias or Erechtheum with the ruined Old Temple in the foreground.

Ionic columns, its great doors flanked on either side by windows opening to the east, the west side was eccentric. Seen from the level of the Old Temple it seemed to have a regular façade. In fact, it was essentially a false front: tall grilled windows filled the space between four engaged columns, their bases resting slightly higher than their eastern counterparts on horizontal moulding, below which the wall continued right down to the level of the Garden of Pandrosus. The actual entrance to the opisthodomos was offset at right angles to the north, where an impressive portico gave onto a long entrance hall (illuminated by the windows of the west façade) from which two doors led into "chapels" on the left, while on the right a third provided access to the Garden of Pandrosus, and straight ahead a narrow flight of steps doglegged upwards to another doorway on the level of the Old Temple's platform—and a third, idiosyncratic portico.[36]

Unusual in that it was accessed only from inside, this was the one part of the new building to encroach onto the Old Temple's foundations, projecting over its ruined peristyle, but stopping short of its

10.3 The Porch of the Caryatids extending over the ruins of the Old Temple with the Propylaea in the background.

cella wall. The intention may have been to harness the site's sacred energy. To Greeks this idea was familiar—besieged by Croesus, Ephesians had stretched a rope between their city and their extramural Temple of Artemis to let the goddess's protective force flow through it; Cylon's followers had done the same, when they tied their rope around the xoanon—and this might explain why, immediately upon completion, the new building was confusingly referred to both as the "temple where the ancient statue is" and as the "Old Temple." Unusually, too, instead of columns, the porch roof was supported by six graceful caryatids, perhaps sculpted by Alcamenes, spiritual descendants of the caryatids gracing Delphi's Siphnian Treaury. Statues of young women, they gazed across the Old Temple's "ground zero" to the Parthenon. Peplos pinned at the shoulder, well-dressed hair cascading down their backs, leg closer to the centre of the composition slightly bent, all adopted the same stance, but each was subtly different, an individual, a character. And, like the landscape over which they watched, they married the traditional with the contemporary. Although in their posture they were reminiscent of archaic *korai* statues, in their execution—with their flowing robes and classical perfection—they were thoroughly modern.[37]

The porch's purpose is unknown, and who, if anyone, the caryatids represent is fertile ground for speculation. No hypothesis is entirely convincing. Pausanias records what he (or his tour guide) interpreted as fragile, blackened statues of Athena, part-burnt by the Persians, preserved as a memorial on the Acropolis. Broken *korai,* archaic statues of young girls, perhaps dedicated by Arrhephoroi, had been buried nearby, between the temple and the Arrhephorion, and while Pausanias does not specify precisely where he saw his blackened statues, being brittle, they must have been protected from the elements. Perhaps they stood, embodiments of a curated past, guarded by their caryatid sisters, inside the porch. Extending out above the ruins of the Old Temple, combining past and present, it would have made a powerful image.[38]

The new temple could easily have seemed disjointed. Instead, thanks to Mnesicles' genius, it possessed compelling logic, its unity of form enhanced by such refinements as the delicate garlands of alternating lotus blossoms and palmettes encircling not just the top of every column shaft (themselves studded with glass and jewels) but the entire temple, where they ran around the walls beneath the slim Ionic frieze. Formed of individually carved marble figures, this frieze was very different from the Parthenon's. All that remains are a few women, perhaps gods, their broken torsos dressed in delicately moulded drapery; a horse; a figure seated on a throne decorated with a sphinx: all too out of context and too damaged to suggest what myth or festival they represented, but unusually they were attached by dowels onto a dark grey background—a band of Eleusinian limestone that encircled the entire building.[39]

It was a remarkable complex. As Temple of Athena Polias, it was home to the goddess's xoanon, no longer simply an adjunct overshadowed by Pheidias' glitzy gold-and-ivory agalma in the Parthenon, but given pride of place and lit by an immortal flame, a golden lamp which burned continuously day and night, whose reservoir of oil was so capacious that it needed to be filled just once a year, and above which a bronze palm tree stretched up to the roof, drawing off the smoke, and glinting in the light. The palm tree was a nod to Apollo, but Athena shared this temple, as she had shared its predecessor, with other gods and heroes, too, not least Poseidon-Erechtheus and Hephaestus. And it contained other holy places—King Cecrops' tomb, shared with the sacred snake, now covered by part of the Caryatid Porch and accessed by a narrow entrance from the Garden of Pandrosus; a patch of virgin rock left unpaved at the North Porch, with an opening in the roof above it, the site either of Poseidon's "token" (marks of his trident) or where Zeus' thunderbolt had crashed to earth; and Athena's olive tree in the Garden of Pandrosus. Meanwhile, further to enhance this sacred zone of the Acropolis, the land between the Garden of Pandrosus and the Arrhephorion was reworked—the ground raised and levelled, the Arrhephorion demolished and rebuilt—to make one linked, coherent unit. The Arrhephoroi and their rituals were linked through sculpture to the Parthenon. Now they were linked through the manipulation of real physical space to the new Temple of Athena Polias. There could be no clearer sign of the importance of their role in Athenian religion.[40]

For centuries, the area of the Acropolis occupied by the new temple had been known as the Erechtheum, so it was little wonder that this name stuck or that Erechtheus' standing increased at this time. In 422 B.C., less than three years after the temple was begun, Erechtheus was the subject of a drama by Euripides, which as usual linked contemporary events to mythology. Set during the legendary war against Eleusis, it sees Erechtheus receive the oracle that only if he sacrifices one of his three daughters will Athens win; as his wife, Queen Praxithea, patriotically approves this action, all three daughters willingly lay down their lives; Erechtheus kills Eleusis' King Eumolpus, but Poseidon is so enraged that he drags Erechtheus beneath the earth and rocks Athens with a massive earthquake. For Athenians still reeling from the earthquakes of 425 B.C. (followed by at least one other in 424 B.C.), these parallels surely added potency to the final scene. Most of the text of Euripides' *Erechtheus* is lost, but enough survives to show that it contained a speech from Athena, who begins by addressing Poseidon—"Poseidon, Lord, I call on you to turn your

10.4 The Porch of the Caryatids.

trident from this land. Do not uproot my country. Do not destroy my lovely city." She goes on to command Praxithea:

> Build a temple with a stone enclosure for [Erechtheus] your husband at the city's heart. Here citizens [of Athens], remembering his killer, will add the name "Erechtheus" to that of esteemed Poseidon, and make sacrifice of oxen. As for you [Praxithea], who have restored the city's foundations, I give you the duty of offering burnt sacrifices on my altar as my priestess.

Euripides frequently ended tragedies with a foundation myth, but what is striking here is his linking of Attica, earthquakes, the building of a sanctuary to Poseidon-Erechtheus and the inauguration of a line of priestesses of Athena, the name of whose current officeholder Lysimache ("Dissolver of Battle"), was loaded with contemporary significance.[41]

Athena's speech contains a further command. Praxithea must bury all three daughters together since "they did not recklessly forsake the oaths that they had made their sister. As a result, their souls have not gone down to Hades. Instead, I have given their spirits a home in heaven, and a glorious name, the Hyacinthidae, by which all Greece shall know them." They would be honoured, the goddess continues, with annual sacrifices, "maiden-dances," and a sacred precinct which must not be entered lightly, especially not by Athens' enemies, since they would bring victory to whichever army brought them offerings. It is the first recorded mention of a ritual which saw Athenians make sacrifice to them before going out to battle (perhaps a recent institution), and although the precinct's site is unknown, it is tempting to locate it near the Arrhephorion, especially since this was now connected to the temple. The idea that self-sacrifice might bring citizens heroic immortality was by now deeply familiar, but it was clearly worth reminding some Athenians of the importance of correctly performing their religious duties.[42]

The Temple of Athena Polias effected both a material and a profoundly sacred transformation of the landscape. While the imperialistic Parthenon still dominated the Acropolis and its skyline, overshadowing the Old Temple's ruins, the new temple became its spiritual counterweight. The arrangement of the buildings, too, told a powerful narrative: the Old Temple, the venerated, burnt "ground zero," remained the sacred heart of Athens, the only monument to face Athena's altar. Now, though, it was flanked by not one but two successors, each embodying an aspect of Athenian identity: the Parthenon and its treasury, conceived by Pericles; Pheidias and their intellectual friends, embodying its wealth and restless mind; the Temple of Athena Polias with its plethora of sanctuaries encompassing its piety.

The Temple of Athena Polias would not be finished until 406 B.C. (when almost immediately it was partially destroyed by fire), but another, smaller temple on the Acropolis begun at the same time was built considerably more rapidly. Inheriting the Parthenon's role as temple of victory, the new Temple of Athena Nike (Victorious Athena), almost identical in design to Callicrates' Temple of Artemis Agrotera and the Delian Temple of Apollo, was sited atop the Propylaea's southwest bastion, 28 feet above ground level, as if on a tall plinth. Planned for years, its construction delayed by work on the adjacent Propylaea,

10.5 The Temple of Athena Nikē.

it fitted perfectly with the spirit of the new programme. The site was of profound historical significance. It was from here that King Aegeus was believed to have leapt to his death, convinced that Theseus, his son, had lost his life in Crete, and foundations of Bronze Age fortress walls still lay exposed in the vicinity, while windows through the marble cladding of the recent bastion exposed traces of its Bronze Age predecessor as well as Bronze Age niches, carefully restored, which may have held cult statues. Visually, too, the bastion, with its band of Eleusinian limestone set beneath the temple base, was reminiscent of the plinth of the iconic Harma monument, set up after the democracy's first victory.[43]

The theme of victory pervaded the temple's sculptures: like the Parthenon's west *metopēs,* the west pediment showed the Amazonomachy; like the Parthenon's east *metopēs,* the east pediment showed the Gigantomachy. The east frieze, too, (just like the Parthenon's) was inhabited by gods, and, although today it is impossible to tell what they are doing, it is striking that, while on the Parthenon they are the focus of a peaceful civic parade, here they are associated with scenes of warfare. Most eye-catching is the fighting shown on the south frieze, since here for the first time the two sides were clearly meant to be identified through weaponry and armour as contemporary Greeks and Persians. While some suggest the battle is Plataea, that victory was won not by Athenians alone, but Greeks led by a Spartan general, and so is unlikely that it is this that is being celebrated here. More plausibly, despite the presence of Persian cavalry, it is Marathon, its composition perhaps modelled on the celebrated panel in the Painted Stoa.[44]

Echoes of another artwork can be found here, too. The pose of one Athenian is modelled on the statue of the tyrannicide, Harmodius. Perhaps, he is the war archon, Callimachus, to whom Herodotus (writing at around this time) imagined Athens' general, Miltiades, saying: "Callimachus, today you must choose either to enslave Athens or free her, and so leave for all future time a legacy *such as not even Harmodius and Aristogeiton left behind*" (my italics). On the Temple of Athena and Hephaestus, the tyrannicides' statue had been referenced in the stance of Theseus; here (if it is, indeed, Callimachus) it was embodied by a human hero, who laid down his life for Athens. The message of the Parthenon that heroized the sacrifice of Athens' citizens lived on.[45]

Battles appear on the north and west friezes, too, but this time between Greeks, some dressed in short tunics, others heroically nude, most helmeted or bearing shields, many dead or dying. There is little or no iconography to help identify what battles are being shown. Even for Greeks it may have been impossible. Many may have thought they signified their ongoing war with Sparta and her allies, and if this was their intention, it was a startling departure from tradition—not only the first Greek temple sculptures to glorify contemporary warfare, but showing many of these modern warriors as nude, the conventional visual shorthand for heroes.[46]

Remarkably, the commissioning of these three temples—on Delos for Apollo; on the Athenian Acropolis for Athena Nike and Athena Polias—inspired by fear that Athens had offended her gods, coincided with a turning point in Athens' fortunes. As summer 425 B.C. turned to autumn, Cleon led Athenians to victory at Pylos in the southwest

Peloponnese. For the first time in history, a Spartan army surrendered. More than 100 prisoners of war were brought in chains to Athens, and with them came their shields, the ultimate sign of their humiliation. Before marching to battle, Spartans were given shields by wives or mothers, who repeated an age-old formula, "with it or on it"—come home carrying your shield or carried on it, dead. Only a coward threw away his shield, since to let it fall into an enemy's hands was shameful. Which made it even more remarkable that, just months after the new building programme was unveiled, ranks of captured Spartan shields were being displayed, hung on the very bastion on which the Temple of Athena Nike was starting to take form. And when that winter no plague came, it must have seemed that Athens was at last back on track.[47]

11 BATTLE LINES

War is the father and the king of every man. He shows some to be gods, and others to be men. He makes some slaves, and others he makes free.

—HERACLITUS, IN HIPPOLYTUS, *REFUTATION OF ALL HERESIES,* 9.9

The capture of the Spartan prisoners was a turning point. So long as Athens held them hostage, her enemies would call off their annual invasions of Attica. Empty of refugees, the city was no longer such an incubator for disease. And now that wagons could pass freely between the quarries of Pentelicus and Athens, the new building programme could proceed apace.

Meanwhile, despite ongoing negotiations—Sparta now desperate to end the war; Athens, newly confident, refusing—hostilities dragged on. Athenian triremes cruised round the southern Peloponnese, seizing the offshore island of Cythera, a useful base from which to launch attacks on Spartan territory, and (with Pylos in Athenian hands) a real threat to the Spartans, who were so worried that helots might seize the moment to stage a fresh revolt that they promised freedom to 2,000 of the bravest. On the day of the liberation ceremony, they led these men, garlanded, in procession round the temples—after which, in Thucydides' disturbing words, they "made them disappear, and no one knew how any of them died."[1]

Still, not everything was going Athens' way. An expedition to take Megara failed. So did a poorly coordinated offensive against Boeotia, an overly elaborate pincer movement that fell at the first hurdle, leaving Athenians forced to retreat overland from their bridgehead a few miles beyond Attica's northeast frontier. Harried by Boeotian troops, some escaped, but many more were forced back to the temporary fort which they had hastily thrown up at Delium, around a sanctuary of Apollo, named from Delos. But if they hoped the god would save them, they were wrong. As corpses bloated in the choking sun, many thousand Athenians found themselves besieged. And then the flamethrower was wheeled into place, a new, horrific weapon in Boeotia's arsenal, which spewed rivers of fire into the tinder-dry stockade (the sanctuary, defiled by the Athenian military presence, being now considered a legitimate target). Fleeing through clouds of missiles to the beach where their fleet was waiting to evacuate them, some could not help but think they had been warned. As Thucydides laconically observed, early that summer "there was an eclipse and the same month, around the time of the new moon, there was an earthquake." Perhaps predictably, Euripides responded with another tragedy based on the Antigone story, about the horrors of war and the burial of bodies, but voices like his were few.[2]

There was no letup. Led by the charismatic Brasidas, an army of Sparta's allies and expendable freed helots (who had escaped the massacre) marched north and in driving snow seized icy Amphipolis. Thucydides the historian was nearby. Like his namesake, he was a politician, that year one of Athens' generals. But sailing in choppy seas off Thasos when the news arrived, he was too late to intervene. Accused of incompetence by Cleon, he was forced into exile—and thus granted leisure to follow the war's course, interview key players and eyewitnesses, and write his history, a "possession for all time," in which the only role gods played was in the minds of credulous humans.[3]

The war had reached stalemate. Athenians held Spartan hostages; Sparta held Athenian Amphipolis; it was time to discuss peace. In spring 423 B.C. a year's armistice was signed, predicated on retaining the status quo, and with the option of extending it into a more long-lasting treaty. But news travelled slowly. Between the truce being signed and news reaching him, Brasidas accepted the surrender of one of Athens' colonies. Even after learning of the armistice, further nearby

11.1 The Temple of Athena Nikē from the Propylaea.

colonies declared for Sparta. The truce was over. Early the next year Cleon sailed north, determined to repeat his triumph at Pylos and retake Amphipolis. He failed. In battle by the city walls both he and Brasidas were killed. Each was an advocate of war. With their deaths more dovish voices cooed, and in 421 B.C. Athens, Sparta, and most of their allies signed a fifty-year non-aggression treaty, known today from its chief Athenian negotiator as the Peace of Nicias. (Athens and Thebes made a separate truce.) Bar acknowledging a few minor gains and the return of certain captured territories—together with the Spartan hostages—all sides agreed to freeze things as they were. Ten years of fighting had achieved very little, certainly not Pericles' aim of seeing Athens unopposed, an economic powerhouse, mistress of the sea.[4]

Still, peace had been achieved, and, when the Temple of Athena Nike was consecrated the next year, Athenians might just about have managed to confuse stalemate for victory. It was not their only confusion. The temple's wooden statue showed the goddess holding in her right hand a pomegranate (the fruit of Persephone, a link with Eleusis' message of rebirth), and a helmet in her left to show that war was over. But over time people thought she represented Nike, Victory, herself. Her iconography and Athena's were almost the same, except for one thing: Nike had wings. So, asked why they made this statue wingless, later Athenians explained that it was so that she would never fly away but stay forever where she was. They had quite literally clipped her wings.[5]

This was not the only temple dedicated in these early months of peace. Athens was still reeling from the aftermath of plague. The loss of life had been enormous; many survivors were suffering paralysis of their extremities and other complications. Ex-combatants, too, had come home nursing wounds. Health and well-being were everyone's concern. So, the Assembly voted to introduce a new god to the city: Apollo's son, Asclepius. The god of medicine, Asclepius possessed a healing sanctuary at Epidaurus, and it was from here (part of the peace dividend, since it lay deep in Peloponnesian territory) that they brought him to Athens in the guise of a sacred snake, timing his arrival to coincide with the Eleusinian Mysteries—a sign of its importance. Lined up at Piraeus' harbour, priests in ritual vestments greeted the state trireme that had fetched him, accompanying the god's procession between the Long Walls to his new home on the south slope of the Acropolis. Among the welcoming committee was Sophocles, the dramatist—later to be honoured both as Asclepius' priest and as the hero Dexion ("Receiver") for temporarily accommodating the serpent in his house until the sanctuary was finished.[6]

The cult of Asclepius combined faith and science. While new medical techniques were being advanced by practitioners such as Hippocrates, whose meticulous observation and recording of symptoms for the benefit of future doctors mirrored the historian Thucydides' determination to "find precise information about the past to help interpret the future," many treatments still relied on faith and magic—including in sanatoria within Asclepius' sanctuaries, where cures were thought to be effected by sacred snakes that glided over sleeping patients, and votive plaques of limbs and organs were offered in hope of healing. But Asclepius' cult, where rational and irrational could coexist in harmony, was an exception.

Elsewhere the culture wars raged on, and as usual it was in the theatre (just east of Asclepius' sanctuary) that they were waged most intensely. One of the most revealing of all plays was Aristophanes' comedy, *Clouds*. When first staged in 423 B.C., it flopped, but Aristophanes felt that it was so important that, six years later, he revised the script for publication or private performance, and this version survives. Here, Aristophanes attacks the sophists, their scientific, rational worldview, and their professed ability to make any argument seem plausible. The plot revolves around a yeoman farmer, Strepsiades, who, married to "the niece of Megacles"—in other words, an Alcmaeonid heiress—is plunged into debt thanks to his son's addiction to chariot racing. Assailed by creditors, he attends a sophist's "phrontisterion," or "thinking factory," but fails to grasp even the basics of its arcane teaching. His son, Pheidippides, is more receptive, but when he turns his newly acquired logic against Strepsiades, the old man drives out the sophists and burns down the phrontisterion.[7]

Even a thumbnail sketch shows much about Athens of the 420s and 410s B.C.: the profligacy (perceived or real) of young aristocrats; increasing strains between generations; fear that revolutionary rhetorical techniques might threaten social order. But this is only the beginning. Embedded in the play is a more existential fear that the sophists are denying the gods' existence and indoctrinating their impressionable young pupils with dangerous beliefs. Tensions between god-fearing traditionalists and radical philosophers had been developing for decades, but now they were coming to a head. Realities of war, plague, earthquake, and famine had forced Athenians to make a choice. Either they agreed that these were natural disasters explicable by science, or they believed that they were punishments sent by gods, angry at being dishonoured.

As an Athenian writing for Athenians, Aristophanes chose to satirize not any of the controversial incomers from other cities, such as Protagoras or Gorgias, but an Athenian famous for his eccentricities—the shabby, barefoot, bulging-eyed, and deeply disputatious Socrates. In *Clouds,* he is very different from how his student, Plato, would remember him, more natural scientist than philosopher, a disbeliever in traditional gods of Greece. Repeatedly in the script, he or his students insist that "Zeus does not exist," or that "the modern

11.2 The Temple of Poseidon at Sunium.

position is that gods do not exist." For Aristophanes' Socrates, the only real gods are the clouds, from which his comedy is named. It is a characteristically clever turnaround: while genuine philosophers were setting out to identify the gods with natural phenomena, Socrates chides Strepsiades for thinking that divine clouds are merely "mists, dew and smoke." Rather, "they are the only goddesses. The rest is nincompoopery." It is these gods-cum-natural-phenomena, Aristophanes' clouds declare, who were responsible for recent eclipses and even lightning strikes on temples, including at Cape Sunium.[8]

While much of the play might be interpreted as a good-natured, light-hearted romp, its underlying seriousness comes into focus in the violent denouement. By now Strepsiades has concluded that sophistic teaching is a danger to society and rejects Socrates' teaching. So, when Pheidippides asks his father, "Does Zeus exist?," he replies emphatically, "yes," prays to "beloved Hermes"—"don't be angry with me, don't destroy me, no! Forgive me. I lost my reason to a load of bullshit"—climbs onto the phrontisterion's roof, smashes it to pieces and sets it alight. As Socrates and his pupils flee to safety, Strepsiades roars his final, devastating words:

What were you thinking to offend the gods like this,
and scrutinize the temple of the moon?
Chase them! Throw stones at them and beat them up!
You know that they deserve it, and especially because they wronged the gods.[9]

In Greek, the word translated here as "to offend" has powerful overtones. It is *hubrizete,* "commit hubris against," and it underscores the visceral intensity of Aristophanes' rejection of sophists and Socrates, the man whom he has chosen as their representative. If this was how his first *Clouds* ended, Aristophanes (with an eye to winning first prize) must have expected most of its audience to share Strepsiades' outrage. Perhaps they did. The play's failure could have had nothing to do with its content—poor performances and production values, or rival plays raising more laughs on the day. But it sheds important light on schisms fracturing Athenian society and suggests how most might worry that the gods could vent their anger on the many to punish the sceptical few. Sophists scoffed at such fears. In *Clouds,* Strepsiades, not the brightest character, refers to Socrates as "the Melian," a throwaway gag, wilfully confusing him with another philosopher, Diagoras, who did come from Melos and was remembered as an atheist. One anecdote recalls Diagoras mid-ocean in high seas, harangued by fellow sailors, convinced that, because gods hated him, all would be shipwrecked. Pointing to other vessels wallowing in equal difficulty, he asked, "So is Diagoras also aboard them?"[10]

Aristophanes aimed his satire, too, at the sophists' pupils, a generation of entitled young men, sufficiently wealthy to afford their fees, sufficiently leisured to have time for further education, and sufficiently ruthless to do all they could to bend Athens to their will. Chief among them was Alcibiades, whose character and attitudes so resembled those of Aristophanes' Pheidippides, that he was probably the model. A close associate of Socrates (who saved his life at Potidaea, as he saved Socrates at Delium), Alcibiades had shared his boyhood home with Pericles and Aspasia. He had heard its intellectual visitors discussing their inflammatory ideas. As his early years had coincided with the Periclean building programme, he was familiar with the ideas behind it and, while architectural technicalities would probably have bored him, he almost certainly found inspiration in the temples and their sculptures and their potential as vehicles to project the power and preeminence of Athens and her citizens—because to him power and preeminence were everything: his own power and his own preeminence.[11]

Charismatic, certain of his own abilities, determined to win at any cost, Alcibiades acted as a lightning rod for schisms splitting the city, and his emergence in the 420s B.C. coincided with the new post-plague morality. In some ways the embodiment of late fifth-century-B.C. Athens, he was arguably the logical outcome of all the contradictions of the past century: the system of great rival families; the rise of Athens as a ruthlessly imperialist democracy; and the tension between reason and religion. Pericles had been conscious of these inconsistencies but, when it came to domestic politics, wisely tried to steer a middle path. Alcibiades, on the other hand, an egocentric showman, courted controversy, flaunting his wealth, parading his unconventionality, and embroiling Athens in unprecedented religious scandals. A devotee of Homer, he embraced the motto, "always to be best and to surpass all others." Buy now, at the age of thirty, when he might have hoped to live up to this creed by being appointed general, Athens was negotiating peace and dashing his hopes of adventure.

This, however, did not deter Alcibiades in the slightest. Instead, careful not to break the treaty, he encouraged Athens to wage proxy wars, in which he played the role of puppet master. At one Assembly meeting—ominously interrupted by yet another earthquake—he won a vote supporting Argos against Sparta, and soon he was leading a huge Argive army through the northern Peloponnese, forcing reluctant cities to join his coalition prior to an attack on Corinth. At last, Sparta rallied. In 418 B.C. she won a crushing victory, and Alcibiades' ambitions to secure a foothold in the south of Greece evaporated. Blatantly disregarding the oaths of peace that Nicias and the Athenians had sworn with Sparta, he had risked plunging his city once more into total war. But remarkably, the treaty held. Spartans had no wish to reignite hostilities. For them, oaths were sacred.[12]

For most Athenians, too—men such as the venerable Nicias himself, who viewed Alcibiades and his aggressive, quick-tongued, and quick-witted friends as a real danger to the religious and political stability of Athens. By spring 416 B.C., antipathy between the factions and their leaders was running so hot that the Assembly approved an ostracism vote. It was a chance to choose between two very different ideologies, a referendum pitting the religious values and traditional morality personified by Nicias against the revisionist new rationalism embodied by Alcibiades. But politics, like war, has ways of circumventing constitutions. Since, in the lead-up to the ostracism it became clear that the decision was too close to call, Alcibiades made Nicias an offer: join forces and vote down a third party instead. So, another man, Hyperbolus, found himself ostracized. The process resolved nothing. Instead, it revealed a fatal weakness at the heart of the democracy. So long as politicians played by the rules, there was a chance of social stability. Xanthippus, Aristeides, Themistocles: all previous victims of ostracism had accepted the decision in good part. But once one charismatic demagogue had contrived to evade it, its power was gone forever. An ostracism vote was never held again.[13]

Alcibiades' corruption of the noble Nicias smacked of sophistry, where any argument could be bent to seem convincing, regardless of its ethics. A nasty episode later that year exposed sophistic amorality still further. Melos in the Cyclades had long been neutral, but it had let Spartan ships anchor in its harbour and shown some sympathy to Sparta, thanks to which, ten years earlier, Athenians had tried—but failed—to take it. In spring 416 B.C. (since it was not covered by the peace treaty), they tried again, blockading the island, besieging the city, and setting out the arguments for why they should prevail. In exile, Thucydides may have heard reports from eyewitnesses, though his presentation of this controversial episode, couched in the form of a dramatic script, is so unusual that it suggests that he meant it to stand out, an ethical debate on one of the most burning issues of the day, his own considered distillation of the arguments, not a verbatim historical report. He has the islanders appeal to justice. But the Athenians are unimpressed: "What men call 'justice' is a construct that applies only between equals: those in power do as they wish; the weak must simply put up with it." And when the Melians declare their "faith in gods that they will not give us a worse fate than they give you, since we have justice on our side and you do not," the Athenians respond,

> What we think about the gods, and what we know for certain about men, is that it is everywhere a law of nature that wherever they hold power they use it to dominate. We did not invent this law, nor are we the first to follow it. We found it already in existence, and it will still exist forever when we're gone. We know that you or anyone who had the same power we enjoy would do exactly as we do. As for the gods, we're not afraid of them and we see no reason why they should not support us.[14]

Perhaps Thucydides expected such cynical arguments to shock readers, but the notion that, to win, the powerful will use every means at their disposal no matter how unfair or irreligious was espoused with gusto by both Athens and her darling, Alcibiades, who flaunted his privilege, taunting the People with his outrageous behaviour, coquettishly relying on his good looks and charisma to get what he wanted, breaking every rule. Like his aristocratic ancestors, his passion was for horses. In 418 B.C. his chariot team triumphed at the Panathenaic Games. But his eye was on a bigger prize, Olympic victory, and two years later he made sure he could not lose. Given that the Games were part of a religious festival, competitors relied not only on their strength or skill but on the favour of the Olympic patron, Zeus, to win. Not Alcibiades. His strategy was more cynical. To own a chariot was evidence of stratospheric wealth, but at Olympia in 416 B.C. Alcibiades raced seven, which guaranteed his chances of success: since only one needed to win, the other six could block or impede rivals.[15]

The praise-poet Pindar had written: "Whoever wins fragile fame from winning in games or fighting in battle wins eulogies and praise from fellow citizens and countless foreigners alike, the greatest prize of all." For Alcibiades, this fame was everything. Feted for his victory, luxuriating in a palatial tent, ostentatiously providing food and wine for everyone—competitors, trainers, spectators, many thousands—at a banquet on the central day of the entire festival, he made sure that he, not Zeus, became the focus of attention. When he returned home, a hero, he commissioned two paintings to celebrate a string of victories. One showed him triumphant, garlanded by goddesses, incarnations of the Pythian and Olympic Games, while in the second, the goddess of Nemea sat enthroned "more beautiful than any woman alive," embracing Alcibiades as he lounged in her lap. Twenty years earlier, the Parthenon Frieze had celebrated the bond between Athenians and gods. Before that, other artworks, including panels in the Painted Stoa, showed gods fighting alongside mortals. But never had a living citizen been pictured publicly (no doubt heroically nude) in such intimate, erotic entanglement with a goddess. Among the first self-commissioned portraits hung in democratic Athens, six centuries later it was still on display in the Propylaea.[16]

Worse was to come. Early in 415 B.C., two Sicilian cities, Egesta and Leontini, asked Athens for military support in local conflicts. Their pleas were music to Alcibiades' ears. Twice in the past twelve years, Athens had intervened in Sicily without success. This time, he hoped, it would be different. Moreover, the defeat of Leontini's target, wealthy Syracuse, could bring great profit. When a fact-finding mission confirmed Egesta's ability to foot the bill, Alcibiades easily persuaded the Assembly let him lead the taskforce—but, still as divided as they were two years before, it then appointed Nicias to be his colleague. Both men were horrified. Motivated equally by personal loathing and strategic doubts, Nicias launched a vitriolic attack on Alcibiades, foregrounding intergenerational suspicions, calling Alcibiades a "young man in a hurry," "too young for high command," motivated by his "own selfish ends," and suggesting that the expedition needed to be twice the size that Alcibiades proposed. His strategy misfired. The Assembly approved Nicias' inflated, tactically inept estimates and began its preparations.[17]

Nicias was not Athens' only Cassandra. That year, responding to Athenians' increasing ruthlessness, typified by their negotiations with Melos and the brutal treatment of its defeated islanders (massacring its men, enslaving its woman and children), Euripides staged a trilogy which spread one story over all three tragedies, a structure not seen since the days of Aeschylus. Its subject was the Trojan War. The outer plays traced Troy's fate from prosperity to destruction, and its queen's fall from power to slavery. But the central tragedy, a dark, disturbing work, told of an honourable Greek general brought down by false accusations by his rival, the morally corrupt Odysseus. The trilogy explored fears about the dangers of sophistry, of confusing right and wrong, and the lengths to which unscrupulous men might be prepared to go in order to succeed. These fears are seen in *Trojan Women,* the final play, whose prologue shows Poseidon and Athena plotting to destroy the Greeks as they sail home from Troy, since, as Athena explains, "they have insulted me [*hubristheisan,* "committed hubris against"] and my temples" by raping the Trojan princess, Cassandra at Athena's altar. (As Thucydides' Athenians say on Melos, "Those in power do as they wish.") When Poseidon agrees to send a storm to batter the Greek fleet, Athena concludes, "In future, Greeks must learn to respect my shrines *and honour all the gods*" (my italics). So, the victorious Greeks impose their will over the captive Trojan women, ignorant that many will themselves soon be destroyed, a chilling reminder of the fragility of human power and human life.[18]

With the fleet's departure for Sicily immanent, religion became increasingly weaponized, as political factions showed their willingness to go to any length to neutralize opponents. From the start, there were dissenting voices. Sounds of lamentation, as women observed the annual Festival of Adonis by wailing, beating breasts, and burying corpse-dolls, were interpreted as direful omens—and many priests opposed the expedition, including Callias, torchbearer in the Eleusinian Mysteries, grandson of the peacemaker with Persia. But warmongers wheeled out their own religious experts, from the oracle of Zeus Ammon in far-off Egypt which claimed "Athenians were fated to take

11.3 A relatively intact herm.

all the Syracusans" to homespun soothsayers promising that they would conquer the whole of Sicily.[19]

Then, one June dawn, the city awoke to mayhem. Statues of Hermes standing at street corners and in front of urban sanctuaries and homes had been vandalized, their heads and genitalia smashed in a clearly coordinated attack. The psychological impact was devastating. These herms were an integral part of Attica's identity. As god of transitions and transactions, Hermes played a central role in city life and death from overseeing commerce in the Agora to leading dead souls to the Underworld. Even more alarmingly, he was the god of travel, and with the fleet poised to sail, his goodwill was crucial. In *Trojan Women*, Poseidon had described whoever desecrated shrines and tombs as "brainless," adding "he will make his own home a wasteland and in time will be destroyed." Who, then, was responsible for this present desecration, and what was their intention?[20]

Unsolved, this coldest of cold cases remains perplexing. Theories abounded; accusations flew. Suspects included Corinthians, trying to stop Athens attacking their colony, Syracuse; but others looked closer to home, accusing rich young revellers. Often after symposia (drinking parties held in wealthy houses), roisterous groups would roam the nighttime streets, singing, chanting, on occasion going too far. But while previously there were isolated instances of mutilating statues and defacing shrines, this vandalism of the herms was different. It seemed too thorough. Conspiracy theories took hold, with talk of young men meeting in the moonlight in the Theatre of Dionysus, before dispersing through the city in small, determined groups. But their identities were shadowy, their motives unclear. Some said they were Nicias' supporters, determined to obstruct the expedition (an unlikely notion, given Nicias' well-known piety); others that they were rich Athenians angered at the imposition of a wealth tax; still others that they were young sophisticates, mocking religion and the gods.[21]

With the city stunned, a Commission of Enquiry offered immunity from prosecution to anyone with information about this and other sacrilegious acts, and in doing so it opened a Pandora's box. At the last Assembly before the expedition sailed, there came the startling accusation that in a private house with a cabal of young elite Athenians, Alcibiades had profaned the Eleusinian Mysteries in the presence of an uninitiated slave, repeating words, performing gestures, revealing truths forbidden for the uninitiated to see and hear. Now, with all uninitiated citizens removed, the slave was brought to testify. His evidence was damning. With friends acting as torchbearer and herald, he said, Alcibiades had played the role of hierophant, the priest responsible for revealing the Mysteries' most arcane secrets. As more witnesses came forward to corroborate his testimony, Athens entered freefall.[22]

Most citizens believed that former generations had been pious and god-fearing. It was this, as well as bravery and ingenuity, that had let Athens build democracy, defeat enemies, acquire empire—because the gods acknowledged her uniqueness and reciprocated her respect. Throughout the decades following the tyrants' overthrow and Persian defeat, this idea was repeated in art and sculpture, including in and on the Parthenon. The gods had shown their disapproval of the agnostics who conceived that building by sending plague and earthquakes, but Athens had endeavoured to restore the balance with new temples for Athena and Apollo. Now, though, if these accusations were true, elite citizens had wantonly committed sacrilege, desecrating herms (Alcibiades was now implicated in this scandal, too) and profaning the Mysteries. It was blasphemy on a cataclysmic scale.

The truth can never be known, but there are three possibilities, each instructive. The first is that Alcibiades and his friends did parody the Mysteries, thinking themselves so superrational that they could show contempt for popular religion by mocking one of Greece's greatest sacraments, deliberately flouting its strict rule of nondisclosure, proof of the deep schism between Athens' elders and her younger generation. If Aristophanes' *Clouds* and Thucydides' versions of Nicias' speeches that condemn them mirror reality, it is entirely plausible that such young devil-may-care aristocrats might consider such behaviour to be clever and exciting.

A second possibility is that the accusations were *partially* true, that the slave did witness an initiation ceremony but that, rather than a blasphemous parody, it was a genuine induction. In Athens, there were several "hetaireiai," exclusive political clubs, each with around twenty-five members, who supported one another in the Assembly and business and met regularly to socialize. To prevent sensitive dealings being made public, each "hetaereia" had strict rules and regulations—as well as an initiation ceremony for new members, elements of which (including officeholders' titles) were likely influenced by the greatest initiation ceremony of all, the Eleusinian Mysteries. Uninitiated himself, the slave could not know what actually was said or done at Eleusis, but the fact that he was believed suggests that many Athenians thought Alcibiades capable of such blasphemy, though popular suspicion was probably compounded by the belief that "hetaereiai" ("societies of friends") were hotbeds of oligarchic sympathizers and a threat to democracy.[23]

The third possibility is that Alcibiades and his companions were entirely innocent. The slave could easily have been commanded or persuaded to make the accusation by a malicious citizen, fuelled by personal hatred, and counting on the atmosphere of panic and suspicion following the vandalizing of the herms to wound an enemy. Given the circumstances, it could never be proved conclusively. It was his word against that of Alcibiades, and the stakes could not be higher. If Alcibiades were found guilty, his political and military career—perhaps even his life—would be over.

Alcibiades demanded an immediate trial. But time was running out: the fleet was ready; sailing could not be delayed. So, the Assembly reached a compromise: Alcibiades would assume his command; an investigation would determine whether charges should be brought; and, if necessary, he would be recalled to face impeachment. The odds were being stacked against him. Alcibiades' core support came from men of fighting age, and, with many of these accompanying him on campaign, a jury back in Athens was more likely to find against him. As it was, the public mood was hardening against the sophists. When Diagoras, the "atheist" philosopher, was accused of impiety, including that he, too, revealed secrets of the Eleusinian and other Mysteries, he wisely fled to Corinth, where he learned that the Athenians had placed a bounty on his head, a cash reward for any man who killed him. So, when shortly after the fleet set sail Alcibiades was summoned home for trial (prosecuted by the long-dead Cimon's son), he, too, absconded—to Sparta, where he ingratiated himself with his unlikely hosts by trading what he claimed were military secrets.[24]

Again, Alcibiades was playing the Homeric hero and so exposing a further flaw in Athenian society. For generations, Trojan epics had pervaded Attic life, and they were still being heard each year at Panathenaic Games, where rhapsodes recited the entire *Iliad* and *Odyssey*, in which warriors driven by a passion "always to be best and to surpass all others" worsted enemies no matter what the cost. Achilles, the *Iliad*'s protagonist, was the prime example. Insulted by Agamemnon, he withdrew from battle to skulk in his tent, moodily strumming his lyre, and praying that Zeus would "hem in the Greeks by their ships' sterns, by the salty sea, and there let them be slaughtered, so that they might all appreciate their king [i.e., himself, Achilles], while Atreus' son, wide-ruling Agamemnon, might realize his folly in refusing to give honour to the best of all the Greeks." Now, Alcibiades resolved to do the same, and wear down Athens, convinced that one day she would beg him to return. Such behaviour might make for a gripping plotline in an epic poem, but it was never meant to be the blueprint for democratic life, and over the following years it became increasingly apparent that the reality was considerably less heroic. Even without Alcibiades' interference, Athens was sliding to disaster.[25]

Learning of his escape to Sparta, the Assembly condemned Alcibiades to death, erecting an inscription, a "stele of disgrace" on the Acropolis, which named and shamed both him and others implicated in the mutilation of the herms and profanation of the Mysteries. But this was not enough to cleanse the city of his malign influence. In an act of great theatricality—and piety—every priest and priestess in Athens, including those who ministered the Eleusinian Mysteries, paraded at sunset onto the Acropolis, where they turned to face the west, and as the sun sank red above Salamis' far hills, in a defiant act of ritual, shook out their robes and chanted curses, calling down the gods' wrath on Alcibiades and his associates.[26]

But if his enemies had hoped to stop the expedition against Sicily, they had miscalculated. Allowing Alcibiades to sail, they had committed themselves to war, and there was no going back. For two long years, old Nicias, increasingly tortured by kidney stones and consequently drugged heavily with opium, squandered men, materiel, and military advantage, bogged down in a protracted siege of Syracuse. When Athens sent a fresh fleet and army, equal in size to the first expedition, he botched a nighttime assault so badly that many of his hoplites, unable to distinguish friend from foe, slaughtered one another. Soon, Syracusan warships swung into place to block the entrance to their Great Harbour. Athenian captains and oarsmen demanded action. But their ships, so long in water, were sluggish, difficult to handle, and they themselves, so long ashore, were out of practice. The shallow bay gave little room for real manoeuvre, and as the day wore on and even eager fishing boats kept darting out from friendly shores like shoals of minnows to support sleek, hungry Syracusan triremes, the Athenians lost hope. The besiegers found themselves besieged, encamped near fetid swamps, plagued by malaria, their once-proud triremes rotting in the shallow seas. Still Nicias refused to withdraw, terrified of how he would be met in the Assembly, but at last he bowed to the inevitable and gave the order to strike camp.[27]

Then, as sick, exhausted troops and oarsmen prepared for the evacuation, between 9:41 and 10:30 on the night of 27 August 413 B.C., there occurred . . . a total eclipse of the moon. Had Pericles been general, he would have explained this as a natural phenomenon, and if his men demurred, he would have turned the episode to his advantage, arguing that the gods were on their side, veiling the moon's light to help conceal their flight. Not Nicias. For years he had relied on his soothsayer to interpret every omen. But his soothsayer had died on the campaign, and there was no one who could calm the nervous, superstitious, sick old general, who stood down his men, forbidding an evacuation for a full month—the time required for the "polluted" moon to purify herself. Even the most god-fearing thought this an overreaction (traditionally business was suspended for just three days following a lunar eclipse), but Nicias was taking no chances. With all thought of escape forgotten, he obsessively made sacrifice, commanding augurs to examine piles of steaming entrails for some message from the gods, convinced that they were on his side, even as the Syracusans blocked the harbour.[28]

Now even Nicias was forced out of his torpor. Giving the order to strike camp, but unable to escape by sea, he set course inland, his one objective to get as far from Syracuse and save as many lives as possible. But he could not save the badly wounded, whom he was forced to leave behind; and he could not bury the dead. Instead, flouting every moral code, he abandoned them all. For endless days, the remnants of the army trudged and stumbled along dusty roads until, thirsty and exhausted and surrounded by Sicilians, thousands died shot down in a sluggish riverbed. Survivors were herded back to Syracuse, where some were sold as slaves but very many more were corralled to face an unforgiving death within the sheer walls of a stone quarry (a bitter irony for men who set store on stone temples). But, despite the recent siege, Syracusans still admired some aspects of Athenian culture—they freed those prisoners who could perform the latest verses of Euripides, including his Trojan trilogy with its vision of a great city's fall. When they returned home traumatized, the freed captives made a pilgrimage to see the old tragedian and thank him for their salvation.[29]

The expedition's failure with its loss of more than 200 triremes and 10,000 men was the greatest disaster that Athens and her empire had endured in forty years. Not since the Egyptian debacle in the 450s B.C., where (as at Syracuse) besieging Athenians were outwitted and besieged, had one campaign seen such enormous casualties. It rocked Athens to her core. Writing his history, Thucydides saw the entire episode—from the fleet's showy send-off from Piraeus, "to date the most expensive and impressive expedition put together by one single Greek city," to the horrors of the final massacre—as a clear example of how hubris leads to catastrophe, and while some feared that the mutilation of the herms and profanation of the Mysteries had angered the gods, dooming the expedition to failure, others blamed defeat on Nicias' superstition, his reaction to the eclipse, and his insistence that religious observation should trump military sense. With each side blaming the other, society disintegrated further.[30]

Recently in Sparta, too, a pious man's reaction to a natural phenomenon had resulted in unforeseen consequences. When a further earthquake shook southern Greece, Sparta's King Agis, to purify his city, stopped sleeping with his wife. But ten months later, she bore a child, whom in private she called her "little Alcibiades." Given the Athenian's reputation as a womanizer, the conclusion was not hard to draw. The cuckolded Agis ordered his death. But Alcibiades had disappeared. He had led a Spartan fleet out to Ionia, to foment revolution among Athens' subject states, and by the time that Agis' assassins reached the east Aegean he had been tipped off. The next that he was heard of, he was in Sardis offering advice to Persia's satrap, advising him how best to play Athens and Sparta off against one another until all Greece was so exhausted that the Great King could invade.[31]

For, by 413 B.C., war had broken out again. Athens had so clearly breached the terms of the peace treaty that the Spartans were forced to retaliate. This time their approach was much more tactical. All too familiar with the threat posed by Athens' occupation of Spartan Pylos, a military outpost and a haven for fugitive helots, King Agis seized Decelea, a town just 15 miles from Athens, which enjoyed close ties with Sparta. Nestled beneath Mount Parnes it commanded the entire Attic Plain, and once fortified, became impregnable, providing Agis with the perfect base from which to launch year-round attacks on towns and villages and farmsteads from Acharnae to the walls of Athens. Sparta's previous invasions were as predictable as the seasons, but now no one knew when or where a raid might happen. With permanent evacuation impracticable, Attica was plunged into a state of heightened terror. To compound matters, Agis offered sanctuary to runaway slaves. As time went by, some 20,000 took the road to Decelea, including many of those toiling in the silver mines at Laurium, the source of much of Athens' wealth.[32]

Meanwhile, Athens' ships, many built at frantic speed to replace those lost at Syracuse, sped to Ionia to meet the Spartan threat to coastal cities and the neighbouring Aegean islands, and try to stop Sparta, or perhaps Persia, seizing the Hellespont, so vital for Athens' food supply. Faced with so many threats, and with the empire apparently at breaking point, Athens had already revised her constitution, investing ten commissioners (probouloi) with extraordinary powers to oversee the building of new triremes, respected elders, who included Sophocles and Hagnon, founder of Amphipolis. But many richer citizens wanted a more radical overhaul of the democratic constitution, returning it to what it had been prior to Pericles' reforms of the 460s. They found an unexpected ally—Alcibiades, whose agents reassured them that, if they made Athens an oligarchy, albeit with a relatively wide powerbase, he would persuade Persia to support them in the war, while he himself would return to lead Athens to victory. They were empty promises. Persia's satrap was as slippery as Alcibiades, and the price he asked was too high for Athenians to countenance: the surrender of Ionia and the neighbouring islands to the Great King; an agreement that the Persian fleet could operate unchallenged in the East Aegean. Alcibiades knew that such outrageous propositions could never be accepted, but it was a marker of Athens' sudden weakness. Five years earlier, the wind had still been in her sails. Then, her annexation of Sicily, even her defeat of the great Carthaginian empire, and certainly her recognition as hegemon of mainland Greece had seemed entirely possible. Not now. Now she was fighting for survival.[33]

Opinion in Athens remained divided. At the dramatic festival of 411 B.C., Aristophanes staged *Lysistrata,* a comedy where women of Greece deny their husbands sex until they have thrashed out a peace treaty, an unlikely scenario for many reasons, but one that spoke to the city's desperation. Weeks later, the killings began. A group of young thugs knifed a leading democratic advocate to death. Fear gripped the city. The oligarchic faction managed to intimidate the Council and Assembly into concentrating power into the hands of just 5,000 citizens, the wealthiest Athenians who complained that they were shouldering the greatest burden of the war and thus should have the greatest say in politics. With the Council Chamber placed under armed guard, hard-line oligarchs sent delegates to Decelea to negotiate with Agis, but the Spartan would not listen. Instead, he staged a show of force before the city walls and ramped up the pressure ever further.

On the naval base on Samos, too, the oligarchs had made a move, picking off key democrats in both the city and the fleet. Among their victims was Hyberbolus, ostracised from Athens (although not her territories) six years earlier. But the navy, drawn predominately from the demos, Athens' poor, faced down the oligarchs, and when news reached Samos of the coup in Athens, the sailors declared themselves their city's democratic government in exile. Decades earlier, Themistocles had said that Athens was not bricks and mortar but her citizens, and that wherever they settled they would take Athens with them. Now, in a very different set of circumstances, the navy was proving his words true. Far from home, they were reasserting their faith in their democracy and their determination never to be cowed. But paradoxically, they recognized the need for a strong, charismatic leader, and they knew that one was close at hand.

In the *Iliad,* with the Trojans breaching his defensive wall and setting fire to the Greek ships, Agamemnon begs Achilles to return. Now Athens' democrats-in-exile asked Alcibiades to come to Samos as their general. It was the moment that he had been engineering for four years, and he embraced it with the passion of a lover. At a meeting of the sailors' Assembly, he made a string of what he hoped were plausible excuses for his treachery in aiding both the Persians and Spartans, before grandiosely promising that thanks to him the Great King would commit Persia's fleet to fight for Athens against Sparta. It was all lies, but no one cared. Nor did they seem to worry that the man they had appointed as their leader still stood accused of crimes against religion, or that he bore a great deal of responsibility for the Sicilian disaster.[34]

With Athens, the city, controlled by ruthless, hard-line oligarchs, and Athens, the democracy-in-exile, blindly following the dangerously psychopathic Alcibiades, the bipolar situation, developing for decades, was rapidly nearing its endgame. But first, things needed to get worse.

12 CATHARSIS?

And so, farewell my city. You once were bathed in fortune.
Farewell your well-smoothed towers.
Athena, daughter of Zeus, decreed your destruction.
If she had not, you would still be standing proud.

—EURIPIDES, *TROJAN WOMEN*, 45–47

As surviving records for 409/8 B.C. reveal, even while Athens was being torn apart by conflict, work on the Temple of Athena Polias (today called the Erechtheum) continued unabated. With the course of Eleusinian limestone already in position, worked blocks of marble were being hoisted into place; a column capital was waiting to be fixed on an interior pilaster; "three stones for the roof above the maidens" needed to be dressed; there was much still to do, but essentially the building had taken shape. Meanwhile, the great cycle of annual festivals kept turning. Sacrifices were performed on the Acropolis; dramas were staged in the theatre; processions meandered through the streets, though, thanks to the ongoing threat of Spartan raids, initiates no longer paraded to Eleusis overland but sailed round the coast. And each summer, two young Arrhephoroi climbed down the wooden stairway through the rock, exchanged their unknown, sacred objects in the Gardens of Aphrodite, and ascended once more through the limestone birth canal back onto the Acropolis.[1]

Yet, in the past two years so much had changed. Despite his promised Persian aid failing to materialize, Alcibiades had led the newly optimistic navy to a string of morale-boosting victories, systematically eliminating Spartan bases in the Hellespont until, in spring 410 B.C., he smashed the Spartan fleet at Cyzicus and killed its admiral, Mindarus. The threat to Athens' grain supply was lifted, while the interception of a Spartan letter home raised Athenian spirits further. "Ships lost," it read. "Mindarus dead. Men starving. Don't know what to do." In Athens, the news led to the oligarchic government's collapse, and its leaders' prosecution or exile. Now a new generation of radical democrats dominated the Assembly, who legislated a decree condemning to death any who proposed to overthrow the democratic constitution; and when Sparta tried to sue for peace, her delegation was rejected out of hand.[2]

To celebrate, Athenians commissioned a new religious artwork, a low parapet topped with railings surrounding three sides of the bastion, still studded with Spartan shields, on which the Temple of Athena Nike stood. It contained some of the most exquisite sculptures yet seen on the Acropolis. Roughly 137 feet in total length, and just over 3 feet high, each face of the marble balustrade was carved in medium relief with scenes showing Athena looking on as flights of female winged Victories brought bulls to sacrifice at altars and built trophies out of Persian and Greek weaponry and armour. Superlative in execution, these figures were exquisite, their garments clinging to their bodies to reveal the form beneath. This technique, known as "wet drapery," had been used to great effect on the Parthenon's pedimental sculptures, but here it was honed to perfection. So was the composition. As some Victories restrained energetic bulls, or lounged, relaxed, caressing captured shields, or bound their sandals, or removed them, their garments glided sinuously across their supple limbs to hang in gathered folds, accentuating rest and movement, adding rhythm to the composition as a whole. Sisters of the fluttering and glittering winged Victories which formed the temple's acroteria, they proclaimed a renewed confidence, and when Alcibiades, architect of victory, eventually returned in person, he received a hero's welcome.[3]

The summer of 407 B.C. marked a high-water mark. Revelling in his return, Alcibiades made the most of these few months, wooing the People with self-excusing speeches of dubious sincerity. Already his friend, Critias, another of Socrates' aristocratic students, had ensured that the Assembly pass a law not just recalling but exonerating Alcibi-

12.1 Nikē adjusting her sandal from the Nikē Balustrade.

ades—a vital piece of legislation, since when the navy on Samos recalled him, it had done so independently of the official government. Grateful to Alcibiades for reversing Athens' fortunes, and convinced this meant that the gods favoured him, Athenians also voted to return his property, seized when he went into exile, remove the "stele of disgrace" from the Acropolis to sink it deep beneath the sea, and reverse the curses that the priests and priestesses had intoned towards the setting sun.[4]

Meanwhile, Alcibiades himself set about blaming his misfortunes not on the Athenians but on what he described as a "malevolent daimon" that stalked his every move. He was not alone in claiming a personal daimon, a spirit which stayed by him night and day, whispering instructions, directing his behaviour. It was not a new idea, though for some the notion of a daimon was simply a way to explain human conscience. Even Heraclitus had weighed into the argument, suggesting that "man's character is his daimon." But for Socrates (or Plato, on whose record we rely), daimones were more than this, spirit-beings which bridged the gap between the human and divine, conveying prayers and messages between gods and men, precursors of angels. It is most unlikely that Alcibiades had anything of this sort in mind. For him, a daimon was simply a convenient excuse, a pretext to absolve his bad behaviour. But for others it may have struck a more dissonant chord: by his "malevolent daimon" did he mean the curse of the Alcmaeonids?[5]

Alcibiades was not alone in appealing to religion. His enemies did, too. By accident or intention (the ceremony could conceivably have been brought forward or delayed), his arrival home had coincided with the day of the Plynteria, one of the holiest dates in the religious calendar, when Athena's xoanon was stripped of her crown and jewellery, and of the yellow and blue peplos it had worn for ten months since the last Panathenaea. Then in the moonlight, statue and robe were wrapped, hidden from prying eyes, and carried to the sea by a select group of devotees: the priestess of Athena Polias, young girls, probably including Arrhephoroi, and leading all of them a woman carrying a basket of fig cakes. At the shore, two girls carried the statue a short way out into the sea and washed it, while another priestess washed the peplos, ritually cleansing it of all impurities; and when it was all done, they all returned to the Acropolis, to the Temple of Athena Polias, which had itself just been swept out, re-dressed the xoanon, and set it carefully in place. For Athenians it was a day of deep concern. Not only the xoanon, but the goddess herself, they thought, had left the city, and without her protection they could do nothing. So, every sanctuary was closed and roped off to prevent access; no business was transacted; and no new enterprises were begun. For Alcibiades to come home on this day of days was, at the very least, an unfortunate miscalculation. Perhaps, his enemies suggested, it was an omen that foretold disaster.[6]

Nonetheless, the Assembly showered Alcibiades with praise, awarded him gold crowns, and made him general with absolute authority, supreme commander on both land and sea, possibly the first time under the democracy that an Athenian had held this office, whose power came dangerously close to that of tyrant. He used it to prolong his stay at home, his reason: to escort initiates from Athens to Eleusis—overland. The importance of that procession led by Alcibiades himself and accompanied by battalions of well-armed hoplites, the worshippers dancing and singing hymns, the priests dressed in their pomp and finery, cannot be exaggerated, nor can the significance of its return to its old route along the Sacred Way for the first time in six years. For Alcibiades and his supporters, it was a triumph. For his detractors, who had never forgiven what they still believed to be his sacrilege, it must have seemed the most grotesque of blasphemies.[7]

It was also irresponsibly hubristic. By October, when the fleet at last set sail, the seas were dangerous. More dangerous still was the situation developing in the east Aegean with the arrival of a new Spartan commander, Lysander. While Alcibiades had been basking in praise, Lysander had been cutting deals with Persia's prince and winning his support along with generous supplies of money—which was something the Athenians distinctly lacked. Laurium was haemorrhaging slaves, its production was declining, and the ongoing war was sapping resources. With money so scarce, Alcibiades did not engage the enemy. Instead, he toured local subject cities demanding that they fill his coffers. But he made a fatal error. The old friend he left in charge of the Athenian navy disobeyed orders and in early 406 B.C. recklessly engaged the Spartans in the Bay of Ephesus. Many triremes were destroyed, and he himself was killed. When Alcibiades learned of the disaster, he did what he had done before: rather than face the inevitable reprisals from his enemies back home, he ran away, this time to the northern Hellespont, where he had already raised a private army and built a string of forts, to brood, an aging warlord on the fringe of Athens' empire.[8]

Dangerously self-absorbed he may have been, but without Alcibiades, the Athenians again lost their way. That summer, in waters near the Arginusae islands off Ionia's west coast, they engaged the now resurgent Spartan fleet with 155 triremes. Simply to have launched so many ships had been a great achievement. With numbers severely depleted, the Assembly had been forced to enlist slaves as oarsmen, offering to free all who served, and compensate their owners accordingly. New triremes had been built and new crews trained. The expense had been enormous, and money had been tight—to fund the war effort, the Assembly had voted to melt down golden statues of the goddess Nike on the Acropolis and turn them into coin. It was a drastic move. While it had always been acknowledged that in times of trouble precious metals used in statues of the gods might be considered bullion, until now there had been no need. But with Persia bankrolling Sparta, and the Athenian exchequer empty, there was no option. As for the choice of statues, perhaps Athenians hoped that, dedicated to Nike and thus imbued with her divine power, the resulting coins would bring them victory.[9]

If so, they were right. Thanks to the skill and resolution of the eight Athenian generals, they smashed the enemy battle line and, clouds massing and hulls bucking in the choppy waves, chased the scattered Spartan warships lest they join with other squadrons currently blockading Mytilene. But the pursuit took them far from Arginusae, and twenty-five of their own crippled vessels, whose surviving crews were clinging to the debris in the driving, lashing rain. Satisfied the Spartan threat was over, the fleet turned back, but now the storm was so ferocious that there was little it could do to save the drowning or retrieve the corpses of the dead, and when the generals returned to Athens initial triumph turned to bitter accusation. This was the second time in seven years that war dead were denied a proper burial. The first time, in Syracuse, there was nothing the Athenians could do, and still the pain of that humiliation, and the concern of families for their relatives whose souls had not been granted rest, burned deeply. Now, however, there had been every opportunity to collect the dead, but (albeit for good military reasons and bad weather) the generals had failed to do so.[10]

Unconstitutionally, it was decided to try them not in a lawcourt but in the Assembly, not individually but together on a common charge. The verdict was a foregone conclusion. All eight were sentenced to death, two in absentia. Among those executed was a man whose rise to high command had been extraordinary, given that as a youth he entertained no hopes of even being a citizen. As Pericles, son of Pericles and Aspasia, heard his sentence on Pnyx Hill, looking out across the valley to the Acropolis, the Parthenon and Propylaea, he cannot but have felt conflicted. It was his father who had helped make Athens great again. It was his father who in many ways had been responsible for war with Sparta. It was his father who, associating with the greatest intellectuals of his age, had thought to use religion as a tool to bolster Athens' standing and to represent her citizens as demigods, but in so doing helped provoke division. And now he was himself paying with his life.[11]

The generals' execution marked a new low in Athenian democracy. But life was to become still grimmer. These were dark days for the Greek world. In Sicily the Carthaginians were back. Three years earlier, they had returned to Himera, the site of their defeat in 480 B.C. Now they took revenge. They sacked the city and burnt its Temple of Athena to the ground. They overran Selinus on the south coast, too, massacring 16,000 citizens. And then they turned on Acragas, where a string of temples glittered on a ridge between the city and the sea. After a lengthy siege, they took it, slaughtering many who had fled for safety to the altars and "industriously ransacking and pillaging" the temples themselves. Sicily seemed destined to fall. So did Ionia. Despite protestations that they were fighting to "liberate the Greeks," the Spartans showed little loyalty to the Ionians—they had been willing to see them forcibly removed to northern Greece after the Persian invasions; their attitude had not changed since; and with Lysander doing all he could to cultivate the Persian prince in exchange for money and munitions, it seemed unlikely that Ionia would be free much longer.[12]

In Athens, the sense of an old world ending was exacerbated by the deaths of her two most celebrated tragedians, Euripides and Sophocles. For two generations, these bold playwrights, so unalike, had been the city's moral compass, challenging their democratic audiences, speaking truth to power. Despite his reputation as a sophistic thinker, earned partly because he did not shrink from putting "modern" revolutionary ideas into the mouths of many of his characters, Euripides projected a surprisingly traditional worldview, where gods ruled supreme, and mortals crossed them at their peril. Fascinated by advances in science and psychology, he did not suggest that these negated a divinely influenced world order, and, although many of his dramas composed during war with Sparta explored mental suffering, one of his last was a hymn to the power and potency of Dionysus.[13]

Written in Macedonia in self-imposed exile but imbued with beliefs encountered at Eleusis, *Bacchae* demonstrated humankind's powerlessness before the gods. "Though gods may inhabit the high stratosphere," his chorus sings, "they still can see the smallest act of man. Clever is not wise, nor thoughts no man should entertain." The idea was repeated by a messenger reporting the shocking power of Dionysus, who has driven one woman so mad that she rips her son apart with her bare hands: "The best thing is wisdom and piety towards the gods. I think the wisest course for men to follow is to remember this." *Bacchae* makes other powerful observations, too, not least about how easily a charismatic leader can infatuate his followers so completely that they act out of character, ignoring social norms and conventional morality, blindly engineering their own destruction. It was a chilling commentary on contemporary values.[14]

Outliving his rival by just a few months, Sophocles, too, addressed religion in his last play. *Oedipus at Colonus* revisits the myth of Oedipus who, exhausted by age and exile, arrives at Colonus, a few miles north of Athens, to be welcomed kindly by King Theseus. But it is not the Athens that was so familiar to its first audience. Instead, heavy with nostalgia, Sophocles' vision recalls a bygone world, when his city lived up to its ideals of helping the oppressed, standing up for what was right, worshipping the gods. As Theseus vows to protect Oedipus from harm, the chorus sings an ode in which the whole of Attica appears to thrum with the divine. It is worth quoting four stanzas:

Stranger, here in this country of fine horses
you have reached the most commanding place on earth—
bright, shimmering Colonus, where
the nightingale, constantly returning, trills her shrill song,
fluttering beneath the green-black branches,
the ivy dark as wine,
and the untrodden vegetation of the god
so heavy with its berries, deep in shade,
untouched by any storm wind.
Here Dionysus, Bacchic god,
forever treads the ground,
together with the nymphs who nursed him.

Nurtured by heavenly dew,
the narcissus with its rich clusters of flowers
blooms fresh each day, the ancient garland
of the two great goddesses [Demeter and Persephone].
And the crocus blooms, that shines like gold,
while constantly the springs of the Cephisus gush
out their flowing waters, constantly
drenching the Attic plain with their pure waters,
imbuing with fertility the deep swelling soil.
The dancing Muses love this place,
and Aphrodite, charioteer, guiding her team with golden reins.

And there is something here of which I never heard in Asia
or in the mighty Dorian Peloponnese,
a budding plant, unconquerable, and self-renewing,
a thing of terror to our enemies.
It burgeons on this land—
the grey-leafed olive, nurse to all our children.
Neither young men nor old can tear it
with their hand, for the unblinking eye of
its protector, Zeus, and of Athena
grey-eyed goddess, watch over it forever.

And I have further praise for this, our mighty mother city,
the gift of a great deity, the great pride of our nation,
horse-strength, colt-strength, strength of the sea.
O, son of Cronos, lord Poseidon, you have
enthroned her in proud majesty,
for it was here on our streets that you first
clamped the bit that you had forged to pacify wild horses.
And your ships with rising, falling oars
speed past the shore, slicing the sea-spray,
and fifty sea nymphs, dancing, follow in their wake.[15]

There are clear parallels between this vision and the sculptures of the Parthenon, not least the emphasis on the Eleusinian gods Dionysus and Demeter, and Aphrodite, highlighted on either side of the east frieze's divine assembly and opening the choral ode with its subsequent praise of Zeus, Athena, and Poseidon and the inventiveness of Athens. For the ninety-year-old Sophocles, the words perhaps encapsulated all that his city might have been, but thanks both to political ambition and the divisions of the past three decades, when the elite appeared to disregard old values, it never could achieve. In his play, Oedipus' life ends in mysterious circumstances, at a location known only to Theseus, who is instructed to pass this sacred knowledge only to his son "and he to his heir and so on forever," since such would be its power that it would protect the city from attack, "a terrifying mystery that none should speak of."[16]

But the blind king has a warning. Transformed into a hero, he will protect Athens, as will the gods—but only for so long as Athens behaves piously, since "for every city that conducts its affairs properly, many thousands wantonly behave hubristically (*kat'-hubrisan*). The gods can see at once, although they may be slow to punish those who turn away from the divine to madness. Son of Aegeus, do not wish this on yourself." But Sophocles' audience knew that Athens had not behaved piously, not least in regard to the location of Oedipus' grave. According to Pausanias, it was situated near the Areopagus, precisely where, two centuries before the play was staged, Megacles the Alcmaeonid rounded up Cylon's followers for slaughter and so provoked the curse upon his family and Athens, by association. Once more in this, his last and most profound of plays, Sophocles revisits an obsession, the hubris of and curse upon the Alcmaeonids including Pericles and now, in the next generation, Alcibiades, which ruined Athens.[17] Sophocles was lucky. He did not live to see his warning come true. Just months after his death, on a scruffy beach on the Hellespont's European shore, thanks to its commanders' cavalier attitude and lax discipline, Athens' fleet was caught unawares by the now superior Spartan navy. Only a few ships escaped. Most were destroyed, and many of their oarsmen killed. In that one afternoon Athens lost control of the waterway on which she depended for her grain. With no time or resources left to re-equip her navy, defeat was inevitable. The only real question was how long the starving city could hold out before it was forced to surrender—although there was another question, too, for those who remembered that great cause célèbre of the rationalist philosophers sixty-two years earlier, when Anaxagoras examined the famous meteor "about the size of a wagon load" that crashed to earth with such fanfare, for him a natural phenomenon, for others an omen presaging disaster. The site of its impact crater, Aegospotami, was none other than the beach on which Athens had squandered her fleet. Surely it was too much of a coincidence not to be a sign from gods.[18]

In the aftermath of victory, Lysander rounded up as many Athenians as he could find—from survivors of the battle to settlers in Ionia or the islands—and sent them back to Athens, to swell the numbers there, even as their food supplies ran out. No longer did all good things flow into the great port of Piraeus. Instead, the wharves stood empty, and an eerie silence blanketed the docks. Since before the days of Themistocles, Athenians had relied on the sea. Their navy was so powerful, and their city walls and Long Walls were so strong that they could style themselves an island thalassocracy, the hub of a great military and trading empire, destined to rule all Greece. But ambition had blinded them. Convinced by first Themistocles, then Pericles, then Alcibiades, they had overestimated their own capabilities, becoming catastrophically complacent, preferring the heroic creed of always being best and surpassing all others to the motto carved at Delphi, "Nothing in excess." And now they must face the consequences.[19]

Besieged, they contemplated death or slavery. These were the fates which they had meted out on other captured cities. There was no reason why they should be treated differently. At last, delirious with hunger and devoid of hope, they accepted the inevitable and on Pnyx Hill in full view of the Acropolis where the Parthenon and Temple of Athena Nike glittered tauntingly, reminders of past victory, they voted to surrender. At a meeting of the victors, the Boeotians, always Athens' cruellest enemy, pushed for the harshest punishment: to enslave the population, raze the city to the ground, turn Attica into grazing land for sheep. Not even the Persians had countenanced such things. But at a party later the same day, a Phocian sang a haunting song, "Electra, Agamemnon's daughter, I have come to your ramshackle courtyard in the countryside." The delegates all recognized it, lines from Euripides' *Electra,* where the once proud princess, condemned to live in a squalid cottage with a peasant husband, toiled day and night, resentful, dreaming of revenge. As the melody continued, many were moved to tears. And the mood among the victors shifted. They could not destroy "so famous a city, which had produced such great men" as Euripides.[20]

The story may be apocryphal, but Athens and her citizens were spared. Only one part of the city was destroyed: the Long Walls to the sea, so central to empire, commerce, and defence. On a September morning in 404 B.C., the seventy-sixth anniversary of victory at Salamis, a day chosen deliberately by the pitiless Lysander for maximum humiliation, Athenians turned out in force to tear down the Long Walls. Along the straight road to the sea, the Spartans had positioned flute girls, their melodies set off by the grim counterpoint of rubble crashing to dry ground as dust clouds cast their veil over the wreckage of a century-old dream. For years Athenians had expressed ambition and identity in stone and marble—in temples, stoas, odeons, initiation halls, in statues and religious sculptures, *metopēs,* and friezes—but now they were defeated, and their aspirations ended in a calculated act of demolition.

Democracy was ended, too. To govern Athens, Sparta imposed a new administration, whose officers were drawn from the Athenian elite—thirty oligarchs, known as the Thirty Tyrants, many of them educated men, including some involved in the short-lived coup just seven years before. Leading them was Critias, uncle of the philosopher Plato, whose ancestors had been friends of the great lawgiver, Solon, and who was himself a devotee of Socrates, a clever writer and philosopher, the man who had steered Alcibiades' recall through the Assembly. An author of prose works on rhetoric and politics, Critias was well known as a poet and playwright, and while none of his works survives in complete form, fragments reveal his deep religious scepticism. Among them is a passage from his drama, *Sisyphus:*[21]

> There was a time when human life was anarchic, bestial and brutal, without reward for good men or punishment for bad. I think that it was then that humankind established laws to punish wrongdoers, so that justice might be king and keep their wrongdoing [in Greek, "hubris"] in chains. Whoever broke the law was punished. But then, since laws prevented them from openly committing violent crimes, they began to do these things in secret, until (I think) some clever and resourceful man conceived for humankind

> the idea of being frightened of the gods, so that terror might seize wrongdoers if they did or said or even thought anything bad in secret. In this way he introduced religion, the idea of a spirit [in Greek, "daimon"] burgeoning, alive and never withering, that hears and watches with its mind, thinking and taking notice, and appearing like a god, which hears everything mankind might say and watches all they do. If you hatch any wicked plan in secret, the gods will find you out, since they are quick and clever. And with words like these he introduced the most seductive doctrine, concealing truth in lies.[22]

Much of this develops Anaxagoras' ideas and his concept of nous, mind, the pervading spirit of the universe. Critias uses the term *nous* to describe how the divine hears and watches "with its mind," and the passage continues by describing how whoever invented gods deliberately situated their home in the skies, because this is where terrifying phenomena such as thunder, lightning, and comets come from: "These were the fears with which he [the inventor of religion] hedged about the human race. Through them and with beguiling words he housed the divine in a suitable setting and quenched lawlessness with laws. . . . And so, I think, some human first persuaded mortals to believe in the existence of a race of gods."[23]

It was perhaps the most radical anti-religious statement yet formulated by someone aspiring to be a statesman. Of course, being contained now in a fragment, its context is lost, and it may be that the speaker's interlocutor comprehensively demolished the argument with an equally impassioned protest that the gods existed. From what we know of Critias, however, this is unlikely. He was man with little time for niceties, and as leader of the Thirty Tyrants, he unleashed a reign of terror. For eight long months at his command, as 300 thuggish "whip-bearers" scoured Athens' streets in search of trouble, citizens were rounded up and summarily executed. Others were found, lying in their blood, victims of backstreet assassinations. Still others had their houses broken into, their property and money stolen by the Tyrants' fawning lieutenants. One of his own colleagues, speaking out against the cruelty and violence, was put to death on Critias' orders. And, lest opposition rally round him, assassination was arranged for Alcibiades. But resistance grew. In the foothills of Mount Parnes a partisan army won a dramatic victory, before sweeping south to take Piraeus, and then Athens. Critias was cut down in street fighting; the Tyrants were overthrown; and, with Sparta and her allies, exhausted by the long war, keen for a peaceful resolution, a new democracy was put in place, which accepted that for Athens to have any future her People must be reconciled.[24]

With a few exceptions, supporters of the oligarchs were pardoned—an extraordinary decision, showing political maturity unseen for many years, arguably since the days when Aristides and Xanthippus were recalled from exile before the Battle of Salamis. The brutality of the Tyrants' reign, the long decades of escalating war with Sparta and her allies (officially it lasted twenty-seven years, if the Peace of Nicias was discounted as a lull in fighting, though by such reckoning it might be said to have gone on for more than half a century), the humiliation of defeat: the effect of all these was profound, and the conclusion of many was that they must draw a line beneath the past and reimagine what it was to live in a democracy.

This did not mean that the Athenians, still at heart as energetic and determined as before, lived in total harmony with one another or with rival states. Just eight years after her defeat, Athens joined unlikely allies—Thebes, Corinth, Persia—in a lengthy war with Sparta, which ended in peace brokered by the Persian Great King, part of whose terms was the return of the Ionian Greek cities to his empire. Soon another enemy would loom on the horizon, Macedon's King Philip, and Athens would again be split between those eager for appeasement and those who violently opposed him. Among the latter was an able orator, Demosthenes, who modelled himself on Pericles, and whose funeral oration of 338 B.C. for the dead of Chaeroneia, a battle in which, as Philip hacked his path to victory, Demosthenes himself threw down his shield and ran away, is one of the few surviving genuine examples of the genre. But nothing could withstand the march of Macedon, and by 334 B.C. Philip's son, Alexander, having subjugated

12.2 A *metopē* from the Temple of Athena at Troy.

Greece, wheeled his huge army eastwards in a campaign which would see him conquer Persia.

There was much that motivated Alexander, not least his sense of history and passion for the *Iliad.* Like aristocratic Athenians of the fifth century—like Alcibiades—Alexander lived by Homer's sentiments. Under his pillow he kept a copy of the *Iliad,* annotated by the great polymath, Aristotle: "Always to be best and to surpass all others" was a mantra that inspired all he did. His passion for Homer translated into an obsession with the Trojan War. At the start of his Persian campaign, he visited the site of Troy, imagining himself a modern Achilles, part of a continuum stretching through history, where the Trojan War was a precursor to the Persian Wars of the fifth century B.C., which were in turn a prelude to his own attack on Persia. Holding equal place in his equation—on a par with Achilles and himself—were the Athenians, who had done so much to save Greece from occupation and subsequently carried on the war in Persia. Small wonder, then, that Alexander accepted and embraced the vision emblazoned in the sculptures and paintings of the building programme spearheaded by Pericles, that those (like him and like Achilles) who achieved fame in battle were glorious heroes, whose reputation would live on forever.[25]

So, when Alexander won his first victory on Persian soil, he made a point of sending 300 suits of captured Persian armour back to Athens to be displayed, an offering to Athena, on the Acropolis as "spoils from the barbarians," and, according to some Greek historians, when Alexander took the Persian palace complex at Persepolis, he burned those buildings raised by Xerxes and Darius to the ground "in revenge for the destruction of the Greek [i.e., Athenian] temples." And, although his vision of a colossal Temple of Athena towering over Troy's acropolis never came to pass, when his successors, who had already set up a "Panathenaic festival" nearby, constructed a new Doric Temple of Athena at Troy, they modelled its *metopēs* on those of the Parthenon. Thus here, as on the Athenian Acropolis, the Trojan War occupied the north side, the Amazonomachy the west, the Centauromachy the south and the Gigantomachy the east. As on the Parthenon, one of the myths was rooted in the soil on which the temple stood, although at Troy its symbolism was severely weakened: there was no "sacred journey" from the real location of the west façade to the divine setting of the east. In part this was down to the exigencies of geography, but perhaps, too, an understanding of the layout of the sculptures of the Parthenon had been already lost.[26]

It was a rare acknowledgment of the Parthenon. If surviving evidence is representative, the building was scarcely mentioned in contemporary literature. While it played a role in Aristophanes' *Lysistrata,* its importance there was as the city's treasury, not as Athena's temple, and while Demosthenes, harking back as always to what he thought to be a golden age, did reference it three times, on each occasion he listed the Parthenon in second place to the Propylaea, emphasising its outstanding architecture rather than its religious significance. And other than that, nothing. In part the reason was political. Less than a decade after the Parthenon was finished, with its jingoistic *metopēs* celebrating triumph over Persia and its frieze proclaiming the Athenians' mystic heroism, ambassadors from Athens were going cap in hand to Persia begging for help against Sparta, plague had killed one in three Athenians, and earthquakes had done damage to the temple. By the time of Alexander and his successors, the context in which the

Parthenon was built was less immediately important. What mattered now was that it stood for Greek victory over Persia. Once more the Parthenon fitted the zeitgeist.[27]

Yet the world had changed drastically. When Alexander offered to fund a new Temple of Artemis at Ephesus, the local authorities refused his help, protesting that "it was inappropriate for a god to make offerings to gods." Just two generations after Athens fell to Sparta, powerful rulers, whom fifth-century-B.C. Greeks called tyrants and we would call dictators, were being addressed not simply as heroes, as Pericles imagined the Athenians, but fully fledged deities. Following Alexander's not-so-divine death, Athenians thought it politic to call one of his successors, Demetrius, bleakly nicknamed "the Besieger," their "saviour god." Moreover, they let him take up residence in the Parthenon's opisthodomos, next to the cella of his "sister," Athena, who, wrote Plutarch, "welcomed him, even though he was not a courteous guest and did not conduct his life with the modesty befitting the virgin [goddess]"—he shared the room, once treasury of Athens' empire, with at least four mistresses simultaneously, all of them celebrated prostitutes, two of whom were worshipped as goddesses in their own sanctuaries.[28]

The Parthenon's subsequent history is too complex to explore properly here. However, its location and grandeur ensured that it retained a powerful focus for Athens' changing population. When late Republican Rome's civil wars spilled over into Greece, it survived horrors of siege and slaughter, and under the Roman Empire Athenians, now basking in their city's reputation as a seat of learning, knew how to bend with the wind. In A.D. 61, having dedicated a statue to the then emperor, they set up an inscription in bronze lettering above the Parthenon's east *metopēs,* which began: "The Council of the Areopagus, and the Council of the Six Hundred, and the People of the Athenians, erect this statue to the supreme Emperor Nero Caesar Claudius Sebastus Germanicus, Son of God."[29]

Yet, questions of religion remained as potent and divisive as they were in the fifth century B.C. Christianity swept the Roman world. In A.D. 391, its Emperor Theodosius banned pagan worship, and in the next century the Parthenon became a church where the Virgin Athena was transformed into the Virgin Mary. The building was reorientated: its main doors now at the west side led through the opisthodomos to the east-facing nave, with a high altar in front of the old doors, and walls glowing with religious paintings. As for Pheidias' agalma, its fate remains a mystery. Already in 296 B.C., it had been stripped of gold by a worthless general in need of money for his troops. Refurbished, it may have suffered badly in a fire in the third century A.D. If it still survived into the fifth century, it may have been transported east to Constantinople, where one tantalizing reference places it as late as the tenth century, but in truth we simply do not know.[30]

In 1458 Ottoman Turks took Athens and converted the Parthenon into a mosque. Despite the addition of such features as a minaret, much of the original structure remained intact, and by the mid-seventeenth century it was attracting Western visitors and artists, including Jacques Carrey, a Frenchman, who sketched its sculptures. But in 1687 on 26 September—the 2,166th anniversary of the Battle of Salamis—disaster struck. Besieged by a Venetian army, which had landed on Greek soil at (of all places) Eleusis, the Turks were using the Parthenon as a gunpowder magazine, so when a mortar scored a direct hit, the consequences were catastrophic. The explosion blew off the roof, destroyed most of the cella walls and dislodged many sculptures. Then, when the victorious Venetians tried to dismantle the still-surviving east pediment, its statues of Athena and Poseidon toppled to the ground and smashed. Shortly afterwards, the Turks returned and built a second mosque within the rubble of the first, the heart of a now-thriving village.[31]

By 1801, when Britain's Ambassador to Constantinople, Thomas Bruce, the seventh Earl of Elgin, visited with artists supposedly intent on making exact drawings and replicas of the surviving sculptures, he reported that the local governor was so charmed that he issued paperwork, which permitted "setting up ladders around the ancient temple of the Idols, moulding with mortar (that is, with plaster) the said ornaments and visible figures, measuring the remains of other ruined buildings, and undertaking when necessary to dig the foundations to find inscribed blocks that may have survived in the gravel," instructing that "no one will meddle with their ladders and instruments and that no objection will be made to the removal of some pieces of stone with inscriptions, and figures." Elgin's ensuing removal of most of the frieze, along with parts of the pedimental sculptures and south *metopēs* just twenty-one years before the wars of Greek independence, has since proved controversial. In 1983, Greek actress Melina Mercouri spearheaded a campaign for their return from London's British Museum to Athens, calling them "an integral part of a monument that represents the national spirit of Greece." Since then, restoration work on the Acropolis has helped preserve both the buildings and fabric of the rock itself, consolidating the Parthenon's now iconic ruined silhouette, while since 2009 the stunning Acropolis Museum has housed remaining sculptures of the Parthenon and its related buildings, including the Old Temple, with a sensitivity and sense of drama of which Pheidias would have been proud.[32]

Of the rest of the fifth-century-B.C. building programme, only the Temple of Athena and Hephaestus overlooking the Agora remains more or less intact, thanks to its early conversion to a church. Below, all that remain of such public buildings as the Council House and stoas including the once-stunning Painted Stoa are scant foundations, while close to where Harmodius and Aristogeiton struck down Hipparchus and the site of the tyrannicides' statue, Athens' railway cuts an ugly scar through the once-sacred Agora. On the other side of the Acropolis, nothing of Pericles' Odeon survives; the Temple of Olympian Zeus, begun by the Peisistratids, abandoned by the Athenian democracy, but completed by Rome's philhellenic Emperor Hadrian, lies in artfully curated ruins; while, beyond, above a busy road modern houses crowd the scant foundations of the Temple of Artemis Agrotera, destroyed by Ottomans as recently as the 1770s. Poseidon's ruined temple still stands on "Sunium's marbled steep/where nothing, save the waves and I/may hear our mutual murmurs sweep," but of its nearby sister Temple to Athena or the Temple of Nemesis at Rhamnous, little remains. Even at Eleusis, where thousands processed each year to celebrate the Mysteries, scarcely anything survives of the once numinous Telesterion. In 1803, when Edward Clark visited the site, he found it mere rubble. Nonetheless, local villagers resisted his attempt to remove a statue which they claimed was Saint Demetra, protesting that it protected their crops. In vain. Clark sailed with it for England. His ship was wrecked, but his cargo was recovered, and today the statue is displayed in Cambridge, while at Eleusis the once fertile fields have been built over; traffic clogs the road to Athens by the track of the ancient Sacred Way; and oil refineries cast their glow across the night sea to Salamis.[33]

~ ~ ~

We do not know what consequences (if any) fifth-century-B.C. Greeks thought might await those who revealed the rituals of the Eleusinian Mysteries—the punishment that Alcibiades feared was not spiritual but political, a weaponizing of religious outrage to achieve a purely secular win. Even ten years later (in his *Frogs* of 405 B.C.), Aristophanes was confident that he would suffer no reprisals for parodying Eleusinian practices on stage (presumably with many non-initiates in his audience). Nor can we tell how many Athenians genuinely believed in gods worshipped at Eleusis and in other sanctuaries and temples throughout Attica and wider Greece. But what is certain is that the fifth century B.C. was a time of radical and sometimes violent debate about the nature or existence of these gods, and that this argument spilled over dangerously into politics.

It was in the first year of the next century, that these debates reached their (albeit temporary) denouement. Less than five years after their defeat and four since the fall of the Thirty Tyrants, most Athenians were chastened by recent events. Not Socrates. Placing integrity above expediency, the barefoot philosopher, now in his early seventies, continued to haunt the Agora, raising awkward questions, and expressing dangerous opinions. Exposing the intellectual and moral weaknesses of fellow citizens, he had long been a thorn in their side, in his own terms, a "gadfly," and he saw no reason to stop now.[34]

Yet for some Athenians, Socrates, as teacher of Critias and Alcibiades, embodied everything that led to all the suffering of the past three decades and more. No matter that the Thirty Tyrants tried to ban him from conversing with men younger than thirty or that Socrates refused to follow illegal orders to arrest a retired general. No matter either that, in the dying years of fifth-century-B.C. Athenian democracy, Socrates, serving that day as president of the Assembly, refused to let the generals of Arginusae be tried in a group action (though he could not prevent the case being heard next morning). Such details were irrelevant. What mattered was his association with the brash jeunesse dorée who had strutted their entitled way through recent history, apparently with no care for any but themselves—perhaps his close association, too, with the Alcmaeonids. His wife may well have been a member of the family. She certainly bore a good Alcmaeonid name: Xanthippe.[35]

But it was not just recent politics which were stained by Socrates' fingerprints. The religious and moral schisms which had split Athens since early in the 420s were associated with him, too. As early as 423 B.C., Aristophanes portrayed him questioning the gods, encouraging the worship of clouds, teaching those who could afford his fees to win debates with worthless arguments. Even then, Aristophanes imagined the provoked Athenians rising in anger against Socrates and burning down his phrontisterion. In the ensuing quarter of a century, his pupils had been implicated in irreligious acts—Alcibiades parodying the Mysteries; Critias arrested on suspicion of involvement in the scandal of the herms, and going on to write his deeply sceptical or atheistic plays.[36]

In the first years of the war with Sparta, some believed that plague and earthquakes were signs of divine anger provoked by the arch rationalism of sceptics such as Pericles. Now that this war was over, with so much effort made to heal deep rifts and draw a line under the past, many found it grating to see Socrates behaving as he always did, apparently remorseless and untroubled by the part that he had played in Athens' downfall, still espousing dangerously oligarchic views. So, in summer 399 B.C., he was brought to trial on charges relating to both politics and religion. He had, it was alleged, corrupted the young men of Athens (Alcibiades and Critias and other oligarchs). But also, he did not believe in the gods of the Athenians and had introduced new gods to the city—a reference to the daimon or daimonion, which he claimed guided his life, "a kind of voice, which always stops me doing things, but never forces me to act." For Socrates' detractors, the word that mattered here was "me." His daimonion was personal to him. Unlike the gods of Athens, it did not "belong" to the whole polis. It set Socrates apart. It was undemocratic.[37]

By a slim majority of the 501 jurors, Socrates was found guilty. But in the subsequent debate when each side proposed a punishment, Socrates' suggestion was so outrageous (that he receive free meals for life in recognition of his service to the city) that the prosecution's demand for his execution was approved by more jurors than had found him guilty. Normally sentence would have followed swiftly, but religion lengthened Socrates' life. The day before his trial, Athens had dispatched her sacred ship to Delos for annual celebrations of how Theseus had killed the Minotaur and freed his city. While the ship was gone, no executions could take place, so it was only the next month, when it returned, that the warden of the public jail brought Socrates the tiny cup of hemlock that would kill him. According to Plato, just before Socrates died, he reminded his friends gathered at his bedside that "we owe a cockerel to Asclepius," a sacrifice to the god of medicine and health (in whom was accused of not believing), a thank-offering for being cured of life. Ironic, provocative, and darkly clever, these words, spoken at the start of the fourth century B.C., encapsulate the spirit of the fifth. They are the last words of an entire generation.[38]

Socrates' death lanced the boil that had been festering for decades. His guilt or innocence has been debated for centuries, but in the context of his age it represented a cleansing. Each year, at a festival of Apollo called the Thargelia, Athenians performed the ritual of the *pharmakoi,* leading the ugliest man and woman through the streets, a string of dried figs slung about their necks, before driving them from the city, whipping them and beating them with sticks (perhaps even to death). They were symbolic scapegoats, their ugliness a sign that (unlike those beautifully formed young men and woman who populate Greek sculpture) they were hated by gods and freighted with evils, their removal from public life a communal catharsis. In was the same with ugly old Socrates. Even his trial was made to coincide with the month, Thargelion, in which the ritual took place. Perhaps he was aware of the connection. The word, *pharmakoi,* is close to *pharmakon* meaning "drug" or "medicine," and it may have been with this in mind that he linked his execution with Asclepius.[39]

The month's delay, however, meant that it was not until midsummer that he died. The precise date is unknown, but as Socrates awaited execution in those long hot days of June, above him on the Acropolis the two Arrhephoroi were getting ready for the ritual which for them, too, marked an end, when they would dress in their white robes for the last time and make their way down through the darkness of the cleft that burrowed through the rock, and out onto the Peripatos Road round to the Gardens of Aphrodite, exchange their sacred caskets, climb back to the Acropolis, remove their robes, relinquish their office, and emerge back into society, exchanging service to the virgin goddess for marriage and childbearing. And, for many centuries to come, successive new pairs of Arrhephoroi would take their place.

With Socrates removed, the cycle of religious ritual continued as (for the moment) did the cycle of democracy. But as citizens trooped onto Pnyx Hill, gathering since well before the dawn to listen to the current crop of politicians use age-old tropes to validate tired arguments, the space in which they found themselves was very different to the space which Nicias and Pericles and Ephialtes, and before them Cimon, Aristeides and Themistocles had known. The Thirty Tyrants had left their mark upon the face of Athens. The only building programme they carried out was on the Pnyx. Expending great effort and much money to relocate the Speaker's Platform and reorientate the seating, they had reversed its axis. The People's focus now was solely

12.3 The floodlit Acropolis of Athens from the Areopagus.

on the rostrum, whereas once they could look out towards the city and the pale blue hills and silver olive groves, across the Agora and Areopagus and the Acropolis with its proud temples silhouetted as the sun rose high above the Attic plain. Already the fifth century with its wars and sacrifices, its miraculous achievements in the realm of art and architecture, literature and music, even in that most controversial discipline of all, philosophy, was acquiring the aura of a golden age, at odds with reality perhaps, though exhilarating, nonetheless—especially when viewed, as now, through the dark prism of defeat and the perverted bloodlust of the Thirty Tyrants. Pericles' and Pheidias' vision of the citizen as hero had been a heady dream. But the sun had set on that old world. The time for dreams was over.[40]

ACKNOWLEDGMENTS

I have been musing on the ideas that this book contains for more than forty years, since a visit to the British Museum when the realisation first dawned on me that the way the gods are ordered on the east frieze of the Parthenon was far from being haphazard. Over those years, I have discussed those ideas with too many friends and colleagues to acknowledge individually here, but special thanks must be accorded to Sam Moorhead, with whom I once penned an article, "Rising to Resurrection" for *The British Museum Magazine,* and Alex Zambellas, whose infectious enthusiasm and profound understanding of all things Hellenic continue to inspire. Thank you to Alex, too, as well as to Paul Cartledge, for reading a proof of this book and for making wise suggestions, not all of which I followed. . . . My profound thanks go, too, to members of the Parthenon Restoration Service, and especially Vasileia Manidaki, who gave generously of her time and knowledge, showing me the House and Passage of the Arrhephoroi. When I embarked on this project, I hoped to "tire the sun with talking" about art and sculpture with the incomparable Ian Jenkins, who had been so encouraging and supportive in the past, but his sudden death meant that this was not to be. He is greatly missed.

This book itself has taken five years to complete. I would like to thank my agent, Bill Hamilton of A. M. Heath, who first championed it; at Harvard University Press, Ian Malcolm, who took it up; Andrew Kinney, to whom he passed the baton as my editor; and Grigory Tovbis, who saw it across the finish line. Thank you also to the two anonymous academic reviewers, whose comments were invaluable. Maps are a crucial part of any work like this, and I have been fortunate to work once more with the brilliant cartographer, Isabelle Lewis, to whom I am profoundly grateful—as I am to all who have contributed to the production of the book, to Susan Karani Virtanen for her meticulous copyediting, Anne McGuire for her mind-blowingly thorough tidying of the endnotes, Stephanie Vyce for her help with the illustrations, Ingrid Paulson for the interior design, John Gall for the cover design, and Rebekah White and Colleen Lanick for their work marketing and promoting the book.

Last, but certainly not least, thank you to the home team, my friends and family; my mother, Kate; and my wife and best friend, Emily-Jane, my foundation, my pillar and my coping stone, like Athena the protectress of our domestic city-state, who "shields her people as they march to battle and come home again." And finally a heartfelt thank you to our two cats, Stanley and Oliver, who have spent a quarter of their long lives, Pheidias-like, supervising the completion of this book, and whose fortitude and wisdom have surely earned them both "a good name that will not grow old."

NOTES

INTRODUCTION

1 See p. 21. The precise number of annual Assembly meetings in the fifth century B.C. is unknown, but in the fourth century it seems to have been around forty. See E. M. Harris, "How Often Did the Athenian Assembly Meet?," *Classical Quarterly* 36, no. 2 (1986): 363–377.

2 See pp. 30 and 34.

3 *Kistai:* N. Robertson, "Athena's Shrines and Festivals," in *Worshipping Athena: Panathenaia and Parthenon,* ed. J. Neils (Madison: University of Wisconsin Press, 1996), 60.

4 See p. 35.

5 The "religious crisis" of late fifth-century-B.C. Athens will be explored in the second half of this book. See R. Parker, *Athenian Religion: A History* (Oxford: Clarendon Press, 1996), 209–214.

6 See pp. 179–181.

7 Pericles as "first man": Thucydides, 2.65. Educator of Greece: Thucydides, 2.41. Plague and reactions to it: Thucydides, 2.47–55.

8 Three million people visited the Acropolis in 2022: Sarah Cascone, "Greece Will Curb Rampant Tourism at the Acropolis," ArtNet News, August 7, 2023, https://news.artnet.com/art-world/acropolis-to-limit-summer-visitors-2346868. Parthenon accounts: L. Kallet, "Wealth, Power, and Prestige: Athens at Home and Abroad," in *The Parthenon: From Antiquity to the Present,* ed. J. Neils (Cambridge: Cambridge University Press, 2005), 53–56. "The beauty": Demosthenes, 22.72. Intention behind the Parthenon: while J. B. Connelly, *The Parthenon Enigma: A Journey into Legend* (New York: Knopf, 2014) sees evidence of the intention in a fragment of Euripides' *Erechtheus,* I find her arguments unconvincing for reasons which will become apparent throughout this present book. "Her appearance": Thucydides, 1.10.

9 "At the time": Plutarch, *Pericles,* 13.

10 Acropolis: Pausanias: 1.22–27. The description of the Parthenon and statue (including the digression on griffins) can be found in two brief sections (5–7) in Pausanias 1.24. Statue: Pliny, *Natural History,* 34.54. "The Parthenon": Diogenes Laertius, 7.67.

11 "A curious anomaly": as will be seen, I disagree with Connelly (*Parthenon Enigma,* xxii) that "the Parthenon was first and foremost a religious building." Triumphant general: Plutarch, *Demetrius,* 26.

1. LAYING THE FOUNDATIONS

1 The precise number of Assembly meetings per annum is unknown, but in the fourth century BC it seems to have been around 40. See E. M. Harris, "How Often Did the Athenian Assembly Meet?," *Classical Quarterly* 36, no. 2 (1986): 363–377; V. Azoulay, *Pericles of Athens,* trans. J. Lloyd (Princeton, NJ: Princeton University Press, 2014), 40. Red paint: Aristophanes, *Acharnians,* 20. Scythian archers: B. Bäbler, "Bobbies or Boobies? The Scythian Police Force in Classical Athens," in *Scythians and Greeks: Cultural Interactions in Scythia, Athens and the Early Roman Empire (Sixth Century BC–First Century AD),* ed. D. Braund (Exeter, UK: University of Exeter Press, 2005), 114–122.

2 Pericles' oratory: Thucydides, 2.65; Eupolis, fr. 102 K.-A., in R. Kassel and C. Austin, eds., *Poetae Comici Graeci,* vol. 5, *Damoxenus–Magnes* (Berlin: De Gruyter, 1986); Plutarch, *Pericles,* 8.

3 Sacrifices, prayers, and curses: R. Parker, *Polytheism and Society at Athens* (Oxford: Oxford University Press, 2005), 99–100 (discussing evidence from Aeschines, 1.23), 405; J. Larson, *Ancient Greek Cults: A Guide* (New York: Routledge, 2007), 11. "Who wants to speak?": Aristophanes, *Acharnians,* 45.

4 Capacity of mid-fifth-century-B.C. Pnyx: J. Paga, *Building Democracy in Late Archaic Athens* (Oxford: Oxford University Press, 2021), 141; M. H. Hansen, "How Many Athenians Attended the Assembly?," *Greek, Roman and Byzantine Studies* 17 (1976): 115–134; but see G. R. Stanton and P. J. Bicknell, "Voting in Tribal Groups in the Athenian Assembly," *Greek, Roman and Byzantine Studies* 28, no. 1 (1987): 51–92. J. M. Camp, *The Archaeology of Athens* (New Haven, CT: Yale University Press, 2001), 46, suggests—surely optimistically—that it held 8,000–13,000.

5 Pericles' appearance: several ancient busts survive, including one currently in the British Museum (1805,0703.91). Size of head and "Squill Head": Plutarch, *Pericles,* 3. "Olympian": Plutarch, *Pericles,* 8. Ambiguous meaning of *demos:* P. Cartledge, *Democracy: A Life* (Oxford: Oxford University Press, 2016), 3. Pericles' use of surrogates: Plutarch, *Pericles,* 4; Azoulay, *Pericles,* 47–48.

6 Cimon: see primarily Plutarch, *Cimon;* also D. Stuttard, *Phoenix: Cimon, Miltiades and the Rise of Athens* (Cambridge, MA: Harvard University Press, 2021). Thucydides Melesiou: J. D. Davies, *Athenian Propertied Families, 600–300 B.C.* (Oxford: Clarendon Press, 1971), 231–234.

7 Process of taking the bill before the Assembly: J. S. Boersma, *Athenian Building Policy from 561/0 to 405/4 B.C.* (Groningen: Wolters-Noordhoff, 1970), 4–5. 40,000–60,000 citizens: M. Munn, *The School of History* (Berkeley: University of California Press, 2000), 64. Boersma, *Building Policy,* 49, suggests that the entire population rose from 140,000 (including slaves and a few thousand metics) in c. 480 B.C. to 315,000 (including slaves and 28,500 metics) in 431 B.C. 6,000 on Pnyx: L. Kallet, "Wealth, Power, and Prestige: Athens at Home and Abroad," in Neils, *Parthenon from Antiquity,* 46; Paga, *Building Democracy,* 140–142.

8 Material contained in this and the next four paragraphs will be examined in greater details in Chapters 3, 4, and 5.

9 Imports: Hermippus in Athenaeus, *Deipnosophistai,* 149. Preserving old layout of city: Boersma, *Building Policy,* 10.

10 Fragile statues: Pausanias, 1.27.6. Olive-wood statue: Pausanias, 1.26.6; Eusebius, *Praeparatio Evangelica,* 10.9.15; Apollodorus, 3.14.6; Plutarch, *De daedalis Plataeensibus;* Philostratus, *vita Apollonii,* 3.14; Tertullian, *Apologia,* 16.3.8 (which comments on the similarity between the shape of statue and the Christian cross); John H. Kroll, "The Ancient Statue of Athena Polias," *Hesperia Supplements* 20

(1982): 65–76; J. Larson, *Greek Heroine Cults* (Madison: University of Wisconsin Press, 1995), 42; Connelly, *The Parthenon Enigma: A Journey into Legend* (New York: Knopf, 2014), 68. "Light infused": Pindar, fr, 76. N. Robertson, "Athena's Shrines and Festivals," in Neils, *Worshipping Athena,* 29, argues that the xoanon and the ancient (aniconic) olive wood statue were not one and the same.

11 Description of statue: T. L. Shear Jr., *Trophies of Victory: Public Buildings in Periklean Athens* (Princeton, NJ: Princeton University Press, 2016), 360–362. Colours of robe: Euripides, *Hekabe,* 465–474; Evy Johanne Håland, "Athena's Peplos: Weaving as a Core Female Activity in Ancient and Modern Greece," *Cosmos* 20 (2004): 155–182; J. L. Shear, *Serving Athena: The Festival of the Panathenaia and the Construction of Athenian Identities* (Cambridge: Cambridge University Press, 2021), 348. Symbolism of yellow dress: Parker, *Polytheism,* 243. J. Shear, *Serving Athena,* 35; and Parker, *Polytheism,* 268–269, discuss evidence suggesting that the peplos was presented annually only during and after the second century B.C. The question does not affect the arguments in this current book. Enceladus on peplos: Scholiast on Aristophanes *Knights* 566a (II), repeated by *Suda* s.v. πέπλος.

12 Old Temple of Athena and sculptures (first carved from island marble, putting Athena center stage): Boersma, *Building Policy,* 20. Paintwork: Dimitrios Pandermalis, Stamatia Eleftheratou, and Christina Vlassopoulou, *Acropolis Museum Guide* (Athens: Acropolis Museum Editions, 2015), 108.

13 "Everything is full of gods": Thales, quoted by Aristotle, *On the Soul,* 411a7; Parker, *Polytheism,* 1; M. R. Lefkowitz, "Women in the Panathenaic and Other Festivals," in Neils, *Worshipping Athena,* 79. P. Cartledge: "The Greek *polis* or citizen-state, including therefore the Athenian democratic *polis,* was a city of Gods as well as—and before it was—a city of Men." P. Cartledge, "Sixth- to Fourth-Century BCE History and Society: A Brief Introduction," in *Looking at Greek Drama,* ed. D. Stuttard (London: Bloomsbury Academic, 2024), 28.

14 J. Shear, *Serving Athena,* 18–19.

15 Topography: Camp, *Archaeology of Athens,* 3. Acropolis: Camp, *Archaeology of Athens,* 248; J. M. Hurwit, *The Athenian Acropolis: History, Mythology and Archaeology from the Neolithic Era to the Present* (Cambridge: Cambridge University Press, 1999), 3–11.

16 Sanctuary of Zeus: R. J. Hopper, *The Acropolis* (London: Weidenfeld and Nicolson, 1971), 142. Poseidon as lord of elemental geological forces: Larson, *Greek Heroine Cults,* 57. And horses: Larson, *Greek Heroine Cults,* 58, 65–66. Larson argues that Poseidon means "Spouse of the Earth."

17 Athena's birth: Herodotus, 8.55; Isocrates, *Panathenaikos,* 193; Apollodorus, *Library,* 3.14.1; Connelly, *Parthenon Enigma,* 40. "Wise Zeus": *Homeric Hymn 28: To Athena,* 4–15.

18 *Homeric Hymn 11: To Athena.*

19 "Not worse": words from the ephebic oath found in Lycurgus, *Against Leocrates,* 97–101. For its application in the fifth century, see R. Thomas, *Oral Tradition and Written Record in Classical Athens* (Cambridge: Cambridge University Press, 1991), 85. Contest between Athena and Poseidon: Apollodorus, 3.14; Larson, *Greek Heroine Cults,* 67; Connelly, *Parthenon Enigma,* 40.

20 In one version, it was the rest of the Olympian gods who made the judgement, with Cecrops called as a key witness. Tokens: Pausanias, 1.26.6; Strabo, 9.1.16; Connelly, *Parthenon Enigma,* 108. J. Z. van Rookhuijzen suggests that the marks of Poseidon's trident were originally the three caves clearly visible on the northwest rockface of the Acropolis. Van Rookhuijzen, "The Parthenon Treasury on the Acropolis of Athens,"

American Journal of Archaeology 124, no. 1 (2020): 3–35. Olive tree exported from Acropolis worldwide: Herodotus, 5.82.2; compare Euripides, *Trojan Women,* 801–803; see S. Mills, *Drama, Oratory and Thucydides in Fifth-Century Athens: Teaching Imperial Lessons* (London: Routledge, 2020), 66.

21 The flood and its aftermath: Connelly, *Parthenon Enigma,* 40–41.

22 Nexus of dead maidens: the idea that these maidens are key to the Parthenon's iconography is central to Connelly's arguments (*Parthenon Enigma*). Pandora: *Suda,* Παρθένοι. Aglaurus: A. H. Sommerstein and A. J. Bayliss, *Oath and State in Ancient Greece* (Berlin: De Gruyter, 2012), 17. Death of Erechtheus: Euripides, *Ion,* 281.

23 Poseidon-Erechtheus: Connelly, *Parthenon Enigma,* 323; Larson, *Greek Heroine Cults,* 116; J. D. Mikalson, "Erechtheus and the Panathenaia," *American Journal of Philology* 97, no. 2 (1976): 141–153, 143.

24 The myth of Demeter and Korē is widespread in classical literature, but the "canonic" Eleusinian version is contained in the *Homeric Hymn to Demeter.* "Build me a great temple": *Homeric Hymn to Demeter,* 271–274. "How to take care": *Homeric Hymn to Demeter,* 476–482.

25 Eleusinian Mysteries: H. W. Parke, *Festivals of the Athenians* (London: Thames and Hudson, 1977), 55–71; R. Parker, *Athenian Religion: A History* (Oxford: Clarendon Press, 1996), 97–99, 327–368; Larson, *Greek Heroine Cults,* 71–76; E. Simon, *Festivals of Attica: An Archaeological Commentary* (Madison: University of Wisconsin Press, 1983), 24–35; H. Bowden, *Mystery Cults in the Ancient World* (2010; repr. London: Thames and Hudson, 2023), 34–61; C. Sourvinou-Inwood, "Festival and Mysteries," in *Greek Mysteries: The Archaeology and Ritual of Ancient Greek Secret Cults,* ed. M. B. Cosmopoulos (London: Routledge, 2003), 25–45; K. Clinton, "Stages of Initiation," in Cosmopoulos, *Greek Mysteries,* 50–70. Cobbled road: J. M. Camp, *Archaeology of Athens,* 130.

26 Birth of Hephaestus: Hesiod, *Theogony,* 927–928. Attempted rape of Athena: Apollodorus, *Bibliotheca,* 3.14.6. Earthborn Erechtheus: Homer, *Iliad,* 2.547–548. Sacrifices to Pandora: L. R. Farnell, *Cults of the Greek States* (Oxford: Clarendon Press, 1896), 290; J. Shear, *Serving Athena,* 137, 152. Garden of Pandrosus: Larson, *Greek Heroine Cults,* 40. For discussion of Pandora/Pandrosus, see Connelly, *Parthenon Enigma,* 278–282; M. Valdés Guía, "Some Aspects of the Tradition of Pandora in Athens: Women and Autochthony," *Studi e Materiali di Storia delle Religioni* 88, no. 2 (2022): 669–689.

27 Athenians as autochthonous children of earthborn Erechtheus: see, for example, Pindar, *Isthmian,* 2.19; Sophocles, *Ajax,* 202; Lysias, 2.17–20; Isocrates, *Panegyricus,* 24; N. Loraux, *Born of the Earth: Myth and Politics in Athens,* trans. S. Stewart (Ithaca, NY: Cornell University Press, 2000); V. J. Rosivach, "Autochthony and the Athenians," *Classical Quarterly* 37, no. 2 (1987): 294–306; M. Fullerton, "Archaism and Autochthony on the Post-Periklean Acropolis," in *From Kallias to Kritias: Art in Athens in the Second Half of the Fifth Century B.C.,* ed. J. Neils and O. Palagia (Berlin: De Gruyter, 2021), 31–49; S. Lape, *Race and Citizen Identity in the Classical Athenian Democracy* (Cambridge: Cambridge University Press, 2010); R. Parker, "Myths of Early Athens," in *Interpretations of Greek Mythology,* ed. J. Bremmer (London: Croom Helm, 1987), 187–214. See also Connelly, *Parthenon Enigma,* 38–39, 80.

28 Sacred snake: Herodotus, 8.41; Philostratus, *Imagines,* 2.17.6. Erechtheus-Erichthonius: the relationship between the two is complicated; see Plutarch, *Moralia,* 843b; Connelly, *Parthenon Enigma,* 38 and 132–133, suggests they split in the

mid-fifth-century B.C., when they may have become younger and older versions of the same hero ("In Athenian eyes, there was only one hero, Erechtheus").

29 Cleft in rock: O. Broneer, "Excavations on the North Slope of the Acropolis in Athens, 1933–34," *Hesperia* 4, no. 2 (1935): 109–188; O. Broneer, "A Mycenaean Fountain on the Athenian Acropolis," *Hesperia* 8, no. 4 (1939): 317–433; Hopper, *Acropolis,* 29–30; Hurwit, *Athenian Acropolis,* 10. Praxiergidae washing robes: Plutarch, *Alcibiades,* 34; Parke, *Festivals of the Athenians,* 152–155; Simon, *Festivals of Attica,* 46–48; Robertson, "Athena's Shrines," 48–49.

30 Arrhephoroi: Parker, *Polytheism,* 219–223; Parke, *Festivals of the Athenians,* 140–145; Larson, *Greek Heroine Cults,* 45–46; Larson, *Greek Heroine Cults,* 39. Writing in the Roman age, Pausanias (1.23.7) maintains that "not a lot of people know about" this ritual but this does not mean that it was equally unknown in the fifth century B.C. Ceremony of Arrhephoroi: Simon, *Festivals of Attica,* 39–46; Robertson, "Athena's Shrines," 60–62; E. Kadletz, "Pausanias 1.27.3 and the Route of the Arrhephoroi," *American Journal of Archaeology* 86, no. 3 (1982): 445–446. Staircase: "Arrephorion," Acropolis Restoration Service (YSMA), n.d., https://www.ysma.gr/en/monuments/arrephorion/; Connelly, *Parthenon Enigma,* 27–28, 33; and Robertson, "Athena's Shrines," 60, who, noting that Pausanias (1.27) links the ceremony to the Panathenaic Festival, suggests it happened on the night before the Panathenaic procession. Others place it at a different time of the year, and later in this book I shall suggest that the Parthenon Frieze provides a different link between the Arrhephoroi and the festival. See also Camp, *Archaeology of Athens,* 19. Gardens of Aphrodite: Pausanias, 1.19; Connelly, *Parthenon Enigma,* 33–34. Aphrodite was regularly associated with gardens: J. Larson, *Greek Heroine Cults,* 114.

31 Statue by Alcamenes: I. Leventi, "Female Iconography of Attic Votive Reliefs of the Late 5th Century BC," in Neils and Palagia, *Kallias to Kritias,* 278. Phallic offerings: E. Pala, "Aphrodite on the Akropolis: Evidence from Attic Pottery," in *Brill's Companion to Aphrodite,* ed. A. Smyth and S. Pickup (Leiden: Brill, 2010), 201–202. Pala notes that "it appears that on the north slope of the Akropolis, Aphrodite was the goddess par excellence. In the late sixth and early fifth centuries B.C., the entire slope was apparently transformed into an open-air sacred precinct." See also Broneer, "Excavations," 119–129.

32 120 days of festivals: T. Whitmarsh, *Battling the Gods: Atheism in the Ancient World* (New York: Knopf, 2015), 21. Connelly, *Parthenon Enigma,* 254, suggests there were between 130 and 170 festival days. Thesmophoria: Parke, *Festivals of the Athenians,* 82–87; Parker, *Polytheism,* 270–283; L. B. Zaidman and P. S. Pantel, *Religion in the Ancient Greek City,* trans. P. Cartledge (Cambridge: Cambridge University Press, 1992), 102–104; Larson, *Greek Heroine Cults,* 70. Parallels between Thesmophoria and Arrephoria: Parker, *Polytheism,* 273. Arrhephoroi as surrogates: Larson, *Ancient Greek Cults,* 10. Impious destruction: D. Castriota, *Myth, Ethos and Actuality* (Madison: University of Wisconsin Press, 1992), 134.

33 Great Panathenaea: J. Neils, ed., *Worshipping Athena: Panathenaia and Parthenon* (Madison: University of Wisconsin Press, 1996); J. Shear, *Serving Athena;* Parker, *Polytheism,* 253–269; Parker, *Athenian Religion,* 89–91; Parke, *Festivals of the Athenians,* 33–50; Simon, *Festivals of Attica,* 55–72; Connelly, *Parthenon Enigma,* 250–277. Backstory: J. Shear, *Serving Athena,* 34.

34 Gigantomachy: Apollodorus, 1.6.1–2 (see also Parthenon's east *metopēs*); Hurwit, *Athenian Acropolis,* 30–31. Heracles: Pindar, *Nemean,* 1.67–69, 7.90; Euripides, *Heracles,* 177–179.

35 Art: J. Shear, *Serving Athena,* 43, 49. Enceladus: Euripides, *Ion,* 206–211; Euripides, *Hercules,* 908.

36 See, for example, Simon, "Theseus and Athenian Festivals," in Neils, *Worshipping Athena,* 206.

37 Apollodorus, *Epitome,* 1.21; Isocrates, *Orations,* 12.93; Plutarch, *Theseus,* 30; Diodorus Siculus, 4.70.3–4; and the Parthenon's south *metopēs.* Theseus and Centaurs: Simon, "Theseus and Athenian Festivals," 14. Other versions of the myth suggest that Theseus abducted Hippolyta's sister, Antiope, but they need not concern us. On the place in Athenian art and thought of the Centauromachy: Castriota, *Myth, Ethos,* 34–43; of the Amazonomachy: Castriota, *Myth, Ethos,* 43–58.

38 "First man": Thucydides, 2.65. Area of Attica: Paga, *Building Democracy,* 3.

39 Slavery in ancient Greece is an increasingly contentious issue, and many books have been written on the subject, among them S. Forsdyke, *Slaves and Slavery in Ancient Greece* (Cambridge: Cambridge University Press), 2021; M. Finley, *Slavery in Classical Antiquity: Views and Controversies* (Cambridge: W. Heffer, 1960); P. Hunt, *Slaves, Warfare, and Ideology in the Greek Historians* (Cambridge: Cambridge University Press, 1998); N. R. E. Fisher, *Slavery in Classical Greece* (London: Bristol Classical Press, 1993). Thales: Diogenes Laertius, *Lives of the Eminent Philosophers,* 1.33; Castriota, *Myth, Ethos,* 57.

40 The most significant work on Greece's view of the "barbarian" remains E. Hall, *Inventing the Barbarian* (Oxford: Clarendon Press, 1989). "A kinship": Herodotus, 8.144.

41 "Always to be best": Homer, *Iliad,* 6.208, 11.784. Makeshift shack: I. Jenkins, *Greek Architecture and Its Sculpture* (Cambridge, MA: Harvard University Press, 2006), 117; Boersma, *Building Policy,* 50. J. M. Hurwit, "Space and Theme: The Setting of the Parthenon," in Neils, *Parthenon from Antiquity,* 22–25, argues that more of the Old Temple remained standing after the Persian destruction than is commonly thought. Connelly, *Parthenon Enigma,* 74–75, believes that the "façades and part of its westernmost room (known as the opisthodomos) seem to have remained standing while its roof and interior collapsed."

42 Peace with Persia: the so-called Peace of Callias has been questioned. Herodotus (7.151) mentions a mission undertaken by Callias to the court of the Great King at Susa, but not its purpose. Such a peace treaty would account for the significant changes to Athenian foreign and domestic policy around this time, and fourth-century authors such as Demosthenes (*De Falsa Legatione,* 273) and Isocrates (4.118–120) believed in its authenticity, as did Plutarch, *Cimon,* 13, and Diodorus, 12.4. See, for example, R. Meiggs, *The Athenian Empire* (Oxford: Clarendon Press, 1972), 129–151; E. Badian, "The Peace of Callias," *Journal of Hellenic Studies* 50 (1987): 1–39; E. F. Bloedow, "The Peace of Callias," *Symbolae Osloenses* 67 (1992): 41–68; G. L. Cawkwell, "The Peace between Athens and Persia," *Phoenix* 51 (1997): 115–130; L. J. Samons II, "Kimon, Kallias and Peace with Persia," *Historia* 47, no. 2 (1998): 129–140.

43 Heroes: Parker, *Greek Religion,* 103–123; Parker, *Polytheism,* 445–451; Larson, *Greek Heroine Cults,* 3–20; E. Kearns, "The Heroes of Attica," *Bulletin of the Institute of Classical Studies* suppl. 57 (1989). Heroes shown in art with horses: Parker, *Athenian Religion,* 140; Castriota, *Myth, Ethos,* 218.

44 Parke, *Festivals of the Athenians;* Simon, *Festivals of Attica.*

45 Income: D. M. Pritchard, "Public Spending in Democratic Athens," *Ancient History* 46 (2016): 30–50; A. Moreno, *Feeding the Democracy: The Athenian Grain Supply in*

the Fifth and Fourth Centuries BC (Oxford: Oxford University Press, 2007); A. Monson, "Taxation and Tribute," in *The Cambridge Companion to the Ancient Greek Economy,* ed. S. von Reden (Cambridge: Cambridge University Press, 2022), 264–278.

46 Greek view of temples: T. Spawforth, *The Complete Greek Temples* (London: Thames and Hudson, 2006), 6–15.

2. POWERHOUSES

1 For a useful definition of a sanctuary, see X. Duffy, *Commemorating Conflict: Greek Monuments of the Persian Wars* (Oxford: Archaeopress, 2018), 24. Spring sacred to a river god and water nymphs: Plato, *Phaedrus,* 230b–c. Early temples: see A. Pierattini, *The Origins of Greek Temple Architecture* (Cambridge: Cambridge University Press, 2022). Cult rooms, for example, at Mycenae: see T. Spawforth, *The Complete Greek Temples* (London: Thames and Hudson, 2006), 20–21. Development of temples: A. Mazarikis Ainian, *From Rulers' Dwellings to Temples: Architecture, Religion and Society in Early Iron Age Greece* (Jonsered: Paul Åströms Förlag, 1997, ch. 5. Dating to around 1000 B.C., the earliest peripteral temple-like Greek building was at Lefkandi in Euboea, but it is uncertain whether its purpose was purely religious.

2 Painted panels: thus, for example, the C7th Temple of Apollo at Thermon: see Spawforth, *Complete Greek Temples,* 173–174.

3 Corcyra and temple: C. Gates, *Ancient Cities: The Archaeology of Urban Life in the Ancient Near East and Egypt, Greece and Rome* (London: Routledge, 2003), 211–213; M. Robertson, *A Shorter History of Greek Art* (Cambridge: Cambridge University Press, 1981), 16–17. Altar: approx. 82 feet × 9 feet. Sea battle: Thucydides, 1.13; Herodotus, 3.48–52.

4 J. K. Darling, *Architecture of Greece* (Westport, CT: Greenwood Press, 2004), 184–186.

5 Is there a deliberate "joke" in how Medusa, whose glance turns men to stone, has herself been turned to stone by the sculptors? Medusa on Corcyra pediments: J. B. Connelly, *The Parthenon Enigma: A Journey into Legend* (New York: Knopf, 2014), 50.

6 Fired-clay plaques: Spawforth, *Complete Greek Temples,* 177.

7 Temple statistics: 177 feet × 71 feet; 17 columns on the long sides, 6 on the short, each over 23 feet tall. B. Powell, "The Temple of Apollo at Corinth," *Hesperia* 9, no. 1 (1905): 44–65; R. F. Rhodes, "The Seventh Century Temple and the Earliest Greek Architecture at Corinth," in *Corinth, The Centenary: 1896–1996,* ed. C. K. Williams and N. Bookidis (Princeton, NJ: American School of Classical Studies at Athens, 2003), 85–94; W. B. Dinsmoor, *The Architecture of Ancient Greece* (New York: Norton, 1975), 88–90; C. Pfaff, "Curvature in the Temple of Apollo at Corinth and in the South Stoa and Classical Temple of Hera at the Argive Heraion," in *Appearance and Essence: Refinements of Classical Architecture: Curvature,* ed. L. Haselberger (Philadelphia: University Museum, University of Pennsylvania, 1999), 113–125; Spawforth, *Complete Greek Temples,* 64–65.

8 See D. Stuttard, *Greek Mythology: A Traveller's Guide from Mount Olympus to Troy* (London: Thames and Hudson, 2016), 152. Heroes could visit the Underworld for reasons that were honourable (Orpheus begging for the life of his beloved Eurydice) or nefarious (Theseus and Heracles each trying to bring one of its residents up to Earth). See T. Whitmarsh, *Battling the Gods: Atheism in the Ancient World* (New York: Knopf, 2015), 48.

9 Dates of Olympic treasuries: J. M. Barringer, *Olympia: A Cultural Guide* (Princeton, NJ: Princeton University Press, 2021), 63, 77–79. Relationship between temples and treasuries: J. Larson, *Ancient Greek Cults: A Guide* (London: Routledge, 2007), 8: "The temple (*nāos,* Attic *nēos*) was not a house of worship, but a dwelling place for the deity and a storehouse for the god's possessions, to which access was often restricted."

10 Prometheus: Hesiod, *Theogony,* 536–541. Cleisthenes: Herodotus, 6.121. Artistic hub: Pliny, *Natural History,* 36.9. Sacred war: Plutarch, *Solon,* 11; M. C. Scott, *Delphi: A History of the Center of the Ancient World* (Princeton, NJ: Princeton University Press, 2014), 71–73. Terrace: J. Luce, *L'aire du pilier des Rhodiens (fouille 1990–1992) à la frontière du profane et du sacré* (Athens: Ecole française d'Athènes, 2008), 79–81; J. F. Bommalaer, "Delphica 2: Les périboles de Delphes," *Pallas* 87 (2001): 14–19; Scott, *Delphi,* 71–74. Temple: Luce, *L'aire,* 98–104.

11 Treasury: R. T. Neer, "Delphi, Olympia and the Art of Politics," in *The Cambridge Companion to Archaic Greece,* ed. H. Shapiro (Cambridge: Cambridge University Press, 2007), 244–246. Cleithenes' Pythian chariot victory: Pausanias 10.7.6. Around 575: *Brill's New Pauly,* s.v. "Hippocleides." Contest for Agariste: Herodotus, 6.126–130.

12 Pericles' great grandparents: Herodotus 6.131; J. K. Davies, *Athenian Propertied Families, 600–300 B.C.* (Oxford: Clarendon Press, 1971), 455–460. Cylon affair: Herodotus, 5.71; Thucydides, 1.126; Plutarch, *Solon,* 12. T. Rood, "The Cylon Conspiracy: Thucydides and Uses of the Past," in *Thucydides between History and Literature,* ed. A. Tsakmakis and M. Tamiolaki (Berlin: De Gruyter, 2013), 119–138.

13 Seventh-century Temple of Athena Polias: Connelly, *Parthenon Enigma,* 69. In 2016 a mass grave at Phalerum was identified as that of Cylon's co-conspirators: R. A. Waterfield, *Creators, Conquerors, and Citizens* (Oxford: Oxford University Press, 2018), 76; T. Ghose, "Shackled Skeletons Could Be Ancient Greek Rebels," Live Science, April 15, 2016, www.livescience.com/54432-mass-grave-unearthed-in-greece.html.

14 Plutarch, *Solon,* 12. Curse: V. Azoulay, *Pericles of Athens,* trans. J. Lloyd (Princeton, NJ: Princeton University Press, 2014), 18. Cretan exorcist (Epimenides): Herodotus, 5.71; R. Parker, *Athenian Religion: A History* (Oxford: Clarendon Press, 1996), 50.

15 Subsequent weaponizing of religion: Whitmarsh, *Battling the Gods,* 124. Alcmaeon's chariot victory: Herodotus, 6.125; Isocrates, 4.25.

16 Alcmaeon at Sardis: Herodotus, 6.125; Azoulay, *Pericles,* 20. Hippocleides' archonship: Davies, *Athenian Propertied Families,* 295. Temple: J. S. Boersma, *Athenian Building Policy from 561/0 to 405/4 B.C.* (Groningen: Wolters-Noordhoff, 1970), 13, 180–181. Alcmaeon (and Hippolcleides) at Sicyon: Herodotus, 6.127–130. Hippocleides and the building of the temple: Connelly, *Parthenon Enigma,* 52–53; J. Neils, "The Panathenaia: An Introduction," in *Goddess and Polis,* ed. J. Neils (Princeton, NJ: Princeton University Press, 1992), 20. Hippocleides and festival: H. W. Parke, *Festivals of the Athenians* (London: Thames and Hudson, 1977), 33; A. L. Boegehold, "Group and Single Competitions at the Panathenaia," in *Worshipping Athena: Panathenaia and Parthenon,* ed. J. Neils (Madison: University of Wisconsin Press, 1996), 96. "Deliberately chosen": N. Robertson, "Athena's Shrines and Festivals," in Neils, *Worshipping Athena,* 56.

17 Around 100 cattle: Shear argues persuasively that the term "hecatomb" was loose and does not imply exactly 100 victims. J. Shear, *Serving Athena: The Festival of the Panathenaia and the Construction of Athenian Identities* (Cambridge: Cambridge University Press, 2021), 89.

18 Inauguration of Great Panathenaea: J. Shear, *Serving Athena,* 5; H. A. Shapiro, "Democracy and Imperialism: The Panathenaia in the Age of Pericles," in Neils, *Worshipping Athena,* 215. Modelled on Homeric games: M. Meyer, "Of Gods and Giants: Myths and Images in the Making," in *Images at the Crossroads: Media and Meaning in Greek Art,* ed. J. M. Barringer and F. Lissarrague (Edinburgh: Edinburgh University Press, 2022), 218. Panathenaea and Gigantomachy: J. Shear, *Serving Athena,* 34. Amphorae: J. Shear, *Serving Athena,* 29, 316. Amphoras: D. Kyle, "Gifts and Glory, Panathenaic and Other Athletic Prizes," in Neils, *Worshipping Athena,* 106–136; R. Hamilton, "Panathenaic Amphoras: The Other Side," in Neils, *Worshipping Athena,* 137–162; M. Tiverios, "Shield Device and Column-Mounted Statues on Panathenaic Amphoras: Some Remarks on Iconography," in Neils, *Worshipping Athena,* 163–172.

19 Gigantomachy and the 566 Greater Panathenaea: J. Shear, *Serving Athena,* 44–45. *Pyrrhichē:* J. Shear, *Serving Athena,* 45–46. Invention of chariot: J. Shear, *Serving Athena,* 51.

20 Athena and *apobatēs:* J. Shear, *Serving Athena,* 55–57. Temple and its sculptures: Connelly, *Parthenon Enigma,* 53–60. Dimensions of cella: 34.45 feet by 34.94 feet, Boersma, *Building Policy,* 180. Sixth-century Athenian building programme: Parker, *Athenian Religion,* 67–74.

21 Androgynous lion/lionesses: Dimitrios Pandermalis, Stamatia Eleftheratou, and Christina Vlassopoulou, *Acropolis Museum Guide* (Athens: Acropolis Museum Editions, 2015), 108. In early history such images may have signified the rising constellation, Leo, triumphing over sinking Taurus at the Spring Equinox, and the rebirth of the year: see, for example, W. Hartner and R. Ettinghausen, "The Conquering Lion, the Life Cycle of a Symbol," *Oriens* 17 (1964): 161–171.

22 Tripartite being: Connelly, *Parthenon Enigma,* 57.

23 Gifts: Herodotus, 1.50–51. Gifts included a golden statue of a lion, weighing more than a quarter of a ton, massive gold and silver bowls, jewels, necklaces, and an almost life-size statue of a woman. Model of Sardis temple: Marble Naiskos of Cybele, Digital Resource Center, Archaeological Exploration of Sardis, https://sardisexpedition.org/en/artifacts/r2-7.

24 Croesus and Ionia: Herodotus, 1.6, 1.92. Archaic Temple of Artemis at Ephesus: I. Jenkins, *Greek Architecture and Its Sculpture* (Cambridge, MA: Harvard University Press, 2006), 54–58. Temple of Hera: H. Kyrielies, "The Heraion at Samos," in *Greek Sanctuaries: New Approaches,* ed. N. Marinatos and R. Hägg (London: Routledge, 1993), 125–153. The stylobate is 356 feet × 180 feet. Polycrates: A. Carty, *Polycrates, Tyrant of Samos: New Light on Archaic Greece* (Stuttgart: Franz Steiner, 2005).

25 Peisistratus' rise to power: Herodotus, 1.59. Mirroring Athena as *apobatēs:* J. Shear, *Serving Athena,* 57. Parker, *Athenian Religion,* 83–84, calls this a "piece of theatre" believing that the Athenians embraced Peisistratus' theatricality. Mirroring Heracles' arrival on Olympus: M. Barbato, *The Ideology of Democratic Athens: Institutions, Orators and the Mythical Past* (Edinburgh: Edinburgh University Press, 2020), 115.

26 Peisistratus' palace: Boersma, *Building Policy,* 17. Loans: admittedly he did at the same time impose a 10 percent tax on all agricultural produce.

27 Boersma, *Building Policy,* 15–17.

28 Ion: M. B. Cosmopoulos, *Bronze Age Eleusis and the Origins of the Eleusinian Mysteries* (Cambridge: Cambridge University Press, 2015), 10; G. E. Mylonas, *Eleusis and the Eleusinian Mysteries* (Princeton, NJ: Princeton University Press, 1961), 27. Connection between Ion and the Eleusinian Mysteries: F. A. Zeitlin, "Mysteries of

Identity and Designs of the Self in Euripides' 'Ion,'" *Proceedings of the Cambridge Philological Society* 35, no. 215 (1989): 159–164. Ion's command against Eleusis and his death: Pausanias, 1.31.3, 7.1.5; Strabo, 8.7.1; Connelly, *Parthenon Enigma,* 31–32. Athens as metropolis of Ionian ethnos: Solon, fr. 4a (West); J. M. Hall, *Ethnic Identity in Greek Antiquity* (Cambridge: Cambridge University Press, 1997), 51–56; J. Shear, *Serving Athena,* 291. Early claims over Ionia: T. Harrison, *The Emptiness of Asia: Aeschylus'* Persians *and the History of the Fifth Century* (London: Duckworth, 2000), 108–110; L. Kallet, "Wealth, Power, and Prestige: Athens at Home and Abroad," in *The Parthenon from Antiquity to the Present,* ed. J. Neils (Cambridge: Cambridge University Press, 2005), 61. "Heady scent of fatty sacrifice": *Homeric Hymn to Apollo,* 58–59. Altar of Horns: M. F. Olivieri, "Sacred Landscape in the Sanctuary of Apollo of Delos: Peisitratus' Purification and the Networks of Culture and Politics in the VI Century BC Aegean," in *Sacred Landscapes in Antiquity: Creation, Manipulation, Transformation,* ed. Ralph Häussler and Gian Franco Chiai (Oxford: Oxbow, 2020), 333–344.

29 *Homeric Hymn to Apollo,* 146–155.

30 Olivieri, "Sacred Landscape," 333–344.

31 Thespis: Plutarch, *Solon,* 29; Horace, *Ars Poetica,* 275–277; Themistius, *Oration,* 26, 316d. See also A. W. Pickard-Cambridge, *Dithyramb, Tragedy and Comedy,* 2nd ed., rev. by T. B. L. Webster (Oxford: Clarendon Press, 1962), 69–89; V. Liapis, "On the Origins of Greek Drama," in *Looking at Greek Drama,* ed. D. Stuttard (London: Bloomsbury Academic, 2025), 39–76.

32 Great Dionysia: Parke, *Festivals of the Athenians,* 125–136; E. Simon, *Festivals of Attica: An Archaeological Commentary* (Madison: University of Wisconsin Press, 1983), 101–104; R. Parker, *Polytheism and Society at Athens* (Oxford: Oxford University Press, 2005), 317–318.

33 Dionysus Dimētōr: Diodorus Siculus, 3.62.

34 Peisistratid Telesterion: Boersma, *Building Policy,* 185. Building programme: Boersma, *Building Policy,* 23–26. Temple of Olympian Zeus: Connelly, *Parthenon Enigma,* 63.

35 Anacreon: H. A. Shapiro, "#Leagros: An Athenian Life," in *The Cambridge Companion to Ancient Athens,* ed. J. Neils and D. K. Rogers (Cambridge: Cambridge University Press, 2021), 11. Altar of Twelve Gods: L. M. Gadbery, "The Sanctuary of the Twelve Gods in the Athenian Agora: A Revised View," *Hesperia* 61, no. 4 (1992): 477–489; J. M. Camp, *The Archaeology of Athens* (New Haven, CT: Yale University Press, 2001), 32. Herms: Camp, *Archaeology of Athens,* 37; Parker, *Athenian Religion,* 80–82.

36 Festival at Brauron: Scholiast on Aristophanes, *Birds,* 873. Adding Homer to Panathenaea: R. Lane Fox, *Homer and His* Iliad (London: Allen Lane, 2023), 13, 186. Prizes (albeit from a later date): *IG* II^2 2311; see G. Nagy, *Plato's Rhapsody and Homer's Music: The Poetics of the Panathenaic Festival in Classical Athens* (Cambridge MA: Center for Hellenic Studies, Harvard University, 2002), 51n16; G. Nagy, "Epic," in *The Oxford Handbook of Philosophy and Literature,* ed. R. Eldridge (Oxford: Oxford University Press, 2009), 24. "Educator of all Greece": Thucydides, 2.41.1.

37 Coins: S. B. Pomeroy, S. M. Burstein, W. Donlan, and J. T. Roberts, *Ancient Greece: A Political, Social, and Cultural History* (Oxford: Oxford University Press, 1999), 172; J. Kroll, "From Wappenmünzen to Gorgoneia to Owls," *American Numismatic Society Museum Notes* 26 (1981): 10–15. Hipparchus and the Panathenaea: Plato, *Hippias* 228B; Aelian, *Varia Historia,* 8.2.

38 Assassination of Hipparchus: Thucydides, 6.57; [Aristotle], *Athenian Constitution,* 18; V. Azoulay, *The Tyrant-Slayers of Ancient Athens: A Tale of Two Statues,* trans. J. Lloyd (Oxford: Oxford University Press, 2017), 15–21; C. W. Fornara, "The 'Tradition' about the Murder of Hipparchus," *Zeitschrift für Alte Geschichte* 17, no. 4 (1968): 400–424. Myths of self-sacrificing girls: J. Larson, *Greek Heroine Cults* (Madison: University of Wisconsin Press, 1995), 52.

39 Thucydides, 6.58.

40 Choirs of young girls: J. Shear, *Serving Athena,* 85, 98. Basket carriers: A. Zarkadas, "Boreas and Oreithyia: The Abduction of a *Kanephoros* in the Panathenaic Procession," in Neils and Palagia, *From Kallias to Kritias,* 360. White flour: Aristophanes, *Eccleziasusai,* 732–734. "No better than she ought to be": Thucydides, 6.56; S. Nevin, *The Idea of Marathon: Battle and Culture* (London: Bloomsbury Academic, 2022), 7; J. Shear, *Serving Athena,* 259.

41 Thucydides, 6.56–57. [Aristotle], *Athenian Constitution,* 18, records how Aristogeiton agreed to tell Hippias the names of his fellow conspirators on condition that Hippias seal his promise with a handshake. When Hippias agreed, Aristogeiton mocked him for shaking the hand of the man who killed his brother—at which Hippias, in anger, killed him. Another story tells of a courtesan, Lenaea, "Lioness," lover of one of the assassins, who was tortured by Hippias but bit off her own tongue rather than divulge the other conspirators' names. A statue of a tongueless lioness on the Acropolis was said to commemorate her: Plutarch, *On Talkativeness,* 505E; Polyaenus, 8.45; Pliny the Elder, 34.19.72.

42 Herodotus 5.62; [Aristotle], *Athenian Constitution,* 19.

43 Hippias executes opponents: Thucydides, 6.59; [Aristotle], *Athenian Constitution,* 19. Temple of Apollo: Scott, *Delphi,* 94–99.

44 Peisistratus' irresistible offer: Herodotus 5.63; Parker, *Athenian Religion,* 127; Scott, *Delphi,* 100–101. Marble: Boersma, *Building Policy,* 22.

45 Maxims: Pausanias, 10.24.1. Pediments: Scott, *Delphi,* 102; L. Athanassaki, "Song, Politics and Cultural Memory: Pindar's *Pythian* 7 and the Alcmaeonid Temple of Apollo," in *Archaic and Classical Choral Song: Performance, Politics and Dissemination,* ed. L. Athanassaki and E. Bowie (Berlin: De Gruyter, 2011), 250; W. R. Agard, "Athens and Delphi, 800–485 B.C.," *The Classical Weekly* 17, no. 27 (1924): 209. "Look at the battle": Euripides, *Ion,* 205–218. Also linking the Athenian and Delphic temples: at each side of the Apollo temple's east pediment were sculpted lions savaging prey, which, while a common enough motif, mirrored the subject matter of the pedimental sculptures on Athens' Temple of Athena Polias.

46 Suborning the priests: Azoulay, *Pericles,* 20. Spartan invasions of Attica: Herodotus, 5.63–65.

47 Hippias in Sigeum: Herodotus, 5.94.

3. BUILDING DEMOCRACY

1 Isagoras: Herodotus, 5.70–75; Pausanias, 3.4; J. Ober, "The Athenian Revolution of 508/7 B.C.E.: Violence, Authority and the Origins of Democracy," in *Cultural Politics in Archaic Greece: Cult, Performance, Politics,* ed. C. Dougherty and L. Kirke (Cambridge: Cambridge University Press, 1993), 215–232.

2 Reforms: P. J. Rhodes, ed., *Athenian Democracy* (Edinburgh: Edinburgh University Press, 2004); D. Stockton, *The Classical Athenian Democracy* (Oxford: Oxford

University Press, 1990). Meaning of "demos": P. Cartledge, *Democracy: A Life* (Oxford: Oxford University Press, 2016), 3.

3 Herodotus, 5.66; Aristotle, *Politics,* 6.4; [Aristotle], *Athenian Constitution,* 21; Aristotle, *Politics,* 6.4; Cartledge, *Democracy,* 61–75; J. H. Oliver, "Reforms of Cleisthenes," *Historia: Zeitschrift für Alte Geschichte* 9, no. 4 (1960): 503–507; J. Ober, "'I Besieged That Man': Democracy's Revolutionary Start," in *Origins of Democracy in Ancient Greece,* ed. K. A. Raaflaub, J. Ober, and R. Wallace (Berkeley: University of California Press, 2007); D. W. Bradeen, "The Trittyes in Cleisthenes' Reforms," *Transactions and Proceedings of the American Philological Association* 86 (1955): 22–30; D. M. Lewis, "Cleisthenes and Attica," *Historia: Zeitschrift für Alte Geschichte* 12, no. 1 (1963): 22–40, 25; R. Parker, *Athenian Religion: A History* (Oxford: Clarendon Press, 1996), 102–103.

4 [Aristotle], *Athenian Constitution,* 21; Parker, *Athenian Religion,* 118; H. W. Parke and D. E. Wormell, *The Delphic Oracle,* vol. 1, *The History* (Oxford: Blackwell, 1956), 148; H. Bowden, *Classical Athens and the Delphic Oracle* (Cambridge: Cambridge University Press, 2005), 95.

5 Generals: V. Azoulay, *Pericles of Athens,* trans. J. Lloyd (Princeton, NJ: Princeton University Press, 2014), 29. Rivalry between Cleisthenes and Isagoras: J. Ober, "The Athenian Revolution of 508/7 B.C.E."

6 "Perhaps ten to one": calculating numbers of Helots and Spartans is notoriously difficult. T. Figuera draws up a useful table, showing different scholars' calculations. Figuera, "The Demography of the Spartan Helots,"' in *Helots and the Masters in Laconia and Messenia: Histories, Ideologies, Structures,* ed. N. Luraghi and S. E. Alcock (Washington, DC: Center for Hellenic Studies, 2003), 331. Estimates range from 7:1 (E. Cavaignac, "La population du Peloponnese aux Ve et IVe siecles," *Klio* 12 (1912): 272–274) to 16–29:1 (V. Ehrenberg, *The Greek State* (Oxford: Blackwell, 1960), 31), with 10:1 as the mean. For the present discussion, the exact proportion is unimportant. However, the Spartans were heavily outnumbered, and this worried them. Menacing enemy: Aristotle, *Politics,* 1269 a 37–39.

7 Herodotus, 5.70. Pollution ritual (= Thargelia): H. W. Parke, *Festivals of the Athenians* (London: Thames and Hudson, 1977), 146–149; E. Simon, *Festivals of Attica: An Archaeological Commentary* (Madison: University of Wisconsin Press, 1983), 76–79.

8 Cleomenes on Acropolis: Herodotus, 5.72. Cleomenes' response to the priestess, "Well, madam, I'm an Achaean, not a Dorian," has been interpreted as an appeal to Homeric tradition, since in the *Iliad* Agamemnon, brother of Sparta's King Menelaus, ruled over the Achaeans (in epic poetry a catchall term meaning simply "Greeks") including the Athenians. As successor to Menelaus and Agamemnon, Cleomenes was asserting his right to do as he pleased on the Acropolis. See P. Cartledge, *Thebes: The Forgotten City of Ancient Greece* (London: Pan Macmillan, 2020), 82–83. J. S. Boersma, *Athenian Building Policy from 561/0 to 405/4 B.C.* (Groningen: Wolters-Noordhoff, 1970), 15, suggests that the books of oracles were those delivered specifically to Hippias and the Peisistratids. Aftermath of siege: Herodotus, 5.73. Among Isagoras' executed supporters, Herodotus records "Timesitheus of Delphi, of whose courage and achievements I could tell great things," a remark as tantalizing as Conan Doyle's about the Giant Rat of Sumatra (*The Adventure of the Sussex Vampire*).

9 Herodotus, 5.75. Efficiency of call-up lists: J. Paga, *Building Democracy in Late Archaic Athens* (Oxford: Oxford University Press, 2021, 6.

10 Herodotus, 5.76; L. A. Tritle, "Kleomenes at Eleusis," *Historia* 37, no. 4 (1988): 457–460.

11 Herodotus, 5.77. Site of battle with Boeotians: my suggestion that it was at Harma is prompted by the Athenians' choice to mark victory by dedicating a bronze chariot (see the next paragraph in the text). Harma means chariot. Indeed, the town was said to have been named after an incident involving a chariot following the war of the Seven Against Thebes, a myth looming large in the creation of Athenian identity. Site of battle with Chalcidians: it is hard to square Herodotus' claim that both victories were won on the same day with his statement that the Athenians crossed over to Euboea to do battle with the Chalcidians, given the logistics that this would have involved, and the fact that their landing would have been opposed by the Chalcidians. It is more likely, as suggested here, that the Chalcidians had already reached the mainland, ready to rendezvous with their Boeotian allies. Belief in new constitution: Herodotus, 5.78, waxes eloquent about how Athens' rise (to which these victories greatly contributed) could be attributed to *isonomia:* only when fighting for themselves did Athenians begin to excel in war; previously, under tyrant overlords, they had shown little enthusiasm for fighting and "deliberately shirked their duty" (ἐθελοκάκεον).

12 Herodotus, 5.77. "On the left": undoubtedly the original statue group was plundered or destroyed by the Persians in 480 B.C., but, as with the tyrannicides' statues (see text below), the Athenians likely considered it so important that they erected a replica. Part of the inscription survives (*IG* I[3] 501a/501b). Chariot dedication: Paga, *Building Democracy,* 63–65.

13 "The first time": A. E. Raubitschek, *Dedications from the Athenian Akropolis* (Cambridge, MA: Archaeological Institute of America, 1949), 193; Paga, *Building Democracy,* 63. Symbolism of Eleusinian limestone: Paga, *Building Democracy,* 186–187. Some still consider Eleusinian limestone to have been used for purely aesthetic purposes; for example, J. M. Camp, *The Archaeology of Athens* (New Haven, CT: Yale University Press 2001), 114.

14 Shift in policy: Paga, *Building Democracy,* 33. These buildings included a temple to Athena Nikē (Victorious Athena). Albeit with a tiny footprint (8 feet × 12 feet), its position on the Bronze Age bastion meant that it dominated the approach to the Acropolis: see Paga, *Building Democracy,* 31, 41. Temple and sculptures: J. B. Connelly, *The Parthenon Enigma: A Journey into Legend* (New York: Knopf, 2014), 64–70.

15 Tyrannicides and Panathenaea: J. Shear, *Serving Athena: The Festival of the Panathenaia and the Construction of Athenian Identities* (Cambridge: Cambridge University Press, 2021), 77–79. Temple and pediments: Boersma, *Building Policy,* 20; Paga, *Building Democracy,* 43–49. Delphi and Athens: some of the same sculptors may have worked on both buildings—the Temple of Apollo was completed in 507 B.C.; work on the Temple of Athena Polias began perhaps half a decade later.

16 Other late sixth-century sculptures showing the Gigantomachy are Temple F at Selinous, the Megarian Treasury at Olympia, and the Siphnian Treasury at Delphi.

17 Tyrannicide statue: V. Azoulay, *The Tyrant-Slayers of Ancient Athens: A Tale of Two Statues,* ed. J. Lloyd (Oxford: Oxford University Press, 2017), 23–26; D. Williams, "Les Images de le Cité," in *Images at the Crossroads,* ed. J. M. Barringer and F. Lissarrague (Edinburgh: Edinburgh University Press, 2022), 151–155. "Great was the light": Simonides, fr. 76 (Diehl). Cult of Harmodius and Aristogeiton: J. Shear, *Serving Athena,* 20.

18 "Honours equal to those of gods": Parker, *Athenian Religion,* 123. Relocation of Agora: N. Robertson, "The City Center of Archaic Athens," *Hesperia* 67, no. 3 (1988): 283–302; Paga, *Building Democracy,* 78. Choice of location of Agora: H. A. Shapiro, "Democracy and Imperialism: The Panathenaia in the Age of Pericles," in *Worshipping Athena: Panathenaia and Parthenon,* ed. J. Neils (Madison: University of Wisconsin Press, 1996), 220. Agora as quasi-sacred space: Paga, *Building Democracy,* 95; Camp, *Archaeology of Athens,* 44. Boundary stones: Paga, *Building Democracy,* 90–93. Lustral basins: K. Mitchell, "Allocating Athens: Locating the Significance of the Boundary in the Ancient Town Plan," in *Proceedings of the ACSA European Conference, Berlin, 1997,* https://www.acsa-arch.org/chapter/allocating-athens-locating-the-significance-of-the-boundary-in-the-ancient-town-plan/. Rules and regulations: Paga, *Building Democracy,* 89–90.

19 Tyrants' palace: Boersma, *Building Policy,* 15; Paga, *Building Democracy,* 86. Bouleuterion: Paga, *Building Democracy,* 97–102, 293–298. Iconoclastic architecture: Paga, *Building Democracy,* 101.

20 Royal Stoa: Paga, *Building Democracy,* 102–107, 293–298.

21 Grandstand collapsing: scholion on Aristophanes, Thesmophoriazusae, 395–396. Suda π 2230 Adler s.v. Pratinas; αι 357 s.v. Aeschylus. R. Frederiksen, E. R. Gebhard, and E. Sokolicek, eds., *The Architecture of the Ancient Greek Theatre* (Aarhus, DK: Aarhus University Press, 2015), 42. Temple of Olympian Zeus: Paga, *Building Democracy,* 133–135.

22 Pnyx: Camp, *Archaeology of Athens,* 46; Paga, *Building Democracy,* 140–144.

23 Paga, *Building Democracy,* 159–161; T. Shea, "The Archaic and Classical Cemeteries," in *The Cambridge Companion to Ancient Athens,* ed. J. Neils and D. K. Rogers (Cambridge: Cambridge University Press, 2021), 152–153.

24 Roads: S. Fachard and D. Pirisino, "Routes out of Attica," in *Autopsy in Athens: Recent Archaeological Research on Athens and Attica,* ed. M. M. Miles (Oxford: Oxbow, 2015), 143–144; P. Siewert, *Die Trittyen Attikas und die Heeresreform des Kleisthenes* (Munich: C. H. Beck, 1982); Paga, *Building Democracy,* 25, 170. Late Archaic auditoria are at coastal Thorikos: Paga, *Building Democracy,* 216–217; and at Icarion on Mount Pentelicus: Paga, *Building Democracy,* 228, 231. A similar auditorium may have existed at Marathon, while Rhamnous' agora probably served as a venue for deme assembly: Paga, *Building Democracy,* 205–208. Fortlets: Paga, *Building Democracy,* 243. Spiritual threshold: Paga, *Building Democracy,* 243. "Winged goddess": Mesomedes, *Hymn to Nemesis,* 1–2. Rhamnous: Paga, *Building Democracy,* 200–207. Brauron: Paga, *Building Democracy,* 235–241. Sunium: Paga, *Building Democracy,* 219–227. Cape Zoster: Paga, *Building Democracy,* 211–214. Eleusis: Paga, *Building Democracy,* 179–187; Boersma, *Building Policy,* 24–25 (who places the construction of the Telesterion earlier, under Peisistratus).

25 Telesterion and the significance of the use of Eleusinian limestone in these contexts: Paga, *Building Democracy,* 182–187.

26 Herodotus, 5.70–74. "At Cleisthenes' suggestion": R. M. Berthold, "The Athenian Embassies to Sardis and Cleomenes' Invasion of Attica," *Historia* 51, no. 3 (2002): 259–267.

27 "Eyesore of Piraeus": Plutarch, *Pericles,* 8. Raids: Herodotus, 5.81.

28 Epidaurus and offerings to Athena: J. Larson, *Ancient Greek Cults: A Guide* (London: Routledge, 2007), 181. Statues: Herodotus, 5.83–84. "Around 625 B.C.": J. D. Mikalson, *Herodotus and Religion in the Persian Wars* (Chapel Hill: University of North Carolina Press, 2003), 21; Herodotus, 5.85–87.

29 Statues sweating, trembling, groaning: Plutarch, *Camillus,* 6.

30 Aphaea and her temple: J. Larson, *Greek Heroine Cults* (Madison: University of Wisconsin Press, 1995), 173. According to Pausanias (2.30.3), Aphaea was the Aeginetan equivalent of Cretan Dictynna ("Goddess of the Nets"), originally a nymph, a daughter of Zeus called Britomaris, saved from King Pericles' lust by Artemis, who transformed her into a goddess. Temple: Biers, 157.

31 Temple of Aphaea's pediments: D. W. J. Gill, "The Temple of Aphaia on Aegina: The Date of the Reconstruction," *Annual of the British School at Athens* 83 (1988): 169–177. Telamon at Troy: Apollodorus, 3.6.4. "Made desolate": Homer, *Iliad,* 5.642.

32 Aeacidae and Aegina: S. M. Bocksberger, *Telamonian Ajax: The Myth in Archaic and Classical Greece* (Oxford: Oxford University Press, 2022). Shrine of Aeacus on Aegina: Pausanias 2.29.6–8. Loan of Aeacidae relics to Thebans: Herodotus, 5.81. Athenian Shrine of Aeacus: Herodotus, 5.89.

33 The existence of a *Theseis* is uncertain. See E. Cingano, "Epic Fragments on Theseus: Hesiod, Cecrops and the *Theseis,*" in *Fragments, Holes, and Wholes: Reconstructing the Ancient World in Theory and Practice,* ed. T. Derda, J. Hilder, and J. Wapisz (Warsaw: University of Warsaw Press, 2017), 309–333; Larson, *Greek Heroine Cults,* 112. According to F. Jacoby, *Atthis: the Local Chronicles of Ancient Athens* (Oxford: Clarendon Press, 1949), 220, the *Theseis* "from a time in which early epic poetry had perished, makes a second Herakles of the only Attic hero who was known outside Athens, and to achieve this end it borrowed extensively from the Herakles story." Theseus: A. G. Ward, *The Quest for Theseus* (London: Pall Mall, 1970). Theseus' political role in Athens: H. J. Walker, *Theseus and Athens* (Oxford: Oxford University Press, 1995). Theseus and Heracles: Parker, *Athenian Religion,* 85.

34 The best modern book about Persia, its rise and its customs, is L. Llewellyn-Jones, *Persians: The Age of the Great Kings* (New York: Basic Books, 2022).

35 "Lied to one another": Herodotus, 1.153.

36 Herodotus, 30–36; A. R. Burn, *Persia and the Greeks* (London: Edward Arnold, 1962), 195–197; A. Keaveney, "The Attack on Naxos: A 'Forgotten Cause' of the Ionian Revolt," *Classical Quarterly* 38, no. 1 (1988): 76–81.

37 Aristarchus in Sparta: Herodotus, 5.49–51. Aristarchus in Athens: Herodotus, 5.97.

38 Herodotus, 5.99–100. Sardis: C. Greenewalt, "Sardis: A First Millenium B.C.E. Capital in Western Anatolia," in *The Oxford Handbook of Ancient Anatolia,* ed. S. Steadman and G. McMahon (Oxford: Oxford University Press, 2011), 1112–1130; N. Cahill, "The City of Sardis," in *The Lydians and Their World,* ed. N. Cahill (Istanbul: Yapi Kredi Yayinlari, 2010); E. R. M. Dusinberre, *Aspects of Empire in Achaemenid Sardis* (Cambridge: Cambridge University Press, 2003. The Archaeological Exploration of Sardis, Digital Resource Center, https://sardisexpedition.org/, is recommended.

39 Herodotus, 5.101–102. According to Diodorus (10.25), "the Persians learnt temple-burning from the Greeks, committing the same atrocities against those who first outraged Justice."

40 Spoke no more: Herodotus, 5.103. Defeat of Miletus: Herodotus, 6.6–20. Playwright dramatized: Herodotus, 6.21; P. Green, *The Greco-Persian Wars* (Berkeley: University of California Press, 1998), 27.

41 "I sliced off": Darius' Behistun Inscription, 2.12.

42 Herodotus, 6.95.

43 Darius' envoys to Athens: Herodotus 7.133. Persians touring Greece: Herodotus, 6.49.

44 Naxos: Herodotus, 6.96. Delos: Herodotus, 6.97.

45 Eretria: Herodotus, 6.101–103.

4. BURNT OFFERINGS

1 Battle of Marathon: Herodotus, 6.102–120. Much is unclear, including the location of the Greek camp, which on balance I locate at the base of Mount Agrieliki. I agree with modern scholars who dismiss Herodotus' estimation of the Persian army as comprising 200,000 men. More likely figures are: Persian infantry, ca. 25,000; cavalry 1,000 facing ca. 9,000–10,000 Athenian hoplites and 1,000 Plataeans. See C. J. Butera and M. A. Sears, *Battles and Battlefields of Ancient Greece* (Barnsley, UK: Pen and Sword, 2019), 1–15. "Ask the Athenians": Herodotus, 6.105. Goat sacrifice: Xenophon, *Anabasis,* 3.2; Plutarch, *De Malignitate Herodoti,* 26; Aelian, *Historical Miscellany,* 2.25.

2 Heracles: Pausanias, 1.15. Theseus: Plutarch, *Theseus,* 35. Echetlus: Pausanias 1.32. Epizelus: Herodotus, 6.117.

3 Herodotus, 6.120. Like epic heroes: this idea would become popular in funeral orations for war dead (e.g., Plutarch, *Pericles,* 8; Demosthenes, 60.34; Hyperides, *Epitaphios Logos,* 43). List of war dead: Pausanias, 1.32; *Supplementum Epigraphicum Graecum* 49.370, 51.425, 53.354, 55.413, 56.430, 431, 432; X. Duffy, *Commemorating Conflict: Greek Monuments of the Persian Wars* (Oxford: Archaeopress, 2018), 70–71. Normal burial in public cemetery: J. Paga, *Building Democracy in Late Archaic Athens* (Oxford: Oxford University Press, 2021), 159. Hero cult: Pausanias, 1.32.3.

4 Marble column: J. M. Camp, *The Archaeology of Athens* (New Haven, CT: Yale University Press, 2001), 48. "At Marathon": Simonides, 21 (Page), quoted (150 years later) in Lycurgus, *Against Leocrates,* 109. See also J. H. Molyneux, *Simonides: A Historical Study* (Wauconda, IL: Bolchazy-Carducci, 1992), 150.

5 "Miltiades set up": Simonides, 5 (Page). See Molyneux, *Simonides,* 151; R. T. Neer, "Delphi, Olympia and the Art of Politics," in *The Cambridge Companion to Archaic Greece,* ed. H. Shapiro (Cambridge: Cambridge University Press, 2007), 234; A. Gartziou-Tatti, "Gods, Heroes, and the Battle of Marathon," *Bulletin of the Institute of Classical Studies,* suppl. no. 124 (2013): 91–110.

6 Cave of Pan: Duffy, *Commemorating Conflict,* 88–89. Dedications to Pan: Camp, *Archaeology of Athens,* 50–51. Vow to Artemis: Xenophon, *Anabasis,* 3.2.12; Plutarch, *On the Malice of Herodotus,* 26; see also P. J. Rhodes, *A Commentary on the Aristotelian Athenaion Politeia* (Oxford: Clarendon Press, 1981), 650; H. W. Parke, *Festivals of the Athenians* (London: Thames and Hudson, 1977), 55. Artemis Agrotera: J. Larson, *Ancient Greek Cults: A Guide* (London: Routledge, 2007), 102.

7 "Athenians to Apollo": *IG* I^3 1463. "Complete": the Treasury may have been begun following Athens' victory over Boeotians and Chalcidians in 506; W. C. West, "Greek Public Monuments of the Persian Wars" (PhD diss., University of North Carolina, 1965), 18–19; Duffy, *Commemorating Conflict,* 74. Athenian Treasury at Delphi: see M. C. Scott, *Delphi: A History of the Center of the Ancient World* (Princeton, NJ: Princeton University Press, 2014), 112–113; R. T. Neer, "The Athenian Treasury at Delphi and the Material of Politics," *Classical Antiquity* 23, no. 1 (2004): 63–94; Neer, "Delphi, Olympia and the Art of Politics," 249.

8 "Callimachus of Aphidnae": *Inscriptiones Graecae* (Berlin: De Gruyter, 1873), 12, 609. See C. M. Keesling, "The Callimachus Monument on the Athenian Acropolis

(CEG 256) and Athenian Commemoration of the Persian Wars," in *Archaic and Classical Greek Epigram,* ed. M. Baumbach, A. Petrovic, and I. Petrovic (Cambridge: Cambridge University Press, 2010), 100–130; Neer, "Delphi, Olympia and the Art of Politics," 235; Duffy, *Commemorating Conflict,* 76–77. The reconstructed monument is in Athens' Acropolis Museum (Acr. 690).

9 "Old Parthenon": W. B. Dinsmoor, "The Date of the Older Parthenon," *American Journal of Archaeology* 38, no. 3 (1934): 408–488; Paga, *Building Democracy,* 73–74; J. S. Boersma, *Athenian Building Policy from 561/0 to 405/4 B.C.* (Groningen: Wolters-Noordhoff, 1970), 176; Duffy, *Commemorating Conflict,* 93–94; J. B. Connelly, *The Parthenon Enigma: A Journey into Legend* (New York: Knopf, 2014), 71. Quarries on Mount Pentelicus: P. Valavanis, "The Acropolis," in *The Cambridge Companion to Ancient Athens,* ed. J. Neils and D. K. Rogers (Cambridge: Cambridge University Press, 2021), 66.

10 Alcmaeonidae flashing signals: Herodotus, 6.115. Miltiades on Paros and subsequent trial: Herodotus 6.132–136; S. Nevin, *Military Leaders and Sacred Space in Classical Greek Warfare: Temples, Sanctuaries and Conflict in Antiquity* (London: I. B. Tauris, 2017), 49–59.

11 Piraeus after the fall of Miletus: Paga, *Building Democracy,* 260. Aegina attacks sacred ship: Herodotus, 6.87. Economic impact of fall of Miletus: A. Avramidou, "Athens and Neapolis in the 5th Century B.C.," in *From Kallias to Kritias: Art in Athens in the Second Half of the Fifth Century B.C.,* ed. J. Neils and O. Palagia (Berlin: De Gruyter, 2021), 346.

12 Herodotus, 7.144. Plutarch, *Themistocles,* 4.

13 Ostracism: [Aristotle], *Athenian Constitution,* 22; Diodorus Siculus, 11.55; A. E. Raubitschek, "The Origin of Ostracism," *American Journal of Archaeology* 55, no. 3 (1951): 221–229; D. Kagan, "The Origin and Purposes of Ostracism," *Hesperia,* 30, no. 4 (1961): 393–401; S. Forsdyke, "Exile, Ostracism and the Athenian Democracy," *Classical Antiquity* 19, no. 2 (2000): 232–263; P. Cartledge, *Democracy: A Life* (Oxford: Oxford University Press, 2016), 70–71. Ostracism of Xanthippus: Ostracism: [Aristotle], *Athenian Constitution,* 22; O. Broneer, "Notes on the Xanthippos Ostrakon," *American Journal of Archaeology* 52, no. 3 (1948): 341–343.

14 Triremes: J. S. Morrison, J. Coates and N. B. Rankov, *The Athenian Trireme,* 2nd ed. (Cambridge: Cambridge University Press, 2000).

15 J. R. Hale, *Lords of the Sea: The Epic Story of the Athenian Navy and the Birth of Democracy,* (New York: Viking, 2009), 20–28. Marble eyes: see D. N. Carlson, "Seeing the Sea: Ships' Eyes in Classical Greece," *Hesperia* 78, no. 3 (2009): 347–365.

16 Events in Persia: Herodotus, 7.1–7. New invading force: Herodotus, 7.61–88. "Could not count it": Herodotus, 7.146–147. Few states willing to resist: Herodotus, 7.145; P. A. Brunt, "The Hellenic League Against Persia," in *Studies in Greek History and Thought* (Oxford: Clarendon Press, 1993), 47–83. Only 31 poleis out of many hundreds opposed Persia: V. Azoulay, *Pericles of Athens,* trans. J. Lloyd (Princeton, NJ: Princeton University Press, 2014), 5. Recall of ostracized Athenians: [Aristotle], *Athenian Constitution,* 22; Plutarch, *Aristeides,* 8; M. Jameson, "A Decree of Themistocles from Troizen," *Hesperia* 29 (1960): 198–223.

17 Herodotus 7.140.

18 Herodotus, 7.141. Cithaeron is a mountain in Boeotia near Plataea and Thebes. Some suggest that this oracle was rewritten either at the time by Themistocles to give backing to his strategy or by a post bellum writer to suit the outcome of the war.

19 Herodotus, 7.142–143.

20 Cimon: Plutarch, *Cimon,* 5; D. Stuttard, *Phoenix: Cimon, Miltiades and the Rise of Athens* (Cambridge, MA: Harvard University Press, 2021), 134–135. Snake: Herodotus, 8.41.

21 Evacuation of Attica: R. Garland, *Athens Burning: The Persian Invasion of Greece and the Evacuation of Attica* (Baltimore: Johns Hopkins University Press, 2017), 46–50.

22 P. Green, *The Greco-Persian Wars* (Berkeley: University of California Press, 1970), 109–145. Thermopylae: Herodotus, 7.201–225; Diodorus, 11.4–11; P. Cartledge, *Thermopylae: The Battle That Changed the World* (New York: Harry N. Abrams, 2006); Butera and Sears, *Battles and Battlefields,* 49–63. Herodotus: Artemisium, 7.175–195, 8.2–22; Diodorus, 11.12–13; Plutarch, *Themistocles,* 7–9. Boreas: Herodotus, 7.189.

23 Herodotus, 8.27–39, 51–54.

24 Herodotus, 8.51–54; Garland, *Athens Burning,* 66–68. Xoanon removed: writing in the second century A.D., Pausanias, 1.22, describes the xoanon, implying that it must have survived the torching of the Acropolis, and therefore must have been removed during the evacuation of Athens.

25 Herodotus, 8.54–55.

26 Smuggling Aeacidae relics: Herodotus, 8.64; Green, *Greco-Persian Wars,* 171. Greek war council: Plutarch, *Themistocles,* 11; Herodotus, 8.62.

27 Herodotus, 8.65; Plutarch, *Themistocles,* 15; Green, *Greco-Persian Wars,* 176.

28 Themistocles' ruse: Aeschylus, *Persians,* 355–379; Herodotus, 75–76; Plutarch, *Themistocles,* 12. "Forward Greeks!": Aeschylus, *Persians,* 402–404. Battle of Salamis: Herodotus, 83–90.

29 Owl: Plutarch, *Themistocles,* 12. Cychreus: Pausanias 1.36.1. Bridges destroyed: Herodotus, 8.117.

30 Battle of Himera: Herodotus, 7.166; Diodorus Siculus, 11.20–26.

31 Signs of occupation: Garland, *Athens Burning,* 89–90. Removal of statue of tyrannicides: V. Azoulay, *The Tyrant-Slayers of Ancient Athens: A Tale of Two Statues,* trans. J. Lloyd (Oxford: Oxford University Press, 2017), 32–34.

32 Trophy on Salamis dedicated to Zeus Who Turns the Enemy to Flight (Zeus Tropaios): Pausanias, 1.36.1; *IG* II/III^2 1028. Sophocles' role in victory celebrations: *Life of Sophocles,* 3. Ship dedication at Sunium: Paga, *Building Democracy,* 227.

33 Herodotus, 8.140–142.

34 Herodotus, 8.144.

35 Herodotus, 9.19–70; Diodorus, 11.28–32; Plutarch, *Aristeides,* 11–19; Green, *Greco-Persian Wars,* 239–271.

36 Battles of Plataea and Mycale fought near sanctuaries of Eleusinian Demeter: Herodotus, 9.65, 9.97, 9.101; Strabo, *Geography,* 14.1.3.

37 "If the greatest": Simonides, 8 (Page), in D. L. Page, *Further Greek Epigrams: Epigrams before A.D. 50 from the Greek Anthology and Other Sources, Not Included in Hellenistic Fragments or The Garland of Philip* (Cambridge: Cambridge University Press, 1981).

38 "To save all Greece": Simonides, 12 (Page). "In striving": *IG* VII 53. The full epitaph (attributed to Simondides) reads:

> In striving to sustain the day of freedom for both Greece and Megara
> we received the lot of death—
> some at Euboea beneath Pelion, where the sanctuary is
> named after the holy archer, Artemis;

> others on the crags of Mount Mycale; others before Salamis . . .
> still others on the flatlands of Boeotia, where they dared
> to try their strength against the horsemen.

See P. G. Ruano, "*IG* VII 53: An Epigraphic *Rara Avis* in the Corpus of Greek Metrical Inscriptions," *Mare Nostrum* 7, no. 7 (2016): 35–55. "These men": Simonides, 9 (Page).

39 "Stranger, report this": Simonides, 22b (Page); "Here, against three million," Simonides, 22a (Page).

40 Thespians: Herodotus, 7.202. Malians: Diodorus, 11.4. Thebans, Phocians, Locrians: Herodotus, 7.202–203; Diodorus, 11.4.

41 Each community was identified not by the name of its city ("Athens") but of its citizens ("the Athenians"). Herodotus (8.81) imagines the column representing one three-headed serpent, but autopsy (the remains of the column are today in Istanbul), as well as later drawings such as those of 1574 contained in the Freshfield Album (Trinity College Library MS O.17.2) suggest he was mistaken.

42 Thucydides, 1.90–93; Diodorus, 11.39–40; Plutarch, *Themistocles,* 19. Walls: Boersma, *Building Policy,* 45–46; L. Costaki and A. M. Theocharaki, "City Streets, Wells, and Gates," in Neils and Rogers, *The Cambridge Companion to Ancient Athens,* 54–55; A. M. Theocharaki, "The Ancient Circuit Wall of Athens: Its Changing Course and the Phases of Construction," *Hesperia* 80, no. 1 (2011): 71–156.

43 Thucydides, 1.90.

44 Boersma, *Building Policy,* 44. Material built into north wall: Connelly, *Parthenon Enigma,* 74; Boersma, *Building Policy,* 46.

45 Arrephorion: Hurwit, *Athenian Acropolis,* 200–202; D. Eggelezos, "Re-burial of the Arrephorion on the Athenian Acropolis: An in situ Rescue Intervention against Degradation," in *Geotechnical Engineering for the Preservation of Monuments and Historical Sites,* ed. E. Bilotta, A. Fiora, S. Lirer, and C. Viggiani (Boca Raton, FL: CRC Press, 2013), 367. M. Brouskari, *The Monuments of the Acropolis* (Athens: Ministry of Culture, 2001). My especial thanks to Vasileia Manidaki of the Acropolis Restoration Service, the Architect in charge of the Arrephorion Project, for showing me the Arrephorion in November 2023 and discussing with me its development and architecture.

46 I am grateful to Vasileia Manidaki for pointing out to me these details of the Garden of Pandrosus.

47 Propylaeon Gateway: Boersma, *Building Policy,* 202. Temple of Athena Nikē: Boersma, *Building Policy,* 178.

48 Chariot group: Herodotus, 5.77. The statue which Herodotus saw cannot have been the original, which would have been looted or destroyed by the Persians (see Chapter 3). Statue of Tyrannicides: Azoulay, *Tyrant-Slayers.*

49 Ruins of Athens: Thucydides, 1.89.

5. CITY OF GODS

1 Herodotus, 9.106; Diodorus, 11.37.

2 Herodotus, 9.115.

3 "Athenians dedicated this": *IG* I[3] 1464. J. J. Coulton, *The Architectural Development of the Greek Stoa* (Oxford: Clarendon Press, 1976), 234; J. Walsh, "The Date of the Athenian Stoa at Delphi," *American Journal of Archaeology* 90 (1986): 319–336;

G. Umholz, "Architraval Arrogance? Dedicatory Inscriptions in Greek Architecture of the Classical Period," *Hesperia* 71 (2002): 261–293.

4 Herodotus, 9.116–120; V. Azoulay, *Pericles of Athens,* trans. J. Lloyd (Princeton, NJ: Princeton University Press, 2014), 60.

5 "After defeating the Persians": Simonides, 17a (Page). "Greece's liberators": Diodorus Siculus, 11.33. Pausanias and his replacement: Plutarch, *Aristeides,* 23; Plutarch, *Cimon,* 6; Thucydides, 1.95; [Aristotle], *Athenian Constitution,* 23.

6 Plutarch, *Aristeides,* 25; [Aristotle], *Athenian Constitution,* 23; A. H. Sommerstein and A. J. Bayliss, *Oath and State in Ancient Greece* (Berlin: De Gruyter, 2012), 205–208.

7 Iron: [Aristotle], *Athenian Constitution,* 23. Symbolism of iron bars: Herodotus, 1.165. Name of League: see, for example, P. J. Rhodes, *A History of the Classical World, 487–323* B.C.E. (Malden, MA: Blackwell, 2005), 18.

8 Hellenotamiae: Thucydides, 1.96; A. G. Woodhead, "The Institution of the Hellenotamiae," *Journal of Hellenic Studies* 79 (1959): 149–152. Temple dimensions: 45 feet × 98 feet, with 6 × 11 Doric columns. See T. Spawforth, *The Complete Greek Temples* (London: Thames and Hudson, 2006). The Delian League differed from its Peloponnesian equivalent. Sparta's allies provided men, not money.

9 Diodorus, 11.50. The chronology is notoriously difficult to unpick. Diodorus assigns this discussion to 475 B.C., but the suspicion is that, since he organizes his data annalistically, he has postponed his consideration of the event to a year in which little else happened, simply to have something to write about.

10 Sparta's Persian Stoa: Pausanias, 3.11.3; Vitruvius, 1.1.6. Neither author mentions accompanying inscriptions, but, since Vitruvius wrote four centuries and Pausanias six after the stoa was first built, and both could identify the statues' subjects, it was likely some kind of signifier. "If you should ask": DNa inscription of Darius I.

11 Siphnian Treasury: M. C. Scott, *Delphi: A History of the Center of the Ancient World* (Princeton, NJ: Princeton University Press, 2014), 105–108; R. T. Neer, "Framing the Gift: The Politics of the Siphnian Treasury at Delphi," *Classical Antiquity* 20, no. 2 (2001): 273–344. Temple of Olympian Zeus at Acragas (dimensions 361 feet × 173 feet): Spawforth, *Complete Greek Temples,* 127–128. Proportions of Himera and Syracuse temples: approximately 180 feet × 75 feet with 6 × 14 columns. Temple at Himera: Spawforth, *Complete Greek Temples,* 132–133. Temple at Syracuse: Spawforth, *Complete Greek Temples,* 122–123.

12 Temple of Olympian Zeus: J. Barringer, *Olympia: A Cultural History* (Princeton, NJ: Princeton University Press, 2021), 120–137; L. Drees, *Olympia: Gods, Artists, and Athletes,* trans. G. Onn (London: Pall Mall, 1968), 114–116; Spawforth, *Complete Greek Temples,* 152–154; Darling, *Architecture of Greece,* 207–209.

13 Spawforth, *Complete Greek Temples,* 148–149; Darling, *Architecture of Greece,* 172–173; D. W. J. Gill, "The Temple of Aphaia on Aegina: The Date of the Reconstruction," *Annual of the British School at Athens* 83 (1988): 169–177.

14 Plutarch, *Cimon,* 7; Aeschines, 3.183–185. Herms: J. M. Camp, *The Archaeology of Athens* (New Haven, CT: Yale University Press, 2001), 65. See also D. Stuttard, *Phoenix: Cimon, Miltiades and the Rise of Athens* (Cambridge, MA: Harvard University Press, 2021), 194. For a discussion of the verses, see F. Jacoby, "Some Athenian Epigrams from the Persian Wars," *Hesperia* 14 (1945): 157–211; H. T. Wade-Gerry, "Classical Epigrams and Epitaphs," *Journal of Hellenic Studies* 53 (1933): 71–82.

15 Plutarch, *Theseus,* 36; Plutarch, *Cimon,* 8; R. Parker, *Athenian Religion: A History* (Oxford: Clarendon Press, 1996), 168. Theseus granted Oedipus asylum to and, when Oedipus' son, Polyneices, failed to regain his throne, forced reluctant Thebans to bury the bodies of their enemy's dead. Demophon protected Heracles' orphaned children from Eurystheus, King of Tiryns. "In the heart of the lower city": Plutarch, *Theseus,* 36. H. A. Thompson, "Activities in the Athenian Agora, 1960–1965," *Hesperia* 35 (1966): 37–54, 41, and J. S. Boersma, *Athenian Building Policy from 561/0 to 405/4 B.C.* (Groningen: Wolters-Noordhoff, 1970), 42, identify it as the Heliaea in the south of the Agora, while Camp, *Archaeology of Athens,* 66, places it in the Plaka east of the Agora. Paintings: D. Castriota, *Myth, Ethos and Actuality* (Madison: University of Wisconsin Press, 1992), 33–34.

16 Cimon's victory at Eurymedon: Plutarch, *Cimon,* 12–13; Diodorus, 11.61; Thucydides, 1.100; Stuttard, *Phoenix,* 221–227. Palm tree: Pausanias, 1.15; Plutarch, *Nicias,* 13; Scott, *Delphi,* 128.

17 Painted Stoa: Pausanias, 1.15; J. M. Camp, *The Athenian Agora: Excavations in the Heart of Classical Athens* (London: Thames and Hudson, 1986), 68–72; Boersma, *Building Policy,* 55–57; R. E. Wycherley, "The Painted Stoa," *Phoenix* 7 (1953): 20–35; E. B. Harrison, "The South Frieze of the Nikē Temple and the Marathon Painting in the Painted Stoa," *American Journal of Archaeology* 76 (1972): 353–378. Pausanias records that there was a fourth painting showing the (otherwise unknown) Battle of Oinoe, but this seems likely to have been added later.

18 Artworks: Castriota, *Myth, Ethos,* 76–89 (where Castriota calls the stoa a "hall of victories"); T. L. Shear Jr., *Trophies of Victory: Public Buildings in Periklean Athens* (Princeton, NJ: Princeton University Press, 2016), 14–17. Polygnotus' Sack of Troy: Pausanias, 10.25. Aethra: Hyginus, *Fables,* 79, 92. Problematic nature of subject matter: Castriota, *Myth, Ethos,* 97–101. [On the left]: Pausanias, 1.15.

19 Harpokration s.v. Πολύγνωτος.

20 Examples from the Acropolis include: archaic orientalizing statues Acr. 681, Acr. 269, Acr. 679, Acr. 680; more fluid, energetic bronze and marble statues: Acr. 691, NAM × 6480. Critius: Acr. 698. Ageladas of Argos: Pausanias, 6.8, 7.24, 10.10. Teacher of Pheidias: Suidas, s.v. *Schol. Ad Aristoph. Ran.,* 504; Tzetzes, *Chiliades,* 7.154; 8.191. Teacher of Pheidias, Myron, and Polycleitus: Pliny, *Natural History,* 34.18. Myron's "Discus-Thrower": Pliny, *Natural History,* 34.19. "Gradually": Philo of Byzantium, *Belopoeica,* 4.1. "If one casual": Plutarch, *Moralia,* 45C.

21 Pausanias, 10.10; Scott, *Delphi,* 128–129; "Marathon Monument," *Bulletin of the Institute of Classical Studies* 56, suppl. 105, part 1 (May 2013): 303–318.

22 Statue at Plataea: Pausanias, 9.4; "Athena Areia," *Bulletin of the Institute of Classical Studies* 56, suppl. 105, part 1 (May 2013): 39–43. Height: Pausanias records it as being just shorter than Pheidias' 30-foot-tall statue of Athena Promachus. Statue at Pellene: Pausanias 7.27; "Athena of Pellene," *Bulletin of the Institute of Classical Studies* 56, suppl. 105, part 1 (May 2013): 273–276. Rendering ivory malleable: see, for example, Patricia Saltzman-Mitchell, "A Whole Out of Pieces: Pygmalion's Ivory Statue in Ovid's *Metamorphoses,*" *Arethusa* 41, no. 2 (2008): 291–311.

23 Statue of Apollo the Locust God: Pausanias, 1.24.8; "Apollo Kassel," *Bulletin of the Institute of Classical Studies* 56, suppl. 105, part 1 (May 2013): 417–432. Statue of Lemnian Athena: Pausanias, 1.28.2; "Athena Lemnia," *Bulletin of the Institute of Classical Studies* 56, suppl. 105, part 1 (May 2013): 45–68. The statue is dated to 451–448 B.C. Finest work: Lucian, *Imagines,* 4. Face, nose, cheeks: Lucian, *Imagines,* 6. Pale rosy blush: Himerius, *Oratio,* 68.4.

24 Athena Promachus: Pausanias, 1.28 (which tells how sunlight glinting from the spear could be seen by sailors rounding Cape Sunium—sadly, a physical impossibility); "Athena 'Promachos,'" *Bulletin of the Institute of Classical Studies* 56, suppl. 105, part 1 (May 2013): 277–296; Camp, *Archaeology of Athens,* 53–55. "Ever since the sea": Diodorus, 11.62.

25 L. B. Hunt, "The Long History of Lost Wax Casting," *Gold Bulletin* 13, no. 2 (1980): 63–79; C. Hemingway and S. Hemingway, "The Technique of Bronze Statuary in Ancient Greece," in *Heilbrunn Timeline of Art History,* The Met, New York, October 1, 2003, http://www.metmuseum.org/toah/hd/grbr/hd_grbr.htm.

26 Reception at Olympia: Plutarch, *Themistocles,* 17. Against the tyrant: Plutarch, *Themistocles,* 25. Frustrating Sparta: Plutarch, *Themistocles,* 20.

27 Temple: Plutarch, *Themistocles,* 22. Ostracism: Plutarch, *Themistocles,* 22. In Persia: Plutarch, *Themistocles,* 26–31. Themistocles' decline: G. Cawkwell, "The Fall of Themistocles," in *Auckland Classical Essays Presented to E. M. Blaiklock* (Auckland, NZ: Auckland University Press, 1970), 39–58; G. E. M. de Ste. Croix, *The Origins of the Peloponnesian War* (London: Duckworth, 1972), 173–178.

28 Naxos: Thucydides, 1.137; Plutarch, *Themistocles,* 25. Thasos: Thucydides, 1.100–101; Diodorus, 11.70; Plutarch, *Cimon,* 14; Stuttard, *Phoenix,* 245–249, 254–255.

29 Earthquake: Plutarch, *Cimon,* 16; Diodorus, 11.63; Strabo, *Geography,* 8.5; Pausanias, 4.24; Aelian, *Varia Historia,* 6.7.

30 Plutarch, *Cimon,* 17; Pausanias, 4.24; Thucydides, 1.102.

31 Pericles' background and early life: Azoulay, *Pericles,* 15–27.

32 "When hubris flowers": Aeschylus, *Persians,* 821–822. "They are not slaves": Aeschylus, *Persians,* 242. "The gods": Aeschylus, *Persians,* 347. "Do not campaign": Aeschylus, *Persians,* 790–792. "Silent witness": Aeschylus, *Persians,* 818. "When they got to Greece": Aeschylus, *Persians,* 809–814. See D. Stuttard, ed., *Looking at Persians* (London: Bloomsbury Academic, 2022).

33 "Serving as an archon": membership of the Areopagus was restricted to ex-archons, so the fact that Pericles faced Cimon in the Court of the Areopagus is probable evidence that he had held this office. Military experience: Plutarch, *Cimon,* 13. Family feud: Azoulay, *Pericles,* 26.

34 Plutarch, *Cimon,* 10, 13; Stuttard, *Phoenix,* 233, 236; Boersma, *Building Policy,* 58–59. Academy: Camp, *Archaeology of Athens,* 233. South Wall of Acropolis: Pausanias, 1.28; Boersma, *Building Policy,* 52–53.

35 Trial: Plutarch, *Cimon,* 14; Azoulay, *Pericles,* 24–26.

36 [Aristotle], *Athenian Constitution,* 25; Plutarch, *Pericles,* 9; Plutarch, *Cimon,* 15; Demosthenes, 23.22; C. Hignett, *A History of the Athenian Constitution to the End of the Fifth Century B.C.* (Oxford: Clarendon Press, 1952), 193–213; P. J. Rhodes, *A Commentary on the Aristotelian Athenaion Politeia* (Oxford: Clarendon Press, 1981), 311–319.

37 Tholos and round structures at sanctuaries: Camp, *Athenian Agora,* 94–95; Camp, *Archaeology of Athens,* 69–70. See also A. Steiner, "Feeding the *Prytaneis:* Eating and Drinking in the 5th-Century Tholos," in *From Kallias to Kritias: Art in Athens in the Second Half of the Fifth Century B.C.,* ed. J. Neils and O. Palagia (Berlin: De Gruyter, 2021), 133–145.

38 Antiphon, 5.68; [Aristotle], *Athenian Constitution,* 25.4; Plutarch, *Pericles,* 10; D. W. Roller, "Who Murdered Ephialtes?," *Historia,* 38, no. 3 (1989): 257–266.

39 Athens' Egyptian Campaign: Thucydides, 1.104, 109–110; Ctesias, *FGrH* 688 F14 §36–38; Diodorus Siculus, 11.74, 78–79; also Herodotus, 3.12, 160.2, 7.7.1; Isocrates, 5.86; Plato, *Menexenus,* 241d–e.

40 Thucydides, 1.105–108; Diodorus, 11.78–80. List of casualties: F. H. von Gaertringen, ed., *Inscriptiones Graecae*, editio minor, vol. 1 (Berlin: De Gruyter, 1924), 929; A. G. Woodhead, *Supplementum Epigraphicum Graecum* (Amsterdam, 1958), 58–62. Long Walls: Boersma, *Building Policy*, 57–58; D. H. Conwell, *Connecting a City to the Sea: The History of the Athenian Long Walls* (Leiden: Brill, 2008).

41 Spartan shield at Olympia: L. Drees, *Olympia: Gods, Artists, and Athletes*, trans. G. Onn (London: Pall Mall, 1968), 115; Barringer, *Olympia*, 122.

42 Thucydides, 1.108.

43 Thucydides, 109–110; Diodorus, 11.77; Stuttard, *Phoenix*, 286–287.

44 Jury pay: Aristotle, *Politics*, 1274a8; [Aristotle], *Athenian Constitution*, 27.3–5; M. M. Markel, "Jury Pay and Assembly Pay at Athens," *History of Political Thought* 6, no. 1/2 (1985): 265–297; Azoulay, *Pericles*, 80–81.

45 Moving treasury: Azoulay, *Pericles*, 78; W. K. Pritchett, "The Transfer of the Delian Treasury," *Historia* 18, no. 1 (1969): 17–21.

46 Plutarch, *Cimon*, 18–19; Thucydides, 1.112; Diodorus, 12.3–4; D. Kagan, *The Outbreak of the Peloponnesian War* (Ithaca, NY: Cornell University Press, 2012), 104–105; Stuttard, *Phoenix*, 289–297.

47 Peace of Callias: Plutarch, *Cimon*, 13; Diodorus, 12.4. While the treaty has been questioned since the fourth century B.C., it may be referred to by Herodotus (7.151), and other classical authors trusted its authenticity (Demosthenes, *De Falsa Legatione*, 273; Isocrates, 4.118–120; Plato, *Menexenus*, 241d–e). See, for example, R. Meiggs, *The Athenian Empire* (Oxford: Clarendon Press, 1972), 129–151; E. Badian, "The Peace of Callias," *Journal of Hellenic Studies* 50 (1987): 1–39; E. F. Bloedow, "The Peace of Callias," *Symbolae Osloensis* 67 (1992): 41–68; G. L. Cawkwell, "The Peace between Athens and Persia," *Phoenix* 51 (1997): 115–130; L. J. Samons II, "Kimon, Kallias and Peace with Persia," *Historia* 47, no. 2 (1998): 129–140.

48 "Large or small": Plutarch, *Pericles*, 17. "United under Athens": Kagan, *Outbreak*, 120. Implication of peace on Athens: Boersma, *Building Policy*, 67.

49 Oath of Plataea: Lycurgus, 1.81; compare Isocrates, 4.156. Some are sceptical of its authenticity: for example, P. Cartledge, *After Thermopylae: The Oath of Plataea and the End of the Graeco-Persian Wars* (Oxford: Oxford University Press, 2013). Others are not: for example, L. Kallet, "Wealth, Power, and Prestige: Athens at Home and Abroad," in *The Parthenon from Antiquity to the Present*, ed. J. Neils (New York: Cambridge University Press, 2005), 50–52; and J. B. Connelly, *The Parthenon Enigma: A Journey into Legend* (New York: Knopf, 2014), 82. Sacrifices at Eleusis: Herodotus, 9.19. Cartledge, *After Thermopylae*, 17, suggests that it was during these that any oath would have been made. Timing of rebuilding: Kallet, "Wealth, Power, Prestige," in Neils, *Parthenon from Antiquity*, 52.

6. EMBRACING PAST, PRESENT, AND FUTURE

1 No Classical sources suggest the concept behind the "Periclean" building project. Educated guesses must be based on (1) the buildings themselves, (2) associated artefacts, and (3) contemporary literature, from which Athenian social values may be pieced together. Many theories have arisen to explain primarily the Parthenon and its frieze. My discussion uses physical and literary evidence to seek a reading which is plausible within the context of fifth-century Athenian society and beliefs. Date of "Hephaesteum": see, for example, L. Haselberger, "Bending the Truth: Curvature and Other Refinements of the Parthenon," in *The Parthenon from Antiquity to the Present*, ed. J. Neils (New York: Cambridge University Press, 2005), 101. J. S. Boersma,

Athenian Building Policy from 561/0 to 405/4 B.C. (Groningen: Wolters-Noordhoff, 1970), 60–61, suggests that, sited in the Agora, an area in which Pericles seems to have had little interest, the proposal for the Hephaesteum (perhaps by Cimon) may have been predated the "Periclean" program. If so, its proposer may have been Thucydides Melesiou. Temple and sculptures: T. L. Shear Jr., *Trophies of Victory: Public Buildings in Periklean Athens* (Princeton, NJ: Princeton University Press, 2016), 137–160.

2 Board of Commissioners (*epistatai*): Boersma, *Building Policy,* 5–6. "Overseer of everything" (παντών ἐπίσκοπος): Plutarch, *Pericles,* 13. See I. Jenkins, *Greek Architecture and Its Sculpture* (Cambridge, MA: Harvard University Press, 2006), 80.

3 Temple statistics: 104 feet × 45 feet; 13 × 6 columns. The parentage of both Athena and Hephaestus was eccentric. Athena had no mother (only a father, Zeus). Hephaestus had no father (just his mother, Hera): Hesiod, *Theogony,* 927–928; [Apollodorus], *Bibliotheca,* 1.3.6. Temple: J. M. Camp, *The Archaeology of Athens* (New Haven, CT: Yale University Press, 2001), 102–103. 100,000 tons of Pentelic marble: J. B. Connelly, *The Parthenon Enigma: A Journey into Legend* (New York: Knopf, 2014), 87. Both Pentelic and Parian marble were used for the pedimental sculptures. Parian marble was used exclusively for the friezes, *metopēs,* and acroteria. See H. A. Thompson, "The Pedimental Sculpture of the Hephaisteion," *Hesperia* 18, no. 3 (1949): 230–268, https://www.ascsa.edu.gr/uploads/media/hesperia/146756.pdf. Dual dedication: T. Shear, *Trophies,* 156–160.

4 A. Stewart, "Classical Sculpture from the Athenian Agora, Part 1: The Pediments and Akroteria of the Hephaisteion," *Hesperia* 84, no. 4 (2018): 681–741. H. A. Thompson ("The Pedimental Sculpture of the Hephaisteion," 254–255) believes that the west pediment showed the arrival of Heracles (not Hephaestus) at Olympus. I find his arguments unconvincing. Expulsion of Hephaestus and nursing by Thetis and Eurynome: Homer, *Iliad,* 395–405; *Homeric Hymn to Apollo,* 316–321. Return of Hephaestus: Hyginus, *Fabulae,* 166. The connection between the temple and Athenian ancestors was recognized a century or so later (in 340 B.C.) in the building of a new Temple of Apollo Patroos ("Ancestral Apollo") in front of it at the foot of Colonus Hill.

5 Statue and base: Jenkins, *Greek Architecture,* 127. Friezes: T. Shear, *Trophies,* 151–156; C. H. Morgan, "The Sculptures of the Hephaisteion: II. The Friezes," *Hesperia* 31, no. 3 (1962): 221–235; K. Velentza, "The Ionic Friezes of the Hephaisteion in the Athenian Agora" (BA paper, King's College London, 2015), https://escholarship.org/content/qt4920f86g/qt4920f86g_noSplash_f3664ed6579798dd36fb653f522d993e.pdf?t=nv755y.

6 Gods on Siphnian Treasury: D. Castriota, *Myth, Ethos and Actuality* (Madison: University of Wisconsin Press, 1992), 204–205. *Metopēs:* T. Shear, *Trophies,* 150–151.

7 "Message" of the sculptures: see, for example, J. M. Barringer, "A New Approach to the Hephaisteion: Heroic Models in the Athenian Agora," in *Structure, Image, Ornament: Architectural Sculpture in the Greek World,* ed. P. Schulz and R. von den Hoff (Oxford: Oxbow, 2009).

8 T. Shear, *Trophies,* 55–56; Boersma, *Building Policy,* 74.

9 Solon, fr. 4; R. Parker, *Athenian Religion: A History* (Oxford: Clarendon Press, 1996), 69.

10 There was a precedent for leaving a temple ruined or partly built. The Temple of Olympian Zeus was abandoned incomplete, when Hippias was expelled, a monument to hubris and the fall of his regime. P. Valavanis, N. Dimakis, E. Dimitriadou, and M. Katsianis, "Managing the Open-air Sacred Space on the Athenian Acropolis," in *From*

Kallias to Kritias: Art in Athens in the Second Half of the Fifth Century B.C., ed. J. Neils and O. Palagia (Berlin: De Gruyter, 2021), 23, suggest that the site was left unoccupied to accommodate "the growing number of Athenian spectators" during the Panathenaic sacrifices, but, while this may have been a happy consequence, it is surely not the primary reason. Rivalling Olympia: Jenkins, *Greek Architecture,* 28. Dimensions of processional route: Valavanis et al., "Managing the Open-air Sacred Space," 14. That the Propylaea was begun immediately after the Parthenon was finished is further evidence that the new Temple of Athena Polias (the Erechtheum) was not part of the original building plan, since the structure's presence made access for wagons, etc., harder.

11 Parthenon statistics: 101.31 feet × 228.02 feet; cella 91 feet × 62 feet; opisthodomos 43 feet × 62 feet; 8 × 17 external columns, 34.5 feet tall. Callicrates and Ictinus: Plutarch, *Pericles,* 13.4. Strabo, 9.1.12 and 9.1.16; and Pausanias, 8.41.9, name only Ictinus as Parthenon architect. Design: Jenkins, *Greek Architecture,* 30, argues that there were no blueprints for temples, everything being worked out at foundation level with each course of masonry "being individually tailored to match the previous and to anticipate the next course." Preparations that went into, for example, the platform's enlargement might suggest otherwise. Ictinus' book: Vitruvius, 7, praefatio 12, suggests it was co-authored with Carpion. B. A. Barletta, "The Architecture and Architects of the Classical Parthenon," in *The Parthenon from Antiquity to the Present,* ed. J. Neils (Cambridge: Cambridge University Press, 2005), 88–89, following, for example, G. Gruben, *Grieschische Tempel und Heiligtümer* (Munich: Hirmer, 2001), 186, argues that "Carpion" was a scribe's misreading of "Callicrates." We are unlikely ever to know. The name "Parthenon" (Παρθενών) is problematic. Our Parthenon was apparently not called this in the fifth century, when it was known as either "the temple" (ὁ ναός) or the Hundred-Foot Temple (Ἑκατόμπεδος Ναός—so, Harpocration s.v. ἙΚΑΤΟΜΠΕΔΟΝ). While Demosthenes refers several times (22 *Against Androtion,* 13 and 76; 24 *Against Timocrates,* 184) to the beauty of the Parthenon, he may not mean the building which we call by that name. More specific is the third-century-B.C. geographer Heracleides Criticus, who places the Parthenon above the Theatre of Dionysus. See D. G. J. Shipley, *Geographers of the Ancient World: Selected Texts in Translation* (Cambridge: Cambridge University Press, 2024), 275–288. By the Roman period, authors such as Strabo (9.1.12, 9.1.16), Pliny the Elder (*Natural History,* 24.19.3, 36.4.4), Pausanias (1.24), and Plutarch (*Pericles,* 13) are clearly naming our Parthenon "the Parthenon." See J. Z. van Rookhuijzen, "The Parthenon Treasury on the Acropolis of Athens," *American Journal of Archaeology* 124, no. 1 (2020): 3–35. Equally problematic is the fact that, since Παρθενών is the genitive plural form, it should mean "Temple of the Maidens." Why? Suggestions include (1) that Παρθενών was an otherwise unattested epithet of Athena, (2) that Parthenon was originally the name given to the Erechtheum (because of its Caryatid porch) but that this name somehow migrated to "our" Parthenon, or (3) that the maidens in question were the Arrhephoroi. Peristyle design: T. Shear, *Trophies,* 82–94.

12 Connelly, *Parthenon Enigma,* 232–234, suggests the opisthodomos contained tombs of Erechtheus' daughters. The columns of the opisthodomos were possibly the first topped with Corinthian capitals: P. Pedersen, *The Parthenon and the Origin of the Corinthian Capital* (Odense, DK: Odense University Press, 1989), 21–22. Two-tiered colonnade: Connelly, *Parthenon Enigma,* 92. Cella seeming larger: B. A. Barletta, "The Architecture and Architects of the Classical Parthenon," in Neils, *Parthenon from Antiquity,* 80, 86.

13 Windows: V. Manidaki, "News from the Parthenon Cella: The Question of the Inner Frieze," in Neils and Palagia, *Kallias to Kritias,* 78; P. Valavanis, "The Acropolis," in *The Cambridge Companion to Ancient Athens,* ed. J. Neils and D. K. Rogers (Cambridge: Cambridge University Press, 2021), 69; Barletta, "Architecture and Architects," 85–86. "Colossal" doorway (31.5 feet tall × 15.75 feet wide): V. Manidaki, "News from the Parthenon Cella," 77. Doors: S. Pope and P. Schultz, "The Chryselephantine Doors of the Parthenon," *American Journal of Archaeology* 118, no. 1 (2014): 19–31.

14 Curvature and other refinements: Haselberger, "Bending the Truth," in Neils, *Parthenon from Antiquity,* 101–146; T. Shear, *Trophies,* 94–98; Connelly, *Parthenon Enigma,* 93–95. Columns and width between them: "The column diameter to the axial distance between columns, called the interaxial, is as 4 to 9": Barletta, "Architecture and Architects," 88–89, following, for example, G. Gruben, *Grieschische Tempel und Heiligtümer* (Munich: Hirmer, 2001), 72. The 4:9 ratio: Connelly, *Parthenon Enigma,* 95. For refinements of the Parthenon and other temples, see Haselberger, "Bending the Truth," 101–146. Inclination of columns (by between 2.76 inches and 3.15 inches from the vertical) and their meeting above stylobate: Jenkins, *Greek Architecture,* 79.

15 Plutarch, *Pericles,* 13.

16 Skills involved: Jenkins, *Greek Architecture,* 32–34; Connelly, *Parthenon Enigma,* 86–87. Most expensive temple: L. Kallet, "Wealth, Power, and Prestige: Athens at Home and Abroad," in Neils, *Parthenon from Antiquity,* 54. The cost was between 340 and 380 talents. S. A. Pope, "Financing and Design: The Development of the Parthenon Program and the Parthenon Building Accounts," in *Miscellanea Mediterranea,* ed. R. R. Holloway (Providence, RI: Center for Old World Archaeology and Art, Brown University, 2000), 61–69. This is at the lower scale of estimates. Others suggest a figure of 460–500 talents: see, for example, R. S. Stanier, "The Cost of the Parthenon," *Journal of Hellenic Studies* 73 (1953): 68–76.

17 O. Palagia, "Sculpture and Its Role in the City," in Neils and Rogers, *Cambridge Companion to Ancient Athens,* 287. Mules: Plutarch, *Cato the Elder,* 5.3.

18 Purest iron smelted at Laurium: G. J. Varoufakis, "The Iron Clamps and Dowels from the Parthenon and Erechthion," *Historical Metallurgy* 26 (1992): 1–18, citing C. Conophagos and G. Papadimitriou, "La technique de Production de Fer et d' Acier par les Grecs Ancients en Attique pendans la Periode Classique," *Academie d'Athenes* 56 (1981): 148–172. Precision of work: I. Jenkins, *The Parthenon Sculptures in the British Museum* (London: British Museum, 2007), 20.

19 Nine sculptors: J. Neils, *The Parthenon Frieze* (Cambridge: Cambridge University Press, 2001), 87; J. Neils, "'With Noblest Images on All Sides': The Ionic Frieze of the Parthenon," in Neils, *Parthenon from Antiquity,* 219. "Closely supervised": Boersma, *Building Policy,* 69. "Uniquely for a mainland temple": B. Cook, *The Elgin Marbles* (London: British Museum, 1984), 18–19; A. Barletta, "Architecture and Architects," 78. *Metopēs:* T. Shear, *Trophies,* 108–112; Jenkins, *Greek Architecture,* 82–86.

20 West *metopēs:* K. A. Schwab, "Celebrations of Victory," in Neils, *Parthenon from Antiquity,* 178–183; Castriota, *Myth, Ethos,* 143–151.

21 North *metopēs:* Schwab, "Celebrations of Victory," 183–190; Castriota, *Myth, Ethos,* 165–174.

22 Time and space: A. Suski, "Scandalous Maps in Aeschylean Tragedy," in G. Hawes, *Myths on the Map: The Storied Landscapes of Ancient Greece* (Oxford: Oxford University Press, 2017), 204–220. R. Parker, *Polytheism and Society at Athens*

(Oxford: Oxford University Press, 2005), 377, writes: "It is not in doubt that festivals often play tricks with time, treating the past as if it were present or recurrent, and retrojecting the present into the past." See also D. Williams, "Multi-Layered Time and Place: Temples and Statues in Vase-Painting in Later 5th Century Athens," in Neils and Palagia, *Kallias to Kritias,* 235–262.

23 East *metopēs:* Schwab, "Celebrations of Victory," 168–173; Castriota, *Myth, Ethos,* 138–143.

24 Forbidding sun and moon to shine: Schwab, "Celebrations of Victory," 168.

25 Jenkins, *Parthenon Sculptures,* 69–81. This interpretation of the *metopēs* follows O. Palagia, "The Wedding of Peirithous: South *metopēs* 13–21 of the Parthenon," in Neils and Palagia, *Kallias to Kritias,* 54–61; Castriota, *Myth, Ethos,* 152–165. See also Schwab, "Celebrations of Victory," 173. Curiously, Boersma, *Building Policy,* 68, interprets the central scene as the birth of Erichthonius.

26 Kidnappings: Herodotus, 1.1–5. Heracles in the Gigantomachy: Apollodorus, 1.6.1; Schwab, "Celebrations of Victory," 168–173.

27 Thucydides, 1.112–113; Plutarch, *Pericles,* 18.

28 Thucydides, 1.114.

29 Thucydides, 1.114–115.

30 Solar eclipse: M. Phillipides, "King Pleistoanax and the Spartan Invasion of Attica in 446 B.C.," *Ancient World* 11 (1985): 33–41; P. A. Rahe, *Sparta's First Attic War: The Grand Strategy of Classical Sparta, 478–446 B.C.* (New Haven, CT: Yale University Press, 2019), 225. "Blazing sun god": *Homeric Hymn 28: To Athena,* 13–14.

31 Sybaris and the foundation of Thurii: Diodorus, 12.9–10; Strabo, 6.263; Plutarch, *Pericles,* 11; Nicias, 5.

32 Hippodamus: Aristotle, *Politics,* 2.1267b; Demosthenes, *Against Timotheus,* 22; Andocides, *On the Mysteries,* 45; Suda, ι.555; Boersma, *Building Policy,* 10, 47–48. Lampron: Parker, *Polytheism,* 116. Lampron, Protagoras and Thurii: V. Azoulay, *Pericles of Athens,* trans. J. Lloyd (Princeton, NJ: Princeton University Press, 2014), 120.

33 Massacre: Diodorus Siculus, 12.11–12. One-eyed Hermippus: Suidas, s.v. Μυρτίλος. Hermippus in Athenaeus, *Deipnosophistai,* 149.

34 Cleaenetus: J. K. Davies, *Athenian Propertied Families, 600–300 B.C.* (Oxford: Clarendon Press, 1971), no. 8674 (Cleon) and no. 3773 (Dikaiogenes); Azoulay, *Pericles,* 129–130. Hagnon: Cratinus, fr. 73. 69–71, K-A.; Azoulay, *Pericles,* 130. Pericles funding poor: Plutarch, Pericles, 9.1; Plato, *Gorgias,* 515E.

35 Payment for military: R. T. Ridley, "The Hoplite as Citizen: Athenian Military Institutions in Their Social Context," *L'Antiquité Classique* 48, no. 2 (1979): 508–548, 521–522. Democracy more aggressive than previous constitutions: D. M. Pritchard, "The Symbiosis between Democracy and War," in *War, Democracy and Culture in Classical Athens,* ed. D. M. Pritchard (Cambridge: Cambridge University Press, 2010), 6.

36 Democritus and Prodicus: T. Whitmarsh, *Battling the Gods: Atheism in the Ancient World* (New York: Knopf, 2015), 91–95.

7. ATHENS ON THE CUSP

1 Thucydides Melesiou's generosity: Plutarch, *Nicias,* 2; [Aristotle], *Constitution of Athens,* 28.5. Financing the Parthenon: L. J. Samons II, "Athenian Finance and the Treasury of Athena," *Historia* 42, no. 2 (1993): 129–138.

2 "Greeks must see this": Plutarch, *Pericles,* 12; A. Powell, *Athens and Sparta: Constructing Greek Political and Social History from 478 BC* (London: Routledge, 1988, 60–61.

3 Plutarch, *Pericles,* 12.

4 Plutarch, *Pericles,* 14.

5 "On paper": Thucydides, 2.64; P. Krentz, "The Ostracism of Thoukydides, Son of Melesias," *Historia: Zeitschrift für Alte Geschichte* 33, no. 4 (1984): 499–504.

6 Ceiling: T. L. Shear Jr., *Trophies of Victory: Public Buildings in Periklean Athens* (Princeton, NJ: Princeton University Press, 2016), 105–106; J. de Lara, "3D Physically Based Rendering Applied to the Problem of Translucent Marble Tiles as Means of Illuminating Classical Greek Temples: The Parthenon as Case Study," *Journal of Archeological Science: Reports* 51 (2023): 104–120; K. Ike and T. Otaki, "Natural Lighting Method of the Parthenon: An Experimental Study for Transparency of Pentelic Marble Tile," *Architectural Institute of Japan* 63, no. 504 (1998): 235–243.

7 Five sculptors, twenty-two days: J. M. Camp, *The Archaeology of Athens* (New Haven, CT: Yale University Press, 2001), 98. Grilles: B. A. Barletta, "The Architecture and Architects of the Classical Parthenon," in *The Parthenon from Antiquity to the Present,* ed. J. Neils (Cambridge: Cambridge University Press, 2005), 84. Wax and paint: I. Jenkins, *Greek Architecture and Its Sculpture* (Cambridge, MA: Harvard University Press, 2006), 35–37. Red-background *metopēs* with blue-background triglyphs: Jenkins, *Greek Architecture,* 43; K. A. Schwab, "Celebrations of Victory: The Metopes of the Parthenon," in Neils, *Parthenon from Antiquity,* 160. Metal fixtures: Schwab, "Celebrations of Victory," 161. Frieze: Jenkins, *Greek Architecture,* 94–107.

8 Carving in situ: Jenkins, *Greek Architecture,* 95. Dimensions of frieze: J. Neils, "'With Noblest Images on All Sides': The Ionic Frieze of the Parthenon," in Neils, *Parthenon from Antiquity,* 199; J. B. Connelly, *The Parthenon Enigma: A Journey into Legend* (New York: Knopf, 2014), 152. Sketching and carving the frieze: J. Neils, *The Parthenon Frieze* (Cambridge: Cambridge University Press, 2001), 76–87.

9 A. Stähli, "Parapictoriality," in *Images at the Crossroads: Media and Meaning in Greek Art,* ed. J. M. Barringer and F. Lissarrague (Edinburgh: Edinburgh University Press, 2022), 118–119.

10 West frieze: T. Shear, *Trophies,* 121–122. "First and only time": Jenkins, *Greek Architecture,* 94.

11 Judging horses before cavalry displays: Neils, *Parthenon Frieze,* 128. "Those that cannot": [Aristotle], *Constitution of the Athenians,* 49.1. Cavalry increased to 1,000: I. Jenkins, "The Parthenon Frieze and Perikles' Cavalry of a Thousand," in *Periklean Athens and Its Legacy: Problems and Perspectives,* ed. J. Barringer and J. Hurwit (Austin: University of Texas Press, 2005), 147–161; J. L. Shear, *Serving Athena: The Festival of the Panathenaia and the Construction of Athenian Identities* (Cambridge: Cambridge University Press, 2021), 230. "If you spur": Xenophon, *On Horsemanship,* 11.12.

12 Xenophon, *On Being a Good Cavalry Commander,* 3.2–3.

13 North and south friezes: T. Shear, *Trophies,* 122–127; Neils, "With Noblest of Images," 209–113; Jenkins, *Greek Architecture,* 96–102. Like frames in an animation film: for an excellent visualisation of this, see https://www.zippyframes.com/news/academic/phidias-the-animator-georges-sifianos (accessed August 12, 2025).

14 East frieze: T. Shear, *Trophies,* 127–132; Neils, "With Noblest of Images," 202–209; Jenkins, *Greek Architecture,* 102–106. "Unprecedented": Neils, "With Noblest of Images," 208.

15 Neither Athena nor Ares (Athens' two main war gods) armoured: see E. B. Harrison, "The Web of History: A Conservative Reading of the Parthenon Frieze," in *Worshipping Athena: Panathenaia and Parthenon,* ed. J. Neils (Madison: University of Wisconsin Press, 1996), 208.

16 T. Shear, *Trophies,* 133–135. Girls, stools, and footstool: Neils, *Parthenon Frieze,* 167–169. Identity of male figure: Neils, *Parthenon Frieze,* 169; R. Parker, *Polytheism and Society at Athens* (Oxford: Oxford University Press, 2005), 94–95; J. Shear, *Serving Athena,* 347. Gender of bare-buttocked child: Neils, *Parthenon Frieze,* 169–171. Connelly, *Parthenon Enigma,* 169–172, argues that it is not a boy but a girl, and that the peplos was unlikely to be "manhandled by a priest and boy." Connelly, *Parthenon Enigma,* 176, suggests that the girls look too old to be Arrhephoroi, and (165) that the scene represents King Erechtheus, his wife Praxithea (the first priestess of Athena Polias), and their three daughters ("immediately recognisable to Athenians because of the distinctive presence of three girls"), while the frieze celebrates self-sacrifice for Athens. Those interested should read her book: her arguments are too complex to counter fully either here or in specific endnotes. Archon Basileus: R. Parker, *Athenian Religion: A History* (Oxford: Clarendon Press, 1996), 8, quoting Plato, *Politics,* 290e6–8, observing that "'the solemnest and most ancestral of the ancient rites' were in the charge of the *basileus.*" Temple boy, snake, and statue: Neils, *Parthenon Frieze,* 171; E. B. Harrison, "The Web of History: A Conservative Reading of the Parthenon Frieze," in Neils, *Worshipping Athena,* 204; F. Brommer, *Der Parthenonfries: Katalog und Untersuchung* (Mainz: Von Zabern, 1977), 269–270; H. W. Parke, *Festivals of the Athenians* (London: Thames and Hudson, 1977), 143; E. Simon, *Festivals of Attica: An Archaeological Commentary* (Madison: University of Wisconsin Press, 1983), 66.

17 Generally agreed: For useful caveats see Connelly, *Parthenon Enigma,* 158–159. Arrhephoroi and weaving peplos: J. Shear, *Serving Athena,* 101. Being folded: Neils, "With Noblest Images," 217; Harrison, "The Web of History," 198–202; B. Wesenberg, "Panathenäische Peplosdedikation und Arrhephorie: Zur Thematik des Parthenonfrieses," *Jahrbuch des Deutschen Archäologischen Instituts* 110 (1995): 149–178. Connelly, *Parthenon Enigma,* 159, believes that this interpretation "would certainly be something of an anticlimax." I disagree. Peplos painted: J. Shear, *Serving Athena,* 348.

18 Ring composition: Neils, *Parthenon Frieze,* 52.

19 Hermes and Aphrodite regularly associated in Greek cult: J. Larson, *Ancient Greek Cults: A Guide* (London: Routledge, 2007), 147. Gods' holy days: E. Simon, "Theseus and Athenian Festivals," in Neils, *Worshipping Athena,* 13. Neils, "With Noblest Images," 205–206, suggests the left-hand gods represent land, and those on the right sea, though this is surely an incomplete reading.

20 Semicircle: Neils, "With Noblest Images," 216. Veiling: D. L. Cairns, "Weeping and Veiling: Grief, Display and Concealment in Ancient Greek Culture," in *Tears in the Graeco-Roman World,* ed. T. Fögen (Berlin: De Gruyter, 2009), 37–57.

21 Artemis and Aphrodite on the frieze: Simon, "Theseus and Athenian Festivals," 22.

22 Torch race: J. Shear, *Serving Athena,* 274–275.

23 Zeus only male god with exclusive sanctuary on Acropolis: J. Neils, *Parthenon Frieze,* 192. "Transcending their human statues": Jenkins, *Greek Architecture,* 106, goes further: "the Athenians who ascend in procession to pay homage to their gods may seem themselves to achieve a glorious apotheosis."

24 Metaphysical realm: O. Palagia, "'Fire from Heaven': Pediments and Akroteria of the Parthenon," in Neils, *Parthenon from Antiquity*, 235–236. First time in visual art: T. Shear, *Trophies*, 375. Eleusinian journey into light: Plato, *Phaedrus*, 250b–c. Promise of a better life to come: Cicero, *De Legibus*, 2.14.36.

25 Processional sculptures on Ephesian Artemisium: Jenkins, *Greek Architecture*, 22. Comparisons between friezes of the Parthenon and Persepolis Apadana do not imply that Athens was projecting herself as imperialist: H. A. Shapiro, "Democracy and Imperialism: The Panathenaia in the Age of Pericles," in Neils, *Worshipping Athena*, 222. But see also D. Castriota, *Myth, Ethos and Actuality* (Madison: University of Wisconsin Press, 1992), 185–193. Neils describes the frieze as "a timeless union of the divine and human and the celebration in stone of the golden age of Athens." J. Neils, "Pride, Pomp, and Circumstance: The Iconography of the Procession," in Neils, *Worshipping Athena*, 194.

26 That the frieze represented the Panathenaic procession was first mooted by J. Stewart and N. Revett, *The Antiquities of Athens: Measured and Delineated*, vol. 2 (London, 1787), 12, who asked of its central scene on the east side, "May we not suppose this folded cloth to represent the peplos?" Connelly, *Parthenon Enigma*, 158–159, remarks that "over time, their gentle question has hardened into established dogma," and outlines arguments for and against this identification. Among believers that it *is* the Panathenaic procession are J. Shear, *Serving Athena*, 344 ("the frieze as indubitably the procession at the Great Panathenaia"); and Castriota, *Myth, Ethos*, 192. Among disbelievers are Jenkins, *Greek Architecture*, 105. Welcomed by all twelve gods: Castriota, *Myth, Ethos*, 214–216, points out that this is how Greek art often shows gods and heroes being welcomed onto Mount Olympus at their apotheosis. "Throughout the year": Thucydides, 2.38. From Cerameicus dead zone to divine Acropolis: J. Paga, *Building Democracy in Late Archaic Athens* (Oxford: Oxford University Press, 2021), 172. "Whoever sacrifices": Harpokration, A 239; *FGrH* 3 B I 276–77—both versions of the name, Pandora and Pandrosus, appear in manuscripts. Neils, "With Noblest Images," 209.

27 Specially built studio: while nothing of Pheidias' Athenian studio survives, much of his studio at Olympia remains intact (subsequently converted into a Byzantine church); see L. Drees, *Olympia: Gods, Artists, and Athletes*, trans. G. Onn (London: Pall Mall, 1968), 147–149; J. M. Barringer, *Olympia: A Cultural History* (Princeton, NJ: Princeton University Press, 2021), 59, 132. Given the scale of the agalma, no suitably sized space would have existed for Pheidias to work in; even if it did, given the value of the materials that he was using, it would require tight security. More likely he worked in a purpose-build studio, whose location is currently unknown. Materials of plinth: A. Kosmopoulou, *The Iconography of Sculptured Statue Bases in the Archaic and Classical Periods* (Madison: University of Wisconsin Press, 2002), 236–237. Chosen to resist insect infestation and withstand decay: K. Lapatin, "The Statue of Athena and Other Treasures in the Parthenon," in Neils, *Parthenon from Antiquity*, 272. Network of poles and battens: Lucian, *The Cock*, 24.

28 Triple-crested helmet: J. Shear, *Serving Athena*, 54. Griffins and gold: Herodotus, 4.13.

29 450–500 talents: L. Kallet, "Wealth, Power, and Prestige: Athens at Home and Abroad," in Neils, *Parthenon from Antiquity*, 54. 40 talents spent on gold: Connelly, *Parthenon Enigma*, 85. Removing gold: Thucydides, 2.13.

30 Working ivory: Oppian, Cynegetica, 2.514; Pausanias, 5.12.2; Plutarch, *An vitiositas ad Infelicitatem Sufficiat* 4 (= *Moralia*, 499E); Dioscourides, *De Materia Medica*, 2.87; see Lapatin, "Statue of Athena," 275–279.

31 Pool: Lapatin, "Statue of Athena," 279; Connelly, *Parthenon Enigma,* 92.

32 Repetition of subject matter: for example, Schwab, "Celebrations of Victory," 167.

33 White marble, gold or gilt bronze figures: Kosmopoulou, *Iconography of Sculptured Statue Bases,* 236. Set into Eleusinian stone: Stevens, "Remarks upon the Colossal Chryselephantine Statue of Athena in the Parthenon," *Hesperia* 24, no. 3 (1955): 240–276; W.-H. Schuchhardt, "Zur Basis der Athena Parthenos," in *Wandlungen: Studien zur antiken und neueren Kunst E. Homann-Wedeking gewidmet* (Waldsassen: Stiftland, 1975), 120n5. Others suggest that the figures were set into Pentelic marble: N. Leipen, *Athena Parthenos: A Reconstruction* (Toronto: Royal Ontario Museum, 1971), 27; B. S. Ridgway, *Fifth Century Styles in Greek Sculpture* (Princeton, NJ: Princeton University Press, 1981), 164. However, given the known use of Eleusinian limestone in the statue plinths of the Temple of Athena and Hephaestus and the Temple of Nemesis at Rhamnous, as well as its strategic use of elsewhere within the building project, this is unlikely. "On the statue's plinth": Pausanias, 1.24.7. Hesiod on Pandora: *Works and Days,* 60–82; compare *Theogony,* 560–612; Connelly, *Parthenon Enigma,* 278–280. Pliny the Elder, *Natural History,* 36.4, also says the scene shows Pandora's birth, but unlike Pausanias he does not mention Hesiod, so it is impossible to tell which Pandora he means. Some scholars still maintain that Pandora means Pandora: for example, Lapatin, "Statue of Athena," 269.

34 No fewer than twenty gods: Pliny the Elder, *Natural History,* 36.4. Juxtaposition of the two statues: T. Shear, *Trophies,* 363–370.

35 Agoracritus: P. Valavanis, "The Acropolis," in *The Cambridge Companion to Ancient Athens,* ed. J. Neils and D. K. Rogers (Cambridge: Cambridge University Press, 2021), 72. Pheidias and statue of Zeus: Pausanias, 5.11–12. Wonder of the world: Antipater of Sidon, *Greek Anthology,* 9.58.

36 West pediment: T. Shear, *Trophies,* 114–117; Connelly, *Parthenon Enigma,* 107–108; Palagia, "Fire from Heaven," 242–253; Jenkins, *Greek Architecture,* 92–94. Anthropomorphised river gods: only on temple pediments were rivers shown anthropomorphised: J. Larson, *Greek Heroine Cults* (Madison: University of Wisconsin Press, 1995), 153.

37 Connelly, *Parthenon Enigma,* 112, suggests the pediment "presents the origins of cult practice within the sanctuaries of Athena Polias at Athens and of Demeter and Kore at Eleusis."

38 East pediment: T. Shear, *Trophies,* 112–114; Palagia, "Fire from Heaven," 234–242; Jenkins, *Greek Architecture,* 87–91. "Night of the dark moon": for how the east pediment shows this, see C. Anghelina, "Athena's Birth on the Night of the Dark Moon," *Journal of Hellenic Studies* 137 (2017): 175–183. First time: Connelly, *Parthenon Enigma,* 104. "For long, long hours": *Homeric Hymn 28: To Athena,* 13–15.

39 I. Jenkins, *The Parthenon Sculptures in the British Museum* (London: British Museum, 2007), 60.

40 Arrangement of gods with Eleusinians on left: Palagia, "Fire from Heaven," 240; Connelly, *Parthenon Enigma,* 105.

41 Jenkins, *Parthenon Sculptures,* 36.

42 Further conjectures include an Ionic frieze extending round the front porch: M. Korres, "Der Plan des Parthenon," *Mitteilungen des deutschen archäologischen Instituts* 109 (1994): 52–120; Connelly, *Parthenon Enigma,* 102. Acroteria: Palagia, "Fire from Heaven," 252.

43 "Most decorated temple": Schwab, "Celebrations of Victory," 159; Castriota, *Myth, Ethos,* 184. "Their souls": Euripides, *Erechtheus,* fr. 370, in Euripides, *Selected Fragmentary Plays,* vol. 1, ed. C. Collard, M. J. Cropp, and K. H. Lee (Warminster, UK: Aris and Phillips, 1995). "Those close in birth": Aeschylus, fr. 162; see Parker, *Polytheism,* 143. For Connelly, *Parthenon Enigma,* the myth of the self-sacrifice of Erechtheus' daughters is central to the Parthenon's iconography.

44 Achilles' shield: Homer, *Iliad,* 18, 478–608. Time and Space in Achilles' shield: A. Suski, "Scandalous Maps in Aeschylean Tragedy," in *Myths on the Map: The Storied Landscapes of Ancient Greece,* ed. G. Hawes (Oxford: Oxford University Press, 2017), 204–220. Pheidias drawing inspiration: Strabo, 8.3.30 (where Pheidias claimed that his statue of Zeus at Olympia was inspired by Homer, *Iliad,* 1.528–530).

45 List of treasures: *IG* I³ 343–346, 350–359. Not everything was precious. Also listed are "eight and a half boxes of rotten and useless arrows" (Camp, *Archaeology of Athens,* 81). See K. Lapatin, "Statue of Athena," 279–287.

8. FRACTURES AND FISSURES

1 Telesterion: T. L. Shear Jr., *Trophies of Victory: Public Buildings in Periklean Athens* (Princeton, NJ: Princeton University Press, 2016), 161–195; J. S. Boersma, *Athenian Building Policy from 561/0 to 405/4 B.C.* (Groningen: Wolters-Noordhoff, 1970), 72–73. For excellent reconstructions, see E. Partida and J. Goodinson, "Eleusis: The Telesterion," Anasynthesis, n.d., https://www.anasynthesis.co.uk/index.php/articles/eleusis-the-telesterion.

2 Plutarch, *Pericles,* 13. Pericles as judge: B. Nagy, "The Athenian Athlothetai," *Greek, Roman and Byzantine Studies* 19, no. 4 (1978): 307–314; J. L. Shear, *Serving Athena: The Festival of the Panathenaia and the Construction of Athenian Identities* (Cambridge: Cambridge University Press, 2021), 176. Odeon statistics: 65 feet high, 225 feet × 205 feet. Odeon: Vitruvius, 5.9.1; T. Shear, *Trophies,* 197–228; Boersma, *Building Policy,* 72; R. Beacham, "Playing Places: The Temporary and the Permanent," in *The Cambridge Companion to Greek and Roman Theatre,* ed. M. McDonald and J. M. Walton (Cambridge: Cambridge University Press, 2007), 207–208; V. Azoulay, *Pericles of Athens,* trans. J. Lloyd (Princeton, NJ: Princeton University Press, 2014), 62–64. Vitruvius' statement maintains that the Odeon was built by Themistocles is unlikely: see Boersma, *Building Policy,* 7; J. M. Camp, *The Archaeology of Athens* (New Haven, CT: Yale University Press, 2001), 100–101.

3 Description of countryside: Plato, *Phaedrus,* 229A–230C. Continuing sacrifices: Xenophon, *Anabasis,* 3.2.12. Statue: Pausanias, 1.19. Procession: Plutarch, *Moralia,* 862A. Callicrates as architect: T. Shear, *Trophies,* 347. Temple statistics: 19.6 feet × 41.6 feet; columns 14.6 feet tall. Temple: Camp, *Archaeology of Athens,* 105–106; T. Shear, *Trophies,* 329–341; Boersma, *Building Policy,* 192.

4 Older temples of Poseidon: Boersma, *Building Policy,* 195. Temple of Athena at Sunium: T. Shear, *Trophies,* 243–251. Boersma, *Building Policy,* 184. Temple of Poseidon: T. Shear, *Trophies,* 230–243; Camp, *Archaeology of Athens,* 108–110; Boersma, *Building Policy,* 196. Sculptures: I. Leventi, "Interpretations of the Ionic Frieze of the Temple of Poseidon at Sounion," in *Structure, Image, Ornament: Architectural Sculpture in the Greek World,* ed. P. Schultz and R. von den Hoff (Oxford: Oxbow, 2009), 121–132.

5 T. Shear, *Trophies,* 250–262; M. H. McAllister, "The Temple of Ares at Athens: A Review of the Evidence," *Hesperia* 28, no. 1 (1959): 1–64; A. Stewart, "The

Sculptures of the Temple of Ares in the Agora: Discoveries Old and New," in *From Kallias to Kritias: Art in Athens in the Second Half of the Fifth Century B.C.*, ed. J. Neils and O. Palagia (Berlin: De Gruyter, 2021), 197–209.

6 Themis and Nemesis: J. Larson, *Ancient Greek Cults: A Guide* (London: Routledge, 2007), 179. Temples: T. Shear, *Trophies*, 262–269; Camp, *Archaeology of Athens*, 112–113; M. Miles, "A Reconstruction of the Temple of Nemesis at Rhamnous," *Hesperia* 58, no. 2 (1989): 134–249. Plinth: Pausanias, 1.33; A. Kosmopoulou, *The Iconography of Sculptured Statue Bases in the Archaic and Classical Periods* (Madison: University of Wisconsin Press, 2002), 244–247; E. Kefalidou, "'The Dioskuroi between Athens and Sparta' Once Again," in Neils and Palagia, *Kallias to Kritias*, 321.

7 "Poised and beautiful": Pliny, *Natural History*, 36.4, from whom we learn that Agoracritus was its sculptor, says that the statue was originally intended to represent Aphrodite, sculpted for a competition against another of Pheidias' students, Alcamenes. When Agoracritus lost, he modified his statue to represent Nemesis. Statue: A. Friendly and E. Karapanayiotis, "Nemesis," *Expedition Magazine*, Autumn 1972, 10–14. Description and story about Parian marble: Pausanias, 1.33. Mistaken guide: he was not alone—a Roman-era poem (*Greek Anthology*, 16.222) reads, "I am the stone the Persians hoped to turn into a trophy, but events changed my shape to Nemesis, the goddess rightly ensconced on Rhamnous' shores as witness of victory and Attic skill."

8 Propylaea: T. Shear, *Trophies*, 273–327. Reflecting Parthenon: Jenkins, *Greek Architecture and Its Sculpture* (Cambridge, MA: Harvard University Press, 2006), 111. Alignment: Boersma, *Building Policy*, 70.

9 Date: *IG* I^3 462, l. 3. Mnesicles: Plutarch, *Pericles*, 13; Philochorus, *FGrH*, 328, F38. H. Eiteljorg, "Final Report, CSA Propylaea Project: General Information about the Propylaea," Archaeology Data Service, University of York, June 2013, https://archaeologydataservice.ac.uk/archives/view/propylaea_kress_2013/propgeninfo.cfm.

10 J. B. Connelly, *The Parthenon Enigma: A Journey into Legend* (New York: Knopf, 2014), 225; S. L. Martin-Mcauliffe and J. K. Papadopoulos, "Framing Victory: Salamis, the Athenian Acropolis, and the Agora," *Journal of the Society of Architectural Historians* 71, no. 3 (2012): 332–361.

11 Propylaea as threshold between secular and divine: P. Valavanis, N. Dimakis, E. Dimitriadou and M. Katsianis, "Managing the Open-Air Sacred Space on the Athenian Acropolis," in Neils and Palagia, *Kallias to Kritias*, 14.

12 Abandoning Propylaea: T. Shear, *Trophies*, 311–313.

13 Thucydides, 1.115.

14 Thucydides, 1.116–117.

15 Plutarch, *Pericles*, 28, quoting Duris of Samos, who was born a century or so after the events he described. Plutarch, an enthusiastic advocate of Pericles, dismisses Duris' account as slander. Azoulay, *Pericles*, 60.

16 Pericles' funeral oration after Samos: Azoulay, *Pericles*, 33. "For Athens to be robbed": Aristotle, *Rhetoric*, 1365a. Relationship between the Syracusan tyrant Gelon's speech and Pericles': see P. Treves. "Herodotus, Gelon, and Pericles," *Classical Philology* 36, no. 4 (1941): 321–345. "We cannot see": Plutarch, *Pericles*, 8; these words are echoed by Demosthenes, 60.34 (the fallen are "companions" of the gods); and Hyperides, *Epitaphios Logos*, 43 (it is likely that the war dead receive favours from the gods). "Or widow": we do not know when Callias died. His embassy to Persia is the last we hear of him. "Bravo, Pericles": Plutarch, *Pericles*, 28.

17 Plutarch, *Pericles,* 8.

18 Sophocles: *Vita Sophoclis* (= *Suda* Σ 815); A. H. Sommerstein, *Greek Drama and Dramatists* (London: Routledge, 2002), 41–42.

19 Sophocles, *Antigone,* 453–459.

20 "Speech and rapid thought": Sophocles, *Antigone,* 354–355. "Man's innovation": Sophocles, *Antigone,* 365–375.

21 Death is stronger: Sophocles, *Antigone,* 359–361. Creon representing Pericles in *Antigone:* B. M. W. Knox, *The Heroic Temper: Studies in Sophoclean Tragedy* (Berkeley: University of California Press, 1964), 86; B. M. W. Knox, *Oedipus at Thebes* (New York: W. W. Norton, 1971), 64; V. Ehrenberg, *Sophocles and Pericles* (Oxford: Blackwell, 1954), 95, 98, 145–149; C. Meier, *The Political Art of Greek Tragedy,* trans. A. Webber (Cambridge: Polity Press, 1993), 196–197.

22 Zeus as tyrant: [Aeschylus], *Prometheus,* 224, 312, 736, 942, 958. "Roasted by the sun's blazing rays": [Aeschylus], *Prometheus,* 23. "The will of Zeus": [Aeschylus], *Prometheus,* 34–35. "Zeus wields power": [Aeschylus], *Prometheus,* 150. "Zeus is harsh": [Aeschylus], *Prometheus,* 189–190. "No one is free": [Aeschylus], *Prometheus,* 50. "Are not slaves": Aeschylus, *Persians,* 242. Pericles and religion: Azoulay, *Pericles,* 107–123.

23 Thales: Universal soul: Aristotle, *On the Soul,* 405a19–21, 411a7–9. Water as the first principle: Aristotle, *Metaphysics,* 983b6–32. Anaximander, map: Agathemerus, *Geography,* 1.1–2. Fire as the first principle: Theophrastus in Simplicius, *Commentary on Aristotle's "Physics,"* Commentaria in Aristotelem Graeca, IX, 24.14–25, Diels. Stars: Hippolytus, *Refutation of All Heresies,* 1.6.4–7, Marcovich. Sun and earth of equal size: Aëtius, *Opinions,* 2.21.1, Diels. Anaximenes, air as first principle: Aëtius, *Opinions,* 1.3.4.1–8, Diels. Motion and compression: [Plutarch], *Miscellanies,* 3.3–8, Diels. See T. Whitmarsh, *Battling the Gods: Atheism in the Ancient World* (New York: Knopf, 2015), 56–59.

24 Xenophanes, earth and water: Hippolytus, *Refutation of All Heresies,* 1.14.5–6, Marcovich. Knowledge impossible: Sextus Empiricus, *Against the Professors,* 7.49.4–7, Bury. Homer's error: Sextus Empiricus, *Against the Professors,* 9.193.3–5, Bury. Gods wearing clothes etc.: Clement, *Miscellanies,* 5.109.2, Stählin/Früchtel. "If oxen": Clement, *Miscellanies,* 5.109.3, Stählin/Früchtel. One god: Clement, *Miscellanies,* 5.109.1, Stählin/Früchtel. Directing the universe: Simplicius, *Commentary on Aristotle's "Physics,"* Commentaria in Aristotelem Graeca, IX, 23.11–12, 20, Diels. Migrating souls: Diogenes Laertius, *Lives of the Eminent Philosophers,* 8.36.12–15. See Whitmarsh, *Battling the Gods,* 59–60.

25 "The principles of mathematics": Aristotle, *Metaphysics,* 1–5. Musical intervals: Diogenes Laertius, 8.12. Metempsychosis: compare Diogenes Laertius, 8.36; Aristotle, de Anima, 1.3; Herodotus, 2.123. Pure souls enjoying privileged treatment in death: Diogenes Laertius, 8.31. Journey to acquire wisdom: see, for example, C. Pellò, "'The Lives of Pythagoras: A Proposal for Reading Pythagorean Metempsychosis," *Rhizomata* 6, no. 2 (2018): 135–156. Vegetarianism and taboos: Diogenes Laertius, 8.33–34. "Friendship means equality" and "friends have all things in common": Diogenes Laertius, 8.10.

26 Aeschylus as a Pythagorean: Cicero, *Tusculan Disputations,* 3.23; see R. Seaford, "Thought: Religion, Politics, Philosophy," in *Looking at Greek Drama,* ed. D. Stuttard (London: Bloomsbury Academic, 2025). Pairs of opposites: Aristotle, *Metaphysics,* 986a. Polycleitus: see, for example, J. E. Raven, "Polyclitus and Pythagoreanism," *Classical Review* 1, no. 3/4 (1951): 147–152.

27 Damon's date of birth: see R. W. Wallace, *Reconstructing Damon: Music, Wisdom Teaching and Politics in Perikles' Athens* (Oxford: Oxford University Press, 2015), 186–193. Pythagoreans and music: Wallace, *Reconstructing Damon,* 5. Music's influences: Wallace, *Reconstructing Damon,* 12. "Music is of use": Philodemus, *On Music,* 4. "Poetry is spoken painting": Plutarch, *On the Glory of Athens,* 3. Slavishness, insanity, and hubris: Plato, *Republic,* 388e–400b.

28 Marriage to Agariste: Andocides, 1.16; see Wallace, *Reconstructing Damon,* 51. "From the 460s": based on Damon's intervention (probably in the early 450s) to introduce pay for Athenians serving on juries. Plutarch, *Pericles,* 4. Intellectual powerhouse: Isocrates, *Antidosis,* 15.235. Puppet master: Plutarch, *Pericles,* 4. Jury pay: [Aristotle], *The Constitution of Athens,* 27.4. "The songs he learned": Olympiodorus, *Commentary on Plato's* Alcibiades, 138.4–11 (on Alcibiades, 1 118c).

29 Anaxagoras' arrival in Athens: Diogenes Laertius, 3.3.7. Sun and moon: Diogenes Laertius, 2.3.8. "Existed for all time": DK B10 (DK = H. Diels and W. Kranz, *Die Fragmente der Vorsokratiker* [Berlin: Weidmann, 1910]). "Seeds of all things": DK B11. Thunder, lightning, earthquakes: Diogenes Laertius, 2.3.8–9. Eclipses: Plutarch, *Nicias,* 23. Anaxagoras and Homer: Diogenes Laertius 2.3.11. "Nous": DK B10, B11; Diogenes Laertius, 2.3.6, 2.3.8; Whitmarsh, *Battling the Gods,* 66.

30 Ram: Plutarch, *Pericles,* 6; Azoulay, *Pericles,* 121. Meteor: Pliny, *Natural History,* 2.59.149. "If heavenly bodies": Plutarch, *Lysander,* 12; D. W. Graham, "Anaxagoras and the Comet," *Ancient Philosophy* 33, no. 1 (2013): 1–18.

31 "Praying to statues": DK 22B5. Heraclitus' concept of "Logos" (which, for the lack of any good alternative, is usually translated ineffectively into English as "the Word"), foreshadows the "Logos" of St. John 1.1, "In the beginning was the Word." "The one and only": Clement, *Miscellanies,* 5.115.1, Stählin/Früchtel. "The people's poets" and "the mob": Proclus, *Commentary of Plato's "First Alcibiades,"* 256.3–5.

32 "Speakers who are wise": Plato, *Theatetus,* 167c. "Sound judgement": Plato, *Protagoras,* 318e–319a. "I cannot tell": DK 80B4. Protagoras: Whitmarsh, *Battling the Gods,* 87–91.

33 "Mankind is the measure": DK 80B1. Pericles and Protagoras debate athlete's death: Plutarch, *Pericles,* 36; Azoulay, *Pericles,* 120. Buphonia sacrifice: Pausanias, 1.28.10; Parke, *Festivals of the Athenians,* 162–166; J. Larson, *Greek Heroine Cults* (Madison: University of Wisconsin Press, 1995), 19. "Those who provide": Porphyry, *On Abstinence from Animal Food,* 2.29–30.

34 "Not to be spoken of": Thucydides, 2.45. Ostracism of Alcibiades the Elder: Lysias, 14.39; [Andocides] 4.34. Aspasia's background: A. D'Angour, *Socrates in Love* (London: Bloomsbury, 2019), 191–192; Azoulay, *Pericles,* 101–106. Aspasia brought to Athens: P. J. Bicknell, "Axiochus Alkibiadou, Aspasia and Aspasios," *L'Antiquité Classique* 51, no. 3 (1982): 240–250.

35 Cleinias and his family: Davies, *Athenian Propertied Families, 600–300 B.C.* (Oxford: Clarendon Press, 1971), 9–22. Pericles, Aspasia and Deinomache: Plutarch, *Pericles,* 24. Reputation for leaving parties early: Plutarch, *Pericles,* 7; Azoulay, *Pericles,* 89–91.

36 Kissing: Plutarch, *Pericles,* 24. Rhetoric: Plato, *Menexenus,* 234c–235c. See D'Angour, *Socrates in Love,* 196–197.

37 "In the ancestral way": κατὰ τὰ πάτρια. Festivals of Zeus and the sheepskin: Parke, *Festivals of the Athenians,* 95–96. Thesmophoria: Parke, *Festivals of the Athenians,* 82–88.

38 Tragedy a powerful tool: P. A. Cartledge, "Sixth to Fourth Century BCE History and Society: A Brief Introduction," in Stuttard, *Greek Drama,* 22–34. Decree of 439: A. Sommerstein, "Comedy and Comic Poets," in Stuttard, *Greek Drama,* 99–113.

39 "The greatest tyrant": Cratinus, fr. 258, in *Poetae Comici Graeci,* vol 4., ed. R. Kassel and C. Austin (Berlin: De Gruyter, 1983). "Here comes onion-headed Zeus": Plutarch, *Pericles,* 4 (= Cratinus, fr. 73, in *Poetae Comici Graeci,* vol. 4). Wallace, *Reconstructing Damon,* 53–58. Damon's ostracism: [Aristotle], *Constitution of Athens,* 27.4; Plutarch, *Pericles,* 4. Banning comic poets from vilifying named characters: Sommerstein, "Comedy," in Stuttard, *Greek Drama,* 99–114; Plutarch, *Pericles,* 13. Accusations against Pheidias and Pericles: Azoulay, *Pericles,* 99–101.

40 Plutarch, *Pericles,* 31; Philochorus, *FGrH* 328 F121; Azoulay, *Pericles,* 124; T. L. Shear Jr., *Trophies of Victory: Public Buildings in Periklean Athens* (Princeton, NJ: Princeton University Press, 2016), 315.

41 Plutarch, *Pericles,* 31.

42 Diopeithes: Plutarch, *Pericles* 32; Whitmarsh, *Battling the Gods,* 117–118; Azoulay, *Pericles,* 125. Anaxagoras: Plutarch, *Pericles,* 32; *Nicias,* 23; *Moralia,* 169F; Diodorus, 12.39.2; Azoulay, *Pericles,* 125; T. Shear, *Trophies,* 317–318. Protagoras: Diogenes Laertius, 9.8; Cicero, *de Natura Deorum,* 1.23.6; Whitmarsh, *Battling the Gods,* 90, 120. As R. Parker, *Athenian Religion: A History* (Oxford: Clarendon Press, 1996), 209, observes: "No Greek surely would have supposed that an impious opinion should be permitted to circulate out of respect for freedom of speech." Pericles and the master builder: Plutarch, *Pericles,* 13.

43 Calumnies against Aspasia: Plutarch, *Pericles,* 24; Azoulay, *Pericles,* 101–104. "The goddess of buggery": from Cratinus, *Cheirones* = T. Kock, *Comicorum Atticorum Fragmenta,* 3 vols. (Leipzig: B. G. Teubner, 1880), 1:86. Aspasia's trial (Plutarch, *Pericles,* 32) is disputed by modern scholars.

44 Charges against Pericles: Plutarch, *Pericles,* 23; Diodorus, 12.39.2. Alcibiades: Diodorus, 12.38.3–4; Aristodemus, 16.4; see D. Stuttard, *Nemesis: Alcibiades and the Fall of Athens* (Cambridge, MA: Harvard University Press, 2016), 39.

45 Plutarch, *Pericles,* 16. "New Peisistratids": Azoulay, *Pericles,* 92. The charisma of a winning general: Azoulay, *Pericles,* 32. "He has power": Telecleides in Kock, *Comicorum Atticorum Fragmenta,* 1:220.

9. THE ROAD TO WAR

1 Plutarch, *Pericles,* 20; D. Kagan, *The Outbreak of the Peloponnesian War* (Ithaca, NY: Cornell University Press, 1969), 180–181. The date of the expedition is unknown, but most likely ca. 436–435 B.C.

2 Foundation of Brea: Plutarch, *Pericles,* 11; *IG* I^3, 46. Thucydides, 2.97. Amphipolis: Thucydides, 4.102; Diodorus Siculus, 12.32.3.

3 Thucydides, 1.24–25; Kagan, *Outbreak,* 205–289, 222–227.

4 Thucydides, 1.32–36; Kagan, *Outbreak,* 228–231.

5 Thucydides, 1.37–43; Kagan, *Outbreak,* 231–234.

6 Thucydides, 1.45. Pericles' role in the debate and motives: Kagan, *Outbreak,* 237–244.

7 Plutarch, *Pericles,* 29; V. Azoulay, *Pericles of Athens,* trans. J. Lloyd (Princeton, NJ: Princeton University Press, 2014), 35.

8 Thucydides, 1.45–54; Kagan, *Outbreak,* 245–249.

9 Thucydides, 1.67, 1.139; Aristophanes, *Acharnians,* 515–538; Diodorus Siculus, 12, 39, 4–5; Plutarch, *Pericles,* 29–31; Kagan, *Outbreak,* 251–272.

10 Thucydides, 1.56–61.

11 Thucydides, 1.118; Kagan, *Outbreak*, 311.

12 It may have been one of the first times—if not *the* first time—in the theater that a new style of music was heard where, instead of following the natural cadences of spoken Greek, melodies worked against them. O. Thomas, "Music in Euripides' *Medea*," in *Music, Text, and Culture in Ancient Greece*, ed. T. Phillips and A. D'Angour (Oxford: Oxford University Press, 2018), 99–120.

13 Euripides' novel treatment: D. J. Mastronarde, ed., *Euripides: "Medea"* (Cambridge: Cambridge University Press, 2002), 44–57; A. H. Sommerstein, "Tragedy and Myth," in *A Companion to Tragedy*, ed. R. Bushnell (Malden, MA: Blackwell, 2005), 168. Nothing in the surviving text of *Medea* suggests that her chariot was pulled by snakes or dragons.

14 "In peace time": Herodotus 1.87.

15 Mastronarde, *Euripides: "Medea,"* 824–849 (following the Greek text of Euripides, *Cyclops; Alcestis; Medea*, ed. D. Kovacs (Cambridge, MA: Harvard University Press, 1994).

16 "He has persuaded": Aristophanes, *Thesmophoriazusae*, 450–451. Deeply religious: see M. Lefkowitz, *Euripides and the Gods* (Oxford: Oxford University Press, 2016).

17 K. Diamantakou-Agathou, "From Aspasia to Lysistrata: Literary Versions and Intertextual Diffusions of the Feminine Other in Classical Athens," *Logeion* 10 (2020): 238–260. "Some drunk": Aristophanes, *Acharnians*, 524–531.

18 "Drive out the curse": Thucydides, 1.126–127. Athenian response: Thucydides, 1.128; Kagan, *Outbreak*, 317–321.

19 Thucydides, 2.2–7; Diodorus, 12.41–42; D. Kagan, *The Archidamian War* (Ithaca, NY: Cornell University Press, 1974), 44–49.

20 Thucydides as pupil of Anaxagoras: Marcellinus, *Life of Thucydides*, 22; T. Whitmarsh, *Battling the Gods: Atheism in the Ancient World* (New York: Knopf, 2015), 82, 86 (where he describes Thucydides' *History* as "the earliest surviving atheist narrative of human history"). "A short while": Thucydides, 2.8. No geological evidence for earthquake: J. S. Rusten, "ΔΗΛΟΣ 'ΕΚΙΝ'ΗΘΗ: An 'Imaginary Earthquake' on Delos in Herodotus and Thucydides," *Journal of Hellenic Studies* 133 (2013): 135–145.

21 Seers and oracles: R. Parker, *Polytheism and Society at Athens* (Oxford: Oxford University Press, 2005), 116–135. Eclipse: Thucydides, 28; Plutarch, *Pericles*, 35. Azoulay, *Pericles*, 119, notes that the story "has no historical basis since no eclipse of the sun is attested in that year."

22 Thucydides, 2.14, 2.16; V. D. Hanson, *A War Like No Other* (London: Methuen, 2005), 29–30.

23 Thucydides, 2.17.

24 Thucydides, 2.19–23; Kagan, *Archidamian War*, 49–62.

25 Ceremony honouring war dead: Thucydides, 2.34; Kagan, *Archidamian War*, 64–66; M. Barbato, *The Ideology of Democratic Athens: Institutions, Orators and the Mythical Past* (Edinburgh: Edinburgh University Press, 2020); R. Parker, *Athenian Religion: A History* (Oxford: Clarendon Press, 1996), 131–140. J. B. Connelly, *The Parthenon Enigma: A Journey into Legend* (New York: Knopf, 2014), 218, rightly describes the ceremony as "furnishing another mystic cord of memory, whereby the Athenians were bound to their remote past." Pericles' speech: Connelly, *Parthenon Enigma*, 116–118.

26 Thucydides, 1.22; J. L. Shear, "'Their Memories Will Never Grow Old': The Politics of Remembrance in the Athenian Funeral Oration," *Classical Quarterly* 63, no. 2 (2013): 511–536.

27 "The speech must": Plato, *Menexenus,* 236e. Autochthony and "first praise": Plato, *Menexenus,* 237a–b. "Loved by the gods" and "fought over by them": Plato, *Menexenus,* 237c. Grain and olive: Plato, *Menexenus,* 238a. "Considered it their duty": Plato, *Menexenus,* 239b. See Barbato, *Ideology,* 38–42.

28 "They bewitch": Plato, *Menexenus,* 235a–c. Games: P. Low, "Commemoration of the War Dead in Classical Athens: Remembering Defeat and Victory," in *War, Democracy and Culture in Classical Athens,* ed. D. Pritchard (Cambridge: Cambridge University Press, 2010), 348. Public funeral as time all Athens gathered as one body: J. L. Shear, *Serving Athena: The Festival of the Panathenaia and the Construction of Athenian Identities* (Cambridge: Cambridge University Press, 2021), 332.

29 Funeral speech as propaganda: Azoulay, *Pericles,* 33. "I shall start first": Thucydides, 2.36.

30 "Especially regarding": Thucydides, 2.37. Is this mention of unwritten laws a deliberate rejoinder to Sophocles, who used the phrase in *Antigone* to criticize Pericles and his crucifixion of the Samian rebels? "Taking the city as a whole": Thucydides, 2.41.

31 "With our hard work completed": Thucydides, 2.38.

32 "Gaze every day": Thucydides, 2.43. See Azoulay, *Pericles,* 95–97.

33 "Even if they fell short": Thucydides, 2.42.

34 "We have provided": Thucydides, 2.41.

35 "They [the Athenians]": Thucydides, 1.70.

36 "A tyrant city": Thucydides, 1.124. "Slavery pure and simple": Thucydides, 1.122.

37 "Barely if at all": implied by Thucydides' observation that the platform on which he stood was erected so that he might be heard by "as many of the crowd as possible" (2.34). "Well versed" etc.: Plato, *Menexenus,* 235e. "Improvising": Plato, *Menexenus,* 236b.

38 See C. H. Kahn, "Plato's Funeral Oration: The Motive of the Menexenus," *Classical Philology* 58, no. 4 (1963): 220–234.

39 "Familiar subjects": Thucydides, 2.36.

10. CONVULSIONS

1 Thucydides, 2.47–48. 300,000 people: V. D. Hanson, *A War Like No Other* (London: Methuen, 2005), 6.

2 Thucydides, 2.48–49; Hanson, *A War Like No Other,* 67–80; D. Kagan, *The Archidamian War* (Ithaca, NY: Cornell University Press, 1974), 70–100. M. Papagrigorakis and colleagues diagnose typhoid fever, based on finding DNA of the bacteria causing typhoid fever in dental pulp of corpses of plague victims. M. Papagrigorakis, C. Yapijakis, P. N. Synodinos, and E. Baziotopoulou-Valavani, "DNA Examination of Ancient Dental Pulp Incriminates Typhoid Fever as a Probable Cause of the Plague of Athens," *International Journal of Infectious Diseases* 10, no. 3 (2006): 206–214. But see R. J. Littman, "The Plague of Athens: Epidemiology and Paleopathology," *Mount Sinai Journal of Medicine* 76, no. 5 (2009): 456–467, 456, who points out that "because typhoid was endemic in the Greek world, it is not the likely cause of this sudden epidemic."

3 Thucydides, 2.49–52.

4 "When they saw": Thucydides, 2.53.

5 "The temples": Thucydides, 2.52. "Piled high": Thucydides, 2.52. "War with the Dorians": Thucydides, 2.54; T. Whitmarsh, *Battling the Gods: Atheism in the Ancient World* (New York: Knopf, 2015), 82. "Stalking the high peaks": Homer, *Iliad,* 1.43–52.

6 "All the other disasters": Thucydides, 2.59. Perhaps they also stripped him of command: Plutarch, *Pericles,* 35.

7 Used to his excoriating speeches: Plutarch, *Pericles,* 15. "To anyone": Thucydides, 2.63.

8 "Second to no one": Thucydides, 2.60. "To accept phlegmatically": Thucydides, 2.64.

9 "Other crowds": Sophocles, *Oedipus Tyrannus,* 19–20.

10 Whitmarsh, *Battling the Gods,* 103.

11 "Drive out the pollution": Sophocles, *Oedipus Tyrannus,* 96–98. "Thanks to my reasoning": Sophocles, *Oedipus Tyrannus,* 398. Diopeithes: Whitmarsh, *Battling the Gods,*103.

12 Sophocles, *Oedipus Tyrannus,* 873–890; Whitmarsh, *Battling the Gods,* 104–105.

13 "It was Apollo": Sophocles, *Oedipus Tyrannus,* 1329–1330; Whitmarsh, *Battling the Gods,* 106. "From now on": Sophocles, *Oedipus Tyrannus,* 857–858; Whitmarsh, *Battling the Gods,* 104.

14 Plutarch, *Pericles,* 36.

15 Plutarch, *Pericles,* 37. "Is my bastard": Plutarch, *Pericles,* 24; Eupolis, *Demes,* in T. Kock, *Comicorum Atticorum Fragmenta,* 3 vols. (Leipzig: B. G. Teubner, 1880), 1:282.

16 Plutarch, *Pericles,* 38. Lucky charm: R. Parker, *Polytheism and Society at Athens* (Oxford: Oxford University Press, 2005), 124; V. Azoulay, *Pericles of Athens,* trans. J. Lloyd (Princeton, NJ: Princeton University Press, 2014), 121. Tyche: see V. Giannopoulou, "Divine Agency and 'Tyche' in Euripides' 'Ion'": Ambiguity and Shifting Perspectives," *Illinois Classical Studies* 24/25 (1999–2000): 257–271.

17 Cost of Potidaea campaign: M. Munn, *The School of History* (Berkeley: University of California Press, 2000), 54; Hanson, *A War Like No Other,* 27.

18 "Kill my son": Euripides, *Hippolytus,* 888–889.

19 "If only": Euripides, *Hippolytus,* 1415. "Good, religious attitude. Pray that": Euripides, *Hippolytus,* 1454–1455. "This misery": Euripides, *Hippolytus,* 1462–1466.

20 Fall of Potidaea: Thucydides, 2.70. Mytilene and debate: Thucydides, 3.36–50; Diodorus, 12.55; Kagan, *Archidamian War,* 132–146, 152–167. Cleon's style of oratory: [Aristotle], *Athenian Constitution,* 28.

21 "That your empire": Thucydides, 3.37. General Paches' suicide: Plutarch, *Nicias,* 6; Plutarch, *Aristeides,* 26; Kagan, *Archidamian War,* 167–168.

22 Thucydides, 3.381; Kagan, *Archidamian War,* 179–181.

23 "The moment that constraints": Thucydides, 5.84.

24 "Hand themselves over": Herodotus, 6.108. Fall of Plataea: Thucydides, 2.2–6, 2.71–78, 3.51–68.

25 Vandalizing vineyards etc. Hanson, *A War Like No Other,* 35–37, outlines Athenian's attachment to the land and practical difficulties in permanently destroying trees and vines.

26 Gorgias: see, for example, S. Consigny, *Gorgias: Sophist and Artist* (Columbia: University of South Carolina Press, 2001); R. Wardy, *The Birth of Rhetoric: Gorgias, Plato and Their Successors* (New York: Routledge, 1996). The many works on

sophists include: *The Greek Sophists,* trans. J. Dillon, and T. Gergel (London: Penguin, 2003); S. Montiglio, "Wandering Philosophers in Classical Greece," *Journal of Hellenic Studies* 120 (2000): 86–105; E. Robinson, "The Sophists and Democracy beyond Athens," *Rhetorica* 25 (2007): 109–122.

27 "More than": Thucydides, 3.87. "Around the same time": Thucydides, 3.89. See R. V. Munson, "Natural Upheavals in Thucydides (and Herodotus)," in *Kinesis: The Ancient Depiction of Gesture, Motion, And Emotion,* ed. C. A. Clark, E. Foster, and J. P. Hallett (Ann Arbor: University of Michigan Press, 2015), 41–59.

28 "In my opinion": Thucydides, 3.89. Because of Thucydides' rationalist approach to the earthquakes and the scanty details that he gives, scholars have tended to downplay their impact on Greek psyche.

29 Freak weather: Diodorus Siculus, 12.58.3–4. Earthquakes: Thucydides, 1.23.1, 3.87.4, 3.89.1–5. Earthquakes and damage to Parthenon: T. L. Shear Jr., *Trophies of Victory: Public Buildings in Periklean Athens* (Princeton, NJ: Princeton University Press 2016), 370–374.

30 New religious fervour: R. Parker, *Athenian Religion: A History* (Oxford: Clarendon Press, 1996), 200. Under Cleon's leadership: R. Brock, "Thucydides and the Athenian Purification of Delos," *Mnemosyne,* 4th ser., 49, no. 3 (1996): 321–327. Purification of Delos and revival of games: Thucydides, 3.104. Temple: J. S. Boersma, *Athenian Building Policy from 561/0 to 405/4 B.C.* (Groningen: Wolters-Noordhoff, 1970), 86–87, describes this as "one of the rare buildings from the entire period . . . which was undertaken primarily for religious motives."

31 Temple statistics: stylobate approx. 56 feet × 32 feet; cella 24.5 feet × 32 feet; six columns front and rear. More remarkable were the contents of its tiny cella (24.5 feet × 32 feet). I. M. Shear, "Kallikrates," *Hesperia* 32, no. 4 (1963): 375–424. Bronze statues: Boersma, *Building Policy,* 18.

32 Significance of Oreithyia myth: Parker, *Athenian Religion,* 157; A. Zarkadas, "Boreas and Oreithyia: The Abduction of a *Kanephoros* in the Panathenaic Procession," in *From Kallias to Kritias: Art in Athens in the Second Half of the Fifth Century B.C.,* ed. J. Neils and O. Palagia (Berlin: De Gruyter, 2021), 357–366.

33 Nicias' character: Plutarch, *Nicias,* 2. Nicias' wealth and dedications: Plutarch, *Nicias,* 3. Stilbides: Plutarch, *Nicias,* 23.

34 Plutarch, *Nicias,* 3–4; D. Kagan, *The Peace of Nicias and the Sicilian Expedition* (Ithaca, NY: Cornell University Press, 1981), 153–154. Date of temple: Boersma, *Building Policy,* 88, suggests it was begun in 421.

35 One of Cleon's closest acolytes: his name was Smicythus, for more on whom and the Erechtheum's date see T. Shear, *Trophies,* 376–379.

36 R. J. Hopper, *The Acropolis* (New York: Macmillan, 1971), 97–110; T. Shear, *Trophies,* 381–389.

37 New temple called "Temple where the ancient statue is": I. Jenkins, *Greek Architecture and Its Sculpture* (Cambridge, MA: Harvard University Press, 2006), 119; and "Old Temple" (Archaios Neos): Jenkins, *Greek Architecture,* 117. Work of Alcamenes: Jenkins, *Greek Architecture,* 126. "Spiritual descendants": L. Haselberger, "Bending the Truth: Curvature and Other Refinements of the Parthenon," in *The Parthenon from Antiquity to the Present,* ed. J. Neils (Cambridge: Cambridge University Press, 2005), 104.

38 Blackened statues: Pausanias, 1.12.6. Korai: M. C. Stieber, *The Poetics of Appearance in the Attic Korai* (Austin: University of Texas Press, 2004).

39 Jenkins, *Greek Architecture,* 127; L. Pallat, "The Frieze of the Erechtheum," *American Journal of Archaeology* 16, no. 2 (1912): 175–202.

40 Lamp: Pausanias, 1.12.6. Altars to Hephaestus and Butes: Pausanias, 1.12.5. Cecrops' tomb and caryatids: J. M. Camp, *The Archaeology of Athens* (New Haven, CT: Yale University Press, 2001), 99. Showing off token: J. B. Connelly, *The Parthenon Enigma: A Journey into Legend* (New York: Knopf, 2014), 109. Ground raised: N. Robertson, "Athena's Shrines and Festivals," in *Worshipping Athena: Panathenaia and Parthenon,* ed. J. Neils (Madison: University of Wisconsin Press, 1996), 44.

41 424 B.C. earthquake: Thucydides, 4.52. "Poseidon, Lord": Euripides, *Erechtheus,* F 370.55–57. "For Erechtheus": Euripides, *Erechtheus,* F 370.90–97. For complete fragments of the play and discussion, see *Euripedes, Selected Fragmentary Plays,* ed. C. Collard, M. J. Cropp, and K. H. Lee (Warminster, UK: Aris and Phillips, 1995), 1:148–175; M. Wright, *The Lost Plays of Greek Tragedy,* vol. 2, *Aeschylus, Sophocles and Euripides* (London: Bloomsbury Academic, 2019), 168–171. Importance of Euripides' *Erechtheus* to building of the Erechtheum: T. Shear, *Trophies,* 374–375.

42 "They did not recklessly": Euripides, *Erechtheus,* F 370.70–74. Site of precinct unknown: Connelly, *Parthenon Enigma,* 232–234, suggests the Parthenon's opisth-odomos, but this was scarcely somewhere which was never entered.

43 Fire at Temple of Athena Polias: Xenophon, *Hellenica,* 1.6.1; Camp, *Archaeology of Athens,* 99. Estimates vary for the date when the Temple of Athena Nike was started. Preparations: T. Shear, *Trophies,* 346. Evidence suggests that members of the public were invited to submit designs for the temple's door, and that the Assembly debated whether it should be faced with gold and ivory or just gold: *IG* I^2.88; Boersma, *Building Policy,* 5. Aegeus jumping to death: Pausanias, 1.22.4; Camp, *Archaeology of Athens,* 90. J. Larson, *Greek Heroine Cults* (Madison: University of Wisconsin Press, 1995), 92, suggests that in Classical Greece, veneration of Bronze Age or Mycenaean ruins was relatively common.

44 Frieze: T. Shear, *Trophies,* 352. Comparison with gods of Parthenon: Jenkins, *Greek Architecture,* 117. Interpretations include: (1) the birth of Athena: O. Palagia, "Interpretations of Two Athenian Friezes: The Temple on the Ilissos and the Temple of Athena Nike," in *Periklean Athens and Its Legacy: Problems and Perspectives,* ed. J. Barringer and Hurwit (Austin: University of Texas Press, 2005), 188–189; (2) a celebration of victory: E. B. Harrison, "The Glories of the Athenians: Observations on the Program of the Frieze of the Temple of Athena Nike," in *The Interpretation of Architectural Sculpture in Greece and Rome,* ed. D. Buitron-Oliver (Washington, DC: National Gallery of Art, 1997), 113; Palagia, "Interpretations of Two Athenian Friezes," 177–192; J. M. Hurwit, *The Athenian Acropolis: History, Mythology, and Archaeology from the Neolithic Era to the Present* (Cambridge: Cambridge University Press, 1999), 184–188; and (3) weighing the souls of Memnon and Achilles at Troy, to decide which of the two should live: F. Felten, *Grieschische tektonische Friese archaischer und klassischer Zeit* (Waldsassen-Bayern: Stiftland, 1984), 123–133, 139. South Frieze: T. Shear, *Trophies,* 352.

45 "Callimachus, today": Herodotus, 6.109.

46 T. Shear, *Trophies,* 352–355. Suggestions regarding the battles' identities include: (1) the Trojan War: Felten, *Grieschische tektonische Friese,* 123–133; (2) Erechtheus fighting against Eleusis: Kardara, *Archaiologike Ephemeris* (1961): 84–90; (3) the Seven Against Thebes: Harrison, "The Glories of the Athenians," 113; (4) Megara: E. G. Pemberton, "The East and West Friezes of the Athena Nike Temple," *American Journal of Archaeology* 76 (1972): 304–307; or (5) the Battle of Oenoe: Palagia,

"Interpretations of Two Athenian Friezes," 186. Boersma, *Building Policy,* 86, suggests that one frieze shows the Battle of Sphacteria.

47 M. Lippman, D. Scahill, and P. Schultz, "*Knights* 843–59, the Temple Bastion, and Cleon's Shields from Pylos," *American Journal of Archaeology* 110, no. 4 (2006): 551–563.

11. BATTLE LINES

1 "Made them disappear": Thucydides, 4.80.

2 Delium: Thucydides, 4.89–101; Diodorus, 12.69–70. Flamethrower: H. van Wees, *Greek Warfare: Myths and Realities* (London: Duckworth, 2004), 141. "There was an eclipse": Thucydides, 4.52.

3 Brasidas and Amphipolis: Thucydides, 4.102–107; Diodorus, 12.68; D. Kagan, *The Archidamian War* (Ithaca, NY: Cornell University Press, 1974), 290–302; M. Roberts, *Two Deaths at Amphipolis* (Barnsley, UK: Pen and Sword Military, 2015). Thucydides' exile: Thucydides, 5.26. "Possession for all time": Thucydides, 1.22.

4 Death of Cleon and Brasidas and aftermath: Thucydides, 5.2–12. Peace of Nicias: Thucydides, 5.13–20; Kagan, *Archidamian War,* 342–348.

5 Statue: Suidas, s.v. Nike; Pausanias, 5.26.6. Explanation of wingless "Nike": Pausanias 1.22.4.

6 Asclepius in Athens: B. L. Wickkiser, *Asclepius, Medicine, and the Politics of Healing in Fifth-Century Greece* (Baltimore, MD: Johns Hopkins University Press, 2008); K. Clinton, "The Epidauria and the arrival of Asclepius in Athens," in *Ancient Greek Cult Practice: the Epigraphical Evidence,* ed. R. Hägg (Stockholm: Svenska institutet i Athen, 1994), 17–34; H. Perlstadt, "The Plague of Athens and the Cult of Asclepius: A Case Study of Collective and a Social Movement," *Sociology and Anthropology* 4, no. 12 (2016): 1048–1053. Sophocles as Dexion: *TrGF* 4 T69; R. Parker, *Athenian Religion: A History* (Oxford: Clarendon Press, 1996), 184–185; A. Connolly, "Was Sophocles Heroised as Dexion?," *Journal of Hellenic Studies* 118 (1998): 1–21. Sophocles as priest: T. Whitmarsh, *Battling the Gods: Atheism in the Ancient World* (New York: Knopf, 2015), 22.

7 "Niece of Megacles": Aristophanes, *Clouds,* 46–47.

8 "Zeus does not exist": Aristophanes, *Clouds,* 367, 827, and also, for example, 1240–1241. "The modern position": Aristophanes, *Clouds,* 246–248. "Mists, dew and smoke": Aristophanes, *Clouds,* 330. "They are the only": Aristophanes, *Clouds,* 365. Eclipse: Aristophanes, *Clouds,* 584–585. Lightning strike on Cape Sunium: Aristophanes, *Clouds,* 401.

9 "Does Zeus exist": Aristophanes, *Clouds,* 1470. "Beloved Hermes": Aristophanes, *Clouds,* 1478–1480. "What were you thinking": Aristophanes, *Clouds,* 1506–1509.

10 Socrates from Melos: Aristophanes, *Clouds,* 830. Diagoras: Cicero, *De Natura Deorum,* 3.89; see Whitmarsh, *Battling the Gods,* 120, 112–113; L. Woodbury, "The Date and Atheism of Diagoras of Melos," *Phoenix* 19, no. 3 (1965): 178–211.

11 Alcibiades as Pheidippides: especially convinced by this belief is M. Vickers, *Aristophanes and Alcibiades* (Berlin: De Gruyter, 2015). Socrates and Alcibiades at Potidea: Plutarch, *Alcibiades,* 7; Plato, *Symposium,* 220d–e; at Delium: Plutarch, *Alcibiades,* 7; Plato, *Symposium,* 220e–221a.

12 Assembly meeting: Thucydides, 5.44–46; Plutarch, *Alcibiades,* 14; Plutarch, *Nicias,* 10; D. Stuttard, *Nemesis: Alcibiades and the Fall of Athens* (Cambridge, MA: Harvard

University Press, 2016), 104–105. Battle of Mantinea: Thucydides, 5.65–74; Diodorus, 12.79; Stuttard, *Nemesis,* 115–116.

13 P. J. Rhodes, "The Ostracism of Hyberbolus," in *Ritual, Finance, Politics: Athenian Democratic Accounts Presented to David Lewis,* ed. R. Osborne and S. Hornblower (Oxford: Clarendon Press, 1994); B. Baldwin, "Notes on Hyperbolus," *Acta Classica* 14, no. 1 (1971): 151–156; Stuttard, *Nemesis,* 121–125.

14 "What men call": Thucydides, 5.89. "Faith in the gods": Thucydides, 5.104; Whitmarsh, *Battling the Gods,* 83–84. "What we think about the gods": Thucydides, 5.105.

15 Alcibiades' outrageous behaviour: Plutarch, *Alcibiades,* 1–7. Alcibiades at Olympic Games: Thucydides, 6.15; Plutarch, *Alcibiades,* 11; Stuttard, *Nemesis,* 128–131.

16 "Whoever wins": Pindar, *Isthmian,* 1.50–51. Paintings: Athenaeaus, 12.532d–e. First self-commissioned portraits: M. Munn, *The School of History* (Berkeley: University of California Press, 2000), 60. Displayed in Propylaea: Pausanias, 1.22.6–7.

17 Democratic Syracuse: E. Robinson, "Democracy in Syracuse, 466–412 B.C.," *Harvard Studies in Classical Philology* 100 (2000): 189–205. Debate in Assembly: Thucydides, 6.12.

18 "They have insulted": Euripides, *Trojan Women,* 69. "In future": Euripides, *Trojan Women,* 85–86.

19 Festival of Adonis: Plutarch, *Alcibiades,* 18. Priests and oracle of Zeus Ammon: Plutarch, *Nicias,* 13. Soothsayers: Thucydides, 8.1.

20 Mutilation of Herms: Thucydides, 6.1; Diodorus, 13.2; Plutarch, *Alcibiades,* 18; Nepos, *Life of Alcibiades,* 3; Andocides, *On the Mysteries,* 62; Aristophanes, *Lysistrata,* 1094; D. Kagan, *The Peace of Nicias and the Sicilian Expedition* (Ithaca, NY: Cornell University Press, 1981), 193–195; Stuttard, *Nemesis,* 146–149; Whitmarsh, *Battling the Gods,* 85. Herms in Athens: Munn, *School of History,* 104. "He will make": Euripides, *Trojan Women,* 97.

21 Thucydides 6.28.1; Kagan, *Peace of Nicias,* 195–196; V. D. Hanson, *A War Like No Other* (London: Methuen, 2005), 207; D. Hamel, *The Mutilation of the Herms: Unpacking an Ancient Mystery* ([n.p.]: [CreateSpace], 2012), 7. Wealth tax (*eisphora*): Munn, *School of History,* 100.

22 Andocides, *On the Mysteries,* 11; Thucydides, 6.28–29; Plutarch, *Alcibiades,* 19. See *Antiphon and Andocides,* trans. M. Gagarin and D. M. MacDowell (Austin: University of Texas Press, 1998), 104; Kagan, *Peace of Nicias,* 195; Munn, *School of History,* 106. Under Athenian law, slaves' evidence was acceptable only if given under torture, but the Assembly was not a law court and this was not a formal trial.

23 Hetaereiai: A. W. Gomme, A. Andrewes, and K. J. Dover, *A Historical Commentary on Thucydides,* vol. 5 (Oxford: Clarendon Press, 1981), 5.128–131; Munn, *School of History,* 90.

24 Alcibiades demands trial: Thucydides, 6.29. Alcibiades recalled: Thucydides, 6.60–61. Diagoras: Diodorus, 13.6; Lysias, 6.17; Aristophanes, *Birds,* 1073–1074. Diagoras and Mysteries: Athenodorus, *A Plea for the Christians,* 4.

25 "Hem in the Greeks": Homer, *Iliad,* 1.409–412.

26 "Stele of disgrace": Plutarch, *Alcibiades,* 22; Philochorus, *FGrH,* 328, fr. 134; so-called by Kagan, *Peace of Nicias,* 225. Curses: Lysias, 7.51; Plutarch, *Alcibiades,* 22, 33.

27 Views of generals: Thucydides, 6.49–52; Kagan, *Peace of Nicias,* 212–217. Sicilian expedition: Thucydides, 6.62–88, 6.94–105, 7.1–71; Diodorus, 13.417; Plutarch, *Nicias,* 15–22; Kagan, *Peace of Nicias,* 217–328.

28 Timing of eclipse: NASA eclipse website, https://eclipse.gsfc.nasa.gov/LEhistory/LEplot/LE-0412Aug28T.pdf (accessed 5 September 2025); Kagan, *Peace of Nicias,* 323. Stilbides and Nicias: Plutarch, *Nicias,* 23–24; Whitmarsh, *Battling the Gods,* 85.

29 End of Sicilian expedition: Thucydides, 7.75–87; Diodorus, 13.18–33; Kagan, *Peace of Nicias,* 329–353. Freeing prisoners who sang Euripides: Plutarch, *Nicias,* 29. For an irreverent take on the subject, read F. Lennon's novel, *Glorious Exploits* (London: Macmillan, 2024).

30 "The most expensive": Thucydides, 6.31.

31 Earthquake: Plutarch, *Alcibiades,* 23; Plutarch, *Lysander,* 22. Alcibiades in Persia: Plutarch, *Alcibiades,* 25.

32 Decelea: Thucydides, 7.19; Diodorus, 13.9. Fugitive slaves: Thucydides, 7.27.

33 Probouloi: F. D. Smith, *Athenian Political Commissions* (Chicago: private edition distributed by the University of Chicago libraries, 1920; PhD diss. 2016); D. Kagan, *The Fall of the Athenian Empire* (Ithaca, NY: Cornell University Press, 1987), 5; Hanson, *A War Like No Other,* 236. Suspension of constitution: Thucydides, 8.53–54; M. Munn, *School of History,* 137–138; Kagan, *Fall,* 133. Tissaphernes' demands: Thucydides, 8.56.

34 Begging Achilles to return: Homer, *Iliad,* 9.182–668. Return of Alcibiades: Thucydides, 8.81–82; Plutarch, *Alcibiades,* 26.

12. CATHARSIS?

1 Work continued unabated: see, for example, *IG* I^3 474 dating from 409/8 B.C., which reads, "Following the decree of the People, the supervisors of the temple on the Acropolis housing the ancient xoanon . . . recorded the work on the temple, both completed and yet to be finished, as they inherited it when Diocles was archon during the first prytany of Cecropis, when Nicophanes of Marathon was Council Secretary."

2 "Ships lost": Xenophon, *Hellenica,* 1.1.23; Plutarch, *Alcibiades,* 28. Restoration of democracy: D. Kagan, *The Fall of the Athenian Empire* (Ithaca, NY: Cornell University Press, 1987), 252–256. Decree: Andocides, 1.96–98.

3 Parapet: T. L. Shear Jr., *Trophies of Victory: Public Buildings in Periklean Athens* (Princeton, NJ: Princeton University Press, 2016), 356–358. Dimensions: W. B. Dinsmoor, "The Sculptured Parapet of Athena Nike," *American Journal of Archaeology* 30, no. 1 (1926): 1–31. Alcibiades' return: Plutarch, *Alcibiades,* 32; Diodorus, 13.68.

4 Plutarch, *Alcibiades,* 33; Diodorus, 13.69; M. Munn, *The School of History* (Berkeley: University of California Press, 2000), 167–168; Kagan, *Fall,* 289.

5 "Malevolent daimon": Plutarch, *Alcibiades,* 33; Diodorus, 13.69; Justin, 5.4.13–18; Nepos, *Alcibiades,* 7.6. Kagan, *Fall,* 289; Socrates and his daimon: Plato, *Apology,* 31c–d; Heraclitus, fr B119; K. Robb, "'Psyche' and 'Logos' in the Fragments of Heraclitus: The Origins of the Concept of the Soul," *The Monist* 69, no. 3 (1986): 315–351. Spirit beings which bridged the gap: Plato, *Symposium,* 202e.

6 Plynteria: Xenophon, *Hellenica,* 1.4.12; Plutarch, *Alcibiades,* 34; H. W. Parke, *Festivals of the Athenians* (London: Thames and Hudson), 1977, 152–155; E. Simon, *Festivals of Attica: An Archaeological Commentary* (Madison: University of Wisconsin Press, 1983), 46–48; J. Larson, *Ancient Greek Cults: A Guide* (London: Routledge, 2007), 48. Dark of the moon: N. Robertson, "Athena's Shrines and Festivals," in *Worshipping Athena: Panathenaia and Parthenon,* ed. J. Neils (Madison:

University of Wisconsin Press, 1996), 27. Robertson, "Athena's Shrines and Festivals," 33, suggests that the statue was bathed with water drawn from Poseidon's well on the Acropolis.

7 Plutarch, *Alcibiades,* 33; Xenophon, *Hellenica,* 1.4.20; Diodorus, 13.69; Justin, 5.4.13–16; Nepos, *Life of Alcibiades,* 7; Kagan, *Fall,* 290. Justin, 2.5.4, goes further, saying that Athens awarded Alcibiades "not only all human honours, but divine ones too." "First time under the democracy": According to Plutarch, both Themistocles (*Aristeides,* 8) and Aristeides (*Aristeides,* 11) held the position, but even if this is true they probably did so only on campaign or on the battlefield, where it was necessary for one general to be in overall command. Alcibiades possibly was joint strategos autocrator (supreme commander) with Nicias and Lamachus in the early days of the Sicilian Expedition (Thucydides, 6.8, 26; Diodorus, 13.2; Plutarch, *Nicias,* 12; Plutarch, *Alcibiades,* 18), but that was very different from the position he held now.

8 Battle: Xenophon, 1.5.12–15; Diodorus, 13.71; Plutarch, *Alcibiades,* 35. Alcibiades escapes: Plutarch, *Alcibiades,* 36–37.

9 Melting statues: Aristophanes, *Frogs,* 720; Kagan, *Fall,* 338.

10 Battle of Arginusae and aftermath: Xenophon, 1.6.28–33; Diodorus, 13.97–100; Kagan, *Fall,* 341–353.

11 Trial of generals: Xenophon, 1.6.33–7.35; Diodorus, 13.100–103; Kagan, *Fall,* 354–375.

12 Himera: Diodorus, 13.59–62. Selinus: Diodorus, 13.54–57. Acragas: Diodorus, 13.85–90, 96. "Industriously ransacking": Diodorus, 13.90.

13 Old world ending: such is the thrust of, for example, Aristophanes' *Frogs.*

14 "Though gods may inhabit": Euripides, *Bacchae,* 392–396. "The best thing": Euripides, *Bacchae,* 1150–1152.

15 Sophocles, *Oedipus at Colonus,* 668–719.

16 "And he to his heir": Sophocles, *Oedipus at Colonus,* 1532. "A terrifying mystery": Sophocles, *Oedipus at Colonus,* 1526.

17 "For every city": Sophocles, *Oedipus at Colonus,* 1534–1538. Site of Oedipus' grave: Pausanias, 1.28.7.

18 Battle of Arginusae: Xenophon, *Hellenica,* 2.1.25–29; Diodorus, 13.105–107; Plutarch, *Alcibiades,* 36–37; Kagan, *Fall,* 386–394.

19 Xenophon, *Hellenica,* 2.2.3–19; Diodorus, 13.107; Kagan, *Fall,* 396–405.

20 Plutarch, *Lysander,* 15, quoting Euripides, *Electra,* 167–168.

21 Xenophon, *Hellenica,* 2.2.19–23; Diodorus, 14.2–5; [Aristotle], *Athenian Constitution,* 35. Critias: J. K. Davies, *Athenian Propertied Families, 600–300 B.C.* (Oxford: Clarendon Press, 1971), 322. Friends of Solon: Plato, *Timaeus,* 20e.

22 Critias, *Sisyphus,* fr. 19 = *TrGF,* 1.43 fr. 19, 1–26. See T. Whitmarsh, *Battling the Gods: Atheism in the Ancient World* (New York: Knopf, 2015), 94.

23 "These were the fears": Critias, *Sisyphus,* fr. 19 = *TrGF,* 1.43 fr. 19, 37–42.

24 Xenophon, *Hellenica,* 2.4.

25 Alexander and the *Iliad:* Plutarch, *Alexander,* 8. At Troy: Plutarch, *Alexander,* 8.

26 "Spoils from the barbarians": Arrian, 1.16. "In revenge": Diodorus, 17.72; also Plutarch, *Alexander,* 38. Temple of Athena at Troy: N. MacSweeny, *Troy: Myth, City, Icon* (London: Bloomsbury Academic, 2018), 88–90; C. B. Rose, "The Temple of Athena at Ilion," *Studia Troica* 13 (2003): 45–33; Rose, "Temple of Athena," 35–43.

27 Demosthenes and Parthenon: *Against Androtion,* 13, 76; *Against Timocrates,* 184. Propylaea more admired than Parthenon: R. Parker, *Athenian Religion: A History*

(Oxford: Clarendon Press, 1996), 220. The Parthenon *was* shown on vase painting, however: D. Williams, "Les Images de le Cité," in *Images at the Crossroads: Media and Meaning in Greek Art,* ed. J. M. Barringer and F. Lissarrague (Edinburgh: Edinburgh University Press, 2022), 130–131.

28 "It was inappropriate": Strabo 14.1.22. Demetrius in Athens: Plutarch, *Demetrius,* 23–25; Philippides, fr. 25, in *Poetae Comici Graeci,* vol. 7, ed. R. Kassel and C. Austin (Berlin: De Gruyter, 1983).

29 Subsequent history: M. Beard, *The Parthenon* (Cambridge, MA: Harvard University Press, 2002). "The Council of the Areopagus": see, for example, K. K. Carroll, *The Parthenon Inscription,* Greek, Roman and Byzantine Monographs, no. 9 (Durham, NC: Greek, Roman, and Byzantine Studies, Duke University, 1982).

30 Statue: G. P. Stevens, "Concerning the Parthenos," *Hesperia* 30, no. 1 (1961): 1–7.

31 Venetians, including landing at Eleusis: T. E. Mommsen, "The Venetians in Athens and the Destruction of the Parthenon in 1687," *American Journal of Archaeology* 45 (1941): 544–556; C. Hadziaslani, *Morosini, the Venetians, and the Acropolis,* trans. G. Huxley (Athens: American School of Classical Studies, Gennadius Library, 1987); J. B. Connelly, *The Parthenon Enigma: A Journey into Legend* (New York: Knopf, 2014), xvi.

32 "Setting up ladders": text of Lord Elgin's firman from W. St. Clair, *Who Saved the Parthenon? A New History of the Acropolis Before, During and After the Greek Revolution* (Cambridge: Open Book Publishers, 2022), Appendix A, "An integral part"; Martin Bailey, "Declassified Documents on Parthenon Marbles Reveal Rift between UK Government and British Museum," *The Art Newspaper,* May 10, 2023, https://www.theartnewspaper.com/2023/05/10/british-museum-parthenon-marbles-declassified-documents-lobbying. Melina Mercouri's passionate description of the Parthenon sculptures representing "the national spirit of Greece" charmingly misunderstands their original Athenocentric, anti-Spartan and thus decidedly not Panhellenic purpose.

33 "Sunium's marbled steep": Byron, "The Isles of Greece," in *Don Juan* (London: John Murray, 1821), canto III. Removal of Eleusinian statues: J. L. Lawson, *Modern Greek Folklore and Ancient Greek Religion: A Study in Survivals* (Cambridge: Cambridge University Press, 1910), 79–80; P. L. Fermour, *Mani: Travels in the Southern Peloponnese* (London: John Murray, 1958; repr., Harmondsworth, UK: Penguin, 1984), 180.

34 "Gadfly": Plato, *Apology,* 30e–31a.

35 Alcibiades, Critias, and Charmides: see, for example, Whitmarsh, *Battling the Gods,* 125. Banned from conversing: Xenophon, *Memorabilia,* 1.2.35. Disobeying orders: Plato, *Apology,* 32c–d. Socrates at Arginusae trial: Plato, *Apology,* 32b; Xenophon, *Hellenica,* 1.7.15.

36 Parker, *Athenian Religion,* 199–217.

37 Dangerously oligarchic views: see, for example, Plato, *Crito,* 47c–d; Plato, *Laches,* 184e; Xenophon, *Memorabilia,* 1.2.9. Corrupting young: Plato, *Euthyphro,* 3c–d. Religion: Whitmarsh, *Battling the Gods,* 126. Literature on Socrates trial and death is too vast to list here.

38 "We owe a cockerel": Plato, *Phaedo,* 118a; R. D. Griffith, "Socrates' Dying Words (Plato, *Phaedo,* 118a) as an Aesopic Fable," *Phoenix* 71, no. 1/2 (2017): 89–101.

39 Thargelia: R. Parker, *Polytheism and Society at Athens* (Oxford: Oxford University Press, 2005), 203–204, 481–483. Scapegoats: J. Bremmer, "Scapegoat Rituals in Ancient Greece," *Harvard Studies in Classical Philology* 87 (1983): 299–320.

40 The decision to reorientate the Pnyx following the collapse of the retaining wall may have been practical rather than political: J. Paga, *Building Democracy in Late Archaic Athens* (Oxford: Oxford University Press, 2021), 142–143; J. S. Boersma, *Athenian Building Policy from 561/0 to 405/4 B.C.* (Groningen: Wolters-Noordhoff, 1970), 94.

CREDITS

Illustrations are © David Stuttard unless otherwise noted.

Plan 1. Adapted from Madmedea/Wikimedia Commons/CC BY-SA 2.0
Fig. 1.2. Jastrow/Wikimedia Commons/CC BY-SA 4.0
Fig. 2.1. Neoclassicism/Wikimedia Commons/CC BY-SA 4.0
Fig. 2.3. Zde/Wikimedia Commons/CC BY-SA 4.0
Fig. 3.1. Panoramio/Wikimedia Commons/CC BY-SA 3.0
Fig. 3.3. Bibi Saint-Pol/Wikimedia Commons
Fig. 4.2. Oren Rozen/Wikimedia Commons/CC BY-SA 3.0
Fig. 4.6. Shakko (Sofia Bagdasarova)/Wikimedia Commons/CC BY-SA 4.0
Fig. 5.1. Carole Raddato/Flickr/CC BY-SA 2.0
Fig. 7.6. Dean Dixon/Wikimedia Commons/Free Art License
Fig. 8.6. Shakko (Sofia Bagdasarova)/Wikimedia Commons/CC BY-SA 3.0
Fig. 9.3. Niko Kitsakis/Wikimedia Commons/CC BY 4.0
Fig. 10.1. Giovanni Dall'Orto/Wikimedia Commons
Fig. 11.3. Ricardo André Frantz/Wikimedia Commons/CC BY-SA 3.0
Fig. 12.1. Gary Todd/Wikimedia Commons/CC0 1.0
Fig. 12.2. Neoclassicism Enthusiast/Wikimedia Commons/CC BY-SA 4.0

INDEX

Academus, 60
Acharnae, 38, 139, 237, 294
Achilles, 39, 127, 133, 196, 220, 291, 296, 312; shield of, 196
Acragas, 125, 303
Acropolis: Bronze Age remains, 31, 43, 66, 204, 265, 272; cleft in, 30, 34, 116, 181, 184, 320; north wall, 115; southwest bastion, 271–272, 274, 298; statues buried on, 116, 268; statues on, 21, 39, 105, 117, 132, 264, 268, 272; tokens on, 26, 192, 269
Acropolis Museum, 6, 316
Aeaceum, Athens, 84
Aeacidae, relics of, 84–85, 106
Aeacus, 83–84, 92
Aegeus, 231–232, 272, 307
Aegina, 23, 82–84, 106, 114, 126–127, 234, 237; Athenian refugees on, 104–105; enmity with Athens, 81–85, 94, 98–99, 140; prize after Salamis, 109; pro-Persian stance, 109; surrenders to Athens, 141–142
Aegospotami, 216, 307
Aeschylus, 159, 196, 209, 214, 286; *Oresteia,* 214; *Persians,* 136–137, 142, 212
[Aeschylus], *Prometheus,* 211–212
Aethra, 129, 158
agalma of Athena Parthenos, 147; construction of, 187–190; cost of, 189, 216; lawsuit connected to, 220–221; Parthenon designed to accommodate, 152–154; sculptures on, 191, 196; subsequent fate of, 315
Agamemnon, 54, 114, 251, 291, 296
Agariste, daughter of Cleisthenes of Sicyon, 48, 143
Ageladas of Argos, 130
Agis, 294, 296
agora: Corinth, 46; Megara, 112; Miletus, 208; Pireus, 165; Sparta, 124; Thurii, 165
Agora, Athens, 15, 29, 84, 128–129, 238, 288, 316; Altar of Twelve Gods in, 220; books burned in, 222; cavalry pageants in, 173–175; ostracisms held in, 134; Persian occupation of, 22, 104, 109; relocation of, 76–77; semi-sacred space, 20; Socrates in, 317; statues of heroes in, 178; tyrannicide statue in, 76, 109, 117, 149
Agoracritus, 192, 203
Ahmose II, 63
Ahura Mazda, 86, 124
Ajax, 84
Alcamenes, 34, 149, 267
Alcibiades, 4, 282, 291, 295–298, 300, 301–302, 307–308, 311; condemned by priests, 291, 300; Eleusinian Mysteries, profanation of, 289–290, 301, 317–318; herms, mutilation of, 289; Homer's influence on, 291, 312; "malevolent

Alcibiades (*continued*)
daimon," 300; Nicias, relationship with, 283, 285; at Olympia, 284; ostracism vote, 283; paintings of in Propylaea, 285; in Persia, 294; Sicilian Expedition, 285, 290; Socrates, relationship with, 281, 309, 318–319; sophists, relationship with, 261, 281; in Sparta, 291, 294; ward of Pericles, 218, 224, 255–25, 281
Alcibiades the Elder, 218
Alcmaeon, 48, 50, 54, 63, 87
Alcmaeonid Curse, 49–50, 70, 234–235, 307
Alcmaeonids, 48–50, 60, 63–66, 70, 87, 97–98, 139, 215, 218, 234, 279, 318
Alexander I of Macedon, 109–110, 138
Alexander III of Macedon, 311–314
Altar of the Twelve Gods, 60, 220
Amazonomachy, 36–37, 85, 239, 257; on agalma's shield, 190, 221; in Painted Stoa, 129, 158; on Parthenon, 158, 161, 173, 184, 190, 192, 195; on Temple of Artemis at Ephesus, 55, 185; on Temple of Athena and Apollo at Pallene, 202; on Temple of Athena at Troy, 313; on Temple of Athena Nike, 272; on Theseum, 128–129
Amphipolis, 226, 276–277, 295
Amphitrite, 128, 159, 161
Anacreon, 60
Anaxagoras, 215–217, 222, 235–236, 252, 307, 310
Anaximander, 212–213, 215
Anaximenes, 213
Angra Mainyu, 86, 90
Antenor, 76
Antigone, 210, 276
Aphrodite, 4, 32, 41, 78, 218, 257–258; on Parthenon, 158–159, 178, 181–183, 194, 233, 306; on Temple of Athena and Hephaestus, 150
Aphrodite, Gardens of. *See* Gardens of Aphrodite
apobatēs, 51–52, 55–56, 177, 186
Apollo, 41, 57–58, 63–64, 68, 79, 83, 86, 132, 160, 255, 269; god of Delos, 11, 90; god of Delphi, 54, 95, 101, 264–265; on Parthenon, 159, 178, 181–183; patron god of Ionians, 57, 91, 128, 131, 201; patron god of Sparta, 70, 230, 250; Patroos, 57, 95; plague god, 11, 251, 262; on Temple of Athena and Hephaestus, 150; on Temple of Zeus at Olympia, 126
Archon Basileus, 77; on Parthenon frieze, 179, 184
Areopagus, 23, 37, 49, 56, 105, 158, 321; Council of, 138, 314
Ares, 46, 92, 107; on Parthenon, 159, 178, 181–182
Argos, 56, 101, 133, 139, 282
Aristagoras, 86–87
Aristeides, 100–101, 122–123, 133, 283, 320
Aristogeiton, 62, 75, 273, 316; statue of (*see* Tyrannicides Statue)
Aristophanes, 318; attacks Aspasia, 233–234, 236; attacks sophists, 279–281; *Clouds,* 279–281, 289; *Frogs,* 317; *Lysistrata,* 295, 313
Arrhephorion, 115–116, 179, 268–269, 271
Arrhephoroi, 2, 4–5, 12, 32, 34, 136, 186, 219, 268–269, 297, 300, 320; on Parthenon, 5, 179–181, 183–185, 187, 191
Artaxerxes I, 128
Artaxerxes II, 143–144
Artemis, 37, 41, 54, 79, 95, 257–258, 264; Agrotera, 91, 95, 200; goddess of Marathon, 90–92; identified with Aphaea, 83; identified with Cybele, 54; on Parthenon, 159, 178, 181–182, 194, 258
Artemision. *See* Temple of Artemis at Ephesus
Artemisium, 104, 108
Asclepius, 278, 319–320
Aspasia, 217–218, 245–246, 256, 281, 303; relationship with Pericles, 218;

targeted by Pericles' enemies, 218, 223, 233–234
Athena, 23, 41, 49, 51–52, 56, 72, 96–97, 189, 269, 286, 306, 315; attempted rape by Hephaestus, 29–30; born from Zeus, 24; communes with Pericles, 222–223; contest with Poseidon, 25–27, 36; and Erechtheus, 4, 30–31, 34, 191; in Gigantomachy, 1, 21, 35–36, 75; Hygieia, 223; Nikē, 25; on Parthenon, 158, 160, 178–184, 192–193, 315; on Temple of Aphaea, 83–85; on Temple of Athena and Apollo at Pallene, 202; on Temple of Athena and Hephaestus, 150; on Temple of Athena Nikē, 298; patron goddess of Athens, 10, 22, 25, 37, 77, 102, 105, 108, 111, 131, 152; Polias, 25; Promachus, 25, 89; rejects Parthenon, 11, 262–263; sacred owls of, 21, 128; as trireme figurehead, 100
Athena Polias, priestess of, 1–2, 70, 179, 270, 300
Athenian Assembly, role of, 10, 13–14, 16, 69, 74, 78, 124, 290, 295
Athens: Agora (*see* Agora, Athens); archaic Bouleuterion, 76; Callimachus monument, 96–97, 158; cave of Pan, 95; city walls, 114–115; Colonus Hill, 146; Long Walls, 141, 151, 228, 236, 270, 278, 308–309; Muses' Hill, 23, 160; Nymphs' Hill, 23; Odeon, 199, 220, 316; Painted Stoa, 129, 149, 151, 158, 273, 285, 316; plague at, 5–6, 11, 248–253, 255–258, 260–262, 264, 274, 278–279, 289, 318; Royal Stoa, 77, 80; Sacred Gate, 29; Theseus' hero-shrine, 128, 151, 237; Tholos, 139
Athos, 89, 101, 104, 108

Babylon, 85
Battle of Arginusae, 302; trial of generals after, 303, 318
Battle of Artemisium, 104, 108, 264
Battle of Chaeroneia, 311
Battle of Coronea, 163
Battle of Eurymedon, 128
Battle of Harma, 72–73, 81, 105, 117
Battle of Marathon, 9, 19–20, 40, 92–94, 96–97, 202, 260; in Stoa Poikile, 130, 158; on Temple of Athena Nike, 273
Battle of Mycale, 111, 120–121
Battle of Plataea, 19, 110–111, 122, 129, 136, 144, 273
Battle of Salamis, 9, 19–20, 107–108, 124, 136–137, 199, 309, 311, 315
Battle of Sybota, 229
Battle of Tanagra, 141, 174
Black Sea, 20, 35, 44, 56, 61, 141, 225, 231
Boeotia, 79, 81, 101, 104, 142, 162–164, 261, 275
Boreas, 104, 108, 264
Bosporus, 207, 225
Boulē, role of, 68
Brasidas, 276–277
Brauron, 61, 79
Brea, 226
British Museum, 316
Bruce, Thomas, Earl of Elgin, 315–316
Buphonia, 217
Byzantium, 122, 207–208

Callias, 144, 209
Callias the Younger, 286
Callicrates, 15, 152–153, 200, 263, 271
Callimachus, 96, 273
Cambridge, 317
Cambyses, 85
Cape Zoster, 79
Capture of Miletus, The, 88, 255
Caria, 122, 208–209
Carpathus, 170
Carthage, 20, 166
Carthaginians, 108, 125–126, 303
Cecrops, 26, 30, 116, 204, 264; on Parthenon, 193; tomb of, 34, 269
Centauromachy, 36, 85; on agalma's sandals, 190; on Parthenon, 160–162; on statue of Athena

Centauromachy (*continued*)
  Promachus, 132; on Temple of Artemis at Ephesus, 55; on Temple of Athena at Troy, 313; on Temple of Athena and Hephaestus, 149; on Temple of Poseidon at Sunium, 201; on Temple of Zeus at Olympia, 126; in Theseus' hero-shrine, 128, 151
Cephalonia, 142
Cerameicus, 15, 57, 147
ceremony for war dead, 79, 237–238
Chalcidians, 71–73, 91
Chalcidice, 226
Chalcis, 72
Christianity, 315
Chrysaor, 45
Cimon, 16, 320; death of, 143; feud with Pericles, 137–138, 143–144, 209, 228; influences design of Marathon Monument, 131; intervenes to help Sparta, 135; leads Delian League, 122, 127–128, 133, 135; ostracism of, 138; repatriates Theseus' bones, 127–128, 131; returns from exile, 143; Spartan enthusiast, 138, 162; at Temple of Athena Polias, 103; wins Battle of Eurymedon, 128
City Dionysia, 59, 252
Clark, Edward, 317
Cleaenetus, 166, 259
Cleinias, 218
Cleisthenes of Athens, 60, 63–67, 70–71, 74, 81; reforms of, 68–69
Cleisthenes of Sicyon, 48, 50, 63, 167
Cleomenes, 65, 67, 70–72, 74
Cleon, 259, 263, 264, 265, 273–274, 276–277
Colophon, 213
Constantinople, 315
Corcyra, 44–46, 226–230, 259
Corinth, 45–46, 51, 101, 114, 140, 226–232, 282, 290, 311
Coroebus, 198
Cratinus, 220, 223, 246
Crete, 101, 166, 272
Crimea, 20, 225
Critias, 298, 309–311, 318–319
Critius, 117, 130
Croesus, 47, 50, 54–55, 81, 85, 87, 267
Cronus, 35
Croton, 164, 213
Cylon, 49, 55
Cyprus, 16, 40, 140, 143, 145
Cyrus, 85–86
Cythera, 275
Cyzicus, 298

daimon/daimones, 300, 310, 319
Damon, 15, 214–217, 219–220
Darius, 81, 85–86, 88–90, 100, 313; as character in Aeschylus' *Persians,* 137; tomb of, 124–125
Decelea, 294, 296
dedications: after Marathon, 93–97; after Plataea, 112–114; after Salamis, 109
Delian Games, 57, 263
Delian League, 122–124, 127–129, 131, 133, 135, 143, 168, 201, 229
Delium, 276, 281
Delos, 57–58, 64, 122, 128, 143, 201, 263–265, 276, 316; as Apollo's island, 11, 57, 235; Athenian Treasury moved from, 168; fake news of earthquake, 235; spared by Persians, 90
Delphi, 48, 54, 57, 64, 114, 162, 165, 230–231, 247, 257, 308; Athenian embassy to, 480 B.C., 101–102; Athenian stoa, 121; Athenian Treasury, 95–96, 151; bronze palm tree, 128, 265; Cleisthenes at, 63–64, 68; Marathon Monument, 131–132, 149–150, 181; Serpent Monument, 122; Siphnian Treasury, 125, 150; Temple of Apollo (*see* Temple of Apollo at Delphi); treasuries, 47–48
Demaratus, 72
Demeter, 41, 59, 79–80, 98, 107, 111, 146; in Eleusinian myth, 28–29; on Parthenon, 178, 182–183, 194, 306
Demetrius the Besieger, 314

Demophon, 127, 129, 158, 161
Demosthenes, 7, 311, 313
Diagoras, 222, 281, 290
Diogenes Laertius, 8
Dionysus, 60, 77, 148, 304; and drama, 58–59, 88; at Eleusis, 29, 41, 58–59, 79, 107, 306; on Parthenon, 159, 178, 181–183
Diopeithes, 222
Dracon, 50

earthquakes, 215; on Aegina, 82; in Attica, 11, 260–262, 264, 269–270, 276, 279, 282, 289, 313, 318; before Battle of Salamis, 108; in Peloponnese, 294; reported on Delos, 235; in Sparta, 135–136, 234
eclipses, 235, 280; during Gigantomachy, 164; lunar, 164, 276, 292–293; solar, 235–237
Egesta, 285
Egypt, 20, 35, 85, 166, 212–213, 249, 286; Athenian campaign to, 140, 142–143
Eleusinian limestone, 27, 81, 198, 203; built into Erechtheum, 264, 268, 297; built into Propylaea, 206, 272; used in statue plinths, 73, 117, 149, 187, 190, 202–203, 263
Eleusinian Mysteries, 27–29, 34, 47, 59, 71, 74, 76–77, 80, 146, 278, 304, 317; Alcibiades' parodying of, 289–291, 293, 318; coinciding with Battle of Salamis, 107–108; influence on Parthenon, 182–183, 185, 193, 199; origin myth, 27–29; processions to, 29, 107, 297, 301, 317
Eleusis, 2, 37, 113, 146, 198, 236, 248, 315, 317; limestone from (*see* Eleusinian limestone); military encounters at, 65, 71, 73, 79, 81, 108, 163–164, 237, 246; Mysteries of (*see* Eleusinian Mysteries); myths surrounding, 27–29, 57, 59, 78, 239, 269; oath made at (*see* Oath of Plataea)
Elpinice, 209–210
Enceladus, 1, 21, 35–36, 51, 65, 74, 160
Ennea Hodoi, 226
Ephesus, 54–55, 60, 87–88, 105, 152, 302, 314
Ephialtes, 136–139, 320
Epidamnus, 226
Epidaurus, 82, 278
Epizelus, 15, 92
Erechtheum. *See* Temple of Athena Polias at Athens (Erechtheum)
Erechtheus, 27, 34, 71, 104, 196, 204, 264; ancestor of all Athenians, 30–31, 143, 147–148, 181, 215, 232; birth of, 29–32; birth shown in Temple of Athena and Hephaestus, 149; character in Euripides' *Erechtheus*, 196, 269–270; death of, 27; founder of Panathenaea, 52; identified with Erichthonius, 31; identified with Poseidon, 27, 52, 269–279; as serpent, 31, 103, 179, 191; shrine on Acropolis, 34; war with Eleusis, 27, 71
Eretria, 87–88, 90–91
Erichthonius, 31, 52
Erinyes. *See* Furies
Eros, 32, 41, 233; on Parthenon, 158, 160, 178, 181–183
Eteocles, 210
Ethiopia, 249
Euboea, 72, 79, 90, 163, 261–262
Eumolpus, 27–28, 269
Euripides, 8, 64–65, 276, 304, 308; *Bacchae*, 304; *Electra*, 308; *Erechtheus*, 196, 269–271; *Hippolytus*, 257–258; *Ion*, 65; *Medea*, 231–233, 257; *Trojan Women*, 286, 293
Euripus Strait, 72
Europa, 161
Eurotas Valley, 136
Eurynome, 149

Fars, 124
Furies, 49

Garden of Pandrosus, 30, 116–117, 265–266, 269
Gardens of Aphrodite, 2, 32, 34, 180, 184, 297, 320
Gē, 30, 35
Giants, 35, 46
Gigantomachy, 35–36, 41, 159, 164; on agalma's shield, 190; on Athenian Treasury at Delphi, 96; foundation myth for Great Panathenaea, 35, 51, 177; on Parthenon, 159, 177, 184, 190, 195; on peplos, 21, 179; on second archaic Temple of Apollo at Delphi, 64, 75, 96; on second archaic Temple of Athena, 74–75; on Temple of Athena Nike, 272; on Temple of Athena at Troy, 313; on Temple of Poseidon at Sunium, 201
Gorgias, 261–262, 279
Gorgon, 21, 45, 100, 189
Great Panathenaea, 35, 50–52, 55, 57, 59, 64–65, 190, 199, 263, 300; Aristogeiton's assassination at, 61–62, 74; influence on Parthenon sculptures, 159, 162, 177, 185–186
Grove of Academus, 78, 183, 238

Hades (god), 24, 27–28, 46
Hades (place), 112–113, 131, 196, 271
Hadrian, 316
Hagnon, 166, 226, 295
Harma monument, 73, 81, 105, 117, 272
Harmodius, 62, 75–76, 109, 117, 149, 273, 316
Hebe, 158, 178, 182
Helen, 129, 158, 161–162, 202
Hellespont, 56, 101, 108, 120–122, 166, 216, 225–226, 295, 297, 302, 307
helots, 69, 124, 142, 234, 275–276, 294; revolt of, 136, 141
Hephaestus, 30, 70, 141, 196, 212; in myth, 24, 29–30, 52; on Parthenon, 159, 178, 181–182, 193; progenitor of Athenians, 52, 143, 181, 196, 215, 233, 269; on Temple of Athena and Hephaestus, 148–150
Hera, 24, 30, 223; on Parthenon, 158–159, 161, 178, 181–183; on Temple of Athena and Hephaestus, 148, 150
Heracles, 40–41, 47, 56, 83, 85, 92, 113, 184, 223; on Athenian Treasury at Delphi, 96, 150; and Gigantomachy, 35–36, 160–161; in Painted Stoa, 130; on Parthenon, 160–161, 193, 195; sanctuaries in Attica, 92; on Temple of Athena and Hephaestus, 150–151; on Temple of Cybele at Sardis, 54; on Temple of Zeus at Olympia, 126
Heraclitus, 216, 300
Hermes, 28, 41, 46, 60; on Parthenon, 159, 178, 181–184, 280
Hermippus, 166, 223, 246
herms, 60, 127; mutilation of, 288–291, 293, 318
Herodotus, 82, 121, 165, 232, 234, 273
hetaireiai, 290
Himera, 108, 125–126, 303
Hinduism, 86
Hipparchus, 56, 60–61, 64, 78, 85, 127, 169; assassination of, 61–64, 74–76, 314
Hippias, 56, 60–67, 69–71, 75, 78, 85, 90, 99, 106, 135, 169, 224
Hippocleides, 48, 50
Hippocrates, 278
Hippodamus, 165
Hyperbolus, 283

Iacchus, 29
Icaria, 38, 59
Ictinus, 6, 15, 153–155, 198
Iliad, 39, 61, 84, 93, 127, 150, 196, 251, 291, 296, 312
Indus Valley, 85, 106
Io, 161
Ion, 57, 87, 95, 193, 264
Ionia, 54, 86, 88, 111, 120, 122, 212, 215, 294–295, 304, 308
Ionian Revolt, 87–89, 216
Ionians, 36, 57, 90, 120, 165, 311
Isagoras, 67, 69–71, 74

isonomia, 68, 70, 241
Isthmian Games, 51
Isthmus of Corinth, 104, 106–107, 109–110, 114–115, 262
Italy, 20, 57, 106, 164–165, 213, 228

Jason, 225, 231–232
Jocasta, 253, 255
Judaism, 86

Korē, 27, 59

Lacedaemonius, 228
Lampon, 165, 215
Lasus, 60
Laurium, 15, 37, 98–99, 117, 157, 264, 294, 301
League of Athens and Her Allies. *See* Delian League
Leipsydrium, 63–64, 67
Lemnos, 132, 207
Leocorium, 61, 75
Leontini, 285
Leto, 58, 79, 264
Libya, 20, 166
Lycurgus, 69
Lydia, 47, 50, 54–55, 85, 166
Lysander, 301, 304, 308–309
Lysimache, 270

Macedon, 311
Macedonia, 101, 109, 138, 304
Marathon, estates of Peisistratus at, 56, 90
Marathon Temple at Athens, 97, 105, 115, 152, 156
Marduk, 86
Medea, 161, 231–233
Media, 85
Medusa, 45–46, 53
Megacles (Pericles' uncle), 99, 101
Megacles (son of Alcmaeon), 48, 50, 55–56, 60, 167
Megacles the Elder, 48–50, 307
Megara, 49, 55, 79, 112, 139–140, 163, 229–230, 234, 237, 275
Melos, 281, 283, 286
Memphis, 140, 142
Menelaus, 158
Mercouri, Melina, 316
Messenia, 69, 139
metics, 52, 69, 99, 114, 157, 186, 219, 240
Metis, 24
Micon, 128–129
Miletus, 22, 86–89, 98, 165, 207–208, 213, 218, 223
Miltiades, 60, 92, 94, 98, 103, 131, 273; in Marathon Monument, 181
Mindarus, 298
Mnesicles, 203–204, 206, 265, 268
Mount Aegaleus, 23, 71, 248
Mount Hymettus, 13, 23
Mount Ithome, 136
Mount Lycabettus, 23
Mount Mycale, 111, 207
Mount Olympus, 21, 24, 35, 56, 94, 148, 178, 184, 251, 264
Mount Parnes, 23, 63, 294, 311
Mount Pentelicus, 23, 38, 92, 97, 100, 121, 147, 156, 275
Mount Taygetus, 136
Muses' Hill, 23, 160
Mycenae, 114
Myron, 130
Mytilene, 259, 302

Naqš-e Rostam, 124
Naupactus, 142
Naxos, 56, 86, 89–91, 135; dedications on Delos, 58
Nemean Games, 51
Nero, 314
Nesiotes, 117
New Peisistratids, 224
Nicias, 15, 264, 277, 283, 288–289, 320; on Delos, 264–265; Peace of (*see* Peace of Nicias); and Sicilian Expedition, 285–286, 292–293
Nile River, 140, 142, 249

Oath of Plataea, 110, 144–145
Odysseus, 158, 286
Oea, 82
Oedipus, 252–253, 255–256, 305–307

olive tree ("token"), 4, 26, 30, 34, 106, 108, 116–117, 192, 269
Olympia, 47, 48, 94, 114, 284; statue of Zeus at, 192, 222; Temple of Zeus (*see* Temple of Zeus at Olympia)
oracle of Zeus Ammon, 286
Ouranus, 35

Pallas, sons of, 149, 202, 257
Pan, 91, 94–95, 100
Panaenus, 129–130
Panathenaic Games, 159, 177, 186, 284, 291
Pandora, daughter of Erechtheus, 27
Pandora, first woman, 27, 190–191
Pandora, daughter of Cecrops, as Pandrosus, 30
Pandrosus/Pandora, 30–31, 186–187, 190–191, 193
Panhellenic Congress, 144, 164
Parian marble, 60, 64, 74, 83, 95, 121, 147, 201, 203
Paros, 38, 64, 98
Parthenon, 6, 12, 42; acroteria, 195; ancient descriptions of, 7–8; architectural refinements, 153–155; ceiling, 170; cella, 153; as church, 315; columns, 156–157, 170; construction of, 156; as courtesan, 167–168; destruction of, 315; doors of, 154, 195; earthquake damage, 11, 262–263; footprint extended, 152–153; frieze, 171, 184–187, 315; frieze (east), 177–184; frieze (north), 175, 177; frieze (south), 177; frieze (west), 170–175; grilles, 170, 196; *metopēs,* 157, 161–162, 190; *metopēs* (east), 159, 161; *metopēs* (north), 158, 161; *metopēs* (south), 160, 162; *metopēs* (west), 158; as mosque, 315; opisthodomus, 153, 196–197; paintwork, 167, 170–171; pediments, 192, 194–195; pediments (east), 8, 181, 193–194, 315; pediments (west), 8, 192–194; Pericles' involvement with, 10–11, 18, 42, 48, 167–170; possible interior frieze, 195; roof, 170; windows, 154; workforce, 155
passage of the Arrhephoroi, 2. *See also* Acropolis: cleft in
Pausanias (Spartan general), 110–111, 122, 125, 134–135. 234, 250
Pausanias (traveller), 7–8, 190–191, 268, 307
Peace of Callias, 144, 207
Peace of Nicias, 277, 311
Pegasus, 45
Peirithous, 36
Peisistratid palace, 56–57, 59–60, 76, 139
Peisistratus, 55–56, 58, 67; annexes Delos, 57–58; building programme, 57–58, 60, 263–264; palace of, 56–57, 59–60, 76, 139
Pentelic marble, 97, 187, 201–203, 206
peplos (Athena's), 31; on agalma, 187, 189; on Parthenon, 159, 162, 178–181, 183, 186, 190–191; presentation to Athena, 52, 183; washing of, 31–32, 300; weaving of, 32, 114; on xoanon, 21, 32, 52
Pericles, 11, 19, 22–23, 27, 39, 42, 56, 81, 131, 186, 197, 211, 233, 255, 308; and Anaxagoras, 215–216; and Aspasia, 217–218, 223, 233; as choregus, 136–137; and Cimon, 138, 142–143; citizenship law, 143, 218, 256; in comedy, 219–220, 224, 234, 256; and Damon, 214–215; death of, 256; and Ephialtes, 137–139; family, 48, 66, 98–99, 218, 255, 281, 303; family curse, 48–50, 122, 234–235, 252, 307; as "first man," 6, 16; foreign policy, 139–140, 144, 162–164, 207, 225–230, 260, 277, 282; funeral oration, 239–242, 244–247; involvement with Parthenon (*see* Parthenon: Pericles' involvement with); and jury pay, 142–143, 143, 166; nicknamed "Zeus," 15, 212, 223, 251; oratory, 14, 16, 169, 208, 251, 311; and Panathenaea, 199; and Panhellenic Congress, 144; physical appearance

of, 15, 169, 220; and plague, 251, 255–256; policy in Peloponnesian War, 236–237; and Protagoras, 216–217; put on trial, 223–224, 255; rationalism of, 10–11, 212, 219, 222–223, 235–236, 252, 256–257, 292, 318; represented on agalma's shield, 221–222; Samian Campaign, 207–209, 232; and Thucydides Melesiou (*see* Thucydides Melesiou: clashes with Pericles); and Thurii, 164–165
Peripatos, 2, 32, 320
Persephone, 28–29, 41, 59, 73, 79–80, 107, 277, 305; on Parthenon, 194
Persepolis, 185, 313
Perseus, 45–46
Persian Stoa Sparta, 125
Persian tent, 199, 220
Phaedra, 257
Phalerum, 82, 90, 98, 141
Pharmakoi, 320
Pheidias, 15, 130–133, 150–151, 196, 203, 214, 268, 271, 316; agalma of Athena Parthenos, 152–153, 189–190; in comedy, 220; death of, 222; initial sketches of Parthenon sculptures, 171, 181, 186, 192; Marathon Monument, 131, 181; as "overseer of everything," 146–147, 153, 157, 189; statue of Apollo as "Locust God," 132; statue of Athena Areia, 131; statue of Athena at Pellene, 131; statue of Athena Promachus, 132–133; statue of Lemnian Athena, 132; studio on Acropolis, 187; on trial, 220–222
Pheidippides (Aristophanic character), 279–281
Pheidippides (runner), 91–94
Philaids, 48, 60, 98, 103, 131, 137, 209
Philip II of Macedon, 311
Phocis, 104, 142, 162
Piraeus, 15, 20, 81, 98, 103–104, 132, 138, 141, 151, 228, 248, 293, 311
Plato, 246, 279, 300, 309, 319; *Menexenus*, 239–240, 246
Pliny the Elder, 7, 191
Plynteria, 300
Pnyx, 12–15, 23, 25, 87, 104, 141, 145, 227, 303, 308; capacity of, 18; construction of, 78; reorientation of, 320
Polycleitus, 130; *Canon*, 130, 214
Polycrates, 55, 60
Polygnotus, 129–130
Polyneices, 210
Poseidon, 24, 31, 41, 83, 98, 114, 146, 200, 258, 269–270, 286, 288, 306; contest with Athena (*see* Athena: contest with Poseidon); father of Theseus, 36, 41, 128, 257–258; god of earthquakes, 11, 107, 135, 215, 232, 262; on Parthenon, 159, 161, 178, 181–182, 184, 192–193; Poseidon-Erechtheus, 27, 52, 269–270; well on Acropolis, 26
Potidaea, 229–230, 234, 255, 257–258, 281
Praxiergidae, 31–32
Praxithea, 269–270
Priene, 207
priestess of Athena Polias, 1–2, 4, 21, 32, 70, 74, 103, 191, 270, 300; on Parthenon frieze, 5, 179–181, 183–184
probouloi, 295
Prometheus, 48, 211–212
Propylaea, 203–204, 206–207, 222–223, 227, 265, 271–272, 285, 313
Protagoras, 165, 167, 216–217, 222, 262, 279
Protesilaus, 121
public cemetery, 78, 93, 209, 238, 246
Pylos, 273–274, 275, 277, 294
pyrrhichē, 51–52
Pythagoras, 213
Pythagoreans/Pythagoreanism, 183, 185, 214
Pythian Games, 48, 51, 285

Rhamnous, 37, 79, 146, 202–203, 317
Rhea, 35
Rheneia, 263–264

River Cephisus, 23, 23, 305; on Parthenon, 192
River Danube, 85
River Eridanus, 23, 156; on Parthenon, 192
River Ilissus, 23, 60, 78, 200; on Parthenon, 192
River Pactolus, 87
River Tigris, 88
ruins of "Old Temple," 21, 34, 111, 115–117. *See also* Temple of Athena Polias at Athens: third archaic ("Old Temple")

sacred serpent. *See* Erechtheus: as serpent
Salamis, 19–20, 23, 55, 104–109, 133, 162, 187, 291
Sardis, 50, 54, 81, 87–88, 90, 100, 123, 207, 294; Temple of Cybele at (*see* Temple of Cybele at Sardis)
Saronic Gulf, 23, 81, 83
scapegoats, 70, 320
Scythian archers, 13, 56
Sea of Azov, 226
Selene, 41; on Parthenon, 158
Selinus, 303
Sestus, 120–121, 136, 208
Shrine of Theseus. *See* Athens, Theseus' hero-shrine
Sicily, 20, 35, 37, 57, 61, 101, 108, 165, 303–304; Athens' expeditions to, 261, 285–286, 288, 292, 295
Sicyon, 48, 114, 142–143
Sigeum, 66
Simonides, 60, 76, 94, 112, 214
Sisyphus, 46–47, 52
slavery, 38
Socrates, 11, 15, 279, 318; and Alcibiades, 281, 318; in Aristophanes' *Clouds,* 279–281, 318; and Critias, 281, 309, 318; and daimones, 300; in Plato's *Menexenus,* 240, 245–246; and the Thirty Tyrants, 317–318; trial and execution of, 319–320
Solon, 50, 57, 152, 297, 304
Sophocles, 15, 109; *Antigone,* 210–211; general on Samian campaign, 209; *Oedipus,* 252–253, 255–256; *Oedipus at Colonus,* 305–307; receives Asclepius to Athens, 278
Sōros, 93–94
Statue of Athena Parthenos. *See* agalma of Athena Parthenos
Statue of Athena Promachus. *See* Pheidias: statue of Athena Promachus
Statue of Nemesis at Rhamnous, 202–203
Statue of Zeus at Olympia. *See* Olympia: statue of Zeus at
Strepsiades, 279–281
Strymonian Gulf, 226
Sunium, 37, 79, 90, 98, 109, 146, 200, 280
Susa, 109
Sybaris, 164–165
Syracuse, 108, 126, 285, 288, 292–294, 303

Tanagra, 141
Telamon, 83–84
Telesterion, 29, 317; classical, 198; first archaic, 60; revised classical, 198–199; second archaic, 80–81
Tempe, 101
Temple of Aphaea on Aegina, 83–84; replacement sculptures, 126
Temple of Apollo on Aegina, 83
Temple of Apollo at Corinth, 46–47, 52, 155
Temple of Apollo at Delphi: first archaic, 48, 63; second archaic, 63–65
Temple of Apollo at Didyma, 88
Temple of Apollo on Delos: archaic, 58; first classical, 123, 143; second classical, 263–264, 271
Temple of Apollo Patroos at Athens, 57
Temple of Artemis Agrotera, 200, 263, 271, 316
Temple of Artemis Aristoboule, 133
Temple of Artemis at Corcyra, 45
Temple of Artemis at Ephesus: archaic, 54–55, 152, 185, 264; classical, 314

Temple of Athena and Apollo at Pallene, 201–202
Temple of Athena and Hephaestus, 147, 156, 198, 200–202, 237, 316; sculptures, 147–151, 193, 273
Temple of Athena at Himera, 126, 303
Temple of Athena at Sparta, 135
Temple of Athena at Sunium, 79, 200
Temple of Athena at Troy, 313
Temple of Athena Nike, 271–274, 277; parapet, 298; sculptures, 272–273; statue, 277–278
Temple of Athena Polias at Athens: first archaic, 49; second archaic, 50, 52–55, 60, 80; third archaic ("Old Temple"), 22, 74–76, 80, 85, 97, 103, 105. *See also* ruins of "Old Temple"
Temple of Athena Polias at Athens (Erechtheum), 265, 268–269, 271, 297, 301; caryatid porch, 266–268; frieze, 268
Temple of Cybele at Sardis, 54, 87, 185; burned by Greeks, 88
Temple of Eleusinian Demeter at Athens, 236
Temple of Hera on Samos, 55, 60, 152
Temple of Nemesis at Rhamnous: archaic, 79; classical, 202–203, 317
Temple of Olympian Zeus at Acragas, 125–126
Temple of Olympian Zeus at Athens, 60, 78, 169, 200, 316
Temple of Poseidon at Sunium: archaic, 79, 109; classical, 200–201, 280
Temple of Themis at Rhamnous: archaic, 79; classical, 202
Temple of Zeus, archaic, 57
Temple of Zeus at Olympia, 126, 141
Teucer, 83–84
Thales, 22, 38, 212–213
Thanatos, 46
Thasos, 130, 135–136, 138, 276
Theatre of Dionysus, 77, 199, 278, 288, 314
Thebes, 56, 91, 141–142, 260, 277, 311; in mythology, 37, 210, 239, 241, 252–253, 255
Themistocles: champions fleet, 98–99, 103, 308; and city walls, 114–115; downfall of, 133–135, 139, 169, 283; at Olympic Games, 133; and ostracism, 99; at Salamis, 104, 106–109, 296
Theodosius, 315
Thermopylae, 104, 113
Theseis, 85
Theseus, 41, 47, 92, 113, 184, 319; as Athenian hero, 36–37, 40, 85, 87, 127, 130, 210; on Athenian Treasury at Delphi, 96, 150; bones repatriated, 127–128, 131; in drama, 232, 257–258, 305–306; fights sons of Pallas, 149, 202; in mythology, 36–37, 211, 239, 272; in Painted Stoa, 129–130; on Parthenon, 158, 161, 195; on Statue of Athena Promachus, 132; on Temple of Athena and Apollo at Pallene, 202; on Temple of Athena and Hephaestus, 149–151, 273; on Temple of Poseidon at Sunium, 201; in Theseus' hero-shrine, 128, 151
Thesmophoria, 34
Thespis, 58–59
Thessaly, 56, 101, 111, 133, 139
Thetis, 149
Thirty Tyrants, 309–310, 317–318, 320–321
Thucydides (historian), 7–8, 235–236, 239, 245, 247, 250–251, 261–262; in exile, 283; and Hippocrates, 278; reliability of speeches, 239–240, 244–246, 289; serves as general, 276; survives plague, 249
Thucydides Melesiou, 16, 227–228, 230, 234; clashes with Pericles, 168–170, 215; ostracism of, 170, 218–220
Thurii, 165, 215
Titanomachy, 35
Titans, 35, 46, 59, 125

trireme, design of, 99–100
Troezen, 104, 257
Trojan War, 312–313; in myth, 39, 61, 83, 93, 121, 127, 129, 200, 202, 286; in Painted Stoa, 129; on Parthenon, 158–159, 161–162, 184, 190; on Temple of Athena at Troy, 312–313; on Temple of Artemis at Corcyra, 46
Turks, 315
Twin Towers Gate, 57, 61–62, 77, 238
tyrannicides, 74, 75, 150–151; first statue of, 75–76, 109; second statue of, 117, 130, 147, 149, 151, 222, 273, 316

Venetians, 315
Virgin Mary, 315
Vitruvius, 6

Xanthippe, 318
Xanthippus (father of Pericles), 98–99, 101, 120–122, 136–137, 208, 283
Xanthippus (son of Pericles), 245, 255
Xenophanes, 213, 217
Xerxes, 101, 108–111, 122, 124, 128, 313; in Athens, 105–106; in *Persians,* 136–137
Xerxes' tent. *See* Persian tent
xoanon of Athena, 21, 36, 103, 128, 162; Cimon and, 103; cleansing of, 31, 300–301; description of, 21; dressed in peplos, 21, 36; in Parthenon, 191–192, 195; removed during Persian Wars, 105–106; rope tied to by Cylon's men, 49, 267; in Temple of Athena Polias at Athens (archaic), 52; in Temple of Athena Polias at Athens (Erechtheum), 265, 268; in temporary shrine, 21, 39, 117, 152

Zacynthus, 142
Zeus, 25–26, 28, 35, 40, 45–47, 59, 94, 109, 114, 202, 211–212, 217, 269, 291, 306; aids Cimon's search, 128; existence of questioned, 215–216, 279–280; festivals of, 49–50, 284–285; grants Athena's intervention in Persian Wars, 102–103, 105, 108; myth of fathering Athena, 24, 29; on Parthenon, 158–161, 178, 181–184, 188, 182–193; sanctuary on Acropolis, 24, 43, 105; on Temple of Athena and Hephaestus, 148, 150